JESSE HERMAN HOLMES, 1864-1942:

A Quaker's Affirmation for Man

Jesse Herman Holmes in 1934
Artist — Keith Morrow Martin
Original portrait in the Managers' Parlor, Parrish Hall,
Swarthmore College.

JESSE HERMAN HOLMES, 1864-1942

A Quaker's Affirmation for Man

by
Albert J. Wahl

Richmond, Indiana

Published by
Friends United Press
Richmond, Indiana

Copyright 1979
by
Friends United Press

L.C. #79-63127
I.S.B.N. 0-913408-50-6

Printed in the United States of America
by
Arcata Book Group

To
Elsie Vera Wahl

PREFACE

In 1951, when the author was writing his doctoral dissertation on the Progressive Friends — a Quaker separatist group pursuing general reform in the period 1848-1940 — the logic of the situation demanded that he cut the story at the Civil War time. Only in the last chapter was there any foreshadowing of events to come in the period 1865 to 1940, and only a very brief mention of Jesse H. Holmes as the last leader of this group.

Twenty years later, when the author retired from active teaching, he decided that now he would have the time to finish the story of the Progressive Friends. He and his wife started to do the necessary research, their work carrying them into the library of the Chester County Historical Society, West Chester, Pennsylvania, and into the Friends' Historical Library at Swarthmore College. When they reached the period of Jesse Holmes' leadership of these Progressive Friends they gradually came to the conviction that here was a man who, by reason of his personality and style, and his wide range of activities, deserved a full-scale biography. The present work is the result of that conviction — a "life-and-times" biography which at the same time incorporates the story of the Progressive Friends.

As we delved more deeply into the Holmes' record it became apparent that not only was Jesse a lively and lovable man, full of wit and humor, but that he was married to a wise and witty lady. Her activities, and those of their daughter and two sons, became integral parts of the whole picture and afforded a nostalgic view of family life among middle-class Quakers in the exciting academic atmosphere of Swarthmore College from 1900 to 1942.

It was from his home on the edge of Swarthmore's campus, and from his post as professor of philosophy and religion, that Jesse tried to advance social, intellectual, religious, economic and political reforms. An idealistic pragmatist, he dared to challenge those mindless relics of the superstitious Dark Ages which had developed as conventions in association with Christmas, Easter, weddings, and funerals — and which had been so much commercialized. We see him transforming the Quaker's inner light into an "inner spur" for social betterment; we see him helping to found the American Friends Service Committee; and, through countless speeches and many articles, working to reconcile science and religion, and to unify Quakers and other religious groups. His life's work, so much concerned with affirming Christianity as a religion of reason as well as of faith, has much to tell to those Americans now under the travail of still another intolerant and anti-intellectual movement by revivalists and cultists. Reacting vigorously to the winds of doctrine in major fields of American life, he gradually became convinced of socialism's general worth and ran for local, state and national office on the Socialist ticket. If Norman Thomas became America's conscience during much of this time the same could be said for Jesse Holmes, especially in that circle of influence extending one hundred miles from Swarthmore as a center. Never quite functioning as a highly publicized and truly national figure (except as leader of the Hicksite Quakers), he took his place as one of those liberal intellectuals, who, working on a slightly lower level, supported the giants of reform in their efforts to lift man against the dead weight of the status quo.

The burden of research for our project would have been considerably heavier if it had not been for the unstinting help given us by the staffs of the various libraries we visited. From the beginning Dorothy Lapp and Bart Anderson of the Chester County Historical Society helped us find volume after volume of primary material; their files were wondrous sources of newspaper clippings, letters, photographs, et cetera. At the Friends Historical Library, John Moore, J. William Frost, Dorothy Harris, Nancy P. Speers, Jane Rittenhouse and others were of inestimable assistance, eking out the rather sparse collection of the Holmes Papers with many fruitful suggestions for further material. Thomas Drake, of the Quaker Collection, Haverford College, gave material aid in the early stages of the research on the Progressive Friends. And at one point the Eleutherian Mills Historical Library in Greenville, Delaware, was opened to us so that we might consult the Longwood

Manuscripts there. Peter E. Told, former student of Jesse's, opened up the file copies of *The Swarthmorean*.

The Holmes biography would never have gotten very far beyond what newspapers, books and magazines could yield if it hadn't been for Grace R. Holmes and Jesse Herman Holmes III. Grace, a daughter-in-law of Jesse's, and Herman, Jesse's eldest son, both searched among their household effects and came up with rich finds of memorabilia, including artifacts, photographs, letters and diaries. Herman's wife Jessie gave indispensable help in this search. And all three of them gave us fruitful personal interviews, filling in many gaps in the written material, as was true of other relatives by blood and marriage — Margaret L. Price and Rebecca Timbres Clark. John Kendall and Kenneth H. Dryden, Jesse's nephews, also supplied data impossible to get otherwise, as did Mr. and Mrs. Gilpin Johns out of their records and memories of "Uncle Sassie" and his family.

Former Swarthmore College faculty colleagues of Jesse's — John W. Nason, Brand Blanshard, and Everett Lee Hunt — dug deeply into their memories to supply data, anecdotes, and insights for his meaning as a teacher and as a man. Everett Lee Hunt especially went far beyond the call of duty in this respect.

Many features of the Holmes story would have suffered if it had not been for the help given by former students of Jesse's, most notably Margaret Byrd Rawson, Eleanor Stabler Clarke, Elizabeth Harbold Westkott, and Mr. and Mrs. Harold F. Carter.

The author is greatly indebted to Everett Lee Hunt, to Grace R. Holmes and her son David R. Holmes, and to Jesse and Jessie H. Holmes III, for their willingness to wade through the typescript of the book, and for their many cogent comments and suggestions. Whatever faults remain are certainly not theirs; they are mine alone.

And finally the author wishes to hail his wife, who worked with him so efficiently and so tirelessly across eight years of travel, notetaking and writing. Cook, housekeeper, research companion, typist and occasional critic, without her constant presence this book would not have been possible.

A.J.W.

ACKNOWLEDGMENTS

Grateful acknowledgment is made to the following for permission to quote or paraphrase from the specified selections:

Harold F. Alderfer and Fannette H. Luhrs, *Gubernatorial Elections in Pennsylvania 1922-1942* (State College, Pa.: The Institute of Local Government, 1946), p. 15; Table 29, Appendix. Also for their *Registration in Pennsylvania Elections 1926-1946* (State College, Pa.: The Institute for Local Government, 1948), pp. 44-45.

American Heritage Publishing Co., Inc., for Robert L. Reynolds, "The Coal Kings Come to Judgment," *American Heritage*, XI (April 1960), 61. Copyright © 1960 by American Heritage Publishing Co., Inc. Reprinted by permission from *American Heritage* (April 1960).

American Heritage Publishing Co., Inc., for Richard O'Connor, "Yanks in Siberia," *American Heritage*, XXV (August 1974), 10-16, 80-83. Copyright © 1974 by American Heritage Publishing Co., Inc. Reprinted by permission from *American Heritage* (August 1974).

A.S. Barnes & Company, Inc., for the prayer "At Morning," p. 125 of *The Mind of Robert Louis Stevenson*, ed. Roger Ricklefs (New York: Thomas Yoseloff). Copyright © 1963 by A.S. Barnes & Co., Ltd.

The Evening and Sunday Bulletin (Philadelphia, Pa.) for the Jesse H. Holmes' obituary on May 28, 1942.

Merle Curti, for pp. 578-579, 580-582, 585 of *The Growth of American Thought* (Third Edition). Copyright © 1964 by Merle Curti.

Eric G. Curtis, for excerpts from the *History of George School 1893-1943* (George School: Alumni Association of George School, © 1943).

Friends General Conference of the Religious Society of Friends, *Quaker Torch Bearers* (Philadelphia: Friends General Conference, © 1943), pp. 8-13, 15-16, 17-19, 21.

Friends Journal (formerly the *Friends Intelligencer*), for excerpts from articles, editorials, and news reports from 1900 to 1942.

Greenwood Press (Westport, Conn.), for Mary Hoxie Jones, *Swords Into Plowshares* (1937), pp. 19, 76-78, 319-361. Used with the

"The Hidden Philosophy of the Americans," *Saturday Review,* Vol. 45 (March 10, 1962), pp. 15-16 f; and for Hazel Henderson, "The Japanese Ask: What Price Influence?," *Saturday Review-World* (December 18, 1973), 10, 68-69.

Simon & Schuster, Inc., for Peter Townsend, *Duel of Eagles,* pp. 47-48, 81. Copyright © 1972.

Swarthmore College, for *Swarthmore Remembered,* ed. Maralyn Gillespie (© 1964), pp. 2-6, 40-43, 112, 127-129.

The Swarthmorean, Swarthmore, Pa., for excerpts from its issues, 1900-1957.

Time, Inc., for excerpts from its issues of *Time* for December 10, 1928, and for December 29, 1975.

Wesleyan University Press, for Frances Blanshard, *Frank Aydelotte of Swarthmore,* ed. Brand Blanshard (© 1970), pp. ix, 152-157, 179-181, 186-190, 193-196, 210-212, 226-227, 274-275, 291-292, 396, 399.

West Chester (Pa.) *Daily Local News,* for many excerpts in the years covered by this biography.

John Wiley & Sons, Inc., Publishers, for excerpts from Ralph Henry Gabriel, *The Course of American Democratic Thought* (© 1956).

CONTENTS

PHOTOGRAPHS AND ILLUSTRATIONS

1. An "Hilarious" Memorial Service

On Sunday, May 31, 1942, at four o'clock in the afternoon, the Friends' Meeting House on the edge of the beautiful campus of Swarthmore College became the scene of what one Quaker called "the most hilarious memorial service I ever attended." The many friends, neighbors, and associates of the late Dr. Jesse Herman Holmes, professor emeritus of philosophy and the history of religion at Swarthmore, had gathered there to express their appreciation of what this man's life had meant to them and to their world. "The meeting had an extraordinarily happy tone, as though the joy that such a man had lived outweighed for the moment the sense of grief at his loss." While many of those who rose to speak told jokes and humorous anecdotes about Jesse H. Holmes, they were also there to pay a higher tribute to a man who had spent his life working more for the betterment of mankind than for his own advancement.

Dr. Brand Blanshard, who had succeeded Dr. Holmes as head of the department of philosophy at Swarthmore College, opened the meeting by saying that those present had met to honor and draw strength from one who had been "the heart and headstone of the Swarthmore Meeting of the Religious Society of Friends." Blanshard rejoiced that, while Dr. Holmes' place could never be filled, he was taken while "the tides of his being were still running strong so that their memory of him would be one of a gay and boyishly adventurous spirit, kindly, courageous and chivalrous." And, Blanshard went on, the dispossessed of this world — "whoever they were, whatever their plight" — always had a champion in Jesse Holmes. "His was an uneasy presence for those satisfied and self-satisfied because he truly loved men and justice and implemented his concern with action."

Dr. Leslie Pinckney Hill, distinguished president of the State Teachers College at Cheyney, had entered the meeting house just before the appointed hour to find the auditorium filled to capacity. Only one seat remained vacant, the one on the facing benches which

1

"Ducky" Holmes had so often occupied in Friends' meetings. Dr. Hill took his place there, an act which many considered most fitting in view of Ducky's long work for the uplift of Negroes. Presently he rose to say that not long ago Holmes had expressed the conviction that the great problem which mankind would need to solve after World War Two was how to achieve interracial harmony; there could be no lasting peace unless it was based on "a genuine understanding and love of one's fellow man, with justice and equality for all." But, said Dr. Hill, Holmes' ideas for the achievement of such a peace were ahead of his time; he reminded his listeners of Emerson's judgment that "the proof of a great man is that we will come around to his viewpoint twenty years after he has gone."

Dr. Everett L. Hunt, dean of men at Swarthmore, and a next-door neighbor of the Holmes family for many years, now rose to say that "we have all known people who loved all mankind," but that he wanted "to testify to Dr. Holmes' simple neighborliness. . . ." No doubt he recalled how Jesse had "induced" the Swarthmore College authorities to put a lawn-bowling turf on a vacant lot next to the meeting house and just across the street from the Holmes' residence. Here Jesse and members of the faculty bowled regularly for several years, Jesse keeping the balls on his front porch so that they could be picked up for use at any time. Dr. Hunt further illustrated Jesse's good nature and humor by telling several amusing anecdotes; perhaps too he related how, in that very same room, Jesse had reacted to Joan Fry, an English visitor to the Meeting. Miss Fry had taken her seat; everyone then waited for some forty minutes for her to be moved by the spirit. "Finally she arose and said simply: 'The earth is the Lord's and the fullness thereof.' Ducky was on his feet immediately to say with a rasp in his voice, 'The earth may be the Lord's, but he has a terrible time with his title.' " Dr. Hunt thought that Ducky's whole career might well be described as "helping the Lord to hold on to his title."

It must have pleased the Holmes family very much to hear such stories, and such praise, from an old friend and neighbor. Jesse's wife, Rebecca Webb Holmes, was there, together with her two sons and their wives, Jesse Herman and Eloise, Robert and Grace. A fifteen-year-old grandson was also present, Jesse Herman, the fourth in the Holmes' lineage to bear this name.

But Jesse Holmes IV was to hear much more in praise of his illustrious grandfather. Clarence Pickett, executive secretary of the American Friends Service Committee, paid tribute to Dr. Holmes'

2

long service in that organization, recalling how he had been one of its founders, and "terming him far greater than anyone inside or outside of that group. . . ." He said that Jesse was one of those who, "when caution or daring were being decided upon as courses of action, always chose the daring as the better course of duty."

Dr. Louis N. Robinson, former student of Jesse's and latterly his colleague on the Swarthmore faculty, added his eloquent praise. Dr. Robinson, one of the country's most famous penologists, and currently a new member of the Pennsylvania Prison Board, said that he had taken every course given by Dr. Holmes that he could enroll in, and that, "more than any other of his teachers, he had helped him most in thinking through certain of the great problems of life."

A somewhat similar tribute was voiced by Dr. John W. Nason, former teaching colleague of Jesse, and then president of Swarthmore College. Dr. Nason held that Jesse "was among the selected number of unusually great teachers which the college had possessed. . . ." He likened Jesse to Socrates as a gadfly for the general welfare: claiming "no special wisdom or special knowledge, . . . he questioned the assumptions and challenged the complacencies of our lives, and everyone in the College, Meeting or community who came in contact with him [is] different and better for his quickening process."

Since Jesse in his later years wore a pointed beard and sported a cloak, making him look "strangely like Mephistopheles," perhaps Dr. Nason also recalled one of Jesse's remarks: "I could never see the sense of the old adage about fighting fire with fire. Why give the devil his choice of weapons?"

After Dr. Nason's tribute, other friends and colleagues lent their voices to Jesse's memorial: J. Barnard Walton, of the Philadelphia Yearly Meeting (Hicksite), was followed by Herbert Way of that Meeting's Advancement Committee; by Dr. J. Russell Smith, renowned geographer; by Ethel Brewster, former student of Jesse's and head of the classics department at Swarthmore; by Miss Janet Speakman, Benjamin F. Whitson, Gunther Reuning, and A.F. Armstrong; and by Leslie Chrismer, who gave the appreciation of certain labor groups in nearby Chester.

Patrick Murphy Malin, on leave from the Swarthmore department of economics for service in Washington, D.C., was the last speaker. Dr. Malin had known Jesse Holmes for many years as a faculty colleague and as his associate in the work of the Society of

Friends; he now paid a moving tribute to his old friend's personality and leadership. Jesse, he said, "was one man who never found a fact too uncomfortable for him to face, and that his courage was matched by a capacious spirit which never heard of any evil without feeling a sense of responsibility for its elimination."

Dr. Malin closed the service with a poem about Jesse written by E.C. Walton, Jesse's associate in the reformist public forum held annually by the Progressive Friends of Longwood near Kennett Square until 1940. In this poem Walton not only praised Jesse and the Progressive Friends, but reminded the audience that the key question at Longwood had always been "Do ye serve?"

While this memorial service ended in a mood somewhat different from the tone of hilarity which had marked so much of it, at its close people gathered into little groups to relate still other anecdotes generated by Jesse H. Holmes. Brand Blanshard was in one of these groups, we may be sure. He may well have told how Jesse, a year or so before he died, appeared in Clothier Hall to address the Swarthmore student body, a student body that had not known him as a teacher but which knew him as a living legend in the cause of American liberalism. When he finished his address and sat down, the students applauded him so heartily and so long that he became embarrassed and didn't know how to respond. "It was obvious to all but himself that it was not his cause they were applauding but himself, that indomitable good white head of his, unbeaten, lusty, and unbowed. They knew a man when they saw one."

To find out just what sort of man he was is the purpose of this book.

2. Young Man From the West

Jesse Herman Holmes came out of the West, if Iowa and Nebraska can be called the West. He was born January 5, 1864, in West Liberty, Iowa, only seven miles from the birthplace of Herbert Hoover. His father, a country doctor, assisted at the birth of the future President of the United States, according to Holmes' family legend.

Jesse represented the fourth generation of this American Holmes family, reaching back to the time when a certain William Holmes married Margaret Fell, the daughter of Judge Thomas Fell, of Swarthmoore Hall, Lancashire, England. (After Judge Fell's death Margaret's mother, also called Margaret, married George Fox, founder of the Society of Friends.) A son of this marriage, William Holmes, Jr., accompanied his uncle Edward Fell when he sailed to Maryland in 1730. William somehow found his way to Virginia, where he fell in love with Mary Coos, a member of the Fairfax Meeting of Friends located at Waterford. They were married in Meeting on June 6, 1753, and produced nine children. Joseph Holmes was one of these; he married Elizabeth Hughes to produce Jesse Herman Holmes I in 1813 while living on a farm with a large mill near Hamilton, Loudoun County, Virginia.

This was apparently a prosperous farm. But Joseph Holmes died when his son Jesse was only five or six years old. Jesse I now embarked on a variant course: elementary education in a local school, apprenticeship to a local tailor, and then a period of study under Benjamin Hallowell in a Friends' school in Alexandria. When the Great Separation of 1827 divided Quakers into the two major branches of the orthodox and the liberals, Jesse joined his family on the Hicksite or liberal side. About four years later, when he was twenty-one, he went to New Lisbon, Ohio, where he started a Friends' school of his own. The school apparently prospered enough in its early stages to encourage him to get married to Rebecca

Hanna, an aunt of Mark Hanna, who was to become the famous Cleveland industrialist and manager of William McKinley's political fortunes. Three children were born of this marriage. But again tragedy touched his life: his school failed and his wife Rebecca died of consumption.

While there seems to be no record of what happened to the three children after Rebecca's death, we know that Jesse continued teaching school in Clark County and elsewhere in Ohio. Somewhere along the way he met and married Mercy Lloyd, and with her help conducted still another Friends' school at Salem, Columbiana County. Sponsored and supported by the local Monthly Meeting, it was a coeducational boarding school, offering a program ranging from primary instruction up to what we would now call the junior college level. Jesse and Mercy were hired as "principal teachers," to be assisted by "well-qualified *male* and *female*" instructors. In the fall and winter sessions of 1848-1849 the school had sixty-five "male" students and sixty-three "females," this student body being drawn from Ohio, Pennsylvania and Virginia.

Apparently this teaching experience at Salem did not satisfy Jesse's restless spirit: he now began to study medicine, and, after a short time, moved to Logan County near Bellefontaine, where his wife owned some land. Here he practiced medicine and did some farming until Mercy's death.

But Mercy's death did not cause Jesse to pine away. In 1854 he married Sara Morgan Paxson, whose ancestor, James Paxson, left Buckinghamshire, England in 1682 to join the Quaker community in Bucks County, Pennsylvania. How the Paxsons got to Ohio we don't know; we do know that Sara and Jesse soon left Ohio for Iowa, perhaps because Jesse's antislavery views made life in a turbulent area both unsafe and unpleasant. Settling in West Liberty, Jesse practiced medicine, and fathered Helen Holmes about 1860; she was to marry John Dryden of Nebraska. Four years later Jesse Herman Holmes II, the hero of our story, greeted the wintry winds of Iowa with his lusty birth cries.

Up to the time of Jesse II's birth, his family, on both the paternal and maternal sides, had illustrated very well indeed that westward push, that independent spirit, and that capacity for hard work and endurance which characterized so many pioneer Americans. Jesse II was no exception to this pattern. He attended country school in the West Liberty area, and then went on to graduate from high school in 1879 when he was only fifteen years of age. This precocious promise of greater things to come led the Holmes family to move to Lincoln, Nebraska in that same year, so that he might attend the state university there. He enrolled as a student, but, due to his father's poor health, found that he had to finance his education largely through his own efforts. He spent the summer vacations — and apparently one full year as well — cleaning the exhibits in the university's museum, and working in a dairy and on a cattle ranch. Returning to the academic life, he still pursued paying occupations: e.g., he did such a good job of tutoring a young man implicated in a robbery that the former bandit was able to enter the university.

In 1884 he received the B.S. degree. While his major interest had been in the sciences, he also did considerable work in literature. (Years later his daughter-in-law, Grace R. Holmes, recalled how Jesse would sit on a porch on a summer evening and recite from memory long passages from Shakespeare and other poets and literary lights.) After graduation the need for money drove him to devote a year to tutoring and serving as assistant librarian at his alma mater.

In the fall of 1885, however, Jesse felt that the time had come to push on to higher things. He left his home in Lincoln with one hundred dollars in his pocket, heading east to Baltimore, where he entered Johns Hopkins University in pursuit of a doctorate, taking major courses in chemistry, physics, and with a minor in philosophy. The hundred dollars he had brought with him would not last very long, he well knew, so he got a job as assistant librarian in the university library.

But a librarian's wages also proved inadequate; he found that he had to leave Johns Hopkins to earn his living and gather more capital funds. He took a job in the Sidwell Friends' Select School, Washington, D.C., during the years 1886-1888. This was an "Elementary and High School for Both Sexes;" he was to teach its students "Science, German, and History." During the summer-vacation periods of the school Jesse worked at various jobs to amplify his income. He put in a stint as a railroad surveyor in Colorado, and collected botanical specimens for the United States Herbarium, Department of Agriculture, in the pine barrens of Potomac Valley, New Jersey. (Later on, in a summer-vacation period of Johns Hopkins, he was to collect botanical specimens in Colorado, traveling by horse and wagon over the rough trails of the canyon country, many miles from the nearest railroad. The main object of this adventure was to find grass seeds, which, if crossed with others, would produce a more nutritive grass capable of growing in arid soils.)

Going back to graduate study at Johns Hopkins in the fall of 1888, Jesse took advanced work in chemistry, biology and mineralogy, and was granted the degree of Doctor of Philosophy in 1890. He returned to the Sidwell School that autumn for three more years of service, his teaching assignments being science, geography, and history.

A Fortunate Marriage — the Wren and the Jay

Sometime during the period 1888-1891 Jesse met Rebecca St. Clair Webb, Philadelphia Friend, while she was visiting her Aunt Annie (wife of Dr. Oliver E. Janney) in Baltimore. He immediately fell in love with this gay, witty and vivacious girl, with her wren-like figure and quick movements — a love affair which endured through a long life together, cementing their union in times of heartbreak and blooming still more in their many moments of triumph. (Years later, when he created a large autobiographical rug, he started the series of pictures in the rug with a deer on the upper left-hand margin to represent the happy hours they had together in the Philadelphia Zoo during the courtship. He said that his life never really began until he met and married "Rebe.") The courtship itself was a whirlwind affair, causing Rebe's older sisters to poke gentle fun at her, saying that she had " 'fallen like a ripe plum' to this dashing young Lochinvar out of the West...."

Given such impetuosity, the wedding could not be long delayed. Nor could the threatened heat and humidity of a Philadelphia summer dampen the spirits of the young lovers: they decided to marry themselves in a Quaker ceremony on June 16, 1892. Rebe's parents broadcast an invitation to the festivities:

William B. and Rebecca T. Webb
desire thy presence
at the wedding reception of their daughter
Rebecca S.
and
Jesse H. Holmes

Fifth-day evening, Sixth month sixteenth,
from eight until ten o'clock
1728 Mt. Vernon St.,
Philadelphia
1892

We may be sure that the entire Webb clan was there, welcomed at
the door by the father and mother of the bride. William B. Webb,
well-to-do druggist, and member of the board of trustees of the
Philadelphia College of Pharmacy, had come to the Quaker City by
way of York, Pennsylvania and Baltimore, Maryland, where he
began to learn the business of being a druggist by working in the
drug store of Coleman and Buchanan. Moving to Pennsylvania,
he was graduated from the Philadelphia College of Pharmacy
in 1845, and founded a pharmacy in Philadelphia distinguished over
the years for its skill, accuracy, and feeling of responsibility to its
customers and to the medical profession. Rebe's mother, nee
Rebecca Turner, traced her ancestry through the Turners of
Maryland to the St. Clairs of Scotland and their Rosslyn Castle near
Edinburgh.

No doubt several of Rebe's four sisters were also greeting the
wedding guests; perhaps one was upstairs helping her put the
finishing touches to her wedding gown, described by Rebe as being
of "White corded silk, made with Princess back *au train*. . . ." The
gown was V-shaped front and back, and trimmed with Duchess lace
at the neck and elbows. A white veil, bouquet of white roses, white
gloves and slippers, completed what must have been a vision of
beauty to the eager young bridegroom.

Jesse had left Washington the day before the wedding with
"Ernest and Warner," friends and colleagues at Sidwell School.
After "a very jolly trip" they arrived in Philadelphia and went
directly to the Webbs. Here they took tea and "gazed on the glories
that had arrived" — about 140 wedding presents displayed "to
advantage" in a side room. After some more tea they had a brief
rehearsal; and then the three young men went over to Samuel Carr's
"for to sleep. . . ." (Samuel B. Carr, a teacher, had married
Cassandra T. Webb, one of the bride's sisters.)

The next day Jesse found the Webb house very busy and "turned
upside down. . . ." Cheesecloth draperies had been put across one
end of the parlor and sprays of smilax over these. "The rest of the

9

room was adorned with ferns and daisys [sic] brought in . . . by the
S.A.K. boys and girls (That's the literary society [the Webbs] belong to). . . ." Jesse helped in the arrangement of these items to a
"very beautiful result," and then went on to help Ernest, his best
man, get rigged out for the occasion. "I was very much tickled to
get him into a dress suit and he looked very fine. . . ."

And then came the Big Moment. The wedding party walked to the
cheesecloth bridal bower in the parlor and sat down in a semicircle.
After a short pause, Jesse reported, "Rebe and I arose and
proceeded to marry ourselves — or each other, whichever it is. . . ."
After a brief Quaker meeting, the "awfully hot" room was
ventilated, and everyone crowded around the young couple to
shake their hands and offer congratulations. Jesse wrote later that
"I drew largely on my reserve supplies of brilliant impromptu but
didn't have enough to go 'round. . . ."

The need for more brilliant repartee was at least partially avoided
when the whole company trooped upstairs to a supper table spread
in "unexampled gorgeousness" for some one hundred guests. Rebe
and Jesse had good appetites: they put away chicken croquettes,
chicken salad, and ice cream "just as if [they] weren't a bridal
couple. . . ." The formal reception followed, forcing them to stand,
shake hands, and "talk pretty" until ten o'clock, when they got
ready to leave on their nuptial flight. Their carriage arrived at 10:45.
What happened next bears telling in Jesse's own words:

> I happened to know that some of the young and giddy expected
> to throw rice at us so I held back a little when Rebe went out and
> just as the appointed man was sprinkling some toward her I
> knocked the bag out of his hand . . . and off we went.

And so it was that Rebe and Jesse — she like a wren and he more
like the flashing, aggressive blue jay — started out on their honeymoon. Their destination was Middleville, New Jersey, on the shores
of Swartswood Lake. They missed a train connection or two, but, as
Jesse reported to his mother in Nebraska on the fourth day of his
nuptial adventure, "we didn't care and we're having a jolly
time. . . ." He wrote that they spent some of that time rowing on the
lake, swimming, and walking. More than that, he had engaged to
give a temperance lecture at the local Methodist Episcopal church
the following Sunday evening. (Perhaps here we have a measure of
our man — that he would give a temperance lecture while on his
honeymoon!)

10

A New Job: the George School Experience.

The honeymoon over, Jesse returned in the fall of 1892 to his teaching duties at the Sidwell School in Washington. (We are not sure whether Rebe accompanied him or not; perhaps she stayed with her parents in Philadelphia.) But another teaching opportunity soon opened for him, no doubt more lucrative, and certainly more suited to his training in science. He joined the faculty of the George School, Newtown, Bucks County, Pennsylvania, when it opened its doors to students for the first time in 1893, being hired to teach chemistry, physics, astronomy, and mineralogy.

George School had been founded through the philanthropic generosity of John M. George, heir to the fortune of a prominent Philadelphia Quaker family. With George L. Maris as principal, it fielded a fine faculty in that first year of its existence. Three "professors" and seven "teachers" were to prepare its students for success in "the pursuits and realities of active life. . . ,"and to equip them for admission "into the best colleges." Jesse was one of these professors, along with Charles M. Stabler (mathematics), and Joseph M. Johnston (history). The seven teachers included Mary E. Speakman (reading and composition); George H. Nutt (manual training); Belle Vansant (biology); Agnes Woodman (English); Anne H. Brinton (freehand drawing); Sophie Lange (German and French); and Anne Jackson (librarian).

Pleased to be in such distinguished company, and anxious to make a good impression, Jesse plunged into his first year at George School with his characteristic zest for a challenging task. He must have lived as a proctor in the boys' wing of the newly constructed main building, leaving Rebe with her parents, for we find him serving as leader of the boys doing exercises with Indian clubs, dumbbells, and parallel bars in the basement of Main before bedtime. Since he had an intense interest in current events, he often appeared in Assembly to speak on topics of recent public concern, sometimes continuing such discussions in evening dormitory sessions after the lights went out and students gathered around him in the dark. An outgoing person, he played tennis, and also enjoyed the many social events promoted by students, faculty, and townspeople. (However, at one such neighborhood party, being a man of "discriminating . . . eating habits," he refused to touch "ice cream with a stick in it.") But he must have enjoyed especially that George School banquet, held in March, 1894, when his newly

11

written *Neshaminy,* set to the tune of *Maryland, My Maryland,* was sung for the first time, "taking its cue from Sophie Lange's tuning fork. . . ." *Neshaminy* was to be the school's song, remaining popular for a long time.

Such social activities, of course, were but side-pleasures incidental to Jesse's main job of teaching chemistry, physics, and other physical sciences. His classes in the beginning were quite small, and his methods very progressive. He believed that science should be studied as a method of inquiry, and that no science, considered as subject matter, should be taught in isolation from other sciences. Accordingly, he and his colleague in biology, Belle Vansant, taught so that their separate subjects should be seen by the students as closely related to each other, and to mathematics, in "a natural manner." Both he and she followed their own special interests, their vibrant personalities and enthusiasms generating in their students "a contagious devotion for their work. . . ." Textbooks were used, but considered as of secondary importance; there were extensive assignments to do outside reading in library books. Jesse did not like the "experiments" outlined in laboratory manuals, with their foreordained results; he wanted his students to develop their powers of observation on everyday events, subject the observed data to systematic analysis, and arrive at their own conclusions. In all his teaching he wanted the students to realize how the science they studied applied to the "practical and normal situations" of daily life.

(Since Jesse, using these methods, quickly earned a reputation as "an unusually versatile and inspiring teacher," it came as a shock to many people when he left George School in 1899 to teach philosophy and religion at Swarthmore College. Joseph S. Walton, who followed George L. Maris as principal in 1901, expressed "profound regret" that he had not chosen to continue developing his new and stimulating approach to the teaching of the physical sciences. It seemed to Walton that Jesse had abandoned the greater for the lesser field of service. Still the two men remained close friends and co-workers: they were active in promoting the work of the Friends General Conference (Hicksite) and its Advancement Committee; and they originated a series of summer schools at George School to impart new teaching methods for First-day schools. Jesse was on the faculty of the first summer school of this kind in 1907, teaching a course on the history of religious doctrine, and, we may be sure,

12

showing by example how religious instruction should be conducted.)

It was this emphasis on practicality, plus a feeling of inadequacy in his technical training, which led Jesse to take the course in "Electrical Engineering" offered by the Harvard University Summer School in 1894. This course, designed to help teachers of physics in high schools and preparatory schools, covered nearly the same material as the regular college course entitled "Industrial Applications of Electricity." It was also to include lectures on the theory of electrical machinery — dynamos, motors, et cetera. Prerequisites for the course: a good knowledge of general physics, previous training in electrical testing, and "a good mathematical training up to and including calculus."

Returning to Rebe in Philadelphia after summer school, Jesse took her to Newtown on a house-hunting expedition. They found one on the outskirts of town, a three-story frame structure with porches and a semi-gabled roof.

So, in early September, 1894, Rebe was in the throes of shopping for more furniture and moving to her new home. She described how she went to Van Sciver's in Philadelphia for a library table, how on her return she was met at the Newtown railway station by a delegation from George School, escorted to the school to join Jesse for dinner, and then how they were taken back to their house in a pouring rain. "I never shall forget that night, our home-coming," she wrote. "The mud was ankle deep all around the house, but a few boards had been placed from the kitchen porch to some solid earth. . . ." near the street. Rebe and Jesse got out of their carriage; Jesse tried to find the solid earth and the boards while Rebe stood in the downpour. "Finally we got in, and then the matches wouldn't light, but finally the lamp was lighted, and we went upstairs. . . ." She found that there were only "two springs and a mattress on top . . . in our room. . . ." Since Rebe had only one sheet in her "grip," and the comforts were all on the third floor, they were in some trouble on a cold and rainy September night. In spite of the fact that the stairs to the third floor had been freshly painted, they just *had* to have those extra coverings. Jesse put wooden blocks on every other step, and then, Rebe wrote, "valiantly went forth to conquer fate and the comfortables. I never saw anything so funny as when he came downstairs, his arms full of studd, and making frantic efforts to balance himself on the little blocks of wood, and not get fresh paint all over his clothes. . . ." Rebe said that he looked like a ballet dancer, and that she gave way to "unseemly mirth, but . . . repented. . . and helped him as much as I could." After that they made the bed, unpacked two chairs, and then retired for the night.

In the next week or two, through the swarming of workmen and their own efforts, Jesse and Rebe would be established in comfortable fashion. The house furnishings would be installed — a "library rug. . . , our bedstead and washstand. . . , a table with lamp, some chairs, and my desk. . . . ," as Rebe described them. And we may be sure that their many beautiful wedding presents were displayed and used to their best advantage, among them being a silver-plated tea set and solid-silver cutlery. Pictures were hung; and the many well-bound set of volumes by Hawthorne, Browning, Oliver Wendell Holmes, and Lowell were housed in appropriate book cases. Although their presents had included lots of "jimcrackery," according to Jesse, there were so many fine things that he regarded them as "an embarrassment [sic] of riches — but Rebe don't and after all as long as we have 'em it's no more extravagant and indeed is less so to use fine things then cheaper ones. So I bear it with considerable equanimity."

In general, Rebe found her new situation "very cosy [sic]." But she was somewhat unhappy about the requirements being put on Jesse by his job at George School, as well as by its peripheral demands. "I can't get much out of Jesse — today is Faculty Mt'g, and 7th day he has to attend a horrid old F.D.S. Union [?] in Newtown and speak twice [sic]. . . ." In addition, he was being pressed to write an article for the "Current Topics Committee." She thought that people should have more mercy on a man just moving into a new house. Beyond such irritations, she found that her domestic problems regarding Jesse were only beginning. As the daughter of a well-to-do Philadelphia family she had not been forced to learn all the skills a housekeeping wife might be expected to have; now she found herself faced with a housewifely duty which had ordinarily been performed by a maid. Being quite properly concerned about her husband's appearance when he made his first public speech in Newtown, she surreptitiously pressed the trousers to his best suit. Apparently there wasn't enough time to correct what she had done, for Jesse appeared on the platform with creases on the sides a la sailor pants.

Although Rebe was to be saved from similar mistakes through the services of colored maids, working off-and-on throughout her

14

married life, she learned to do many of the tasks expected of a housewife in the period of economic depression characterizing the mid-1890s. She also learned that it was the essential nature of her husband Jesse to be ever in the thick of things, ever busy in endless lectures, writings, and public, private, and professional ventures of all kinds. During his first year at George School, he had become aware of the considerable effort needed to keep abreast of a system of instruction in which students had five daily classes (four with homework), entailing twenty-three prepared lessons per week. Now, it was becoming increasingly clear, Jesse's new approach to the teaching of science was a demanding one, involving much interdisciplinary research and planning, and many visits to the library to set up the outside reading lists and schedules. And then there were always special projects to promote, such as the exhibits of student work in chemistry, physics and biology to be shown along with George H. Nutt's exhibits of his student's work in manual training in 1895 and 1896. The many visitors to these exhibits — from Pennsylvania, New York, Maryland, and Ohio — were greatly impressed by the accompanying demonstration classes in chemistry and physics put on by Jesse H. Holmes. And, since this sort of thing did not seem to exhaust his energies, he continued his practice of giving interesting comments on current events in school assemblies, along with George H. Nutt and Charles M. Stabler. Temperance, that hardy perennial among public issues, was discussed from the prohibitionist point of view by Jesse; Charles Stabler, a temperance advocate, was more likely to present the other side on this or any other controversial public issue, if only to serve as a foil to Jesse's rapier.

One of the most controversial of all issues in the early years of George School was the apparent conflict between science and religion. Jesse, with his feet planted firmly in both camps, delivered many memorable messages on this topic in public assemblies as well as in Quaker meetings for worship. His teaching and preaching, projected with all the force of his powerful personality, generally appealed to the students because he "left things undecided and stimulated further thinking. . . ." The messages of Charles M. Stabler and George L. Maris, while "undoubtedly on a high intellectual and spiritual level," frequently struck young minds as too conclusive and authoritarian. But Jesse's liberal, open-minded approach sometimes drew fire from his colleagues. Mary E.

Speakman, who livened her classes in English with her brilliant wit and humor, asserted one day in Assembly that Jesse H. Holmes "had 'his wit from his memory and his facts from his imagination,' an attack that Holmes took good-naturedly. . . ." His advanced ideas and experimental attitude disturbed such conservative Friends as William P. Bancroft, who once said, "Jesse, thou frightens me sometimes, but I think thou art about right."

By the time Jesse heard such opinions and comments he was basking in the sunshine of popularity and success. Now thirty-three, the photograph of the George School Faculty for 1896-1897 shows him in a confident mood, wearing a gates-ajar collar with black tie, and already sporting the moustache and pointed beard which were to become so familiar to his many audiences in the Eastern United States up to 1942. The year 1896 was an important one for him. His daughter Elizabeth was born on May 1, weighing in at eight pounds, and, according to her mother's report in July, loved her bath and hated her clothes "as a well-regulated baby should." Shortly after Elizabeth's birth, Jesse was notified that the Phi Beta Kappa chapter at the University of Nebraska had elected him to membership as a distinguished alumnus.

And then J. Russell Smith, destined to be a life-long friend and colleague, joined the faculty at George School as a teacher of history. Like Jesse, Dr. Smith was to leave George School in 1899; he would advance his career in economic geography at the University of Pennsylvania and Columbia University. As we shall see, the paths of the Smith and Holmes families often ran parallel courses in social and reform activities.

A Summer Trip to Europe.

These were heady times for Jesse and Rebe, full of domestic and professional adventures. But as the spring of 1898 approached, the pressures of their lives led to a decision to take a trip abroad in the summer of that year. Leaving their "precious daughter to the tender ministrations of her aunts and grandmother. . . . ," Jesse and Rebe joined Belle Vansant, Emma Bromwell, and Ellen Pyle for a three-month's jaunt through Western Europe, England and Scotland. They left New York June 16, sailing on the *S.S. Werkendam* of the Holland-American Line, bound for Amsterdam.

Although Jesse was "rather of the opinion that a diary is all tomfoolery. . . . ," both he and Rebe kept travel logs, filling them with salty comments on the people they met and the things they saw — a lucky move for the writer, for without these detailed notes we would know very little about their activities on this trip, nor would we get so many insights into the personalities and characters of our travelers.

The first day or two aboard the *Werkenham* were spent in getting adjusted to their new quarters. They were assigned the second table in the dining saloon, Jesse taking the end position. After meals, we may suppose, they walked the deck and sized up their fellow passengers. Ever the extrovert, Jesse soon struck up a speaking acquaintance with a professor from Columbia University and with a graduate student from Nebraska. But he was more interested in the steerage passengers, no doubt rejects from Ellis Island. He found them generally destitute, with "few resources and few comforts. . . . It doesn't seem right that one like myself should have the comforts while [they are without]; but what can one do?"

Two days later this restless, energetic man with reformist impulses found life on board ship almost intolerable. "A more idle and aimless existence [*sic*] than ocean-steamer life would be hard to imagine. In a fit of almost unheard of energy yesterday I took a couple of photographs of the ship and talked photography to several people. . . ." Two days after that he was still complaining: "Nothing really happens. . . . Man becomes accustomed even to nothing. The days pass more easily than at first. We eat and sleep — sleep and eat — read a little and sleep . . . so it goes." He reported that they *had* seen some flying fish and a few "large creatures, yclept porpoises by some who knew not, ..."

Still, things were not as dull as they seemed. Jesse had met several other passengers, among them being the sister of Lillian Blauvelt, a well-known opera star. And "A very rough looking man who looks like a mechanic . . . was pointed out as the perpetrator of Ta-ra-Boom-de-ay and other popular songs. Has made enough out of them to retire on." A week later both Miss Blauvelt and the Ta-ra-ra man [Henry J. Sayres] joined a violinist named Van Gelder in a ship's concert and entertainment. Jesse found Van Gelder's playing "something to remember," although Miss Blauvelt's voice was "too operatic" for him. As for "Ta-ra-ra's performance;" well, that was "about what would be expected — rather clownish and vulgar. . . ." A certain Herr Zick gave an illustrated talk on student life at the

German universities, which Jesse found "interesting but tough." The picture presented by Herr Zick "of the sottish, swinish life of the student . . . was not less vivid because told with entire approval and as one who still joined in the debauchery." The concert-performance closed with the singing of the national anthems of Holland, France, Germany, and the United States. Jesse enjoyed the foreign songs because the people from those countries sang with so much spirit and enthusiasm. The Americans sang *America*, but "fell all over the Star Spangled Banner. Our national hymn is not yet written."

Landing at Amsterdam the day after the concert, the Holmes party toured the city, enjoying the generally foreign air of all things — the quaint, red-tiled houses, the very small donkeys pulling carts, the wooden shoes worn by the people in the narrow streets, and the many varieties of beautiful dogs seen everywhere in great number. But they found the Ryks Museum overwhelming in its size and in the number of things to see. Most noteworthy were the pictures in the International Gallery by Rembrandt, Van Dyck, Reubens, and Murillo.

From Amsterdam they journeyed to the Hague, to Delft and Rotterdam, and to Antwerp, Brussels and Cologne, consulting their Baedekers all the while and visiting the major palaces, museums and cathedrals. They called the cathedral in Cologne its "one great thing"; as Quakers, however, they could not stomach the church of St. Ursula. "Her bones and those of the 1100 virgins massacred with her at Cologne are now a source of income to the church. 'To such base uses,' etc."

Much more pleasant was their trip up the Rhine, although at Bonn their Quaker sensibilities were again offended by the presence of two large cannons, and soldiers everywhere. ". . .we are in a land of armed men. . . ." Upstream from Bonn they were thrilled to see the Drachenfels, Bingen, the Schloss Rheinstein, and the Lorelei rocks. Jesse found the Lorelei formation especially "impressive" because of "old associations." Going to Heidelberg by train, they found it a beautiful place. Walking along the *Philosophen Weg* near Heidelberg, Jesse watched two sturdy young women going down a steep vineyard path, each one carrying a large, heavy rock on her head, "one bare arm up steadying the stone. . . ." But let our young reformer from the farmlands of Iowa and Nebraska tell the rest of the story:

I do not consider the free outdoor work of these women a great hardship, I have seen them in the hay field, driving or helping to pull the dog carts [,] and then they look able for their duties and hearty in them. There is some cant in our condemnation of such wholesome outdoor work for women while we condone the deadly sweatshop and piece work system and the many other ways by which we grind our women into the mire.

In Strassburg they watched the famous clock figures in the cathedral tower. They went on to Basle and Lucerne, where Jesse discovered that he did not need to try out his graduate-school French or German on the hostess of the Hotel de l'Ange since she spoke English as well as he did. The next stop was Interlaken, where Jesse woke Rebe at four o'clock in the morning so that they might see the sunrise against the snow-covered mountains. They dressed rather hurriedly, joined a party of thirty or more tourists, and then stood for forty-five minutes "to see his Majesty deign to rise. At last the tops of the . . . mountains were tinged with rosy light . . . and spell-bound we watched the transformation scene. . . ." Next day the Holmes group took a long carriage ride to Grindlewald, "the Jungfrau being in sight most of the way. . . ." They were beset by children running alongside their carriage, trying to sell flowers, fruit, or lace. They walked from their Grindlewald hotel to a glacier, Rebe calling it "a long, hot stony walk. . . ." to see "a mass of dirty icy snow. . . ." But she found other aspects of this part of Switzerland beautiful and interesting — the "Staiback [sic] Falls," the village of Lauterbaunnen, and the costumes of the Swiss girls. In Berne they watched the bears, then went on to Lausanne and Geneva, where Jesse bought her a "beautiful opal ring" as a souvenir.

Passing up a visit to the Mer de Glace at Chamonix in favor of resting in Geneva, they eventually took a train to Ferny, the home of Voltaire. Then on to Paris, which Rebe thought to be "most wonderful" at night: the Church of the Madeleine, the Place de la Concorde, the lights glittering all around, the "revolving," changing light on the Eiffel Tower. . . , the vast statues looming up in the semi-darkness. . . ." Walking down a boulevard on a Sunday evening, Rebe was impressed by the crowds — "like a great procession —" and impressed too to find the restaurants and cafes so full of people, and the shops open. The following day they strolled the Rue St. Antoine, "the street of the 'hoi polloi'," and then visited

19

Notre Dame, the Palaise Royale, the Louvre, the Garden of the Tuilleries, and the Bourse. Versailles could not be missed; they saw the Little Trianon, "where Marie Antoinette and her ladies used to play at being peasants. . . ." Then they visited the Palace, with its interminable corridors, rooms, and paintings hanging everywhere. Rebe noted that Waterloo was "discreetly left out of" the series of paintings depicting the leading events of French history. Returning to Paris, the Holmes party did the sightseeing chores expected of the tourist — visiting the Pantheon, the Arc de Triumphe, the Tomb of Napoleon, etc. —, and then "we girls" went to the Bon Marche and really "did" the store. They found the store inferior to American stores a la Wanamaker, being on a par with Philadelphia's Eighth Street emporiums. Still, although the inferior merchandise was "very high in price," Rebe "bought *40 pairs* [sic] of gloves. . . ."

Confessing that she was not particularly fond of sculpture, Rebe nevertheless paid another and more leisurely visit to the Louvre. She saw quite "a number of Venuses, including the *Venus de Milo!* [sic]." She found much more pleasure in visiting the Louvre's Salon Carre, where she bought a few paintings.

But now the time had come to go to England. On July 29 the Holmes party returned to their hotel, packed their belongings, and then took an evening train to Le Havre, where they boarded a ship for Southampton. From there they went to Salisbury, finding the cathedral "beautiful", and to Stonehenge, which they thought to be "interesting." In London Rebe praised the room accommodations and condemned the meals in comparison with those they had had on the Continent. On August 1, although it was a Bank Holiday, they were able to pick up their mail at Brown and Shipley's travel agency. Their mail was most welcome, especially so since it brought them greatly needed travel funds. However, Jesse's suitcase, lost somewhere in Germany, had not been forwarded. The next day they went to the British Museum where Rebe demonstrated once again that marble figures left her cold. The Elgin Marbles, brought to London from the ruins of the Parthenon by Lord Elgin, drew this comment: "Personally, I confess that I cannot get up any degree of enthusiasm over mutilated and disfigured statues. A torso, an arm, or a piece of leg, even if the sculpture thereof be inimitable, are unable to thrill me!. . ." She found the Assyrian and Egyptian displays much more interesting, with "statues and bas-reliefs in a state of perfect preservation, dating from 3600 to 800 B.C."

In the next week or so Jesse and Rebe made a flying trip through the Lake Country northwest of London, and then went on to Edinburgh and Glasgow. In constant concern about the adverse effects of industrialization on working people, Jesse thought industrial Glasgow to be rather revolting. The streets were "very dirty," and in a walk to their lodgings, Jesse and Rebe "saw more hollow-eyed men and women, dirty children and squalor in this walk than in any other of the same length in any city." But the trip to Scotland produced one good result: Jesse bought the heavy canvas which he was going to use later on as a base for his justly famous autobiographical rug.

They returned to London by way of York, where they stayed in the City Temperance Hotel. In London, however, there was a mix-up about their room reservations; the Holmes party was forced to split, Jesse and Rebe being assigned to an awkward and unpleasant room at No. 2 Montague Street, Russell Square, while the others reamined at No. 7 Montague Street, where they all took their meals.

Jesse's anger at this new housing agrrangement must have abated considerably in the course of a subsequent shopping trip with Rebe. With her help he selected "a gray business suit, a bicycle suit, ditto stockings, two neckties and a cap [,] amounting in all to between £3 and £4 — about nineteen dollars . . . but perhaps a little more. . . ."

During the rest of their time in England they were, by and large, conventional tourists, doing only a few unconventional things because of their special interests. Jesse's interest in adult education for working people led them to visit the Westminster Adult School; common humanitarian impulses caused them to go to the Foundling Chapel, where "The children looked very lovable — the girls in caps and aprons, the boys in red vests and dark blue coats with shiny buttons. . . ." The children sang "very sweetly," and the preacher told them the story about the same man serving as the artist's model for the faces of Jesus and Judas. No teacher of the sciences could afford to miss seeing Cambridge University, so Jesse and company journeyed out there. They were shown through the laboratories, which were large and convenient but with no otherwise unusual or distinguishing features. Returning to London, they took a bus to Shepherd's Bush, Hammersmith, and Picadilly. Westminster Abbey was not neglected; and the group walked past

Buckingham Palace and St. James Palace, and "blundered" into the residence of the Duke of Sutherland. They saw the crown jewels in the Tower of London, and, after lunch, visited St. Paul's Cathedral, causing Jesse to comment that the tombs and monuments there were "mostly of great killers. . . ." Then on to Windsor Castle, Burnam Beeches, and Stoke Poges, where they viewed the grave of Thomas Gray of *Elegy* fame.

On August 27 Jesse complained that "Girls have no idea of time! We started for the Tate Gallery yesterday morning and by various waits didn't reach it until about eleven and a half or later. . . ." But Jesse enjoyed the Tate Collection very much since it was composed entirely of "modern" works, ". . .and I prefer them greatly to Old Masters. . . ." He especially liked those by Watts — "*Love and Life, Hope* (harping on a single string). . . ," and those by John Millais and Sir Frederick Leighton. That afternoon the group went to the British Museum once again, and then on to the Parliament buildings. The day's tour ended at the Crystal Palace, where they saw a woman put a den of lions through their paces. "I don't like such things," Jesse wrote, although a few days earlier he had spent a very enjoyable three hours at the London Zoo.

The next day being a Sunday, these Hicksite Quakers decided to go to Devonshire House, where English Friends held their Yearly Meetings. Then the party went on to a session of Bun Hill Meeting, which was composed almost entirely of Friends "by convincement" through the teachings of the Bun Hill School. Jesse was "favored to hold forth on the progressive idea of God. . . ." That afternoon they enjoyed a concert at Albert Hall.

But now the summer's trip, so full of rewarding experiences, was drawing to a close. After visiting a few more historic places — Hampden Court Palace and Canterbury Cathedral — the Holmeses crossed the Strait of Dover to Boulogne, where they boarded the *S.S. Spaarndam.* They arrived in New York on September 14. From there it was but a brief trip to Philadelphia to pick up their daughter Elizabeth, and an even briefer trip from Philadelphia to Newtown and the George School.

3. A Change of Course

Presumably refreshed by their summer's jaunt abroad, Rebe and Jesse picked up the threads of that multi-colored fabric they were weaving in Newtown and the George School. Jesse, of course, continued to meet his classes in chemistry and physics, again making those subjects come alive in the students' minds through his imaginative approach and his winning personality.

But, in spite of his growing reputation as an inspiring teacher of science, he felt a nagging sense of incompleteness — a feeling that there were other responsibilities to be fulfilled, other worlds to conquer. We have seen how his proclivities for reform led him to discuss the temperance question in school assemblies; this same interest had led him to become the county chairman of the Prohibition Party. He provoked thought about Henry George's single tax in many a speech, and organized a Sunday-school class for working people in Newtown. Here, and in other places throughout Bucks and neighboring counties, he gave a series of lectures on the Bible and religious subjects, not only trying to reconcile religion and science in these lectures, but weaving into them threads of thought from his wide reading in philosophy and literature. Altogether, one gets the picture of a man with superabundant energy, ever flitting from place to place trying to fill religious, reform, and intellectual voids.

And he was a poet. We have seen how his *Neshaminy*, named for the Neshaminy Creek near George School, became the school song. Leaving further consideration of his poetic efforts to a later chapter, it is sufficient here to say that he had a life-long love for that rhymed cadence we call poetry. In 1941, in his last year of life, he put into a philosophical work he was writing a poem by Whittier which he might very well have quoted in 1898:

> I am — how little more I know —
> Whence came I, whither do I go?

A centered self that thinks and is,
A cry between the silences;
A shaft from Nature's quiver, cast
Into the future from the past;
Between the cradle and the shroud
A meteor flight from cloud to cloud.

Given all this poetic feeling, these diverse interests, talents, and activities, it should not have surprised his many friends and admirers that Jesse applied for a position as instructor in philosophy and religion at Swarthmore College sometime during the academic year 1898-1899. His change of course was more apparent than real, judging from his avocational activities since he married Rebe. His main purpose in life, it had become increasingly clear, was not to teach chemistry and physics in new and challenging ways, but to bring his scientific mind to bear on problems in philosophy, religion and social reform. There ought to be more science applied to the study and practice of philosophy and religion, he thought, just as philosophical and moral or ethical values should guide people when they applied scientific facts and laws to the creation of an industrial America. Perhaps people could be brought to see that there was no irreconcilable conflict between science and the Quaker concept of religion. Jesse believed that, working with more mature minds in a liberal collegiate atmosphere, he could make his post at Swarthmore a platform from which he might work toward the accomplishment of these ends.

The Oxford Preparation for the Swarthmore Job.

The Swarthmore authorities agreed with him. Reasoning from a reformist Hicksite tradition, and knowing Jesse's background, they offered him the position. And it was a measure of their desire to add this intellectual shooting star to the Swarthmore faculty that the Board of Managers, after his acceptance of the offer, granted him a leave of absence for the academic year 1899-1900 so that he might prepare more thoroughly for his new job. His plan was to study philosophy, Hebrew and biblical Greek at Oxford University, and to get a first-hand knowledge of areas involved in the background and origin of Christianity by touring Palestine and Egypt.

One may imagine the flurry of activity in the Holmes family after this good news was received from Swarthmore. The furniture in the

Newtown house had to be moved and stored, steamship accommodations secured for Jesse, and arrangements made to move Rebe, now pregnant with Jesse Herman III, to her mother's home in Philadelphia for her care during Jesse's absence. (Years later, when there was considerable talk about planned parenthood, Rebe exclaimed, "What's so new about that!? Jesse and I planned to have our second child while he was on his trip abroad and while I could enjoy the benefits of my Mother's home with none of the cares.")

The final word from Swarthmore came early enough to allow for some vacation before Jesse's departure for England in the summer of 1899. So he took his family to join their relatives at Carter Hill, on the shores of Kezar Pond about eight miles from Fryeburg, Maine. Here, renting a large farmhouse, the five Webb sisters, and their husbands and children, had since 1896 maintained a summer-vacation retreat from the heat and humidity of their homes in Pennsylvania and Maryland. Rebe, Jesse, and daughter Elizabeth had enjoyed previous visits there. And Jesse enjoyed this one, as shown by the entry in his travel diary on board ship later on: "A week since I was one of a dozen by the long table over a jolly game at Carter Hill. . . ."

We may be sure that this group gave him a rousing send-off when he left to board the Cunard liner *Cephalonia* in Boston the third week of August. And the United States mail moved almost as rapidly as he, for before sailing he received letters from friends, as well as "a dear little package of 'em from Rebe — one for each day of the voyage. . . ." Among the letters from friends were "I love thee" messages from Carter Hill's children, including one obviously written *for* three-year old Elizabeth, and marked with her childish circles and squiggles. One of the older children, Eleanor Janney, wrote a poem which Jesse found among these messages. Subscribed a "Round-Robin from the Carter Hill Folks," it is given here in its entirety. There seems to be no better way of showing something about Jesse's nature, and the nature of the Carter Hill group, than to let them speak in their own lines:

> Now, dear Jesse, when we think
> Of our dear one, far away,
> We would to thee greetings send,
> Words of love we fain would say.
>
> How we miss thee none can tell
> We love thee more than currant jell,

Or apple-sass, or chocolate fudge,
But, dear heart, thee must not judge
That without thee we will die,
Though full often we will sigh
For that fat and pudgy form.
When thee 'gins to feel, the storm
Do not think that thee'll be sick,
But to Christian Science stick.
We miss thee in the morning
When tennis doth beguile,
When bathing, boating, fishing,
Or grabouche we play the while.
But most of all we miss thee
In discussions fierce and wild,
For argument without thee
Is watery, weak and mild.
So we'll think of thee at night,
And we'll never more be happy
'Till thee once more looms in sight.

However amateurish this poem was (Eleanor apologized to Jesse for her awkward efforts at original poetry), Jesse's spirits must have been lifted by it as he settled into his quarters aboard the *Cephalonia*. While he had had some difficulty about the care of his bicycle, his baggage and his banjo were well handled, being safely placed into a large, pleasant stateroom with an upper and a lower berth. The upper berth was to be occupied by Dr. Frank Newman, a Leipzig Ph.D. in chemistry aiming to become a doctor of medicine. Jesse lost little time in decorating the mirror over his dresser with Rebe's picture, and Elizabeth's under it. And, before he made his first entry in his travel diary, he pasted a small photograph of Rebe and one of Elizabeth at the top of the first page. His emotional condition may be seen in his diary entry that the voyage would be the worst part of the whole year, for ". . .the heart strings haven't healed at the raw ends where they were jerked in two." Still, he resolved, he would try "to keep steady and intend to use the year for all there is in it. . . ."

His heart strings were at least partially healed, and his loneliness soon relieved, if we are to judge from his activities in the next few days at sea. After dinner on August 26 he dropped into the smoking room, where he was soon drawn into an animated discussion on the Philippines. "Two Americans were the combatants — the expansionist a middle-aged individual who said 'we done it,' the other a white-haired old sinner with a rather cynical view of humanity. . . ." Two Englishmen were there also, and Jesse was presently engaged with them on "the government of inferior races," these "Sir Oracle" types frequently interrupting him to say, " 'bosh, you know,' " interruptions which he "didn't mind at all. . . ." Jesse wrote to Rebe that he was greatly refreshed by the scrap and slept the "sleep of the (more or less) just" that night. The next morning (a Sunday) he had a leisurely bath, took a walk on deck before breakfast, and then attended Church-of-England services conducted by the captain. Here he met two girls, one of which was taken ill during the services and "had to charge out. . . ." The other girl he took to the bow of the ship for a chat. It was this one, as Jesse informed his pregnant Rebe, that he had picked out to be his girl for the voyage. "She is small (thee knows that's my taste), has rather sharp featured and pleasant manners, [and] is inclined to be helpful to the other ladies in various little ways. . . ." He had also walked the deck with a young Englishwoman, a Miss Weber, who was "home-sick, sea-sick, and love-sick." That evening he and his roommate played whist with the two girls.

At other times Jesse did some banjoing, played "ring-toss" and shuffleboard, and on occasion read a book — including one which particularly pleased him because its author was a student of William James, the famous Harvard advocate of pragmatism. On the third day at sea, perhaps feeling a little queasy, Jesse amused himself by drawing in his travel journal a series of six well-done pencil sketches of himself trying out various treatments or cures for seasickness. On the far left was a sketch of Jesse leaning over the ship's rail, his hat on the deck beside him. The next three frames of this comic-strip series showed a bottle of medicine, then a glass of seawater, and a cup of tea. The fifth frame showed Jesse's ample midriff, but with his belt tightened. And finally there was a rather good likeness of him, pointed beard and all, with his hand pointing to his forehead and a caption underneath the picture reading "mental science." But he was not actually ill; the next day found him in his usual high spirits: he tried a hurdle race over deck chairs with his roommate, taking a rather heavy fall.

It must have been about this time that Jesse read and reread one of those letters Rebe had sent to him in a package — "one for each day of the voyage. . . . " This particular letter must have sustained him throughout the rest of his trip. Rebe wrote that she missed him very much. "Sometimes thee has said that I was cold and undemonstrative . . . but now — when thee is going away for oh, so long, know that my whole heart and soul are thine. . . ." She assured him that she would not be happy or at peace until he was again by her side, "my . . . husband, and the devoted father of our *children* [*sic*]." "And," Rebe went on, "when I have said 'I love thee,' I have said it all . . . but I hate to stop. . . ." She closed her letter with some lines by Lowell:

> What were I, love, if I were stripped of thee,
> If thine eyes shut me out whereby I live,
> Thou, who unto my calmer soul dost give
> Knowledge and Truth and hold Mystery,
>
> ⤙⤙⤙⤙⤙⤙⤙⤙⤙⤙⤙⤙⤙⤙⤙⤙⤙⤙⤙⤙⤙⤙⤙
>
> Without thee I were naked, bleak and bare
> As yon dead cedar on the sea cliff's brow;
> And Nature's teachings, which come to me now,
> Common and beautiful as light and air,
> Would be as fruitless as a stream which still
> Slips thro' the wheel of some old ruined mill.
>   "Thine always,
>   Rebe"

The *Cephalonia* ploughed on through late-summer seas, passing an iceberg and a pod of spouting whales. On September 5 she stopped at Queenstown, then went on to end her voyage at Liverpool on September 6. Jesse disembarked, drove to the railroad station to catch a train for Birmingham — and immediately got into a row with the cabbie about the fare. On the train he discovered that he had forgotten his banjo; but his bicycle was waiting for him at the Birmingham station. Gathering his belongings, he hired another cabbie to take him to the Central Hall, where the Birmingham Friends held their meetings. Here he met some old friends: John W. Graham, Mary Travilla, Sarah Paiste, and Howard M. Jenkins. Through the good offices of these friends he was invited to attend an afternoon garden party on the luxurious estate of the Wilson-Kings outside of Birmingham. "Tea was served in a tent with a high platform floor while a band discoursed sweet music from another tent among the trees. . . ." As the band played on, Jesse wrote to Rebe, he mingled with the guests, not feeling "fully at home in such swell surroundings. . . ." But he must have made a good impression

28   035549 ⑧

on the Wilson-Kings, for he was invited to a supper party and to spend the rest of his stay in Birmingham in their palatial home. Professor McGifford, of Union Theological Seminary in New York, was to be his roommate. McGifford, "A pleasant young fellow," and a kindred spirit, had become quite famous since his searching history of the early Christian period had threatened the traditionalist doctrines of the Presbyterian Church. Jesse said that he had been "roughly handled" by the Presbyterian brethren and that he was likely to be tried for heresy that fall. However, McGifford's troubles were far away; at this point he and Jesse were enjoying the hospitality of the Wilson-Kings — their host "a tall, very fine-looking man with a frank, easy, almost breezy manner. . . ."; his wife a "rich, cultured" Quaker, but perhaps "rather shallow and worldly. . . ." Their supper party was fun, everyone joining in "telling stories, laughing, talking, etc. . . ."

Professor McGifford and many of the people at that garden party were in Birmingham to take part in the Friends' Summer School being held in Central Hall. Jesse attended, of course; he found out that the Summer School consisted of a series of lectures delivered by prominent theologians, both British and American. While Jesse noted the names and topics of the British speakers, especially Miss Joan M. Fry with her talk on two German mystics, he thought that Professors Rogers and McGifford, Americans, "were definitely the stars of the lecture course. . . ." Since McGifford's remarks under the title of "The Primitive Conception of the Church" were so much in accord with his own, Jesse must have applauded his assertion that, in the early times, Christian ideals and actions permeated the daily lives of Church members. But later, in a time of fear of weakness and sin, Catholicism developed as a safeguard, deriving its power from "external human forces and sanction. . . . Men were set up as leaders who abused their privileges, and ceremonious meetings took the place of the simple informal gatherings of the earliest Church. Fear won a victory over faith, and the heroic age of the Church disappeared. . . ." Jesse enjoyed these lecture-meetings; as an inveterate public speaker in his own right, he was especially delighted by the enthusiastic responses to the speakers shown by these English audiences. "A good point is applauded easily and spontaneously and there is a general active cooperation on the part of the listeners which must be very inspiring."

He may have found the next few days even more inspiring since he went on several bicycle excursions into the English countryside with interesting female companions. One of these was with a Miss Agnes Graham, "a little mite of a thing, [who] . . . was kind enough to take an interest in my happiness and welfare. . . . " Jesse and Miss Graham took tea at an adult school nearby, "and also rode from Warwick to Stratford. . . ." Then, in company with others, there was a ride with his hostess, Mrs. Wilson-King, to her family farm a dozen miles outside of Birmingham. There the party enjoyed tea in "daintily furnished" rooms. Following that, there was still another excursion into the country, this time to play tennis on the beautiful lawn of the Albrights. Following that, he mounted his trusty bicycle to visit the large adult school established by one of the Cadburys, that family so prominent in English and American Quakerism. Jesse found the "adult school business to be something tremendous. Attendance at two [sessions] was over 4000 the Sunday I was there. . . ." (That so many industrial workers should give up their Sabbath to go to a school run by Quakers indicated not only their need but the woeful inadequacy of the English system of public education.)

But now the time had come to leave Birmingham to advance Jesse's own education. Arriving in Oxford on a Friday afternoon late in September, he again availed himself of the mutual-aid aspect of the Society of Friends by staying in the home of a Quaker banker for the weekend. On ensuing days he found a rooming house run by a Mrs. Bumpus, and made arrangements to start his studies through Professor Thatcher of Mansfield College and Principal Drummond of Manchester. A call on Canon Driver of Christ Church College resulted in the hiring of a coach for Greek at ". . .3/6 per hour. . . ." Jesse thought this was a bit high until he was assured that 10/0 was the common rate.

These arrangements were made about September 27. From this point on until the middle of January, 1900, Jesse must have been so busy with his studies that he didn't have time to make notations in his travel diary about his work at Oxford. And there are no extant letters to Rebe for this period; it is not until January 16 and 17 that we find him telling her that he had been plugging away at Hebrew, finishing "a chapter in Genesis, besides dosing [sic] in grammar. . . ." He told her that he liked working at Hebrew much better than at Greek, and he feared that he rather neglected the latter. Still, he thought, Greek could be "brought up" more easily at home;

he could work on vocabulary, his greatest need. Some of his time had been spent in writing a set of "Lesson Leaves on the prophets and I have about finished the first. . . ." The "next lot," he thought, could be finished in Swarthmore. (Undoubtedly he planned to use these lesson leaflets in his college classes in religion at Swarthmore; perhaps too they might be used in First-day schools in Swarthmore Meeting.)

Such procrastinations, however, might have been avoided if Jesse had not been diverted by social events and by side-trips from Oxford. Thus, on September 25, before he started serious work on his studies, he took a bicycle trip to Gloucester. He spent the night in a temperance hotel, viewed the cathedral, and then, indulging his interest in social experiments, set out to find a rural socialist colony. There had been a fall out among the members, however; Jesse was told that the founder of the colony had withdrawn and was "lawing" to get his farm back. Returning to Oxford, Jesse almost immediately went on another bicycle trip, this time to visit the Witney School for Adults on invitation from Benjamin Neave, its director. He attended the morning classes, finding these to be more-or-less straight education. The evening meeting, however, was more in the style of a mission, with hymns to enliven the proceedings. Jesse was the speaker, giving " em a straight-from-the-shoulder peace sermon. . . ."

In these meetings with working-class people Jesse felt more comfortable than he had at the garden party given by the rich, middle-class Wilson-Kings. We are not sure how comfortable he felt when he met nobility at the home of the mayor of Oxford on October 13. The invitation to this affair, printed in Spencerian style on a card embossed with the blue-and-gold seal of the City of Oxford, seems worthy of full reproduction:

Town Hall  Oxford

Civitas Oxoniensis

To meet the High Steward of the City and
the Countess of Jersey and their Graces the
Duke and Duchess of Marlborough.

The Mayor and Mayoress
at Home
Friday, October 13th.
Music 9 o'clock
Civic and Academic Robes
An early answer is requested.

Although we don't know whether Jesse enjoyed himself at this reception, or whether he wore academic robes, we do know that he went on several other extracurricular excursions from Oxford. One of these was a rather extended trip by rail about January 14 to visit Mr. and Mrs. Henry Binns near York, a couple he had met in Birmingham. Apparently the Binns couple had another house guest, Frederick Andrews, the headmaster of Ackworth School, for he and Jesse were soon on a train bound for the Andrews' home. He enjoyed Andrews' "charming" talk, especially his stories of his activities in the temperance and other movements. Arriving at the school, Jesse had a "lively game of crockinal" [sic] with the Andrews' school-age daughters, and then had "one of the atrocious meals they call 'supper' — served at 9 o'clock and lacking all the esthetic elements which make a meal a kind of pageant of civilization. . . ." Jesse asserted that the English had no conception of a meal except that it was something to eat. "Their breakfasts are hideous, their dinners brutal, and their suppers vile. . . ." While he thought that perhaps it was too sweeping a generalization, there were still some elements of truth in his conclusion that they concentrated into their teas the social virtues that Americans distributed among all their meals.

Leaving the Ackworth School to return at Oxford, Jesse apparently had to change trains in Birmingham. In any case, he had enough time to visit the Birmingham Art Gallery, where he was very much impressed by the rich display of paintings, especially those by Rosetti. Arriving in Oxford, he no doubt buckled down to his studies for a brief time. But he soon reported to Rebe that on a "bright Sunday" he journeyed out to attend the Witney Meeting. When he got there he found that Benjamin Jackson, the Quaker missionary who had been expected to lead the evening meeting, was ill. Jesse wrote that he was asked to take Jackson's place as the leader. And then in that curiously involuted type of understatement still used by Quakers in 1900, Jesse said, "I didn't feel free to refuse. . . ." (When Rebe read this she probably snorted, "When did he *ever* refuse a chance to speak in public!?")

By this time Rebe's trans-Atlantic relations with Jesse had become a bit strained. In her last month of pregnancy, living with her mother and two sisters in Philadelphia (Lizzie had recently suffered a "backset"), Rebe felt lonely, somewhat neglected, and jealous of Jesse's good times, if we may judge from his long letter to her in the middle of January. Rebe had written of several "tumbles" she had taken recently; Jesse was of course greatly concerned about the dangers of a miscarriage. "Please be careful of thyself," he wrote, "and 'remember the medical man'. . . . Kogo is a little brick and I'm sure he or she will be a credit to us. . . ." He went on: "By the way, does thee know that the only time thee has called Elizabeth 'thy daughter' was on occasions when thee found it necessary to spank her? Why is this thus?" Rebe had written that, in general, their marriage had been a success; any difficulties which had arisen were mostly Jesse's fault. He agreed with her on this — "that'll surely disarm thee." And, he went on, "Thy deadly sarcasm about superior and inferior minds is duly and meekly appreciated. . . ." He thought that Rebe would be "amazed to know" that he was secretly rather cowed by what he found at Oxford — the antiquity, the stability, and the erudition. And, since she had wailed that she hadn't "been anywhere," he confessed that he rather dreaded all the traveling which seemed so charming to her. But, since she couldn't be with him, he praised her courage, patience and self-denial; their separation in these months of her waiting was giving evidence of "unselfishness and devotion that years of ordinary life wouldn't have brought to light. . . ." Writing of his projected trip to the Holy Land, he thought that he would travel light, using only two satchels. But he wouldn't leave until about the first of March; certainly he couldn't leave until he had a cable telling of her welfare and that of the "new darling."

About a month later Jesse received a cable at his Oxford lodgings telling him that the "new darling" had turned out to be a boy. Soon to be named Jesse Herman after his father and grandfather, he was born at his grandmother Webb's home, 1719 North Eighteenth Street, Philadelphia, on February 13, 1900. A short time later, on March 26, grandmother Webb died, leaving Rebe to carry on with her two children in the house now run by her sisters Lizzie and Cassie.

And a Trip to the Near East.

By this time, however, Jesse was in the middle of a three-month's tour of parts of the Near East. Writing to Rebe from Jerusalem, he told her of his recent experiences in Egypt: how he went to Memphis and Sakhara in company with a Unitarian preacher, an English druggist, and three Presbyterian ministers (he found the latter "rather raw"); how the party got off the train near Memphis to find themselves surrounded by "a howling mass of donkey boys. . . .''; and how they set out for Menphis without guides or donkeys, passing two towering statutes of Rameses II along the way. They saw a "miserable mud village" — all that was left of the ancient Heliopolis "where Joseph married the daughter of the Egyptian priest and became learned in the wisdom of the Egyptians. . . ." After a short time in Heliopolis, mainly spent in "chaffering" with the sellers of "doubtful 'antiques'," the party walked toward Sakhara, followed by a diminishing crowd of vendors. Beyond Sakhara Jesse took a picture of a veiled woman who consented to pose in front of a Bedouin tent spread near a plum orchard. "Of course 'backsheesh' was expected and rec'd. . . ." Pausing for lunch under a tree near a spring, the group saw a little girl and a toddling baby, "and what should one of the Presbyterian divines do but go charging at them with arms spread and howling. . . ." The baby was scared "almost into fits," and sought shelter in the arms of a woman nearby. After scolding the "unrepentent [sic] Calvinist," Jesse walked over to the woman holding the sobbing baby and offered some chocolate and crackers. "The woman understood the apology and smiled sweetly in Egyptian. . . ." Lunch over, the party ventured into the "shimmering heat of the desert," passing a few pyramids and the rock tomb where the ancient sacred bulls were buried. By the time the party got back to the railroad station one of them was nearly exhausted. But, Jesse reassured Rebe, ". . .it was *not* I — I could have kept it up for hours longer. Thee knows how I revel in heat. . . ."

The next day, however, drew a complaint: Jesse wrote of a long, tiring ride to Port Said — "7 hours of heat and dust. . . ." At Port Said he took a ship to Jaffa, where he visited the house of Simon the

Tanner; he went up to the roof where, according to the Biblical story, Peter had his vision of the sheet let down from heaven. Going on to Jerusalem, Jesse was thrilled to find the streets "full of the most varied crowd imaginable. A great many pilgrims of the Greek church are here, Russians in great numbers and others from everywhere. The costumes are a wonderful mix. . . ."

When he left Port Said for Jaffa and Jerusalem Jesse had told Rebe that, while he had been "roughing it" so far, now he would begin "a life of ease and luxury" lasting for the next eighteen days. He also told her that, if he had to do it over again, he would "go it alone" rather than be a member of a planned tour. He thought he would enjoy it more; certainly he could save a lot of money.

But when he arrived in Jerusalem he apparently struck a compromise between going it alone and being a member of a group: he hired a dragoman to show him around the city; he also indicated that he was shown the sights as a member of a party of tourists. One morning the dragoman, Isa n Lobat, took him to the Church of the Holy Sepulchre, only to find it closed because workmen were scrubbing it. Jesse was disappointed, we may believe; he was also pleased: "It is a relief to know that some things are cleaned in Jerusalem, for it is the filthiest, smelliest place it has yet been my lot to visit. . . ." Going through these dirty streets on their way to Mt. Zion they were "beset" by a group of lepers who screamed for money "in their shrill, wailing voices. . . ." Not far from the Church of St. James was a Mohammedan mosque containing the room where Jesus allegedly met his disciples for his last supper; it was also supposed to be the tomb of David and Solomon, as well as the scene of the resurrection. Jesse told Rebe that he was trying to be a good tourist, believing all the traditions about the places he visited as much as he possibly could. But, he said, it was difficult to believe that the same event occurred in several different places, or that so many great events were bunched in one place. He thought that he was like the White Queen in " 'Thro the Looking Glass' " [sic], spending some hours every day believing impossible things; he might "attain remarkable results in time."

In the afternoon Jesse's party found the Church of the Holy Sepulchre open and presumably clean. They gazed at the Sepulchre and the chapels for Greek, Catholic, Coptic and Armenian Christians crowded all around it, (Seeing these chapels may have provoked Jesse's remark that "The Church of the Sepulchre . . . is a commentary . . . on the unChristian nature of Christianity. For in it — as in the Church of the Nativity at Bethlehem — it is necessary to keep Turkish guards all the time to prevent the various sects of Christianity from quarreling . . . .") In front of the entrance to the Sepulchre the tourists found a slab of rock on which, as they were told, Jesus' body was laid for the anointing; nearby was the spot where his mother stood with John the Disciple; to the right was a rock symbolizing Calvary, with the place of the cross well marked; below this and to the left was the tomb. In Jesse's opinion, the whole place was "tawdry with gold and ornaments. . . ."

But, Jesse thought, the really impressive thing in the Sepulchre was the stream of tourists and pilgrims from foreign parts and places. There were "Cretans in quilted skin coats with knives in their belts, their fierce instincts quieted for the time. . . ." There were Greek priests in black, with cornice-topped stovepipe hats; they mingled with brown-clad Franciscan monks. Then there were the ever-present Anglo-Saxon tourists, who looked on the scene with "lofty good-humor," got in the way, and outraged other people's tenderest feelings with "calmest insolence." These Anglo-Saxons, one gathers from Jesse's account, looked with some condescension on the "Heavy Russian peasants, men and women, taking the one flight of their barren lives into the great world, stand [ing] about with great blue eyes wide open, unkept and shaggy, but with a grand simplicity and a sturdy strength in their features. . . ." And, Jesse predicted "If Russia ever really arouses herself these people will be a power. . . ."

From this point on he examined those places usually considered mandatory in the tourists' itinerary for Jerusalem and its environs. He went to the house of Pilate, and then traveled the Via Dolorosa to the Wailing Wall, where he saw several hundreds of Jews facing the Wall, either weeping or praying or reading from the Hebrew Bible. "They seemed deeply in earnest and it was a wonderful sight. . . ." After a night of rest Jesse's party went to the Mount of Olives, with its wonderful view of the Dead Sea, the Jordan Valley, and Jerusalem in the distance. On the way down they stopped in the Garden of Gethsemane, rode down into Gehenna, and returned to Jerusalem through the Jaffa Gate. Here they visited the Mosque of Omar and the Dome of the Rock, the latter with its Rock apparently held in place by nothing more than air. In the pavement nearby was another stone, square in shape and with three and one-half nails in it. "Once there were thirty-two. When the rest go the world comes to an end. If you put money on the stone it disappears — into the capacious hand of a Turkish priest — and you are promised a straight passage to Heaven when you die. Of course I didn't miss a chance like that. . . ."

Although Jesse admitted to Rebe that he was getting some pleasure out of all this sight-seeing, he told her that it was essentially a business — a duty to be performed as conscientiously as possible. "I'm *very* tired of travelling; thee hasn't any idea how tired. I'll be *so* glad to come home. . . ." While this feeling was undoubtedly genuine, his letters also show that he suffered twinges of conscience because, while he was able to travel about seeing new and strange sights, his wife had to remain in Philadelphia doing humdrum family chores. He tried to make these letters as entertaining as possible, giving Rebe so many details of the things he saw that she must have felt, at times, as though she were right there enjoying the sights with him. And, when he got to Beirut, Syria, he told her that when he had been in Italy on his way to Egypt he had bought a "mosaic stick-pin. . . , some little silk purses, and a lava cameo from Vesuvius . . ." These at least gave evidence that he was thinking of the folks at home.

But Beirut was in the future. From his base in Jerusalem Jesse had still to make a somewhat rugged trip to Hebron in company with three American ladies, and the river Jordan and the Dead Sea had not yet been seen except from a mountaintop. On the way to the Jordan Jesse's party passed hundreds of Russian pilgrims going to be baptized through total immersion in the waters of that holy river. Later on Jesse saw them undressing on the Jordan's banks in order to put on a single white robe like a nightgown. Men and women were all together — some old, some young; "some stood about on the bank stark naked. . . ." before donning their robes to wade through thick mud into the waters. Jesse quoted a certain Mulvaney to the effect that " 'It was the most ondacent parade ye ever saw.' " Since "A very little of this was enough . . . we drive back to the hotel. . . ." The next morning Jesse and Lobat, his dragoman, set out for Jericho, stopped for lunch at the Good Samaritan Inn along the way, and eventually reached the Dead Sea south of Jericho. Jesse had determined that, since only his dragoman was present, he was going to have a dip in these historic waters. When three ladies drove up at the critical moment he no doubt became a bit perturbed; but, as he wrote to Rebe, ". . .I wasn't going to be balked of a swim in the Dead Sea, so I went . . ."

Returning to Jerusalem, he started for Nazareth, Haifa and Acre. Touring Nazareth with the help of a guide, he thought that there was nothing of genuine or "high antiquity" except the ground and St. Mary's spring. Since the latter was the only spring in Nazareth, he believed that it must have been used by the family of Jesus. But he did enjoy seeing the picturesque activity there — women washing wool, and "stately water carriers with great jars on their heads" coming and going. He also liked the bazaars there as he liked all oriental bazaars. Then on to Haifa, where he met the daughter of Robert Dale Owen, famous deist and founder of the Workingmen's Party in New York in 1829. (Robert Dale Owen was notable also as the son of Robert Owen, founder of an experimental socialist community in New Harmony, Indiana.) From Haifa Jesse went to Acre, famous as a scene of the struggle between Richard Lion-Heart and Sadadin in the Third Crusade. But Jesse was less impressed by Acre's historial associations than by the "filthy hotel" he was forced to stay in. Here he was "eaten by three separate and distinct insects. . . ."; he complained that he "hadn't been free from fleas . . . since leaving Jerusalem — or even longer. . . ." And, if fleas were not enough, Jesse was subjected to harassment by the Turkish police during his stay in the hotel. His room was on the roof of a granary, with a large part of the roof extending from his doorway. One hot and sultry night he took a chair and sat on the roof to cool off and watch the sea. Here he also had a good view of the adjoining roof, which apparently sheltered a harem. "Indeed," Jesse related, "I saw a half dozen baggy balloon looking women on [the] adjoining roof soon after we arrived, but took no special notice. So the fool Turks thought I must have some designs on the beauties of the harem. . . ." In any case, he was questioned about his "suspicious movements" the following morning by the Turkish officials. His explanation about wanting fresh air and the sea view led them to depart rather reluctantly — "probably they thought they could frighten me into bribing them." No doubt Jesse's anger over this incident was soothed somewhat when the Jewish proprietor of the hotel complimented him on his ability to read Hebrew.

Leaving Acre, Jesse was lucky to find a small steamer going to Beirut. The English captain, however, had his problems: he spoke no Arabic, and his Arabic crew knew little English. Jesse reported to Rebe that he shouted his orders in English, accompanied by gestures and vituperations descending into downright profanity. But the steamer moved along somehow; it got to Tyre and Sidon only to find Jesse suffering from digestive complications. He did not go ashore at either of these ports of call. However, when the ship reached Sidon he was refreshed by the "perfectly delicious" odor of the orange blossoms on the shore.

Arriving in Beirut, he registered in a hotel and then went out to see the sights. His report to Rebe was most vivid: he related how he happened onto a Moslem parade celebrating the circumsion of a "little fellow of seven or eight years," with all the pageantry of whirling swordsmen and colorful banners; and how he stumbled onto a wedding celebration in which some forty bedouins of both sexes, all in their best attire, linked arms to sing and dance in a semicircle around a man "blowing a monotonous phrase on a shepherd's pipe. . . ." Many of the men were handsome, pleasant-looking fellows; "the girls were better looking than the baggy harem women" Jesse had seen, and had "an air of self-respect and freedom without boldness" which reminded him of American girls. However, they all had the lower parts of their faces "tattooed blue in various figures and some [wore] pendants in their noses and strings of coins about their heads. . . ."

Aside from these street scenes Jesse didn't find much of interest in Beirut. However, he had heard of a medical-missionary center established at nearby Brumana by English Quakers, so he traveled out to visit it by a tortuous road. The schoolmaster was the same missionary he had met in the adult school in Manchester, England. At the dispensary Jesse met the doctor, a cultivated Syrian Friend, and his young English bride. He was told that natives came to the dispensary and hospital from as far away as Damascus. But, when put on the spring mattresses sent by a well-meaning Quaker, they pleaded for "a board on the floor. . . ."

By this time Jesse too was almost ready for a stay in a hospital. He was in a depression both physically and mentally. Perhaps he had the "Travelers' Trot"; in any case he wrote Rebe on April 12 that he had been "vegetating" in the Beirut hotel for three days because his "interior department" was not well, and he couldn't walk or sight-see as much as he usually did. "Not that I'm ill," he assured her, "only not fully rested. . . ." He had tried to alleviate his boredom in this period of enforced idleness by studying Hebrew and reading paperback books, but still found time hanging heavily on his hands. And then, in this same time, he had received a letter from Rebe which added to his misery. Rebe's mother had died on March 26; the funeral and other cares were apparently wearing Rebe down. We can judge what she said in this letter by Jesse's reply: "I'm afraid thee's taxed beyond thy strength. How glad I will be to take the responsibility off thy tired little shoulders for a while. Well, it won't be long now. . . . I hope I've done right. I know I haven't sought my own *pleasure.*"

This mood of depression, and this ardent desire to get home, caused Jesse to change his travel plans. Earlier he had thought that he would return to England and take a ship to America from there. Now he planned to leave from Genoa on May 3 on a ship of the North German Lloyd Line. He arrived in Philadelphia on May 17 to be greeted by his long-suffering Rebe, his four-year old daughter Elizabeth, and his baby son Jesse Herman III. Jesse thought that baby Herman resembled his grandfather Holmes, " 'especially in his queer little chin.' "

4. In the Renaissance at Swarthmore, First Phase

After Jesse's reunion with his family in May, 1900, he had to give some thought to getting ready for the move to Swarthmore College and the opening of the fall semester. While the available records do not tell us just how that summer was spent, we may imagine that the entire family, including Rebe's sisters Lizzie and Cassie, made their annual trek to Carter Hill in Maine for a period of rest and relaxation. Then, we must suppose, Jesse, Rebe and the children moved into their house on the Swarthmore campus early enough to allow them to get settled before the opening of the fall term.

The very comfortable house they moved into had been planned by William Price, Jesse's brother-in-law, who was destined to become famous as the architect for such well-known buildings as the Traymore Hotel in Atlantic City and the Wanamaker Store in Philadelphia. The house stood at 3 Whittier Place, across the driveway from the Friends' Meeting House. Behind the Holmes' residence was the grassy athletic field, bordered on the two long sides by stately elms, oaks, and maples. (Given this country atmosphere, it was not too surprising that Jesse, that farm boy from Iowa, soon built a cowshed in the backyard so that his children might have a handy source of fresh milk. But his intentions were better than his judgment: the shed proved to be too short for the cow, so that "Bossie" had to stand on the diagonal to get the maximum protection from the elements. This "biased" cow was a longstanding source of merriment in the Holmes' household.)

Leaving the house, it was but a short walk to the main part of the campus. On the way to his classes Jesse would pass the science building, the Hall Gymnasium, and see the little observatory and the Benjamin West building in the distance. His destination would be Parrish Hall, a great greystone building which was the heart of Swarthmore College. From its commanding position on a hill, people on its front porch could look down a long, broad, tree-shaded walk to a commuters' railroad and the business district of the village of Swarthmore. It was a segregated dormitory, with the girls sleeping in the eastern wing, and the boys in the western section. Between these wings were classrooms, the library, a dining hall, and the administrative offices — those parts which "serviced the body, mind, heart and spirit in the manner of a 'guarded' education. . . ."

And, as Jesse soon realized, the administrators needed to run things in a guarded fashion, for the College was so poor that not even their best efforts could prevent an annual deficit. It had only about 200 students in 1902, so its income from tuition payments could not have been very large. Its endowment in that year was only $360,000.

The Dedicated Faculty and Joseph Swain.

But Swarthmore had one essential ingredient which gave its friends hope and joy — a dedicated faculty. Under the administrative oversight of President William Wilfred Birdsall (1898-1902), and President Joseph Swain (1902-1921), these men and women did much to realize the dream of Swarthmore's founders that " 'a liberal education might be obtained by the youth of both sexes.' . . ." under the care of Friends. Philip M. Hicks, '05, a student of Jesse's in those early days, has given us a picture of this faculty: It was "composed mainly of one-man departments whose staffs were notable for competence in their fields, devotion to their teaching, and richness of personality that made us love them the more for their engaging eccentricities. . . ." Hicks had his personal triumvirate of faculty "greats": "Ducky" Holmes, Joseph Swain, and Susan J. Cunningham. "Sue" Cunningham was head of the department of mathematics, and Hicks remembered her as "a woman in white, 'teaching in a whirl of chalk and frown,' and sailing down the corridors like a great galleon with all sails billowing in a breeze of her own making. . . ." She preached "gumption and grit," assailed the shirkers and timid students, told them that the mysteries of mathematics were as " 'plain as the nose on thy face,' " and then welcomed them to her home when they came for special help. She gave the college its first piano; she also helped persuade Joseph Swain to leave his president's job at the University of Indiana in 1902 to direct that struggling institution known locally as the "Quaker matchbox", a well-deserved nickname because of the many romances flourishing each year on the Swarthmore campus.

Joseph Swain was a big man, "six feet four in his stocking feet," and growing bigger in his Swarthmore job. In 1913 he was described as " 'six feet in circumference, right underneath his vest.'. . . ." But he was big in other ways too — a great builder, using his politician's skills to increase the endowment seven-fold, and increasing the faculty as new departments were added and the student body more than doubled. Also, wonder of wonders, under his administration Swarthmore's football team was able to score an occasional victory over Cornell, Columbia, Lafayette, Lehigh, and the University of Pennsylvania.

Such occasional successes in football were the more notable because President Swain had become convinced that scholastic standards should be required of players. There would be no discrimination in his ongoing efforts to raise the intellectual life of the college; a degree from Swarthmore should and would represent high academic achievement no matter who received it. A man of broad culture himself, Swain saw that the best way to attract exceptional students and teachers was to cultivate still more that search for truth inherent in the Quaker faith and method. Indeed, as one of the students in Swain's time put it, "Perhaps the Quaker search for truth and the aim of a liberal arts college are two sides of the same coin. . . ." But one factor stood in the way of true liberality: the old preference that Swarthmore should remain a Quaker college, requiring attendance at Sunday meeting, and with a curriculum designed for Quaker youth. Soon after his arrival Swain, although a Friend himself, was able to persuade the Board of Managers to drop these restrictions. Henceforth the Board of Managers — including such Quaker members as Isaac H. Clothier and William Sproul, governor of Pennsylvania — would serve mainly as the "repository of the institution's conscience," with the President exercising vastly increased executive powers in hiring and firing faculty people, and a strong voice in the setting of their salaries.

These new policies fitted in very well with the beliefs and temperaments of some faculty holdovers from the 1890s. Among

43

these was Elizabeth Powell Bond, dean of women from 1890 to 1906, and known for her "sweetness and light." Like Joseph Swain, she had been brought to Swarthmore through the influence of Sue Cunningham. Miss Cunningham had known Mrs. Bond, then Elizabeth Powell, as an instructor in calisthenics at Vassar College. Coming to Swarthmore, first as matron (1886-1890), then taking on the dean's job, Mrs. Bond enriched Swarthmore through her sympathetic interest in student problems, the starting of the rose garden near Parrish Hall, and through her constant service for the social welfare of man in problems of education, race relations, and international amity. (In 1928 a grateful Swarthmore community dedicated the Elizabeth Powell Bond Memorial Hall to the use of women students.) Closely allied with Dean Bond in her many concerns, but especially with her interest in the world peace movement, was Dr. William Isaac Hull, Joseph Wharton Professor of History and Political Science. He spent a long and eventful life at Swarthmore, serving for forty-seven years as a member of its faculty, all the while trying to advance the Quaker-Christian principle of "peace on earth, good will to men." Sampling his activities in these early years, we find him editing and publishing *The Swarthmorean* in 1905 and 1906, appearing on the platform of the Longwood Progressive Friends in 1913 with a speech on "The New Peace Movement," and vehemently opposing the use of boxing matches to promote the sale of Liberty Bonds and War Stamps in 1918. His wife, Hannah Clothier Hull, was equally active in reform activity — in women's suffrage, in social-welfare work, and in the constant Quaker drive for world peace. She was a close friend of Jane Addams, a winner of the Nobel Peace Prize. Those who knew their close relationship were not surprised when Jane Addams called her Chicago social-welfare headquarters "Hull House." And, as Barbara Kent of Swarthmore said, "Hannah Clothier Hull was a *lady.*"

The more liberal collegiate policy started at Swarthmore by Joseph Swain attracted other professors soon to become famous in American academic and reformist life. One of these was Paul M. Pearson, holding various positions in public speaking at Swarthmore from 1902 to 1930, and founder of that Swarthmore Chautauqua which brought culture and inspirational messages to so many small towns in the Eastern United States and Canada from 1912 through 1929.

Not long after Pearson appeared on campus, Dr. Robert C. Brooks, a short, dynamic, and aggressive man, was hired to teach political science. He had attended Indiana University, where the "sole rule" under former President David Starr Jordan was (according to Brooks) that " 'no student shall kill a professor.'. . ." He studied at Cornell, taught there for a while, and also at the University of Cincinnati. In 1912 he was appointed to the Joseph Wharton Chair of Political Science at Swarthmore. Later on, in an interview with a student reporter, he admitted that he didn't know whether he was a "left-wing Democrat or a right-wing Socialist. . . ." But, he said, "I confess that I am a Democrat with a small 'd' — my fondness for Switzerland bears that out. . . ." At Swarthmore he not only taught politics, but frequently ran for public office — always on the Democratic ticket, and always defeated. By 1930 he had written five books and countless articles.

In 1908, when Professor Brooks was granted a year's leave of absence to make a special study, President Swain offered Scott Nearing and two other instructors in the Wharton School of Business Administration at the University of Pennsylvania the opportunity to take over Brooks' classes on a part-time basis. Nearing's specialty was economics, but, since the "dismal science" was then widely taught as political economy, he anticipated no difficulty in filling Brooks' shoes — or at least one of them. He was a graduate of the Wharton School, which had been endowed by Joseph Wharton, a major force in Bethlehem Steel, under a deed which required the advocacy of tariff protection. (Like some other Friends, Wharton, a tall spare man dressed in austere Quaker garb, must have carried in his bosom a constant conflict between the meeting house and the counting house, between the ideal and the actual. Nearing, in his autobiography, tells of the time Wharton made an "impassioned plea" for world peace in a Quaker meeting in Philadelphia. After the meeting he was approached by his nephew Wharton Barker, an ardent Populist, with a question as to how he reconciled his strong feeling for peace with his gun factory on the Schuylkill River. " 'Nephew,' " replied the nettled armament manufacturer, 'there are some things that are none of thy damn business.' " Of course, as Nearing wrote, Wharton Barker related this story — and Barker had "strong histrionic gifts.") Although Nearing was already in some hot water at the Wharton School for his persistent probing into the distribution of income under the capitalistic system, and for his outspoken extracurricular opinions on child labor, there was apparently no effort from Philadelphia to block his appointment at Swarthmore as a substitute for Robert Brooks. What was to have been a one-year job stretched into three, with Nearing commuting from his Philadelphia home all the time. He must have enjoyed the Swarthmore atmosphere very much, for in the third year he taught without salary, even paying his own traveling expenses. Here he could exercise freely those principles which had governed his life up to this point: ". . .to learn the truth, to teach the truth, and to help build the truth into the life of the community. If there was exploitation and corruption in the society I should speak out against it. . . ."

But the same academic freedom did not prevail at the Wharton School in Philadelphia: in 1915 Nearing was discharged, "without previous notice, without charges, without a hearing, without recourse, from a job [he] had held for nine years." This experience, plus other violations of due process by the ruling powers, turned this son of a respectable Midwestern family into a radical. He became a socialist, then a member of the Communist Party; after disillusioning experiences with the antidemocratic methods of the communists he returned to socialism, joining that group of reformers advocating the enlightened doctrines of Norman Thomas. (It is interesting to speculate whether Nearing's life might have taken a different turn if Swarthmore's budget and faculty needs had permitted him to stay in the cool groves surrounding Parrish Hall.)

A Settee, not a Chair.

Jesse Holmes was not so badly treated. As we shall see, his conversion to socialism was the result of more vicarious experiences, plus his overall Quaker concern for the welfare of man. He agreed with Elbert Russell, we are quite sure, that the Society of Friends, in the better moments of its more liberal members, had "made its chief contribution to the world as a nursery of spiritual, sensitive, original and adventurous spirits. . . ." He rejoiced in the free academic climate of Swarthmore in President Swain's time; he probably was there when Dr. Harry W. Laidler, editor of *The Intercollegiate Socialist,* addressed the economics and political science classes on "Socialism and the War" in January, 1915. Earlier he must have applauded the article in *The Phoenix,* the college newspaper, on September 19, 1911, when it hailed the fact that Victor Berger, a socialist Congressman, had packed New York's Carnegie Hall, speaking from a platform "draped with college flags. . . ." As the article observed:

> Once people were persecuted for unorthodox beliefs; to-day they are asked to explain them. Printing presses, public schools and universities, cheap periodicals, rural mail delivery, trolleys and telephones have made a total wreck of the old idea. The rising generation evidently proposes to do its own accepting and rejecting — with its eyes open.

If Jesse was happy to see this article in *The Phoenix*, he must have been even more elated to know that here was a convenient medium through which he could advance his own controversial ideas. Indeed, the very name of *The Phoenix* was somehow symbolic of the Swarthmore renaissance under President Swain. The paper had been started after a fire severely damaged Parrish Hall in 1881; its name was chosen to suggest that the spirit of Swarthmore had risen from the ashes to new and higher flights of service.

When Jesse reported for his teaching duties in the fall of 1900, he may have felt that he was being asked to give *too much* service for his salary — that, as the socialists might have said, he was being "exploited." He had been hired to teach philosophy and religion; but he found that Swarthmore's poverty and small faculty, coupled with the need to present rich and varied curricula to its students, required him to teach a bewildering assortment of subjects. In 1900, and in a few succeeding years, he taught three required courses in Biblical literature, as well as four separate courses in ancient, medieval and modern history. (It should be added that he shared the responsibility of these history courses with Dr. W.I. Hull.) Then, it became apparent, he was expected to teach the history of religions, the religion of the Hebrews, the origin of Christianity, psychology, and the history of philosophy. Added to these, in future years, were courses in political economy, in early Christianity, in ethics, the life and times of Jesus, modern scientific theories, history of science, and scientific methods and results. Small wonder that Jesse claimed that he did not occupy at chair at Swarthmore — "it was a settee." And, considering Jesse's varied education — in chemistry, history, literature, physics, mineralogy, biology, philosophy, mathematics, languages, and religion — it was not too surprising that he said later on that "every member of the philosophy department should be able

47

to teach any course in the college on short notice. . . ." John W. Nason, philosophy colleague of Jesse's in the 'thirties, and then president of Swarthmore (1940-1953), confessed that this attitude of Jesse's distressed him at times. Still, "he could almost do what he suggested," since he had "a very wide, though not very deep, range of learning. . . ."

Since his classes in religion were his primary responsibility in the early years at Swarthmore, he drew on all his resources to make them as interesting and informative as possible. While they were most likely originally intended for First-day School, it may be that he used those "Lesson Leaves" he had started at Oxford as study guides for the two basic courses listed in the college catalogue under "Biblical Literature." Course I, required for all freshmen, consisted of assigned readings in the Old Testament, supplemented by recitations and by lectures on the history of the Holy Land. Course II, required for all sophomores, was similar in method but went over into the New Testament. A third course in Biblical Literature, elective for juniors and seniors, involved a detailed study of selected parts of the Bible.

Philip M. Hicks, '05, described his experience as a student in Jesse's two-semester course required of all freshmen and sophomores. "There was little literary criticism in it, and less denominationalism." Using a modified Socratic method of teaching, Jesse made each class "an exercise in leading the student mind to an impartial inquiry into all" that could be discovered about the topic under discussion, "followed by a rational attempt to formulate an answer that [would] not be too ludicrous to follow the words 'I believe.'. . . ." As in his chemistry classes at George School, Jesse's constant aim was to stimulate his students to examine the evidence and arrive at their own conclusions, even if these conclusions were at variance with those beliefs they had brought to Swarthmore from their homes.

In this and other courses, different students reacted in different ways to Jesse, who was rapidly becoming the most controversial figure on the Swarthmore faculty. To the Quakers in his classes, accustomed by the doctrine of the "Inner Light" to do their own thinking in religious matters, his approach was to some extent a familiar one and but to be expected from a Hicksite professor. His handling of religious history made ancient prophets come alive as "vibrant personalities," especially so since their messages were tied in by Jesse with modern social and religious problems crying out for solution.

To some students, of course, the required courses in religion were a bore, and the time spent with ancient Hebrew prophets a waste of time. But to still another group of students, coming from areas where the Bible was the unquestioned Word of God, Jesse's methods produced mixed results. When he expressed his obvious sympathy with Albert Sweitzer's *The Quest of the Historical Jesus,* and Sweitzer's interpretation that Christ was a *man* preaching toward a kingdom of democratic man on earth, some fundamentalist students, often through parental aid and pressure, would ask to be transferred to another course if there was still time. (At this point Jesse might well have been excused if he had used a quotation from one of his resource books: "A bigot is like the pupil of the eye — the more light the more contraction.") One of these fundamentalist students, from a Bible-belt part of Kentucky, was disturbed when Jesse paced the classroom floor, waving his arms, and spoke of "this man Jesus," and "that man Jesus," taking faith away while not giving anything back in its place.

Such tactics, of course, were deliberately designed to set up conflict in order to achieve his main objective — to get his students to *think*. In classroom discussions, he would often take the opposite position to any student's statement in order to force the student to marshall facts and opinions in a logical defense of his position. No wonder that freshmen would become confused and pray for the end of the class so that they could escape. But these were usually momentary confusions, if we are to judge from the testimonies given by his former students: they agreed that Jesse did indeed make them think, and the freshmen from Kentucky said that Jesse produced this result more than any professor he had had at Swarthmore. And through this thinking Jesse made converts to his version of Quakerism. Eleanor Stabler was not at first an enthusiastic supporter of the Holmesian philosophy and methods, but eventually joined his growing group of "disciples." Louis N. Robinson, nationally renowned penologist, wrote as late as 1951 that as a student at Swarthmore he had come under the influence "of that fine man, Dr. Jesse Holmes, and after a painful process of disillusionment . . . came finally into a calm, sea of peaceful religious outlook. . . ." which seemed to him to be the essence of the Friendly Way.

No doubt some of these students, whether converts or confused freshmen, were grateful to Jesse for his easy examination policy. By 1910 the students had caught on to him: they had found out that he always gave the same tests, "based on the conning of the same long blackboard outlines, to each of his four classes. . . ." This, as an article in *The Phoenix* revealed, "was rather more than human nature [had] thus far been able to withstand." No doubt Jesse found that this policy was necessary in view of his heavy teaching load, his incessant lecturing on reform topics on and off the campus, and the fact that the "objective," machine-duplicated examination, so easily scored, was not yet in common use. We can dismiss the foul allegation, also circulating on the Swarthmore campus at the time, that Jesse threw his essay examination papers down the stairs in his home, giving "A's" to those who landed on top. (This same story, with local variations, has been slandering many other professors on scores of campuses throughout the country for a long time. Those of us who were students or teachers in the period since 1910 will attest to this as a fact.)

While Jesse probably never took a course in "how to teach," he knew the psychology and techniques of successful teaching. He constantly practiced the technique of student involvement in class activities, injected humor into class discussions, and used visual aids to bring an optimal reality to his courses in religion and philosophy. By 1916 he had made his classroom, Parrish 31, into a veritable museum of Oriental religious symbols or artifacts. Among many other items in this collection were a Jewish synagogue roll (obtained through Rabbi Krauskopf of Philadelphia), the statue of a teaching Buddha seated on a lotus flower, a Buddhist temple gong from Rangoon, a beautiful copy of the Koran reputed to be three or four centuries old, a brass figure of "Ganesh — the favorite god of the Hindus — showing his elephant's head and riding on his rat," a mummy of an Egyptian sacred cat, some cuneiform tablets from Nippur, and a Buddhist prayer wheel resembling a baby's rattle. In May, 1916, he took his Bible classes, and many other interested people, on a tour of the Holy Land through the medium of lantern slides made from photographs taken during his travels there in 1900. In "one short hour" the magic of his delivery, and "his delightful sense of humor," made the Holy Land "so vivid and real" that his hearers were able to wander through the crooked winding streets of its cities with him, "or stand on the green hills outside

Jerusalem and view the city that has become sacred to a large part of the world." During this presentation Jesse remarked on the fact that one of the girls he saw at Jacob's Well bore a Standard Oil can on her head instead of the expected earthen jar.

The Social Reformer in the Classroom.

The girl with the Standard Oil can on her head was a symbol of the conflict in the homeland of Christianity between a relatively simple handicraft-and-agricultural culture and the increasingly complicated industrial culture beginning to take root in some Mid-Eastern cities. And the Standard Oil can was also a symbol of a conflict in the country of its origin — a conflict in the United States between rival camps of Christians, each bending the Bible to their own purposes. One camp — we may call them the Rockefeller-Carnegie-Frick group — ostensibly believed in a heavenly personal salvation through Christian doctrine; but they also preached the "Gospel of Wealth," claiming that it was their Christian duty to get as rich as possible as soon as possible. Pious churchgoers on Sunday, on Monday they exploited the human and natural resources of America, used shady tricks to wipe out their competitors, and emerged as monopolists pretty well able to dictate the life style of an entire nation. Claiming that Darwin's principle of the survival of the fittest applied to social and economic life, as well as to organisms in nature, they justified their ruthless law-of-the-jungle tactics by closely reasoned arguments summed up as "Social Darwinism." They transmuted Darwin's theory into a holy principle. Listen to John D. Rockefeller:

> The growth of a large business is merely a survival of the fittest. . . . The American Beauty rose can be produced in the splendor and fragrance which bring cheer to its beholder only by sacrificing the early buds which grow up around it. This is not an evil tendency in business. It is merely the working out of a law of nature and a law of God.

In May, 1902, when the United Mine Workers, led by President John Mitchell, went on strike for union recognition and higher wages, mine owners such as George F. Baer turned deaf ears to their appeals. Conditions in the anthracite coal region of Pennsylvania were becoming so desperate by mid-July that William F. Clark, a Wilkes-Barre photographer, wrote to Baer that he hoped God would

51

" 'send the Holy Spirit to reason in' " Baer's heart. Baer's reply deserves to be quoted in full:

Philadelphia and Reading Railway Company
President's Office
Reading Terminal, Philadelphia

17th July 1902

My dear Mr. Clark:

I have your letter of the 16th instant.

I do not care who you are. I see that you are a religious man; but you are evidently biased in favor of the right of the working man to control a business in which he has no other interest than to secure fair wages for the work he does.

I beg of you not to be discouraged. The rights and interests of the laboring man will be protected and cared for — not by the labor agitators, but by the Christian men to whom God in his infinite wisdom has given the control of the property interests of the country, and upon the succesful Management of which so much depends.

Do not be discouraged. Pray earnestly that right may triumph, always remembering that the Lord God Omnipotent still reigns, and that His reign is one of law and order, and not of violence and crime.

Yours truly,

Geo. F. Baer
President

Such arrogance, with the implication that Baer was God's viceregent at the mines, was bound to bring out opposition from people like Jesse and from reformist clergymen. In fact, the opposition had been building for some time in the Age of the Robber Barons. As far back as 1876 the Reverend Washington Gladden, a Congregational minister in Springfield, Massachusetts, had published *On Being a Christian*. Called the first book of the Social-Gospel movement, it asserted that being a Christian had little to do with church rituals, the acceptance of officially declared doctrines, or any mystical emotional experience. A true, steady, day-to-day Christian, Gladden wrote, was one who believed in the fatherhood of God and practiced the brotherhood of man. Such a Christian would be a "socialized individual," bridging the gap between the fierce individualism of the competitors using fang-and-claw methods, and a socialism in which man lost his identity as a person. This individual would have a social conscience and a responsibility for society's welfare. In other words, Christianity would be applied to the world at large; it would become a principle of day-to-day conduct.

The Social Gospel moved on through the work of many people. In 1887 William D.P. Bliss, a graduate of Amherst and the Hartford Theological Seminary, helped to found the (Episcopal) Church Association for the Advancement of the Interests of Labor, known as CAIL. Later on he was the leading spirit in the founding of the Society of Christian Socialists (1889); and, in 1897, as editor, he presided over the publication of Funk and Wagnall's *Encyclopedia of Social Reform.* One of the best articles was his: he was eager to show that the function of the Christian Church in America was not "to sanctify the philosophy of individualistic capitalism, but to take the lead toward a cooperative commonwealth." An experiment along this line, the Christian Commonwealth Colony near Columbus, Georgia, was able to keep going for only three years (1896-1899); its demise was due to crop failures, disease, and the inability of the brothers to deal with renegades within their ranks.

Eight years later Walter Rauschenbusch, a Baptist who had joined the faculty of Rochester Theological Seminary in 1897, made Social-Gospel history through the publication of his book *Christianity and the Social Crisis.* Then came *Christianizing the Social Order* (1912), to be followed in 1917 by *A Theology for the Social Gospel.* These three volumes, plus his activities as a teacher and preacher, made him America's most influential spokesman for this new approach to religion.

What Rauschenbusch had to say was first of all a condemnation of the system of industrial capitalism. Industrial capitalism was evil, not so much because of the sins of the men directing it, but because it had within it four practices opposed to genuine Christianity and democracy. Competition was the first of these; he called it "the law of tooth and nail," and asserted that it was a denial of brotherhood. And this kind of competition resulted only in growing monopolies, which became citadels of the autocratic principle, from which were led the attacks on the democracy of the workers and the government. The third evil practice was that of the middleman, with his short weights and misleading advertising. Finally, in this list of business errors, was the profit motive — a motivation, in the early 1900s, which impelled the powerful monopolies to squeeze tribute from the helpless consumers. " 'If we can trust the Bible, God is against capitalism, its methods, spirit and results,' " said Rauschenbusch.

The second great fault in American society, as he saw it, was the failure of the American churches to live up to their obligations to apply Christ's message to the lives of the great mass of the people. Christ's message was democratic to the last degree: it called for the establishment of social justice by the abolition of unjust privilege of wealth or inherited position; it postulated a society of cooperation and approximate equality among the holders of collective property rights; and it saw the common laborer as " 'the product of today, the creator of tomorrow, the banner bearer of destiny.' " What Christ had meant by his Kingdom of God, Rauschenbusch explained, was a kingdom of the common man on earth. One way to realize this kingdom was through industrial democracy, with workers in industrial corporations helping to make the decisions affecting their lives and fortunes. And it was these applications of Christ's teachings, Rauschenbusch held, which had been forgotten or bypassed in the days of Rockefeller, Carnegie, and Henry Clay Frick. The personal salvation of such men, through their observance of the Ten Commandments, was not enough; the time had come to define the social sins for which their corporations were responsible so that *society* too might be saved. He had applauded the suggestion made by Edward A. Ross in *Sin and Society* (1901), that there ought to be an annual supplement to the Decalogue, so that people would realize that sin evolved with society — that tax-dodging was larceny, child labor was slavery, food adulteration a species of petty thievery, and price fixing by monopolists a conspiracy against the public welfare. The Ross suggestion had been at least partially followed by the Progressives in state and national assemblies from 1901 to 1914; some social sins had been defined and some social criminals brought to justice.

Too often, however, these "social criminals" were thought of only as institutions: oil corporations, meat-packing companies, and governmental bodies whose complicated structures obscured the individual responsibilities of their members to society. The times were ripe for a fresh approach to the problem of how individual Christians should live their daily lives in an increasingly impersonal and industrialized world. Such a fresh approach, Jesse observed, had been found by the Reverent Charles M. Sheldon, whose book *In*

His Steps appeared on bookstore shelves in 1898. In this novel Sheldon suggested that every person, rich or poor, high or low, should ask himself "What would Jesus do?" when faced with the necessity of making a decision affecting not only his own life but that of others. The public hunger for this message was seen in the fact that over fifteen million copies of *In His Steps* were soon sold.

Given such enthusiasm, Jesse reasoned, it should not be difficult to stimulate students in his advanced courses in religion — "History of Religions," "History of Christianity," "Ethics" — to read and discuss not only Sheldon's book, but also books by other Social Gospelites such as Gladden and Rauschenbusch. Perhaps the Social-Gospel fire would spread from his classroom into areas still in the grip of cold and rigid dogmas.

And spread it did, if we may judge by the enthusiastic response of his students. In 1910 they recognized that he had the "most finical job" of any of the Swarthmore faculty, "the teaching of religion in an age of lightning transition. . . ." He was praised as being "so radical" in this instruction "as to employ texts by such harebrained people as Washington Gladden. . . ," and he was so bigoted that he asked a Presbyterian minister to substitute for him in his Bible class. Since one of his aims in life was to break down the barriers separating the various sects and religions, we may be sure that his classes in the history of religions were also made well aware of the different versions of the Golden Rule to be found in twelve great religions practiced throughout the world. And, since the Rule was a major weapon in the Social-Gospel assault on entrenched industrial selfishness, and since sympathy with other people's ideas based on understanding was essential to unity of reform, Jesse had great hopes for this type of teaching. Only the ignorant and hopelessly intolerant — those who had The Word — would accuse him of being a heretic. And his students reported that this *had* happened; indeed, he had been "waxing well favored on this for many moons. . . ." But Jesse had ways of disarming his critics. If one called him a heretic face-to-face, Jesse would place his hands on his shoulders and thank him. If tolerance to the intolerant was the final test, his students thought, Doctor Holmes passed this test every day. Of course, if a particularly obdurate traditionalist insisted that he had The Truth about what to believe in religion, Jesse might reply that "Religious (truth). . .is not 'truth' at all, but a *choice* of a way of life."

The way of life that Jesse believed in was that which would be based on a favorable combination of fact and fancy: the laws governing the natural world, as induced by the world's best scientists, plus the visions of an ideal world passed on to Western civilization through the ideas and efforts of the Hebrew prophets, through Socrates and Plato, and through that long line of idealists represented by Jesus of Nazareth, Saint Francis of Assisi, and George Fox of England. Both of these lines of thought — the actual and the ideal — had come to America in the *Mayflower* and in the many ships bearing steerage passengers and others, which had tied up to the docks in ports on all of America's coasts. The passengers on these ships had been attracted to America by the American Dream — that vision of a better life if the imperatives of nature were combined with a kindlier, more Christian view of man's possibilities in a fresh environment, the new Garden of Eden.

Jesse and Rebe were products of this urgent quest for a better life. So was William James, the Harvard psychologist who so strongly influenced Jesse's thinking, and who was so much like Jesse in his ability to express abstract ideas in vivid, understandable language. And, like Jesse, William James was a Darwinist, believing on the basis of historical studies and experimental data that the "psyche" was a biological process evolving along with its animal housing, all the while adapting itself to its environment. His *Principles of Psychology* (1890) described several original theories of human experience and conduct which were to have profound effects on the course of American psychology, and on literary figures like Gertrude Stein and John Dos Passos. One of these theories he called "the stream of consciousness," meaning that man's perception or understanding of events depended upon a series of states of mind, these mental states being different from time-to-time and place-to-place. Everything was in a state of constant change — the events, as well as the understanding of them; no person would have the same reaction to an event of August 10 as on July 10, because by the time of August 10 his stream of consciousness would have been altered by changing circumstances inside and outside of his body. (Aside from questions of the fallibility of human memory, one can see what effect this theory might have on the credibility of testimony given in courts of law. And, it should be noted, this idea of constant change was not new: Heraclitus, the ancient Greek philosopher, said in effect that "Man cannot step into the same river twice." Further, a logical purist could assert that Heraclitus was wrong; he might say that man cannot step into the *same* river *once.*)

These ideas, of course, combined with those of the emerging Einstein, added up to the concept of the relativity of truth — that the truth about any event depended on the perceptive ability of the viewer, his training in observation, his intellectual background as conservative or radical, his position in the cyclical swing of ideas from time to time, his vantage point for observation, and the state of his digestion. The story about the three blind men reporting the results of their examinations of the elephant was particularly appropriate in more and more college classrooms.

It was in this spirit that Jesse conducted his classes in psychology at Swarthmore. One cannot doubt that he used an updated version of James' *Principles of Psychology* as the required textbook, or that he put *The Will to Believe* on the course reading list. The latter work proclaimed James' conviction that the scientists' account of the physical and biological state of man was only a partial report; much of the other side of human life — the spiritual side — could be assumed " 'on trust, if only thereby life may seem to us better worth living again.' " And Jesse found sympathetic vibrations in James' *Varieties of Religious Experience* (1902), with its praise of certain practical values in Christian Science, religious conversion, and mysticism. There was still another parallel with James: Jesse also dabbled in psychical research, attending spiritualist seances, and tried to be equally quick to detect the frauds in the amazing results claimed by the mediums.

Jesse found another fraud, albeit of a higher or more intellectual order, in John B. Watson's behaviorism. Writing in that loose-leaf notebook which he kept as a compendium of facts, thoughts, and reactions to the passing scene, Jesse called behaviorism an "incomprehensible fad." It was incomprehensible because it asked psychologists to ignore consciousness, which Jesse thought was the one thing Watson or any other person knew anything about. Indeed, what Watson called "behavior" was only one part of consciousness, "and not the largest part either. . . ." While Jesse obviously could not ignore behaviorism's stimulus-and-response explanation for human actions, he could and did react most vehemently against its implications that human behavior was mechanically determined or exclusively directed by the environment, or by man's position as an animal in nature's scheme. Man was an animal, Jesse's experience and training forced him to admit; but he was also a *consciously thinking* animal capable of making *choices* between this or that course of action. These choices depended upon many, many items in man's experience; to eliminate choice would result in the elimination of reform activities and man's hope for a better world. Free will *did* exist if a man was willing to face the consequences of an unpopular choice of action: a man could *choose* to be a socialist if he was willing to suffer the hoots and catcalls of his capitalist neighbors; a man like Jesus could choose to buck the tide of prevailing opinion and die on a contemporary cross. Since Jesse had recorded in another part of his notebook a quotation from Henry Van Dyke — "We should govern ourselves by our admirations, not by our disgusts" — we are reasonably sure that Jesse's unhappiness with Watson's behaviorism allowed him to give this version of psychology only such minimal treatment in his classes as he and his students would consider fair or necessary to understand human behavior.

An Idealistic Pragmatist.

If Jesse violated Henry Van Dyke's principle to a degree in his reaction to behaviorism, he lived up to it most enthusiastically when he made *idealistic pragmatism* his life-long philosophy, teaching it in his classes and hammering home its "truths" in countless lectures, pamphlets, and periodical articles. His philosophy was not "idea-listic" in the Platonic or professional-philosopher sense of a universal, fixed, and Absolute Idea of a chair as distinct from any given physical chair. In this conception only the Idea was Real and indestructible; the "mind" was the repository of such Ideas and was therefore a more important thing to talk about than the transitory matter of which the earth was made. Strangely enough, this position acquired the name of "realism"; it was opposed by the Nominalists in the Middle Ages who claimed that only matter was real. Then thinkers like Berkeley began to insist that matter was nothing but the complex of our sensations. Old Sam Johnson, however, kicked a stone to show that the sensations were caused by something very material indeed.

This mind-versus-matter dualism continued to agitate philosophical debates well into modern times — a debate which Jesse thought to be sterile, illusory, nonsensical, and wasteful of a thinking man's energies. Certain modes of conduct, however, *were*

worth thinking about, and worth making impassioned pleas for —
those principles of charity, brotherly love, voluntary cooperation
and human service which Christ had envisioned in the Sermon on
the Mount, in parables, and which were implicit in the Golden Rule.
These were ideal principles of ethical conduct which could — nay
would — lead to an ideal world if man would but practice them. And,
while Jesse could not approve Josiah Royce's whole theory of the
Absolute, he liked very much indeed that part of it which called for
loyalty to a common community cause as a formula for civilized
living. Individual man, according to Royce, could *choose* to be loyal;
free will *did* exist as it had when Walter Reed and Dr. Jesse Lazear
chose to risk their lives in the common cause of trying to overcome
yellow fever. If men were loyal to opposing common causes, as was
the case in the ultranationalistic period leading up to World War I,
it only showed once again that world ethics were still in an
undeveloped and chaotic state. There was hope, however, in this
principle of loyalty: if men were to respect each other's loyalties —
to be loyal to loyalty — they were already well on the road to the
higher ethic of peace. Perhaps too the understanding and practice of
other ethical principles would grow in a similar way.

Some of these ideas, particularly the one about an evolution of
principles in different fields to a common harmony of world order,
had already been foreshadowed in the thinking of Charles S. Peirce,
Harvard graduate in mathematics and logic. Convinced that there
was an element of "indeterminacy" and "absolute chance" in
nature, he still tried to fuse the logic of idealism with the logic of
material events. He proposed that both of these lines of thought —
the ideal and the actual — might be brought together if people
supposed that both were developing from a world of chancy
disorder to a world of order, and if people would be willing to learn
about principles in both fields through the hard and exacting
methods of experiment practiced by the physical scientists. In 1878,
in an article in the *Popular Science Monthly*, entitled "How to Make
Our Ideas Clear," he laid down the formula for this possible union.
In brief, he suggested that the meaning of any idea is to be found in
its consequences when that idea is put into action. "If two beliefs
lead to different courses of action, they are different in meaning. If
they lead to identical action, they are identical in meaning, however
differently they may be phrased." There was no idea here that a
given belief might be judged as true because its consequences in

action benefited a given individual or his group. No; he thought instead that if different scientific investigators tested an idea, given the same data, they would come up with the same solution to each problem. This solution would be "true"; its object would be "real"; and it could stand as a guide to future conduct. He gave the name "pragmatism" to this theory of truth and meaning. Later on, when popularizers of pragmatism perverted his doctrine to bless the practical success of *any* idea, he changed its title to "pragmaticism" — which, he hoped, would be "ugly enough to be safe from kidnappers."

And yet it was Peirce's friend William James, who, through the effects of his powerful personality and injudicious use of phrases, was chiefly responsible for the twisting of Peirce's formula to mean that if any idea succeeds in practice it is therefore true. This seemed to open the way to a philosophy of success favorable to various types of criminality: If monpoloy practices paid, they were but in the stream of human truth; if embezzlement paid off, it was but an example of " 'truth's cash-value.' " But such applications were popular perversions of James' central theme that ideas, whether from the realm of religion and ethics, or from the world of science, should be tested for their truth. If such testing, such trial-and-error experimentation, did product favorable results for a given hypothesis at a given time, then that idea was true for that time. If more experimentation produced different results, the previous "truth" would need to yield to a new and higher truth. Such practice would open the mind to change and the possibilities of progress. He called his variety of pragmatism *radical empiricism* — "radical," we may suppose, because his method and theory could be used despite popular prejudices to test religious and ethical ideas for truth and meaning, as well to test ideas in the natural sciences; "empirical" because it was the method of trial-and-error, of experimentation, already so well favored in science and industry.

James' radical-empiricist version of pragmatism was beamed mainly at the individual, and it was greatly concerned with religious and psychic phenomena and questions of ethics. But John Dewey, often described as the third great pragmatist, was more concerned with the application of pragmatic principles to the pressing problems of the contemporary social world. Not neglecting the moral issues of the individual, saying that each person had to choose his behavior in the light of its "probable consequences," he made his strongest impression on American life through his assertions that schools, and the ideas taught in those schools, could be made effective instruments for the reconstruction of society through experiments. Calling his version of pragmatism *experimentalism* or *instrumentalism,* he urged a new type of education appropriate to the needs of an industrial and democratic America. He emphasized the child rather than the subject; he called for discussion of problems rather than the taking of rote-memory data from an authoritarian lecturer; he suggested that a classroom of movable chairs could provide a more democratic and informal learning atmosphere than the traditional one in which students were seated in rigid rows; he decried the separation of the so-called "intellectual" aspects of life from its practical or vocational parts. His constant cry was "One learns by experience;" his hope was that through experimental experience Americans would learn to think for themselves and chart a better course for the future. This sort of thinking fitted in with the Social Gospel of Rauschenbusch; it also, for better or for worse, helped to provide the intellectual climate for the experimental policies of the Roosevelt-Taft-Wilson Progressives and the New Deal of the 1930s. And Dewey's whole doctrine challenged the prevailing nineteenth-century assumption that social evolution must proceed without government help; it preached instead that a democratic state, through social experiments, should try to advance the general welfare by positive means. Today we call one such effort the "affirmative action" program.

We may be sure that when Jesse Holmes read these different versions of that search for wisdom that we call "philosophy," he not only learned from them, but rejoiced in the fact that so much of what was said was in agreement with his own thinking. The idealism expressed in the writings of these thinkers often mirrored his own; their practical, experimental attitude toward the solution of individual and social problems reflected his life experiences as a Quaker, a natural scientist, and a social reformer. Once again one feels justified in labelling him as an *idealistic pragmatist* — an idealist as to the goals of life, a pragmatist on the method to attain those goals.

This position of idealistic pragmatism was demonstrated throughout his life in his many activities and in his classes at Swarthmore. Not content with what could be taught along this line through ordinary classroom procedures, he wrote a leaflet called

What is Truth? A Message to Students. In this he told his students that one of Christendom's great weaknesses was the unwillingness of ministers and teachers to put themselves "squarely behind" any message they thought was true; instead they evaded responsibility by making it appear that the truth came "from some earlier and more authoritative source, usually the Bible." Jesse pointed out that George Fox had had the courage to voice his convictions publicly that the Bible was not the direct Word of God, but that God's spirit was "the driving power" in those who wrote it. This same spirit, of course, was behind every sincere presentation of a perceived truth in any field. But authority! ". . .there is no such thing as *authority* — if by that we mean men, books or statements that must be believed because of their sources. . . ." Jesse thought that there was no more dangerous or trouble-making practice than this reliance on authority, leading people to be cowards in thinking, afraid to express "the hot truth straight from their hearts, but must need look about for the canned or warmed over article with some special label, as Luther, or Wesley, or Fox, to commend it. . . ."

While discussing this with his classes Jesse may well have pointed out that the mental effort to formulate a truth from experience is very hard labor; no doubt he quoted Bertrand Russell that "Men fear thought more than they fear death, more than they fear hell." And, to drive home the point about the rigors of arriving at truth independently, Jesse undoubtedly dug into his personal book of quotations to give his classes the thinking of Lewis Gannett:

> I serve a cold God,
> A - He - God
> Without love.
> Other Gods are She - Gods
> Warm Gods
> Loving Gods
> They caress those who serve them,
> My God resents swelling sound,
>   radiant color,
>   fragrant incense.
> He is without voluptuousness.
> I hate my God.
> My God is Truth.

Jesse continued his castigation of unquestioned authority by telling each reader of his leaflet to rely on his own experience.

"Trust your best self," he said. "Play your own part and speak your own message under your own name. . . ." He urged each student to do research so that his message might perhaps be shown to correspond to the truth of other times and other places: "buttress it by quotation, illustration and fair phrasing; but put yourself back of your gospel. . . ." And, he warned, remember that "Truth is not a thing to be established once for all, but to be continually used and continually tested. Truth needs no authority except for the moment, for every moment makes it manifest. . . ." Our belief in gravitation, he said, is not due to Newton, "but because the earth pulls us. . . ." Similarly, our belief in atoms, x-rays, and radioactivity is not due to Dalton, Roentgen, or the Curies, but "because we can use them — because they 'work.' They depend not on authority but on experience."

This was sound pragmatic doctrine illustrated from the world of material things. And Jesse, like William James, extended pragmatism to test religion and the gospel of Jesus. He wrote that if people would but try Jesus' principle that love is the best foundation for human society, they would find out that this teaching was true in cases both great and small through its observable results in human welfare. Unfortunately, Christianity, instead of using pragmatism's test of experience, had "planted itself on the uncertain and shifting foundation of historical interpretation. . . ." The meaning of Christ's life and teachings was lost in endless quibbles about what he did, where he went, and what was the "hidden" significance of his parables. His simple principles of conduct were not really tested for truth. "Truth to be any value — indeed to deserve the name — must so enter into life and conduct as to make some difference, and that difference is the constant test. . . ." Jesse believed that Christ's gospel had this practical character. "Meekness, purity, gentleness — there is no difficulty in finding out their range of experiment. General good will, and conduct based on the best interests of all, will work results easy to observe. . . ." These ideals, and others like them, were those preached in the Sermon on the Mount. And Jesse was optimistic that, in the time of Rauschenbusch's Social Gospel and the James and Dewey versions of pragmatism, the trend in American society was toward the fundamental point of view of the Quakers: that the "truth," the "Inner Light," did not "consist in historical fact, but in the continuous revelation to man of principles of creative life, by which there is to come a nobler, truer manhood, and a nobler, truer society. . . ."

Here was a challenging, stimulating message to the students in Jesse's classes, with its suggestions of the evolutionary and pragmatic nature of truth, and its prediction that through such truth man would build a better world. One of his students, serving in the Friends' Reconstruction Unit in France in 1919, showed in a letter to him that he had caught the message. He wrote that he had become convinced that the Quaker religion, as revealed by Jesse, was one of possibilities: that it was an evolving religion looking to the perfection of society. Eleanor Stabler Clarke caught Jesse's position even more fully: she saw that Jesse was not primarily a scholar in the regular sense, doing extensive research in religion and philosophy in order to write books or to read papers at scholarly conventions; instead he used his classes in these subjects as vehicles to challenge his students to throw off the crippling weight of preconceived or inherited ideas in order to think more clearly and more deeply about the social, religious, and philosophical problems of the times. "We were told," she said, "that 'we [were all] instruments for inventing and creating futures. . . and he told us about the creating of the future that should be." Each person should regard his "Inner Light" as an "inner spur," driving him on to the accomplishment of this purpose.

"Ducky," the Beloved Teacher.

By 1910 the Swarthmore students had decided the time had come to give public honor to Jesse Herman Holmes. In that year they profiled him in a special literary number of *The Phoenix,* entitled "Who's Who and Why in Swarthmore." Under this title was a photograph of Jesse captioned "Ducky," and then "Facts Serious and Frivolous About the Great and Near Great," with the motto "Honor to Whom Honor is Due."

The photograph showed him as a very handsome man in his mid-forties, still sporting a luxuriant moustache and a van dyke-type beard. He had flashing blue eyes, a quick temper — "like a summer storm that passes quickly" —, and a range of expletives that did not go beyond "thunder and turf." For the most part he was a man of "sweet reasonableness," all agreed. Five feet seven inches in height, his "physical angles," according to the students, "incline toward the full 360 ," but "he is very acute mentally. Although rotund in his corporeal contour, he is strictly on the square in other respects, which one would expect of the thoroughly rounded Swarthmore specimen. . . ." A daring freshman had suggested that *The Phoenix* describe a faculty menagerie, with a candidate for the Bantam Rooster [Professor Brooks?], for the Cow, and several for the Chesire Cat. Such flippant burlesque was not quite seemly, thought a more mature *Phoenix* writer. "But when Doctor Holmes gets his head lowered to buck the vested interests in that defiant way, we can almost believe that he was transmigrated from a big burly bison of the plains."

They called him "Ducky" for a number of reasons. Some might have been reminded of a familiar barnyard fowl by his rolling gait; girl students, less impudent, thought that he was so "ducky" that he had a natural right to be so nicknamed. Baseball fans, on the other hand, thought that, after his batting in the faculty game the previous spring, he might be the double of "Ducky" Holmes of the Detroit Americans. But the most widely held theory as to the origin of his nickname was due to the fact that Jesse had a keen interest in lacrosse, always keeping a couple of sticks and a ball in the closet under the stairs at 3 Whittier Place. In the afternoon, after classes, he would put on a white shirt and white duck trousers to join the lacrosse team as a sort of unofficial coach, running around and shouting advice and encouragement on the athletic field behind his house. Indeed, the students claimed that he was so interested in the athletic aspects of college life that he deliberately burned the fence behind his house so that he might have a better view of the field from his study window. His nickname became so firmly established that it even descended to his son Robert when he became a star member of the Swarthmore lacrosse team in the early nineteen twenties.

And his students and friends found a host of other reasons for calling him Ducky. His nephew, William W. Price, remembered the time when Jesse, as his first course adviser, welcomed him to college with a warm smile, "understanding exactly" how a freshman might be confused and frightened by the formidable business of matriculation. Other students found him to be "the acme of public spirit in the college life. . . ." at Swarthmore. In 1910 they said that he ran an employment bureau for needy students who were willing to sweat for cash. It was reported that he "had his house cleaned three times last fall, his grass cut twice a week, and, in short, kept a sort of vaudeville going for the benefit of his proteges...." Genuinely and unobtrusively kind and neighborly, he rang the doorbells of two families in distress and offered them loans of hundreds of dollars. And there were "dozens of amiable eccentrics about who found in him a confidant for their odd enthusiasms and hope from his large tolerance." But, as a Jeffersonian democrat with increasingly socialistic leanings, he had little or no tolerance for the brand of government given Pennsylvania in the early 1900s, thinking it a violation of the basic principles laid down by America's Founding Fathers. Pointing out that he was the only fencer on the Swarthmore faculty, his students called him a militant Quaker delighting in his "internecine" war with the "antipodal Quay cur." They said that he was no more a radical at heart than LaFollette. "Probably the reason why Doctor Holmes in current parlance is dubbed a radical is because people fail to make the distinction between radicalism and that healthy sort of impatience known as idealism, by which ... he is entirely obsessed...." And, the students thought, if Jesse "had written Heywood's comedy of the four P's [?], they would undoubtedly have stood for peace, prohibition, purity and privilege-not."

All this idealism, of course, was brightened by Jesse's zest for life and by his twinkely eyed humor. In his more orderly moments he kept looseleaf notebooks as storehouses of data; several sections of these notebooks were reserved for jokes, humorous stories, and epigrams. Undoubtedly he wove many of these into his classroom lectures and discussions. Ever mindful of the need for the logically correct expression of ideas, he probably told the story about the wife who caught her husband, a professor of English, kissing their cook. The wife exclaimed, "I'm surprised!" "No," said he, "you should be careful of your language. I was surprised, you are merely astonished." Or he might have regaled his students with that wonderfully mixed metaphor from one of the novels of W.L. George: "The cloud that tried to stab their happiness was only a false rumour whose bitter taste could not splinter the radiance nor dim the effervescence of their joy." And still on the question of correct English, he most likely told them that "There isn't much difference between sight and vision, except when you make the mistake of telling a woman one when you mean the other." To correct such a mistake, however, a man might give her a look "you could pour on a waffle." In the early prohibition period he told his classes that "wine, women, and song" had become "grapejuice, your wife, and community singing." If such witticisms and stories drew only mild chuckles from his classes, the quips and sparkling repartee that developed in exchanges between professor and student often sent the classes into spontaneous gales of laughter. *The Phoenix* printed many of these humorous exchanges and incidents, not only because they *were* funny, but, it was evident, because Jesse had become a campus character the students enjoyed reading and talking about. And they had sly fun when, in a series of satirical skits about professors and administrators in the annual Hamburg Show, a student depicted him as delivering a talk on "Playing the Game," all the while twiddling his Phi Beta Kappa key.

These and other testimonies showed that, in general, Jesse was a beloved teacher at Swarthmore. He seemed to understand the students' youthful idealism, their problems, and the fact that there was a need to hold up their self-esteem as members of a democratic society. While the faculty at George School had abandoned the use of plain language in its official minutes for 1898, Jesse continued to address his students with "thee" and "thy" to indicate their essential human equality with himself and all other people. When a girl student panicked at the prospect of taking one of his morning examinations in philosophy, running out to seek refuge in a lunch at Wanamaker's in Philadelphia, he welcomed her back in the early afternoon with just one question: Had she discussed the examination questions with anyone? Assured that she had not, he gave her a copy of the test, put her in a room by herself, and left her. Contrary to the student's fears, she did not "flunk" the test. This same understanding of student psychology was shown in Jesse's article on "The Use of Tobacco in Swarthmore College," published in *The Swarthmorean* on January 18, 1906. Jesse explained that, while students had been heretofore expected to abstain from using tobacco on the campus and in the buildings, a new regulation permitted smoking in Wharton Hall, the men's new dormitory. This new rule was in recognition of the fact that more than a third of the men were over twenty-one, and since many of them had brought the smoking habit with them from their homes, it was simply not good sense to use the method of command and prohibition in the fight against tobacco. Instead, the "method of influence" was to be used through frequent discussions of tobacco's dangers under faculty and student leadership. Jesse offered similar encouragement for the development of responsible action by students when he served as a member of the executive committee of the Young Friends' Association in 1902; and when he, Paul Pearson, and a Mr. Wilbur, started the Student Visitor Movement, apparently a device to get selected students involved in off-campus activities by sending them on speaking-and-service missions. And we can not doubt that the egos of the students in Jesse's advanced classes in philosophy were lifted a bit when they attended a Thursday afternoon tea at the home of their professor. Rebe, the ever-gracious hostess, helped to make the tea informal and pleasurable, as did the tricks of "Terry," the Holmes' mixed-terrier pet. ("Terry's" formal name was Terence O'Toole; he was the first of three Terence O'Tooles to cheer the Holmes clan, the last two being the pets of Robert S. Holmes' children and grandchildren.)

While the biographer's art usually requires the compressing of the subject's life over a long period of time into a few brief pages, thereby making him seem to have been more active than he really was, there can be no doubt that Jesse Holmes was an extremely busy man. In 1904, out of the fame of his many activities, he was invited to deliver the commencement address at his old school, the University of Nebraska. Returning to Swarthmore, he plunged into the life of the campus with a round of activities which can only be sampled here. In 1905, as a member of Swarthmore's Athletic Committee, he, along with others, was appointed to answer a communication from Swarthmore Monthly Meeting of Friends about the athletic conditions in the college. After due consideration he outlined the current system of athletics at Swarthmore "and made many valuable suggestions. . . ." He joined Sue Cunningham in the writing of a tribute to Susan W. Lippincott, who had died in March, 1906, after long years of service as a member of Swarthmore's Board of Managers. In January, 1919 Jesse gave what was termed a "worth while Collection talk." By October of that year *The Phoenix* reported that it was believed that he was out of a job — the job of being chairman of the Committee on Collection Attendance. ("Collection" was the Swarthmore term for what other colleges called "Assembly," "Chapel," etc.) This was due, *The Phoenix* believed, because, in contrast to the earlier "silent Collection, (interrupted only by a perfunctory reading from the rostrum). . . ," and interrupted too by the snores of sleeping students or by their rustling newspapers, a new policy was in force. Since September, it was said, students *wanted* to go to compulsory Collection because now it "had something REAL to offer." Now faculty members and outside talent made it worthwhile. "We enjoy to the fullest the well-rounded speech of Mr. Hicks, the pungent humor of Dr. MacClintock, Professor Goddard's poise, Dr. Holmes' forceful informality, the charm of Dr. Newport's smile-talks, ..." And they enjoyed the "good" outsiders: "[Jane] Addams, Professor [Paul] Douglass, ..." In brief, Jesse's Committee on Collection Attendance would no longer be necessary if the present trend continued.

There can be no doubt that this kind of insight into what students considered worthwhile was due in part to members of Jesse's Committee on Collection Attendance; there can also be no doubt that much of the credit should go to Jesse as their leader. Indeed, his leadership in other innovative drives had made him a sort of father figure to Swarthmore students as early as 1916. William W. Price said that his father had died just before America entered the war of 1914-1918, and that "Uncle Jesse took a father's place in a way, not only for me, but to hundreds of other young men...." This student appreciation of Jesse was openly recognized in 1916 when those in charge of getting out *The Halcyon,* the annual yearbook of the junior class, decided to dedicate that year's issue to "To that counselor and friend, Doctor Jesse H. Holmes...." The accompanying article, written by J. Russell Hayes, Swarthmore '88, may have seemed rather labored and a bit too sentimental to some people. Still, it got home a characterization or two worth remembering. J. Russell Hayes had some gentle fun with his friend and colleague, for he wrote that Jesse had been born in West Liberty, Iowa, a town "noted for its windmills...." And Hayes praised the portrait of Jesse in the front of *The Halcyon* as a "speaking likeness," although "it was taken in one of those rare moments when he was not speaking...." Like that other windy Nebraskan, William Jennings Bryan, Jesse was a Democrat; he was a single taxer and an advocate of women's suffrage — "in general a Fearless Champion...." Jesse didn't mind what you called him, Hayes said, "so long as you didn't call him a Republican!"

Jesse as a rather intense student at the University of Nebraska.
Courtesy Mr. & Mrs. Jesse H. Holmes III, Washington, D.C.

Rebecca S. Webb in her sophomore year at Swarthmore College (1886-87).
Courtesy Mr. & Mrs. Jesse H. Holmes III, Washington, D.C.

5. Family Life, 1900-1912

All of Jesse's many activities on the Swarthmore campus were of course carried on from the home base of his family life — a family life in turn affected by the many other activities into which his abilities and good nature seemed to draw him. His spreading fame as a forceful and interesting speaker on almost any topic brought invitations to speak to Young Friends' Association meetings, to women's clubs, and to other civic groups in such widely separated places as Wrightstown, New Jersey, Gettysburg, Pennsylvania, Rising Sun, Maryland, and Washington D.C. These speeches, plus his increasingly numerous articles in newspapers and periodicals, extended his orbit of influence many miles from his home. And, back in Swarthmore, Jesse was very much the solid citizen, serving on the local national bank's board of directors along with his friends William I. Hull, Joseph Swain, David L. Lukens, Arthur H. Tomlinson, and Morris L. Clothier. Added to these duties were those arising from Jesse's membership in the local school board.

A couple as outgoing and friendly as Rebe and Jesse could expect that their threshold would be crossed by relatives, colleagues and friends in many social visits. It was but in the nature of things that Ernest Holmes and his wife, who had been studying at the University of Paris, should stay with them for a few days in May, 1901, when Rebe was pregnant with Robert (b. December 7, 1901). William L. Price, famous architect and developer of Rose Valley near Moylan, Pennsylvania, loved to drop in on Jesse to argue public issues even if Jesse did sometimes call him "a bald-headed old galoot." But it was for Edward B. Rawson and his wife that a special welcome mat was always laid at the door of the Holmes' residence. "Ed" Rawson and Jesse had met while pursuing graduate studies at Johns Hopkins — Jesse in chemistry and Rawson in pedagogy. While Rawson was more concerned with the professional or technical aspects of teaching, both were born teachers and shared that critical, probing attitude held by unorthodox Quakers. (Ethel Broomell, who had studied under Rawson when he was principal of the Friends' Seminary of New York, and then went on to study under Jesse at Swarthmore, exulted that she had "the privilege of their wonderful understanding of their jobs. . . .") After their respective marriages, the Rawsons and the Holmeses kept in close touch, counting each other as "best friends." In 1902 Rawson visited Jesse and Rebe; in January, 1906, he was undoubtedly their guest when he appeared on campus to talk to students of Latin and Greek on "The Ethics of the Pony." In 1906, when Swarthmore College decided to give courses in education for the professional training of teachers, Rawson was hired to offer "Educational Methods" and "School Management" on Saturday mornings. His wife must have joined him on these weekend trips from New York, for we find her taking her master's degree in religion under Jesse about 1910.

Summers at Carter Hill.

We have seen how the five Webb sisters, and their husbands and children, spent their summers at Carter Hill, eight miles from Fryeburg in the state of Maine. Just why it was called Carter Hill we don't know. But we do know that from 1896 through 1910, the Webb clan enjoyed their vacations in this cool and invigorating country retreat, living in a formerly abandoned farmhouse which had been renovated by John J. Pike, its farmer-owner. When the remodeling was finished, a long loft had been partitioned into four bedrooms, with an outside stairway (called "the Golden Stairs" by Jesse) leading to the farthest room. Downstairs there were more bedrooms, and a large dining room with a long table around which twenty or more people might gather, particularly on festive occasions. These people would be fed from an adjoining kitchen, where Millicent Morgan ("Millie"), a colored cook, would bake thirty loaves of bread a week in a wood-burning stove. The wood bin would be replenished by her son Archie, who also, no doubt, was pressed into service to carry water from the pump in the yard to the laundry adjacent to the kitchen. This laundry, in the absence of an indoor bathroom, served also as a bathhouse for the younger children; here the mothers would soak their offspring in large wooden tubs. Two fireplaces, a living room, and a hall study completed the accommodations in the house proper. Attached to the house, however, was an old stable or barn in the New England style; the space above this stable was converted into two bedrooms when a large new barn was built by Mr. Pike and his two stalwart sons to house the horses and carriages rented by the vacationers.

Behind the barn, and beyond the tennis court, was an apple orchard and an area with scattered blackberry, raspberry and blueberry bushes. To get to this area the Carter Hill folks had to go through an adjacent pasture where the farmer grazed his bulls and cows. (One day a bull pursued one of the older boys, breaking one horn on the stone fence over which the boy had just leaped in his frantic efforts to escape.) Wild strawberry plants were all about, although two weeks later in producing fruit than in Pennsylvania. In front of the house was a large tree, with Jesse's homemade board-swing suspended from a branch by two heavy ropes. Several hammocks were to one side, but still in the shade of the tree; reclining in one of these one could look down the hill to the lower apple orchard and catch a glimpse of Kezar Pond sparkling in the sunshine. (This "Pond" would have been called a lake outside of New England: it was a mile and a half long by one mile wide — deep, cold, and full of fish.) At the end of the path leading down to the lake from the house was a small beach, two diving platforms or floats built by Jesse for the convenience of bathers, and a dock to accommodate rowboats and the *Rebe* — a small sailboat Jesse and Dr. Janney (we'll meet him later) bought for the general pleasure of the community. After an afternoon's outing on the lake one would climb the hill back to the house for supper; and then, in the early evening, sit on the side porch to watch the purpling summit of Mt. Pleasant some three miles away, and the sunset's colors on the lake and on the distant peaks of the White Mountains in New Hampshire.

To get to this idyllic spot from their homes in Maryland and Pennsylvania took a bit of doing by the Webb clan. About June 12 of each year Lizzie Webb and Cassie Carr (who lives with Lizzie after the death of her husband Samuel Carr), closed up their Philadelphia house to go to Maine; they were generally the first arrivals. Jesse and Rebe would rent their house if they could, starting with the middle of June; and then, with the Prices of Rose Valley, they would be off to join Lizzie and Cassie with their children Elizabeth, Herman and Robert, perhaps the family dog, and all their luggage. The trip must have been high adventure to the children — and something of a trial to the parents: by train to the Broad Street Station in Philadelphia; a train to New York or Jersey City; a cab or a ferry to the dock of the Fall River Line in Manhattan; to Fall River, Massachusetts by steamer; and then to Boston, Portland and Fryeburg in a hot and dusty railroad coach. What a relief it must have been to get off the train and climb into the open-air carriage provided for their transportation to Carter Hill by John Pike. The carriage had three seats to hold nine people, and it was drawn by two well-matched black horses. (Mr. Pike was very proud of his horses; once he had four of these black beauties hitched to the carriage to carry the group the eight miles from Fryeburg to Carter Hill. As Ruth Price described it: "He showed them off to us, what high steppers they were, how swift they were, how evenly they carried us over the ground.") Near the end of their journey they would go through the village of East Fryeburg, pass the Pike homestead, and then ascend the lane to be greeted by waving handkerchiefs and glad calls of welcome from Lizzie and Cassie on the porch.

Of the five Webb sisters who shared the expenses and much of the work at Carter Hill, Lizzie was the only one of this matriarchy who never married. Thin, quick and austere-looking, in Philadelphia she served as an invaluable clerk in the Race Street Friends Meeting; here at Carter Hill she exercised her considerable executive talents as the leader in the housekeeping and business aspects of the community. It was she who kept working on Mr. Pike until he built the new barn; and the rowboats and the bathhouse down at the lake shore were largely due to her. She saw to the disciplining of the children, "from simple chores . . . up to the daily blueberry picking and making the beds. . . ." Each summer the Carter Hill folks paid a boy-of-all-work to wait on table and run errands; Lizzie would supervise his work, including his trips down to East Fryeburg to the butchers, and to bring back the Saturday-night baked beans and steamed brown bread and doughnuts. But when these good things were served at the long table, with Lizzie presiding at one end of it, Jesse would dispute her leadership. Often the only mature masculine presence there, he would slap his end of the board in mock anger and cry out, "This is the head of the table!" Lizzie would reply, "No indeed. *I* am the head of the table and thee is the foot." This amiable feud continued until Bill Price, the paid waiter for one summer, settled it in Lizzie's favor. Henceforth, Bill said, Jesse's end of the table would be called Hades, the middle part (where the children sat) the Elysian Fields, and Lizzie's end, Paradise.

One summer Lizzie's almost obsessive concern for good order and cleanliness very nearly prevented her from taking a week's vacation in Bridgeton, some eight miles from Carter Hill. Would the folks she left behind be able to carry on without her? As she hesitated, her sisters, Anne, Emma and Rebe, gathered about her, urging her to go — but not too vehemently, for they didn't want to give the impression that they were anxious to get rid of her. After much gentle assurance that they would be able to manage the household in her absence, she decided to go.

As the week of Lizzie's absence drew towards its close, the Carter Hill house became the scene of great and hilarious activity. With dramatic flourishes of mops, brooms, and dusters, rooms were swept and stairs cleaned. At the same time "there was an air of mystery, an outburst of giggling and laughing after earnest consultations among the sisters. . . ." The children were now told what was afoot; they were to make little signs to be attached here and there telling that "This fireplace has been put in order," and that "The barn floor has been swept." Even little Herman Holmes, who had been remiss in brushing his teeth, now consented to have his teeth washed by Ruth Price so that he might truthfully greet Aunt Lizzie wearing a sign on his back saying " 'This boy's teeth have been cleaned.' "

As Lizzie's carriage approached the house she was greeted by the whole family standing on the porch, waving handkerchiefs and tooting horns. Over their heads, up near the porch roof, was a long white banner proclaiming proudly "This house has been cleaned!" And, when she approached the group for the welcome-home kisses, Herman spun around and showed her the sign on his back. As Ruth Price tells it, "Her expression matched her first words, 'Well, I'm flabbergasted!' "

There was a lot of fun in these Webb sisters; they projected an image far different from that staid and sober one most Americans have formed about Quakers over the years. Indeed, they were not full-born Quakers. Their father had not been a member of the Friends when he married the Quakeress Rebecca Turner. When the daughters came along he brought them up to dance and sing, and Emma played the piano. He served wine at his table and smoked cigars, although these practices were modified as he grew older.

If Lizzie might have appeared a bit straight-laced at times, especially as clerk in the Race Street Friends Meeting in Philadelphia, at Carter Hill she let her hair down. She brought her phonograph along and played Sousa's marches, Arthur Pryor's recordings, as well as grand opera. When she took the Carter Hill children on rides in Mr. Pike's haywagon she enjoyed teaching them rounds — "Three Blind Mice," "My Dame Had a Lame Tame Crane"; at other times there was a lusty singing of "The Spanish Cavalier" and "My Darling Clementine." And she was the only sister to keep a record of the birthdays of all the nieces and nephews, never failing to send them cards.

The other sisters were much the same. Emma (Mrs. William L. Price) also enjoyed the singing of old songs, especially when the group sat on the porch of an evening to sing "Twilight is Stealing" and "There's Music in the Air." Aunt Annie (Mrs. Oliver Edward Janney) wasn't especially musical, but was gay, talkative, and witty; she loved practical jokes. She also loved to tell how, on a trip to England with her husband Dr. Janney, they had had tea with Queen Victoria in Buckingham Palace. Cassie was the dancer of the family. At a birthday party for sister Emma, she did her Spanish dance, clad in Spanish clothes, and snapping her fingers in lieu of castanets. She also did the Highland Fling with Lizzie. An amateur botanist and bird-watcher, she remained "sweetly unperturbed" when twitted about her avocations.

And then there was Rebe, youngest of the Webb sisters. She couldn't dance as well as Cassie; in fact, she once showed up at the opening of college in Swarthmore with a broken toe because she had been trying to dance a jig in the barn at Carter Hill. But she had other talents: lively and talkative, she pleased the people around her not only with her cheerful friendliness, but with her skill at making ice cream, sherberts and mousses. Her maple mousse was a special favorite with the children, perhaps because it could be packed in an ice-cream maker with salt and ice, without the endless turning of the handle as in the making of ice cream. (The ice was supplied by Mr. Pike, who brought it up to them every evening from his icehouse on the shore of Kezar Pond.) And she had developed other talents — the making of doughnuts for the group's Saturday-night special dinner, and the making of fudge and peppermint drops which proved so delicious that the children at Carter Hill pleaded for more.

76

When doing her part of the dusting and cleaning she would wear a red bandana handkerchief around her head. One day, when she appeared outside the house with a red rose in her hair, a certain Benjamin — a visitor to Carter Hill — could not resist bursting into song in celebration of the picture she made.

After Samuel Carr died, Jesse was the leading male influence at Carter Hill, not only because of his personality, but because he was the only husband who by reason of his being a college professor could spend all or most of the three months of summer with the group. Dr. Janney, Anne's husband, could not take more than two weeks from his busy practice in Baltimore to go to Maine; Will Price, wise and witty architect, found that he was in similar straits.

Deprived of adult male companionship of his own class for so much of the summer, feeling some intellectual starvation, Jesse must have looked forward to the times when Dr. Janney and Will Price would spend their two weeks with the group at Carter Hill. And, if Janney and Price could be there at the same time, that would be an extraordinary bonus. It seems entirely fitting and proper that Ruth Price, the fifteen-year-old daughter of Will Price, should report one of those bonus occasions:

> One day, during the last summer of the many we spent on Carter Hill, I chanced to espy the three men of the family . . . sitting outdoors on our little plot of grass under the branches of the big tree. I stole outdoors to hear what was going on, for the men were deep in conversation, and that well-known look of deep satisfaction at the start of an intellectual discussion was upon the face of both Uncle Jesse and my father. However, Uncle Jesse's face frequently wore an eager expression when even a trivial or humorous matter became the core of a discussion. I stood by the trunk of a tree and watched them unobserved. . . . Upon Uncle Ned's face [Dr. Janney] was a look of pleasant seriousness. He was giving the subject. . . his judicial attention.
>
> They were sitting in a circle, as much of a circle as three men can make, their legs folded up crosswise in front of them. At first they were in deep accord, nodd[ing] to each other, agreeing with words of their own to what the others were saying, adding a few words of their own as new thoughts came. It seemed for awhile as though they agreed upon all things[;] then, after a discussion of economical things, possibly the government of the land, in which they were all interested, the conversation veered to another subject. Something was said, and it was now the opinion of two against one, . . .My father was the dissenter, and I could see that they

were now launched into one of those grand controversies where there is much talk, much gesticulating and no one is ever able to persuade the other one to change his opinion. I know it could continue through the morning, so I slipped away.

It was almost inevitable that this argument should be resumed at the supper hour, when Jesse would flash his beautiful teeth in an amiable matching of wits with Will Price and Dr. Janney. There would be brilliant repartee and sly digs to delight those gathered around the long table. Talk among friends was still entertainment in those days.

The ensuing night's sleep, however, might be disturbed in the early morning by Mr. Pike's motorized thresher. In the harvest season he would start his engine as early as six o'clock, waking up Carter Hill's residents and keeping them awake for hours thereafter. While at least one of these residents would sometimes get up, dress, and then go out to watch the harvesters at work, others would simply toss and turn in their beds. Jesse was greatly annoyed; but, knowing that it would do little good to speak to Mr. Pike about the noise, contented himself with mentioning it a few times during meals and composing a little verse:

Early in the morning, before the sun [was] up,
I woke and heard the engine going bup, bup, bup.

No doubt it was on one of those early mornings when one of the girls, aged about twelve, came down the stairs from her second-floor bedroom to the dining area. As she entered the dining area she saw Jesse standing naked in the doorway of his bedroom. They stared at each other. The girl turned around and fled back up the stairs in some confusion. Later, when she came down to breakfast she found Jesse fully dressed and seated at his accustomed place at the table. The girl sat down to start her breakfast. After a moment or two Jesse got up, walked around to her, kissed her, and then, without a word, resumed his place at the table.

Other days were less embarrassing to Jesse, however. Indeed, as the leading spirit at Carter Hill (apart from the housekeeping leadership claimed by Lizzie and Cassie), he took pleasure in inducing such people as Dr. Janney, inclined to be a bit Victorian in his attitude, into engaging in the activities associated with summer vacation resorts. One day he startled Dr. Janney by appearing in his bathing suit. He waved to Uncle Ned, who was standing on the porch in meticulous dress, and invited him to go swimming. Ned protested.

78

" 'I couldn't, Jesse,' he said. 'It would be so undignified. I — really — I couldn't bring myself to clothe myself the way thee is clad.' " But Jesse persisted, and finally Ned went into the house, to emerge in a few minutes wearing a two-piece bathing suit and a straw hat. When he said that he felt absurd, Jesse replied that he would get used to it, "in a tone of voice that meant he was going to *make* Uncle Ned get used to it. . . . " As they started for the lake, Uncle Ned was really embarrassed, his "bare legs fairly quiver[ing] with self-consciousness. . . . " By the end of the visit, however, he was enjoying such public bathing.

And then, since Jesse owned the *Rebe* in partnership with Ned, he would take him for a sail on Kezar Pond. Perhaps they also fished, trolling their lures behind them. At other times Jesse took Rebe and the regular adult residents of Carter Hill for a ride. Once he took out the *Rebe* for a solitary sail, rounding the point of land which hid the farther end of the lake from Carter Hill's view. When he failed to reappear after a reasonable length of time, the folks on shore began to get worried. The lake was choppy; the hour was getting late. Finally they saw the *Rebe* rounding the point — but very, very slowly. The boat was water-logged; it had suffered a calamity; and Jesse was lucky to be able to get it back to the shore's safety.

With clothes soiled by such adventures, as well as by the ordinary day-to-day activities of his family, Jesse often felt impelled to do their laundry in the communal washroom. One can picture him bending over a tub, arms deep in the soapsuds, and chatting all the while with one of the ladies working next to him. On one such occasion he was told that the governor of Rhode Island was waiting to see him outside in the yard. Jesse wiped his arms and hands rather casually, and, still wearing his apron, strode out to meet him. "How are you, governor?" he asked as he extended his soapy hand.

This same friendly informality, this same lack of obeisance to duly constituted authority, was the tone when other distinguished visitors came to Carter Hill. Elizabeth Powell Bond, dean of women at Swarthmore, moved her tall, spare figure through the world with a natural dignity; she claimed that "no lady could dress in less than an hour." Although she threw candy jujubes on the grass outside the house each morning for the children to scramble for, when she settled down at her place at the supper table some sense of restraint must have spread through the children around her. But Jesse knew how to relieve the strain: on one such occasion he called out "with a twinkle in his blue eyes, 'Toss me a biscuit, Liz.' There was something infectious in his spirit, for Mrs. Bond promptly did just that, half-way down the long table. . . ."

This same supper table was graced by two other distinguished guests: Dr. John A. Miller and Dr. Joseph Swain. Dr. Miller, professor of astronomy and mathematics at Swarthmore, had taught Herbert Hoover mathematics at Stanford University from 1891 to 1893; Dr. Swain, also on the Stanford faculty at the time, had helped Hoover gain admission to the university. Swain may have come to Carter Hill not only to get restful relaxation from his duties as president of Swarthmore, but to get away from some of the pressures arising out of his membership in the National Council of Education. However, how much rest this very tall and enormous man got at Carter Hill is problematical: he had to sleep diagonally on a bed while his wife used a cot. And the same general story is told about both Swain and Miller. One version has it that Jesse, in an effort to get Miller started on a discussion on astronomy after supper, asked him about the Milky Way. Miller, puffing his pipe, led the party out to the porch and lawn to point out and discuss some stars. After a while Jesse said, with his "fascinating facetious smile," that he had ordered a display of the aurora borealis to be put on during Miller's visit — an event which also occurred during Joseph Swain's visit, only this time Jesse said that he had "to punch the button" to make it happen.

Perhaps Jesse punched the button for other visitors, who, if less distinguished than Swain and Miller, were equally welcome at Carter Hill. Cousin Eliza Platto, and her daughter Cassie, were frequent guests. Eliza was especially welcome because she taught the Webb sisters how to knit and purl (Aunt Lizzie confused the two, once having done ten or twelve inches of a scarf before she realized that she was purling instead of knitting.) And Mr. Sidwell, founder of the Friends Select School where Jesse had taught before his move to George School, was an esteemed guest at times.

But not all of the guests were so well thought of. One time, after a family of two adults and two children had vacillated about their time of departure, they suddenly decided to leave early one fine morning. Then the Carter Hill folks had to look up train schedules, rush them through their breakfasts, get the horse and carrige out, and send them off to Fryeburg. As they disappeared down the long lane, the group on the porch "fairly hugged each other. . . . Aunt

Rebe sank down, really worn out. She didn't faint. She just sat, suddenly."

Such visitors *were* fatiguing. After a decent interlude of rest, however, various members of the Carter Hill community would find fun and diversion in other activities, such as mountain-climbing expeditions to nearby Mt. Pleasant, or trips to Mt. Kearsarge, Baldface Mountain, or Chicorua in the White Mountains. These trips might be for a day, or for a week, depending on the destination. Returning to Carter Hill, they might attend some of the First-day services Jesse had started with a certain Deacon Chadbourne in East Fryeburg's town hall, or those Quaker meetings held in Carter Hill's barn, with neighbors invited, and followed by box-lunch picnics. (At one of these meetings Jesse started to give an inspired talk, somehow lost the train of his argument, and was guilty of five minutes of gobbledgook before he got back on the track. At another meeting he spoke "simply and earnestly," with "none of the bombastic vigor" he had used in some other speeches.) And there might be a birthday party such as the one given for Emma Price. This started at the breakfast table with gay good wishes and presents; at ten o'clock there was an Alabama cakewalk, with mosquito-netting costumes for the children, as taught them by Millie, the maid-of-all-work; and in the afternoon there was a tennis match, the men wearing skirts and the women, trousers. One can see them now — the men tripping over their skirts, desperately waving their racquets, and the women exploding into peals of laughter.

But it was the children, of course, who had the most fun and the greatest thrills at Carter Hill. There were nine children most of the time: the "Big Four" in 1910 included William W. Price ("Bill" or "Will"), Elizabeth W. Homes ("Libs"), Rebecca W. Janney ("Bocca"), and Ruth Price; these ranging in age from about eleven to about fifteen. The "Little Three," ranging in age from about seven to about ten, were Jesse Herman Holmes (Herman), Robert ("Bobby"), and Katherine ("Kathy"). In an intermediate group were Margaret Price and Eleanor Janney ("Nell").

While Aunt Lizzie and other adults sometimes took the children on outings, Jesse was the leader in the fun and games they enjoyed in and around the house, on hayrides, and in the water sports down at the lake. When the lake was whipped with summer fury he would take them out on the porch to watch the thunderstorms forming over the mountains and rolling toward the house. He taught the older girls how to chin themselves, using a barn ladder as a crossbar; he was chagrined, after having made a swaggering boast, that he couldn't lift his portly figure more than twice, while his daughter Libs and Ruth Price were able to do it five times. (By the end of the summer, Libs had beaten Ruth, being able to chin herself twenty-one times.) Although the tennis court was "bumpy," they enjoyed playing through Jesse's teaching. He set up a croquet court on equally bumpy ground; since it also was tilted toward the lake, games "were won less by skill than by chance." At other times he would come out of the house, scan the lake to judge sailing conditions, and then call out "Come on, it's good sailing weather!" A selected party of youngsters would troop down the hill, get on the *Rebe,* and off they would go, with little Bobby grinning up in the bow. As they sailed along Jesse would lead them in singing "Jubilo" — a song which not only fascinated Jesse and the children with its musical rhythm, but which pleased Jesse through its reform implications:

> Say, darkies, hab you seen my master
> wiv de moustache on his face,
> Go down de road some time dis mawn'in
> like he gwine to leab dis place?
>
> He seen de smoke way up de ribber
> where de Linkum gunboats lay,
> An he put on his coat an' lef' very sudden
> like he gwuine to run away?
>
> De Massa run, — aha! De darkie stay, — oho!
> It looks like de Kingdom's a'comin,
> An' de Day of Jubilo!!

Although Jesse was too impatient to do very much fishing, he sometimes trolled a lure behind the *Rebe* while at the same time enjoying a sail. One one occasion, however, he did take a party of adults on a fishing expedition. A rowboat was attached to the *Rebe* by a rope, and those who wanted to fish were towed to a likely spot. And he may have taught Herman the art; in any case Herman became the group's "excellent fisherman," once bringing in a catch of twenty-five perch and small bass. Herman went out again and again, using a spoon lure or an artificial fly, always returning with a great catch. At first, when Jesse showed him how to clean the fish, Herman "lost some of his ardor"; later, after Jesse had "cajoled" him into cleaning the fish as a matter of course, Herman did a fine job of it without complaining.

If Jesse used cajolery on Herman in the matter of cleaning fish, he had other methods of getting the children at Carter Hill to do the right thing. The children soon found out that they could not invite themselves to go out on the *Rebe* for one of those glorious rides; "one could not coax, wheedle, or nag" him. Such tactics would only draw a withering look or a severe scolding, followed by an "utter withdrawal" of that companionship and geniality which the children prized so much — and wanted to win back. He was sociable with his own children, often getting down on his hands and knees to play bear with Herman and Bobby. And, if they did do something that displeased him, he would not spank or whip them; instead he placed the offender on a chair in his little hallway study, or in his bedroom, and talked to him for half an hour in such a way that the child squirmed and realized the full burden of his guilt. In this way they became generally more amenable, although Herman did continue to absorb large amounts of cookies without permission.

On rainy days, or when the lake was too cold or too windy for sailing, swimming, fishing, the children found other things to do. Although Lizzie disapproved, Jesse taught them card games: slapjack, casino, whist, and five hundred. They enjoyed five hundred, even though Jesse was a reckless bidder at times: in one game he went five hundred in the hole and never got out of it. When card playing lost its charm Jesse started a class in the study of the German language, the class sitting around him on the grass of the croquet court. At first Ruth Price resented the idea of lessons during vacation; in the course of four or five weeks, however, she came to enjoy it — especially when Jesse sang " '*Röslein, röslein, röslein rot, röslein auf der Heide.*' " And, given all the talent at Carter Hill, it was almost inevitable that the older girls should put on plays in the barn. In 1902, when Libs was six, Eleanor Janney staged "Snow White," with all the children taking part. Libs made "a perfect Snow White — hair as black as a raven's wing, cheeks as red as a drop of blood on the snow. Libs was pretty. . . ." Bill Price was the huntsman, and later the prince; Nell took the part of the wicked stepmother, while the rest of the kids were dwarfs. Mothers and aunts made up the audience, being shown to their seats with great ceremony. As Ruth said, ". . .it was fun giving it, and Nell put it on well. . . ."

Nell's production of "Snow White" was so well received that she did it again in another year. But, as she and the other children at Carter Hill grew more mature, with increasing pubsecent urges, her stage productions became more sophisticated. She rigged up a dressing room in the barn, put up curtains, and created a stage setting for a play she had worked up from a vaudeville skit she had seen somewhere. Her crowning effort, of course, was "Lost, a Kiss in Central Park" — a play we are sure amused not only the mothers and aunts but the adult males invited to the show.

At other times the barn was used as a dance hall. The older girls enjoyed dancing — Nell in Baltimore, Ruth in Rose Valley, Pennsylvania. They taught Libs and Bocca the two-step and the waltz, as well as the schottische. Albert, one of the boys-of-all-work, taught them the fox-trot. On the day of one of their big dances they would move the carriages out of the way, and sweep and wax the barn floor. While Jesse would not part with the paraffin that he chewed every day at the recommendation of his dentist, the children found an adequate substitute for the waxing in shaved candle stubs. The wax would be worked into the boards by sliding their shoes. Then Aunt Lizzie's phonograph was brought out, a lighted lantern hung from a rafter, and the dance was on. Even the elders joined in — or at least some of them.

If dancing in a barn lighted by one overhead lantern was not the ultimate in romance, it was nevertheless true that Carter Hill offered a romantic setting in that day of shirtwaists, corsets, and picture hats. Nell enjoyed it most, entertaining three young men there so successfully that she received two proposals of marriage. One of these proposals was eventually accepted, the winning suitor being Walter Robinson Johns. Ruth was only fourteen when she fell in love with a neighborhood swain fifteen years older than herself. She recorded her "ecstatic feelings" in her diary. Libs, however, seemed to have less success; in any event she told Ruth in 1910 that she didn't want to return to Carter Hill next summer. Still, as Ruth wrote later, the romance of Maine lingered on — ". . .the lovely sunny days, the blue high mountains, the quietude of calm fading sunsets, the pine laden air, the sparkling water. . . ."

The Tragedy of Elizabeth.

By the time the Holmes family returned to Swarthmore in 1910 from their last trip to Carter Hill, they had moved to the house next door. Here, at 5 Whittier Place, they were even more comfortable, we must believe; and here the Holmes children could romp with their dog on an equally spacious lawn.

When this move was made, Elizabeth, "inclined to plumpness in her early years" and "sunny and sweet," was almost fourteen years old. Herman, dark haired, was a robust lad of ten; Robert was a curly haired blond of nine. The task of rearing these three in the busy, busy Holmes household was a formidable one, and not without those occasional flare-ups of temper one would expect when five different people live in close and enforced association from day to day. These five people drew their behavior from many different sources. This was certainly true of the children, as Jesse and Rebe realized. They were individuals, not possessions. Perhaps Scott Nearing, part-time colleague of Jesse's in this early period at Swarthmore, had the Holmes family in mind when he quoted some lines from Kahlil Gibran's *Prophet* many years later:

> Your children are not your children,
> They are the sons and daughters of
> Life's longing for itself.
> They come through you but not from you,
> And though they are with you, yet they
> belong not to you.
> You may give them your love but not
> your thoughts.
> For they have their own thoughts.
> You may house their bodies but not
> their souls,
> For their souls dwell in the house of
> tomorrow, when you cannot visit, not
> even in your dreams.
> You may strive to be like them, but seek
> not to make them like you
> For life goes not backward nor tarries
> with yesterday.

Shortly after Elizabeth was born Rebe started a baby book for her, a volume giving many insights into Rebe's character as well as Elizabeth's. From 1896 to 1907 Rebe made intermittent entries into Elizabeth's book, the entries being largely concerned with Elizabeth's birth, early childhood, and her rather frequent illnesses such as colic, whooping cough, and the threat of pneumonia. But in

1907 Elizabeth began to make her own entries, turning her baby book into a diary, which she kept rather faithfully until 1910. This was her sunny period, when in sweet innocence she described those things which stirred the girls in the middle grades of her school.

But now, in 1910, she was beginning to feel the effects of her fatal diabetes. She recorded how, in the fall of 1910, she had gone half-way through the ninth grade, and "then, alas, I got sick, was taken out of school and whisked off to Baltimore to my uncle Ned, to be doctored, . . ." She stayed in Baltimore for two months, spending two weeks of that time in Johns Hopkins Hospital, where she "had a fine time. . . ." Returning to 5 Whittier Place, and finding that her illness would not allow her to go to her regular school, she decided to do a more thorough job of keeping her diary. Of course, as she wrote, ". . .whether I *do* keep a diary will remain to be seen. . . ."

She did keep the diary; in fact, she personalized it, calling it "Dear Little Book," "dear little Journal," and closing entries with "Adieu, kind friend, adieu," and "Good-bye till next time, honey." And the diary contains other evidence, implicitly and explicitly, that she filled its pages not simply to keep busy, but mainly as a release from her adolescent frustrations and her loneliness. In a long passage written on October 16, 1911, Elizabeth tells how she had been reading her mother's journal, in which Rebe told of her many friends of both sexes when *she* was fifteen. The comparison with her own very limited circle of friends, especially of the male variety, left Elizabeth feeling very blue. "If I only had boys to be silly over I guess I'd be as silly as anybody. Oh for a boy to have a case on, that had a case on me!. . ." Then she talked to herself by way of the diary: "Well, never mind, Elizabeth, maybe when thee goes to College thee'll begin having friends. . . ." At this point she broke down and had a good cry, after which she felt a little better. It also made her feel better to know that Rebe understood her problems; she wrote that "Mother is the dearest thing alive, and almost takes the place of a best friend, . . ." Some two weeks later she pasted four photographs of herself on a page of the diary, and then talked to it: "I'm sorry to have to break your fond illusion of my looks, but I must, for it isn't in me to deceive even you, my little book, . . ." Still, she wrote, ". . .I'd like to have one friend that thought I was (ah, I find I am too shy and modest even to mention the word). . . ."

In spite of the dominantly sad tone of the latter part of Elizabeth's diary, it provides some cheery — and certainly very intimate — descriptions of the Holmes' day-to-day family life as carried on in the last three months in 1911 and in January of 1912. In mid-October she wrote that she had fixed up her room so that it looked "quite college girly;" she was "simply crazy about it. . . ." The next day, October 12, was spent going to Philadelphia on a shopping trip with her mother. They got a suit and a hat, winding up the day with "an awfully good dinner in town. . . ." That evening, recording the day's activities, she ended her writing in some excitement — "Horace is downstairs; be still, my fluttering heart!" The next evening a certain "Bill" had supper with them; they were entertained by Jesse, who had just returned from one of his lecturing tours. He told them of his adventures on this trip, sending them all into "convulsions of laughter." The following day, a Saturday, Jesse took her to Philadelphia to see a Dr. Saylor for a physical examination. After the examination they went to a "moving-picture show, as Father and I both enjoy them. . . ." Returning to Swarthmore, Elizabeth went to a dance in Rose Valley with Bill, where she had a fine time in spite of some "rough-house" by the local boys. Since the next day was a Sunday, the family went to First-day School and Meeting. (At this point in her diary she wrote in parentheses "Oh, you cherubim!") She also reported that her father made "a very good speech" in Meeting, after which they all went to the College dining hall for dinner. Returning to Whittier Place, the Holmes family was pleased to receive the Pearsons, the Hulls, and the Walters for an afternoon of pleasant small talk. That evening, after the visitors had gone, Elizabeth studied for an examination in a course in German she was taking by special arrangement with the College. The studying paid off: she proudly reported that she got an "A" in the test. She also indicated that she might have a tutor in algebra later on in the year: "I'm hoping to enter College with my class; if I do, I [won't] mind staying out of school so very much."

It was the nature of Elizabeth's disease that while it prevented her from attending regular sessions of high school or boarding school, it did not, through these last months, prevent her from leading a remarkably active social and athletic life. Her scholarly conscience sometimes impeded her activities, however, as in the time she refused an invitation to stay overnight with friends because she hadn't studied her German for the next day. After German class, though, she went to Mrs. Paul Pearson's house to get help on her

Hallowee'n costume in preparation for a dance at Rose Valley, and then saw a lyman Howe moving picture in the evening. "It was great, but a little hard on the eyes. . . ." On October 26 she attended an afternoon tea given by Miss Bronk, a professor of French; that evening she threw a temper tantrum because Jesse and Rebe wouldn't allow her to go to a "fake hypnotizing" with Bill. (She was "talked to" by her father.) The next day, however, she had a lovely time playing tennis with "Owen and William." A few days later she and Jesse "licked" the boys in two sets, 6-3, 6-3. On the evening of Friday, November 3, getting ready for a Saturday night supper party, she shelled peanuts with Rebe, talking and having a very nice time. After the supper, attended by Anna Miller, Frances and Edward Wright, and "Billy" and Owen, they played "Jenkins-up the first part of the evening and rhyming charades the last part, and we laughed most of the time. . . ." When Jesse and Rebe went out to visit friends, as they did the Pearson's one day, they saw to it that Libs in turn had friends to visit her. On Sunday evenings Jesse would read *Rob Roy* to a family group, or play chess with her. One day, to the boundless delight of Libs, Herman and Robert, he brought them a puppy — the same Terence O'Toole we saw entertaining student visitors in the Holmes' house in an earlier chapter. About the same time Mary Hull gave her a pony, fulfilling one of Elizabeth's long-felt wishes — "Oh, I am the happiest girl alive!" She enjoyed riding Raymond, as she called him; she also enjoyed going to a mass meeting at the College, complete with bonfire, to cheer on the football team. Trips to Philadelphia were "fun" — to have her picture taken (she was apprehensive as to how it would turn out), to attend a stage production of "The Trail of the Lonesome Pine" (it made her cry), or to go shopping for an evening coat at Gimbels. (Her mother favored "a beautiful old rose and black one"; Elizabeth chose "a lovely light blue and black one. . . . ," since all "my clothes are that color this winter. . . .") Perhaps it was because she had been so "scared" when she helped serve refreshments to a meeting of Jesse's Boy Scout troop on November 14 that she evaded the same experience two weeks later by going to Mary Hull's house for the evening. Or perhaps it was because by this time she weighed 105½ pounds, having gained four pounds in two weeks. She thought this "positively shocking." No doubt this concern with her weight and appearance, as well as the requirements of her diabetic diet, led her to eat sparingly of the Thanksgiving dinner at her home attended by Lizzie and Cassie, Dr. Bronk, the Pearsons, and the William Prices in from Rose Valley. After dinner Bill Price sang "Only Me," and then they played charades.

While Elizabeth continued to participate in many activities through December and January, her diary also reveals that her pace was slowing down and becoming more erratic due to the progress of her disease. On Tuesday, December 5, she stayed in bed until lunch, and then went riding on Raymond. She was sleepy that evening, but when she got to bed she couldn't sleep until after midnight. A week later she spent an entire day in bed; getting up only to eat supper and then go to an entertainment at the Faculty Club House in the evening. Jesse and Rebe had taken her on many a trip to Philadelphia to see Dr. Saylor; but, since the insulin treatment had not yet been developed, he could do little to help her. Now, in early December, Jesse and Rebe began clutching at straws: they took her to a Dr. Wesley Dunnington, an osteopath recommended by the Pearsons. Although Elizabeth liked the man "pretty well," she didn't particularly like the treatment he gave her: ". . .just think — two dollars for fifteen minutes of being punched about. I'm having treatments three times a week. . . ." Interspersed among those treatments were Christmas shopping trips, attendance at a lecture on "Peace" by William Starr Jordan, another peace meeting at the Academy of Music in Philadelphia addressed by Henry Watterson (about the last of the old-time orators, according to Jesse), going to the Swains to hear their victrola, and a "card dance" where she danced out her card. But she felt discouarged; she thought that this constant dancing was due to the mechanical card system, not to her popularity. And it was very discouraging not to be able to indulge in small talk: "I can't talk nothingness; I don't know what to say while we're dancing. Bocca talks finely; she [doesn't] seem to have any trouble. . . ." Because she felt so ill in mid-January she missed two days of a series of "gym lessons" she had started at the College, and she now began to call her German classes "horrid."

On February 1, 1912, in what was to be her last entry, this pretty, tormented girl addressed her diary in misery, trepidation, and perhaps a sense of impending doom. "I feel as miserable as any human being can today," she wrote. "I've been in bed with a fierce cold in my head [;] besides feeling bum, I'm not fit to be seen [;] my nose is like a lobster, a particularly large boiled one. . . ." Another reason for feeling bad was the fact that she was scheduled to take a final examination in German at eight o'clock the next morning — "and it's going to be hard, let me tell thee!. . . ." And then Elizabeth apologized to her diary for neglecting it of late: "Does thee suppose I'll ever settle down and do any work for any length of time? I always am enthusiastic at *first*, but sad to say it most always fades from view in a very short length of time. . . ." She hoped that when she got "old and gray" she wouldn't be "so flighty." Then, after telling how she had gone "coasting," and getting "so cold," she wrote, "I'm going to play chess with Father now, so au revoir. I will write more anon — maybe."

Elizabeth lingered for a few more months, being transferred to the home of William L. Price in Rose Valley, Moylan, to spare Herman and Robert the trauma of witnessing her dying agonies. She died there on September 4, 1912 at the age of sixteen. She was mourned by the Swarthmore community, who missed her "bright face and beautiful coloring pass[ing] in and out among us. . . ."

Jesse and Rebe never quite got over her death. Rebe said "All the poetry has gone out of my life." Jesse's grief, on one occasion at least, was expressed more violently. Shortly after her death, when, in a discussion of race relations, a student in one of his classes asked him whether he would let his daughter marry a Negro, Jesse flew into a rage and threw the student out of his class. But, to Jesse's credit, he apologized to the student afterward, explaining his emotional turmoil at the time.

The Holmes' residences on Whittier Place
Photograph by the author, 1973

Parrish Hall in 1973
Photograph by the author.

"Ducky" in 1910
Medium   File   Portraits,   Friends
Historical Library, Swarthmore College.

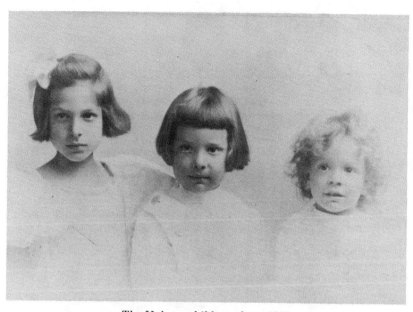

The Holmes children about 1905:
Elizabeth, Jesse Herman, Robert
Courtesy Mr. and Mrs. Jesse H. Holmes III, Washington, D.C.

Elizabeth and Aunt Lizzie when Elizabeth was fifteen. Courtesy Grace R. Holmes.

6. A Time of Adjustment

While Jesse and Rebe would never quite recover from the loss of their daughter, they made valiant efforts to adjust to the new situation by keeping busy. Jesse's normal schedule of teaching and lecturing made this a bit easier for him than for Rebe; in addition, he became an officer in the Chautauqua Association of Pennsylvania and was soon acting as platform superintendent and lecturer in this Chautauqua's summer tours of small towns in the Eastern states. Rebe found some relief in the summer of 1913 when she and her sisters Lizzie and Cassie took a two-month's trip to Ireland, Scotland and England; this was followed in 1914 by a family trip abroad. But her best and most immediate solution lay in her enrollment as a student at Swarthmore in the fall of 1912.

Rebecca Webb Holmes, A.B. — *"Summa Cum Laude."*

She had entered Swarthmore College in 1885 in pursuit of the degree of bachelor of arts, but, because of illness, had to withdraw after she had completed her junior year. For one reason or another she did not return to Swarthmore as a student; when she attended class reunions, however, she quite naturally mingled with her friends as an "ex-'89."

After her marriage to Jesse she taught at George School for several years, and then, with growing children to attend, found it impossible to complete the work for her degree. But when Elizabeth's death posed the need for a psychological anodyne, and with Herman and Robert busy in school, she again enrolled as a student. (Undoubtedly there were also other factors involved in her decision here: the fact that many of her women friends had college degrees, and her desire to catch up academically with her husband as much as possible.) When the family returned from its trip to Europe in the late summer of 1914, they found that they could not

91

move back into 5 Whittier Place immediately (alterations?), but had to board for a while in another house. This arrangement allowed Rebe more time to study; when the family was again able to move into 5 Whittier Place she had to mix studying and housekeeping, and eased up on her normal schedule of entertaining. After all, she said, " 'one must give up something if anything is to be done.' "

Apparently Rebe's main interest was in public speaking since she chose Paul Pearson as her major professor. Other studies included English, philosophy and Bible, her husband being her instructor in the latter courses.

While Rebe received her A.B. degree at the regular Swarthmore commencement exercises in June, 1915, sitting at one time with her old classmates of '89 and at another time with the class of '15, she received a greater honor from her friends, relatives, and neighbors on May 28. These good people, thirty-five women and two men, had conspired to write a petition addressed to Paul Pearson in which they asked of him an extraordinary favor, academically speaking. Typed on official Swarthmore College stationery, complete with the college seal, it was a long document, with the signatures of the thirty-seven conspirators running down through two sheets of paper pasted together:

May 28, 1915

To Professor Paul Martin Pearson, L.H.D.

Dear Friend:

We the undersigned beg leave to present and do hereby present our appreciation of the achievement of your talented student, Rebecca Webb Holmes, and further we beg leave to say and do hereby say that it is our unanimous opinion that, not only she should be given a bachelor's degree (suffragist though she is), but if such a thing is possible, she should be allowed to write her name henceforth, Rebecca Webb Holmes, A.B., *Summa Cum Laude*.

[Signatures]

Although we do not have the details of the party at which this was read and signed, we may imagine that it was held at the Faculty Club House on the campus, and that it was presented to Paul Pearson with much jocular comment and hilarity on the part of Rebe's friends — a good cross-section of the academic and societal Establishment in the Swarthmore of 1915.

A Family Trip to Europe.

Having been granted a sabbatical leave in 1899, even before he started to teach at Swarthmore, Jesse could not expect to receive another one for some time. But in 1913 he received the second one, this time for the spring semester of 1914. During his absence his classes in Bible were to be taught by William T. Ellis of Swarthmore, experienced traveler in the Near East, author of a popular set of Sunday-school lesson booklets, and one of the leading lecturers on the Pennsylvania Chautauqua during the summer of 1913. Jesse's course in the history of philosophy was in the care of Reverend J.M. Wells, pastor of the First Baptist Church of Kennett Square, Pennsylvania. A graduate of Amherst and the Yale Divinity School, Reverend Wells had taught philosophy at Yale for a time.

With his classes so well provided for, Jesse, Rebe, and sons Herman and Robert, now in their early teens, were scheduled to sail for Europe on January 31. Their main object was sightseeing, although Jesse told a student reporter that he also planned to study the life and religions of the several nations they would visit. They hoped to get to England in May in order to attend the London Yearly Meeting, and then spend the rest of the summer touring the English countryside.

While the entire Holmes family enjoyed the trip, Rebe reporting that the boys were thriving on Italian and Austrian food, Italy was the country for her. "Never will I be happy 'till I go again to Rome, Florence, and Venice. . . ." She thought that this was due in large part to the fact that their quarters were so pleasant in each of these places, and that they stayed long enough in each place to feel at home, and to be able to explore each city at their leisure. They found Venice particularly diverting. With it as a base, they went to Murano to see the glass works, and paid a visit to Chioggia, a fishing village on the Adriatic. In Venice itself they visited St.

Mark's Cathedral, had two moonlight gondola rides, and spent several afternoons in St. Mark's Square and on the Piazza. They fed the pigeons in the Square and sat at little tables on the Piazza to drink tea and listen to band concerts. Rebe said that she couldn't "imagine a more attractive scene"; she "could have stayed on there for months! . . ." And Herman enjoyed it too; in fact he said later that the whole trip was the "high spot in my life."

From Venice they went on into Austria, heading for Innsbruck. Here Jesse had a most excellent cup of coffee, a treat which was repeated at breakfast in an open-air restaurant at Botzen on the border. The coffee was so good that Rebe "could hardly drag him away. . . ."

Crossing the border into Germany, the Holmes family traveled to Munich in third-class railway compartments which were "as clean as clean, . . ." And, according to Rebe, "the nicest kind of people" traveled in them. "The 'nicht rauchers' are really 'nicht rauchers,' & the men do not smoke in them 'till asked to desist, as they always did in Italy. . . ." While they found Munich beautiful, there wasn't enough time to "even peep" into the many museums and art galleries. But they had one interesting experience: in their search for a restaurant they stumbled into "a real German drinking hall. . . ." They had a light supper and then stayed on until 9:30 to hear the music and watch the people.

Leaving Munich, the Holmes party went north to Nürnberg, Rothenberg and Marburg. In Marburg, Jesse planned to give German lessons to Herman and Robert; he also planned to accompany a certain young Herr Schellenburg to watch a duel at Marburg University. Rebe was revolted at the idea of this student dueling: "Nearly all the Students have their faces scarred, & it is a 'beastly shame,' I think, for them to spoil their looks so." To Jesse, however, this was but research "in the field" since he was gathering data for a lecture on German university life — possibly for use on the Chautauqua circuit. More research was in the offing, because he planned to leave Rebe and the boys in Marburg for a few days while he went to Jena to study university conditions there. He had a letter of introduction from Dr. Walter Rauschenbusch to a Professor Eneken of Jena which he thought would smooth the way and make the trip worth while.

This was in April, 1914. Although there are no records extant to show that the Holmes family went from Germany to England so that they might attend the London Yearly Meeting in May, we may suppose that this part of their trip was accomplished. But, whether in England or on the Continent, Jesse heard the preliminary rumblings of the guns of August; he brought his family home to Swarthmore before the Uhlans crossed the Belgian border.

And there, in the College's first Collection of the new academic year, he told the students about German university life as he had seen it. Undoubtedly, as a peace advocate, he made much of the war psychology of the saber-scarred German students; no doubt too, this speech was also a trial run for a projected speech on the same subject during his Chautauqua service the following summer.

Origins of the Chautauqua Idea

The Chautauqua that commanded so much of Jesse's time and energy in the period 1912-1929 was part of a movement which had started on the shores of Lake Chautauqua in western New York in the early 1870s. Here Lewis Miller, an Ohio manufacturer and Sunday-school teacher, joined with the Reverend John H. Vincent of the Methodist Episcopal Church in organizing a summer camp meeting for the training of religious workers. By 1874 this had grown into the Chautaugua Assembly, which constantly expanded its varied and highly successful program until in the 'eighties and 'nineties thousands of middle-class people would spend at least part of their summer there, living in clapboard cottages complete with porches and gingerbread trimmings.

Much of the Assembly's popularity was due to the work of William R. Harper, later president of the University of Chicago, and his colleague Shailer Mathews, since they infused Social-Gospel idealism into the program of Bible studies which they directed. Added to the pleasures of such studies were the opportunities to hear distinguished people lecture on historical, economic, and classical subjects in a spacious, well-ventilated auditorium — such men as Herbert Baxter Adams, well-known "scientific historian" from Johns Hopkins; Richard T. Ely, a progressive economist fresh from his studies at German universities; and Professor Mahaffey, renowned Greek scholar from Trinity College, Dublin. And Josiah Royce was there to open up new vistas of idealism in the days of McKinley and the American adventure in Cuba. His Harvard colleague, William James, addressed at least one of the summer assemblies, although during his stay at Chautauqua he was both amused and shocked to note that his audience, hampered by its "dull if high-toned sense of morality," lacked a sense of epicureanism — or even a sense of humor. In addition, there was "a certain shallowness and glibness. . . ." in the people there, a condition which he realized might be rescued by the opening up of glimpses "of the intellectual world beyond their petty personal and domestic affairs."

This evident need for more thought and study had led to the founding in 1878 of a Literary and Scientific Circle which encouraged the Chautauqua habitues to pursue a four-year course of directed readings in the interludes between summer sessions at the lake. These readings, according to George Herbert Palmer of Harvard, would introduce earnest people to " 'Round Tables upon Milton, Temperance, Geology, the American Constitution, the Relations of Science and Religion, and the Doctrine of Rent'. . . ." This was truly a wondrous intellectual feast, but the Chautauqua reading lists for the Circle enriched this even more by listing books from the literary and philosophical classics, and with standard works on the physical and social sciences. Other books were specially written for this overall purpose, and the devotees of self-help popular culture were kept informed of new opportunities along this line by the founding of *The Chautauquan*, a monthly magazine.

(Not so surprisingly, this venture into adult education stimulated the origin and growth of those home-study courses offered by institutions best symbolized by the International Correspondence Schools of Scranton, Pennsylvania. By 1918 there were at least 300 of these private correspondence schools boasting millions of enrollees studying the gamut of knowledge from the most strictly cultural to the most strictly vocational. And the hunger for knowledge on the part of culturally deprived citizens was at least partially satisfied when commercially motivated series of books were offered for sale very cheaply under the imprint of the Standard Library, the Seaside Library, the Lakeside Series, the Leisure Hour Series, and many others of a similar nature.)

But it was not only through books and lectures on intellectual topics that Lewis Miller and Reverend Vincent hoped to reinvigorate the life of the people. The arts and the crafts were part of life too; indeed, Miller was persuaded that William Morris, the English advocate of an individualistic, self-expressive type of socialism, had grasped an important principle when he urged a return to the handicraft ideal of the medieval guilds as a guide to better living in a machine economy. And so the various arts — music, painting, creative writing, and the production of plays — became part of the program at Chautauqua, along with such handicraft projects as basket weaving and the making of rugs and woven textiles. No part of life could be neglected; all of life was a school for the mutual edification and cultural enrichment of farmers, mechanics, teachers, lawyers, businessmen, and housewives of all descriptions.

Small wonder that when Edward Eggleston, of *Hoosier Schoolmaster* fame, visited Chautauqua through an invitation from his friend Reverend Vincent, he was somewhat overwhelmed by all the activities he found there. He strolled through the shaded streets, he watched the bands and parades, he noted the earnestness of students at the lectures, and he couldn't help seeing the romantic antics of young couples. Torn between amusement and awe, he left his impressions:

'You can learn Greek, Latin, Hebrew and for aught I know Choctaw here. You can learn "Americanized Delsarte" and Penmanship and Pedagogy and Exegetics and Homiletics and History and Rowing and Piano Music and fancy bicycling and singing and athletics and how to read a hymn in public and the art of writing family and Business letters and everything else except dancing and whist.'

Most of the farmers and small-town folk in the hinterland could not afford the time or the money to go to Chautauqua to sample this cafeteria-style culture. Instead, the Chautauqua came to them, but not under the official direction of the institution centered at Lake Chautauqua. What did come to them had its origin in 1868, when James Redpath reorganized the remnants of the old lyceums into a highly successful lecture bureau, soon sending out on a circuit such well-known figures as John Gough, the temperance zealot, Thomas Nast, the cartoonist, Russell Conwell, with his "Acres of Diamonds" speech, and John L. Stoddard, who specialized in travelogues. In contrast with the older lyceums' emphasis on informative lectures, the Redpath people went in more for the dramatic, the humorous, and the entertaining type of program. The lectures, however, always had to be free from anything which might threaten the public good, and always had to fit in with the American middle-class regard for religion, the home, neighborliness, and the principles of the Constitution.

These Redpath lyceum programs were generally given in the larger towns during the winter. What was needed, taking a leaf from the Chautauqua book, was a series of summer programs which could be given in or near small towns which did not have the proper auditorium facilities for the staging of lectures, plays, and concerts. These needs were met in 1903, when Keith Vawter, an agent of the Redpath Lyceum Bureau, organized a traveling Chautauqua which brought inspirational lecturers and "clean" entertainment to towns of 500 to 10,000 people every summer, usually for a week. These towns were laid out on a circuit; an advance agent would go to each town in turn to select a site for the large circus tent that would be shipped by railroad. Then, on the opening day, a traveling crew of young men would erect the tent, scatter sawdust on the ground, put up the stage, and set out the folding chairs for the audience. A Chautauqua band would set the mood through stirring marches and semipopular airs; then, with the audience settled down in its seats (perhaps fanning themselves with straw fans in the summer heat), a platform superintendent would introduce the main event of the afternoon or evening. The main event might be Gilbert and Sullivan's "Mikado," or Barrie's "Little Minister," the stage settings for these productions having been brought from the railway station by horse and dray, or later by motor truck. Or the main events might be speeches by such progressive personalities as Theodore Roosevelt, Jane Addams, or Samuel Gompers. William Jennings Bryan was a popular attraction, his silver-tongued oratory and stentorian tones filling the farthest reaches of the sawdust rows.

This Redpath Chautauqua, and others like it, became so popular that by 1912 there were 600 towns on several circuits in six Midwestern states. And there is some evidence that the movement had reached the Far West as well.

On the Chautauqua Circuit

Paul Pearson, professor of public speaking and English at Swarthmore, was well aware of Chautauqua's success in the Middle West. He had taken the job at Swarthmore under an agreement that each year the month of January would be free for his lecture tours;

each January found this short, dynamic man out on a circuit of towns and cities, charming his audiences with his brilliant and entertaining interpretations of modern literature. His tours often took him into the South and Midwest, as in the time he lectured in Georgia and Florida, and then talked his way through Indiana, Michigan, and Iowa. In the summer of 1911 he made another such tour, this time returning to Swarthmore in the fall "filled with" an exciting idea.

This exciting idea was to bring the "movable feast" of the traveling Chautauqua to the small towns along the Atlantic seaboard. Pearson broached the idea to Charles F. Jenkins, a member of Swarthmore's Board of Managers. Jenkins called a meeting of prominent Swarthmoreans; a dozen men, including President Swain, grew enthusiastic as they discussed the possibilities of the idea. While no definite action was taken at this time, the word went out that, if plans matured, about seventy towns in Pennsylvania, New Jersey and Delaware would get the benefits of Chautauqua's entertainment and uplift in the summer of 1912.

Pearson did his best to make the plans mature: in the early months of 1912 he buttonholed his friends and colleagues, including Jesse H. Holmes and Isaac H. Clothier, with constant arguments for the worth of his idea; and he gave assurances that "The dream was not of profit for any of those concerned, but was purely altruistic and . . . a dream of community betterment. . . ."

And Pearson's salesmanship produced results. Whether it was the idealistic appeal of community betterment, or the unvoiced hope for some profit from the venture, a group of Swarthmoreans were persuaded to incorporate themselves as the Chautauqua Association of Pennsylvania (otherwise known as the Swarthmore Chautauqua Association), the corporation being listed as one of the "first class" under Pennsylvania law, since it was an educational institution. Its offices were to be at Swarthmore, and its first officers (and chief stockholders, no doubt) were to be Charles F. Jenkins, E. Pusey Passmore, Rowland Comly, Dr. George Edward Reed, Dr. William I. Hull, T.H. Dudley Perkins, and Dr. Jesse H. Holmes. Pearson was to be the chief director of the association, as well as its "front" man — a job peculiarly suited to his talents.

The new venture got off to a somewhat rocky start in 1912. Instead of the projected seventy towns to be served by Pearson's dream, only forty-one actually saw the circus tents being raised on their vacant lots. The Pearson Chautauqua lost $15,000 that first year, perhaps because Paul had not yet been able to persuade the town authorities to close stores and suspend all business during the hours of entertainment, as was the practice in the West. Still, the loss undoubtedly would have been greater if Pearson had not been able to convince the town leaders to accept a system of "guarantors." Under this system the leaders of a community would guarantee the sale of a required number of "season" tickets, thus accepting a responsibility for part of the cost of bringing Chatauqua to their town. If they sold less than their quota, they lost; if they sold more than their quota, the extra money was applied to the Association's end of the risk. Thus the towns could make no money, and might lose. But the proposition was seldom refused. There were always people, it was said, who were willing to work for the common good. And the lead in this work was taken by the woman's club in each town; only one town possessing a woman's club refused to accept the financial proposition of the Association in the 1912 season.

In the rush of planning for the first summer circuit, the tent crew was recruited from Swarthmore College students largely for reasons of convenience. For the same reason 90 per cent of the students required for the 1913 season were drawn from Swarthmore, although other colleges and universities, such as Princeton, Cornell, Haverford, Penn, Columbia, Penn State and Bryn Mawr were represented. (And Andrew ["Drew"] Pearson, Paul's husky eldest son, served as tent boy that year, in spite of the fact that at age fifteen he was not quite ready to leave Phillips Exeter Academy to enter college.) More students were needed because the program had expanded: now 28 Junior Chautauqua leaders were required to direct morning activities in games, children's play productions, and arts and crafts; a College Players Company had been formed requiring 10 people, with 9 more in the Avon Players Company; there were 4 in the office, 2 in advertising work, one Junior Chautauqua director, and one operator of the lantern for illustrated lectures. Added to these were 52 tent men, including the set-up and wrecking crews.

These crews labored hard, especially in the setting up and taking down of the huge canvas tents. But on a seven-day circuit, after the tent was up, and the stage, sawdust and chairs in place, they had about five days of relative ease, being concerned only with tent maintenance, policing the grounds, and courting the local girls and Junior leaders. Then, after the evening performance on the last day, they had to "wreck" the tent and load everything into a railroad baggage car — a job sometimes running from 10 P.M. to 6 A.M. They must have done their work in good humor, however, since the Swarthmore people were so proud of them; "they are especially desirable," the College newspaper held, "because they in many ways come in contact with the audiences where their gentlemanly, good-natured and cordial manner becomes a definite asset for the Chautauqua...."

No doubt these good-natured tent crews helped smooth the way for the traveling Chautauqua lecturers and entertainment groups as they jumped an average of fifty-seven miles from town to town in 1912. Arriving in a given town on a hot and dusty train, one can imagine a theatrical company unloading its gear, taking it to the tent for storage in a dressing room provided by the tent boys, and then seeking rooms in a nondescript hotel or boarding house. After the performance, perhaps interrupted by a summer storm, the troupe would seek some rest; then, after breakfast the next morning, they would board another train to repeat the same process in another town with an equally nondescript hotel — but with a different group of tent boys. And so on and on throughout a summer, from mid-June to mid-September.

In 1913 some of the attractions appearing on the Swarthmore Chautauqua's platforms were to be Dr. Newell Dwight Hillis, pastor of Plymouth Church, Brooklyn; William Sterling Battis, who would impersonate Dickens' characters in costume; the Florentine Concert Band; Reno B. Welbourne, who would lecture on the wonders of science; seven Tyrolian Yodlers, also in costume; and Paul M. Pearson, giving his lecture-recital on "The Joy of Life." In addition, there were lectures by William Jennings Bryan, Senator Thomas P. Gore of Oklahoma, Judge Ben Lindsay of companionate-marriage fame, Dr. S. Parker Cadman, and a number of others famous in their time and place. Jesse H. Holmes acted as platform superintendent, as he had in 1912, and not only introduced the speakers and entertainers but gave a series of lectures of his own.

As Paul Pearson reported to Swarthmoreans in a special "Joy Night" early in October, the season of 1913 was one to be proud of. While Chautauqua, organized as a nonprofit corporation, was not supposed to make a profit, it had met its expenses during the past summer.

In ensuing years the Swarthmore Chautauqua grew mightily, hampered only to some degree by the Great War. William Jennings Bryan, secretary of state, had been scheduled to speak at Galeton, Pennsylvania in the summer of 1914; he could not keep his date because of what had happened at Serajevo in the Balkans. Other factors, such as the drafting of prospective tent boys, and restrictions on the use of railroads, quite obviously embarrassed operations in 1917 and 1918. But until the United States got into the war there was steady growth; after the war, in 1919, the demand for Chautauqua-style entertainment was so great that a winter circuit was organized, with Claude C. Smith, Swarthmore '14, as its director, and Howard M. Buckman, also of the class of '14, as its advertising manager. In the middle 'twenties Pearson's Pride, as we may call it, expanded its field of operations until it grossed one million dollars a year. Now it had three seven-day circuits, and two five-day circuits were conducting Chautauquas and special Chautauqua Festivals in a belt of sixteen states running from North Carolina to Maine, and on into New Brunswick, Nova Scotia, and Prince Edward Island.

Making scheduled appearances in these Maritime Provinces was sometimes a problem taxing the ingenuity of Jesse in his capacity as platform superintendent and manager of his particular Chautauqua unit. On one occasion, when he became convinced that the regular boat service from Nova Scotia to Prince Edward Island would not get his unit, and all its gear and personnel, to Charlottetown in time for a scheduled performance, he hired a ferry-boat and some fishing smacks for this purpose. The ferry took the major gear — three sixty-foot tent poles, the tent canvas, stage planking, electrical equipment, and perhaps 2000 folding chairs. The fishing boats, "stinking to high heaven," took the performing artists and all their paraphenalia. One can imagine the scene in a rough crossing through Northumberland Strait — some of the deck cargo awry, the tent poles sticking out over the ferry hull, and the Chautauqua crew members and performing talent green with seasickness.

Pearson was fortunate in having so enterprising a unit manager as Jesse Holmes. But most of his Chautauqua's success was due to his own hard work, his managerial ability, and his sense of what people wanted to hear and see, at least in the Age of the Progressives. And his own contributions to the circuit programs helped the cause along. In addition to his early interpretations of literature and his speech on "The Joy of Living," he had developed a speech on "Who Is Great?". In this speech, given many times, he told his audiences that service to humanity was the mark of greatness. " 'The man who looms greatest is the one who, when he knows he is right, has the courage to do what everybody says must not be done, and not to do what everybody says must be done.' "

Robert M. LaFollette, Sr., was such a man; Pearson signed him up, and his well-known courage in fighting corporate interests, plus his dynamic way of speaking, attracted vast Chautauqua crowds, Pearson's showmanship also led to the staging of "Robin Hood" in operetta form, which not only backed up LaFollette's belief in the graduated income tax ("soak the rich"), but pleased the crowds with its tuneful music and romance. In similar vein, the College Players put on "The Fortune Hunter" in 1919, in which Elizabeth B. Oliver's delicious giggles "brought down the house, or rather the tent, at every performance."

While Paul Pearson continued to meet his Swarthmore classes in public speaking and English, he became more and more obsessed with the Chautauqua venture. Not only did he use up most of his own energies in its promotion, but he drafted his son Drew and Drew's younger brother Leon to serve as unpaid clerks in their home, which rapidly became an office. The younger sisters, Barbara and Ellen, were also involved: Barbara became her father's driver and star actress in Chautauqua plays in the late 'twenties; Ellen allowed herself to be "sawed in half" by a magician in one of the vaudeville acts which Paul introduced when the Chautauqua entered its tinselled, tawdry period.

Paul's wife Edna, the daughter of a Jewish dentist-doctor in Kansas, no doubt visited him at times when he was in a favorable location on a circuit. But one gets the impression that she was essentially a homebody, preferring to tend her garden and superintend the making of her famed creamed chicken and punch for the Quaker quarterly meetings at Swarthmore. As chairlady of the Friends Hospitality Committee, she brought smiles and flowers to new arrivals. When her black seventeen-year-old housemaid became pregnant she arranged for the child's delivery, and then permitted the young mother to raise it in the Pearson household. In periods of leisure she concentrated on her painting. (There is a photograph of her sketching her Paul and sons Drew and Leon as they recline against a tree in the yard of their Swarthmore home.) As time went on, and Paul became still more obsessed with Chautauqua, she grew restless and annoyed; she was guilty of making "artless comments" about friends, relatives, and events, even Chautauqua, "which she said had taken her husband from her." Her family thought that this was heresy. How could she criticize the one without criticizing the other, since Paul was the very personification of Chautauqua? To those who knew Paul, "with his wavy, prematurely gray hair, dominant stance, sonorous voice, and easy assumption that people would do what he wanted them to do...," such criticism was unthinkable.

This at least seemed to be the judgment of those who gave both Edna and Paul a gala welcome-home party when they returned from a winter-vacation cruise to Puerto Rico. At the same time magazine articles appeared about him; he was even referred to in newspaper called vacation cruise was but a way to concentrate on the preparation for a summer schedule listing dates with almost a thousand towns in thirteen states.

By 1919, however, Pearson's obsession with his Chautauqua had led to his decision to resign his position as head of the department of public speaking at Swarthmore; he now wished to devote more time to what he obviously considered the greater task. He and Swarthmore were fortunate in that he was retained as a lecturer in public speaking; his department, however, was merged with the English department through an increasing awareness that the study of America's working language involved *all* forms of communication — at that time including grammar, rhetoric, literature, journalism, and public speaking, with art, music, and "body English" also recognized as nonverbal modes of expression.

While Jesse Holmes escaped some of Pearson's obsession with Chautauqua, he had the same general philosophy and predilection for action. Aside from the need for diverting activity after Elizabeth's death, he welcomed the chance to make some money during the summer vacation period by appearing on a stage and doing what he liked best to do — make speeches. His wit, cleverness, humor, and obviously sincere manner eased the way for many a performer on Chautauqua's boards as he introduced him to the audience; the same qualities enlivened his lectures on such topics as hobbies and the profitable use of leisure time. In a lecture on "Luxury and Leisure," he warned people against being obsessed by possessions and urged them to develop their special powers as foils against their drudgeries. Each person could raise some special skill into a hobby, whether in music, painting or other arts, wood carving, the weaving of rugs, embroidery, housekeeping, entertaining, or simply in good conversation. (In these suggestions Jesse was passing on what he and Rebe had found rewarding in their personal lives.) Jesse also drew on his own philosophy and experience when he worked up a lecture on "The Golden Egg" for the circuit. In this speech, greatly enjoyed by both Chautauqua and Swarthmore college audiences, he talked "straight from the shoulder" about the distribution of wealth in America, and the interrelations between city people and country folk. No doubt Rebe heard this speech many times when she visited Jesse at given spots on the circuit, and Herman and Robert too must have heard it during their service as tent boys in the late 'teens and early 'twenties.

Altogether, Jesse spent some fourteen summers in Chautauqua work, although not always with the Swarthmore circuits. In the midsummer of 1920 he returned from a time of work with the American Friends Service Committee in Europe to join a traveling Chautauqua in the Midwest, giving his famous lecture on "The Golden Egg." (In the course of this trip he also found the time to attend several Friends' Yearly Meetings in Indiana and Illinois). In 1921 he apparently returned to Pearson's circuits, this time speaking on "Interpreting the Headlines." The next three summers were spent in the Midwest with the Redpath Chautauqua (1922, 1924), and the White-Myers Chautauqua (1923), lecturing on "Current Events," "Our World," or "War, Its Cost and Who Pays It." These were grueling schedules: in 1924 he toured Iowa, Minnesota, South Dakota and Missouri, speaking once a day and twice on Sundays. He was able, however, to repair at least some of the ravages of these trips through two weeks of vacation on Nantucket Island in 1922 and 1923 when the work was finished.

While the printed records available to the author do not show that one of Jesse's lecture topics in 1923 *was* "Our World," his notes under this heading in his looseleaf notebook give abundant internal evidence that this most probably was included in his program. Through these notes we can enter the mind of this scientist-

105

philosopher and social reformer to get an idea of the substance and the tone of the speech he made to the good people in South Dakota, Missouri, and Kansas while traveling on the White-Meyers circuit.

He started out with a "space perspectus," showing that our world — the planet Earth — was a small spinning, orbiting spaceship in a very large universe. Earth measured only 4 inches in comparison with the sun, which was 33 feet in diameter and 8 light-years away; the star Betelgeuse was 50 light-years away.

Having reduced Earth to size, Jesse then outlined the various peoples crowding it — the blacks in Africa, the browns and yellows in Asia, and the whites in Europe and America, together with their warring religions, and the constant conflict between opposing cultures and economic systems which had produced "sore spots" in China, the Balkans, Russia, and in the Ruhr Valley of Germany. And Europe was a battleground, even after the war to make the world safe for democracy, between the two major camps of the radicals and the conservatives.

Turning to America, Jesse outlined some of its many problems and proposed ways of solving them under the democratic system. He was particularly concerned with the problem of taxation and analyzed the various types of taxes then levied on Americans: consumption (sales) taxes, taxes on capital and income, corporation and inheritance levies, and of course the tariff. To solve this problem, and others constantly cropping up in a dynamic society, people had to become better citizens. To do this they had to learn the rules of the game, had to develop their citizenship skills through involvement — through practice. But in all of this there was no room for the grandstand player. Each and every person had the duty to keep informed about the principles, facts, and opinions guiding the American experiment in self-government. Every adult should get this intellectual ammunition in the fight against tyranny by reading good daily newspapers, a *"good political"* [sic] weekly magazine, and a number of monthlies. Having read all these he could then engage in intelligent discussion, and, through public affairs forums, take part in those processes of reform which had made America the hope of the world.

This was the Chautauqua style a la Jesse Holmes. It combined the practical with the idealistic, it was inspirational, and it left people feeling good as they walked away from the circus tent down tree-shaded streets or toward their waiting "flivvers."

The Decline and Fall of Paul Pearson's Chautauqua.

But it was these automobiles, becoming ever more abundant in the 1920s, which could also take people to the cheaper and more thrilling movies in neighboring towns and cities; at home people tuned in more and more to such radio shows as "Amos and Andy" and the "A&P Gypsies." Indeed, it was the growing popularity of the automobile, the movies, and the radio, which, combined with the growth of a more cynical public attitude in the Age of Prohibition and the Flapper, led to the death of the traveling Chautauqua.

Pearson felt the knell of impending doom in 1925, when revenues from several circuits began to lag behind expenses. In the spring of 1926 he launched the Chautauqua Endowment Campaign, hoping to raise $2,000,000 for Chautauqua's use. He appealed especially to alumni, both of Swarthmore College and of the Chautauqua of old. The results were "more than encouraging, . . ." And, in 1927, Jesse spoke at a workers' Chautauqua in Passaic, New Jersey, indicating that Pearson apparently was trying to reach down through the middle class to a broader base for greater support.

But all of Pearson's efforts proved abortive: the Swarthmore Chautauqua "broke down as a vehicle of educational uplift during the summer of 1929. . . ." Not even the extra assessments put on the guaranteeing businessmen in the years 1926-1929 could avert financial disaster, for they simply grew less enthusiastic with each succeeding year. As the end of Chautauqua became imminent, Pearson went around "making cheerful noises" and threw himself still more into the program. James A. Michener, a recent Swarthmore graduate, recalled from his experience as a tent boy that summer: " 'There was something doing every day in a seven-day circuit. Paul Martin Pearson could handle any one of the twelve programs except maybe play the tuba. . . .' " Now he helped in coaching and producing the play which the local people put on after a week's rehearsal; then there would be " 'a speech by the president or somebody equally formidable and on Sunday a joint religious service as climax. . . .' " Michener remembered Pearson's daughter Barbara as " 'a glorious girl'," but " 'the good doctor, that stocky sanctimonious man with white hair, sticks in my mind as an amiable fraud, a theological Paul McNutt, a megalomaniac. . . .' "

Michener was no doubt a bit too rough on Paul Pearson here, a distraught man desperately trying to save his enterprise from utter

107

ruin. Paul's behavior in previous years at Swarthmore had revealed few, if any, of these qualities. But the end of Chautauqua was near, there was no doubt about that. On July 15, 1931, a public sale of the Swarthmore Chautauqua Association's physical assets brought its activities to an effective close. July 17 saw the last issue of the Chautauqua *News Letter*. A noble experiment in popular culture expired, leaving behind many beautiful memories with those who had been fortunate enough to live in America during Chautauqua's heyday.

Paul's reputation as an administrator, plus Herbert Hoover's concern that a Quaker should hold the job, led to his appointment as governor of the Virgin Islands in 1931. Hoping to make the Islands an "American Bermuda", Paul soon ran into trouble with the poor and illiterate natives, with American businessmen seeking concessions, and through the machinations of Democratic politicians after Roosevelt became President. Things got so bad that he was finally persuaded to write a letter requesting a transfer to another government agency. As a result he took a position as head of the public-housing section of the Public Works Administration.

Although now in failing health, Paul did a workmanship job for the PWA. Under his supervision the country's first integrated public housing project was completed in Chicago. But the job he held was something of a comedown for a man who had been a very popular professor at Swarthmore, had headed the Swarthmore Chautauqua, and who had been governor of the Virgin Islands. All this political infighting was too much for him: he died in 1938, a broken-hearted man. His widow died soon thereafter. Forces beyond their control had wrecked these gentle Quakers.

7. A Friendly Service of Love, Part I

If Paul Pearson's ultimate defeat was due mainly to forces beyond his control, the same fate was suffered by millions of others in the time of the Great Boom of the 'twenties and the Great Depression of the 'thirties. The ordinary man was seemingly a captive in an economic system directed from faraway places — a system too often like a runaway roller-coaster car, in which he, a helpless passenger, was hurtled up and down the hills and valleys of the business cycle to an ultimate economic crash.

This pattern of Boom and Bust certainly was well illustrated in the United States in the period 1922-1939. And, both here and abroad, the Great Depression of the 'thirties could be traced to the dislocations of productive, constructive enterprise brought on by the World War of 1914-1918, which in turn was brought on by the failure of the European system of power politics which had developed since the Franco-Prussian War of 1870. This system was a composite of five interrelated and mutually infective forces, each adding more explosive components to the European powder keg: *extreme nationalism*, which turned love of country into an ethnocentric, paranoid disease; *militarism*, which turned Europe into an armed camp of mutually suspicious neighbors; *balance-of-power alliances*, resulting by 1907 in a Triple Alliance (Germany, Austro-Hungary, Italy) cutting across the Triple Entente (Russia, France, Great Britain); *secret diplomacy*, in which top-hatted and beribboned diplomats directed the activities of secret agents and spies scurrying through dark places of Europe in the best cloak-and-dagger tradition; and *imperialism*, in which rival industrial nations tried to get exploitative control over "backward" areas of Africa, India, Asia, and the Southwest Pacific for raw materials, markets for finished products, and for investment purposes. It was the time when Kipling said that it was the "white man's burden" to lift up his "little brown brother"; it was also the time when Social Darwinism held that the race was to the swift and the battle to the strong. The operation of these five components of *Machtpolitik* by rival nations and rival imperialisms brought Europe and America to one crisis after another, passed over for a time through the desperate efforts of diplomats as they played chess with the lives and fortunes of people they hadn't seen and didn't know.

These crises were symptoms of an increasing tension and nervousness among the governments of Europe — a state of nervousness which had not really been healed by the Hague Peace Conferences of 1898 and 1907, or by the establishment of the Permanent Court of Arbitration at the Hague. While these peace efforts resulted in agreements to ban the use of poison gas in war, to prohibit the aerial bombardment of cities, and to adopt the Geneva Convention rules for the treatment of the wounded, the nervous nations refused to limit the steady growth of conventional armaments. And they would submit only minor disputes to arbitration by the World Court. It became increasingly evident that competitive nationalism, bolstered by the alliance system, was still preferred over cooperative internationalism.

And so, caught in the web of their own entangling alliances, the nations of Europe stumbled into that madness known by Americans as "The War to Make the World Safe for Democracy." After the assassination of the Archduke Ferdinand of Austria in June, 1914, an incident in the nationalistic and Pan-Slavic aspirations of Bosnian patriots, there seemed no way to prevent war. All the old hatreds between Slavs, Teutons, and Latins flared up anew; all the old promises of help between members of each major alliance group were now called for redemption. Austria, backed up by Kaiser Wilhelm's "blank check" promise of support, made impossible demands on Serbia, followed by open war; Russia mobilized in support of Serbia; Germany declared war on Russia and invaded Belgium; France, and then Great Britain, declared war on Germany and Austria. The powder keg had exploded, and it was only a matter of time until other nations in Europe and the world were sucked into the conflagration.   The millions of young men consumed in the fires of Tannenburg, Verdun, the Marne, and the Somme had little if any choice about whether they should refuse service or go "over the top"; they had been psychologically conditioned by national patriotism to believe in their proper role as "servicemen", and they had been drafted by prearranged conscription plans. Only in those countries valuing individualism, civil liberties, and religious freedom was a choice possible: here young men could choose to suffer the sneers and calumnies of patriots by refusing to serve in the armed forces for reasons of conscience.

Origins of the American Friends Service Committee.

England was such a country. From 1647, when George Fox began preaching, the English Quakers had made peace and nonresistance an active part of their way of life. In 1693 William Penn published (anonymously in 1693; openly in 1694) his plan for a league of nations, hoping, through a "European Dyet, [or] Parliament . . . ," to persuade countries to settle their disputes by discussion and co-operation rather than through the rough arbitration of war. This idea was ahead of its time: English Quakers found that often the best they could do in a time of professional armies was to give testimonies to themselves and to any others who would listen about the irrationality of war by Christian peoples. But when the Franco-Prussian War devastated sections of northeastern France they found a new way to serve on melioristic grounds: they organized a Friends' War Victims Relief Expedition to bring material and social help to the inhabitants of the area overrun by the Prussians. As they moved about on their errands of mercy they wore a brassard bearing a red and black eight-pointed star as the symbol of their organization.

This same symbol identified Quaker relief workers called into action in 1914. When the guns of August began to roar there were over 22,000 Friends in Great Britain and Ireland; their leaders issued a "Message . . . 'To Men and Women of Good-will in the British Empire. . . . ,' " reminding these people that " 'the method of force is no solution to any question,' " and asking those " 'whose conscience forbade them to take up arms to serve in other ways in the great crisis. . . .'" This call — " '. . .to be courageous in the cause of love and in the hate of hate. . . .' " — was soon answered by many volunteers willing to work in the four major fields of service developed by the English and Irish Quakers. A Friends' Ambulance Committee was quickly set up to organize volunteers into

111

ambulance units to be sent behind the lines in France. A War Victims Relief Committee was formed to do the same general kind of work in devastated areas of France as its predecessor had done in 1870. At home, those foreigners caught in the swirling crosscurrents of war were to be assisted by the Emergency Committee for Helping Aliens; and a Friends' Service Committee was developed in due course to counsel and assist "those who were suffering for their faith as conscientious objectors" due to the operation of the English Conscription Law. (Inevitably, the English called them "Conchies".)

These committees worked very hard during the summer and fall of 1914, and in November Dr. Hilda Clark (a granddaughter of John Bright), along with T. Edmund Harvey, led the first group of Friends to France. When they got to the areas churned up during and after the battle of the Marne, this group of twenty-five workers found that "relief" required far more than the distribution of food and clothing — it involved the revival of agriculture and local industry, the reconstruction of houses and public buildings, and medical services of many kinds. Three kinds of people were to be helped: the residents of ruined villages still trying to carry on a day-to-day existence; refugees in these villages from other areas; and the repatriates — the civilians captured by the Germans now being returned to France through Switzerland at the rate of one to two thousand a day.

The greatest and most immediate need, of course, was among those people living in or near the war zone. Children and expectant mothers suffered most from the disruption of their normal lives, so a children's hospital was established at Bettancourt in a chateau loaned to the Friends by the Countess Morrilot, and a maternity hospital established at Chalons. District nursing centers were created at Chalons, Bar-le-Duc, Troyes, Sermaize and Paris; and a relocation service began to take children from such war areas as Rheims to safer places in the remote countryside.

Those French remaining in the ruined agricultural villages were helped in reconstruction and agricultural work not only by the issuance of new farm implements but by Friends who lived in these villages and took part in the physical labor of this rehabilitation. In Sermaize 103 portable wooden houses were assembled from precut parts made in England and shipped to France; in these and other houses the French women were encouraged to make embroidered articles which sold very well in England. In all this work of relief, every effort was made to encourage the French to help themselves after their first desperate needs had been met. And they did just that, for the British Friends had brought them hope.

News of the good work being done by the English and Irish Friends soon led American Quakers to help the cause along financially, their contributions reaching about $5,000 a month. Then, in 1915, Rufus M. Jones, leader of the more orthodox or conservative Friends in the Philadelphia area, raised the money to cover the expenses of American volunteers who wished to serve for a year with the Friends' Ambulance Unit in France. Jones chose four men for this service: Edward Rice, Jr., and Felix Morley, graduates of Haverford College; and Carl Fowler and Howard Carey, graduates of Earlham College in Richmond, Indiana. The reports of their experiences, mainly through letters sent to their friends back home, helped to shape the greater cooperation of the future via the founding of the American Friends' Service Committee and its subsequent activities.

Some of the American Friends who had helped pay the expenses of the four ambulance men continued their testimonies against the follies of war in other ways. In June, 1915, Jenkin Lloyd Jones, of the Abraham Lincoln Centre in Chicago, was the principal speaker at the yearly meeting of the Progressive Friends of Longwood. His subject was "Peace — Over all Nations is Humanity". In his speech he said that, in 1915, five great problems agitated the public consciousness: race, sex, labor, drink, and peace — ". . .and all but the last were [on] the high road to solution. . . ." But men, he said, could not be scared into peace by making war more terrible. And, "The greatest fallacy of the twentieth century is that war can be averted by getting ready for it. . . ." Further, World War I had been caused by foolish men who had "read history wrongly"; out of this war, however, would come a peace based on the "common ties of humanity. . . ."

This theme of deep-lying common ties was implicit in a cable sent to America in that same year by the London Yearly Meeting: "Who shall separate us?," asked the English Quakers of the American Friends, who had been divided into the two main camps of the Orthodox conservatives and the Hicksite liberals ever since the Great Separation of 1827, with at least three splinter groups breaking away from the two main branches since that time. The question for the American Friends, of course, was not so much "*Who* shall separate us?" as "What *has* separated us?" And the answer was simple: an original dispute in 1827 over the hierarchical control of Quaker affairs by conservatives had hardened through eighty-eight years of institutional inertia into attitudes of mutual suspicion and noncooperation.

But now a small minority on each side saw that there was a need of unified action in the face of the very great threat to that principle of peace they had treasured so long. So a few leaders called for a Friends National Peace Conference to be held at Winona Lake, Indiana, in July, 1915. Friends of all branches were invited to send delegates. As Henry Ferris exulted in an editorial in the *Friends' Intelligencer* four years after the event, "It was for many reasons an inspiring occasion, for it proved beyond a doubt that the ice was breaking in our Society, and that many concerned Friends of all branches were ready at least to *work* together." Ferris told how a railroad carload of delegates from both Orthodox and Hicksite meetings in Philadelphia went to Winona Lake together, and how much they enjoyed this trip.

One of the greatest concerns of the Winona Lake Conference was the series of war bills being considered in Washington, all of them certain to affect Friends. It was felt that Quakers should develop some agency which would keep them informed about the doings of Congress, and possibly to propose alternatives or amendments. A Continuation Committee was appointed to this purpose, composed of every branch of the Society, with a charge to maintain headquarters in Washington, and to keep all types of Friends advised of developments. This committee did effective work, perhaps most importantly in joining with the special peace committees of the two Philadelphia yearly meetings in formulating peace-campaign plans.

In the time between the Winona Lake Conference and the Hicksite Philadelphia Yearly Meeting in May, 1916, Quakers were exceedingly active in the cause of peace. In partnership with "the Friends of the other branch," the Hicksites supplied money for the expenses of a lecturer who brought the cause to the students in Pennsylvania colleges. A Fellowship of Reconciliation was established, which aimed "to end the war by ending the spirit of war...." William I. Hull was on its executive board, making 93 addresses in its behalf; and Jesse Holmes made 50 speeches in a similar vein for the same purposes. Paul Pearson put "powerful peace addresses" on 160 programs of his Chautauqua in 13 states. A Peace Shop was opened, largely through the efforts of Lucy Biddle Lewis and Hannah Clothier Hull; this developed into an important propaganda center, featuring posters and window exhibits, study classes, and an open forum. And the Peace Section of the Philanthropic Committee of the Hicksites was never so busy, sending pamphlet material to all parts of the United States and Canada to be used in preparing speeches and debates. School children in the Philadelphia area were very helpful in circulating a petition supplied by this Philanthropic Committee against Senate Bill 1695, which provided for military training. This petition, bearing 3000 signatures, was then sent to Senator Chamberlain. And the Church Peace Union, of which William I. Hull was a trustee, helped to sell pamphlets and leaflets freshly spawned by the war crisis. Thus, 5000 copies of Anna Allen Pratt's *Lesson of the Hundred Years of Peace* were issued; Elizabeth Lloyd's *Song of the Twentieth Century* sold well, as did William I. Hull's *Preparedness — the Military and American Programs*. But William Price hit the jackpot — 25,000 copies of his *Peace Man or War Man* rolled off the press into the eager hands of peace advocates.

In March, 1916, the Philadelphia Arch Street Yearly Meeting addressed a letter to the Hicksites centered at Race and Cherry streets, in which they expressed a desire to have any peace committee appointed by the Hicksites cooperate with their own special Peace Committee. This letter was read to the Hicksite Yearly Meeting at their May session, and affirmative action quickly followed. The Women's Meeting led the way by appointing an Emergency Peace Committee to serve during the war crisis, the membership to consist of those active in the Peace Section of the regular Philanthropic Committee, plus other leaders in the peace movement. The ladies also authorized the appropriation of $1500 from the Yearly Meeting's Treasury for the new committee's use. The Men's Meeting agreed on the principle of these actions, but modified the mode of selecting the Committee's membership. The General Nominating Committee was given the job of proposing people to serve in this special group, and on May 19 came up with a list of thirty-one names which was approved without further ado. Jesse H. Holmes was to be the chairman; other Committee members included such prominent peace advocates as Henry Ferris, editor of the *Friends Intelligencer,* Hannah Clothier Hull and her husband William I. Hull, Lucy Biddle Lewis, Paul M. Pearson, William L. Price, and Joseph Swain, lending his support to the group as president of Swarthmore. The Emergency Peace Committee was also granted the privilege of using the Cherry Street end of the meeting-house complex for its purposes, subject to the approval of the Representative Committee as to times of use.

Undoubtedly Jesse Holmes' chances of being named chairman of this special Hicksite committee on peace had been improved by his letter to the editor published in the *Friends Intelligencer* just before the Yearly Meeting convened. In this letter, entitled "Our Duty in Keeping Peace," Jesse lashed out at the foolhardy principle of trying to preserve peace by preparing for war, just as Jenkin Lloyd Jones had done at Longwood a year earlier. He wrote that it was "necessary and important to oppose what has been called 'preparedness,' because it aims to prepare for that which we condemn — war. . . ." He asserted that "It is a part of the insanity of the war method that it can never accomplish its purposes. . . ." This was true because, under the ever-mounting spiral of the armaments race, nations would tend to become still more frightened of each other instead of being reassured by their ever-larger armies. Rather than have America "travel that endless road," Jesse thought that more care ought to be given to cultivating better international relations — "We must try to see with the eyes and hear with the ears of citizens of neighbor nations, to the end that we shall not misjudge them, as we so easily may."

And, he continued, our neighbors to the south had reasons to be suspicious of Uncle Sam's purposes in the light of our highhanded acquisition of the Panama Canal Zone at Colombia's cost, as well as in our war with Mexico in the 1840s. Contemporary Mexico was in the "throes of anarchy" and needed all the sympathy and help we could give her; the Monroe Doctrine ought to be restated in terms of brotherhood. And, if this same spirit of brotherhood could not be extended to the Japanese — "a nation self-conscious, proud, and perhaps looking for affronts" — at least jingoistic leadership in the United States, which was so prone to give offense, could be toned down or eliminated. The Japanese, still smarting from the "Gentlemen's Agreement" of 1907 (by which Japan had its arm twisted to prevent the emigration of laborers to America); and from the Webb Act in California (which in 1913 forbade aliens ineligible for citizenship to own agricultural land in that state), must have applauded Jesse's assertion that "Insult is not a proper aid to diplomacy...."

Similarly, he counseled calm, careful dealing with the "terribly smitten nations across the Atlantic.... In sorrow, in love, in patience, it is our duty to keep alight and aloft the torch of Christian civilization...." The American policy ought to be based on faith, not fear; it ought to constantly call for "right against violence, justice against privilege, Christianity against paganism...." Americans ought to retain a strong faith in God and in men; as citizens and "real patriots" they should lend their support to "those influences which will establish an America which can be trusted, not feared, and which will be a light to heathen Europe."

In the interval between the big annual convocations of Hicksites held in Philadelphia in May, 1916, and May, 1917, these Quakers, both as individuals and as members of the Yearly Meeting's two peace committees, were very busy indeed. Some of them served on both of these committees — the special Emergency Peace Committee chaired by Jesse Holmes, and the Peace Section of the Philanthropic Labor Committee. While the Peace Section's report of the work done in this interval explained that, due to the other special committee's creation, not as much was done as might have been true otherwise, they had accomplished quite a bit. They had sent peace literature to 1,964 normal school graduates in the spring of 1916; they had distributed 2000 copies of the Peace Declaration adopted by the Friends' General Confrence at Cape May, including copies mailed to President Wilson, all the members of Congress, and the governors of all the states; and they had purchased 300 lapel-sized ploughs made from swords (along with the die for their manufacture), to be worn by pacifists "as a silent protest against war."

Most of this work was done in the spring and summer of 1916. And Jesse Holmes, as chairman of the special committee, was no doubt also extremely busy at this time. Still, either in the late summer or early fall of 1916, he found enough free time to write a trenchant article for the *Friends' Intelligencer,* soon to be published in pamphlet form and obtainable at Quaker addresses on Arch Street, Philadelphia. Entitled "What Is a Pacifist?", this article mounted a strong attack on that Social-Darwinist belief, so fondly held by "Teddy" Roosevelt and leaders of his stripe on both sides of the Atlantic, that conflict, war, and warlike competition alone brought out those "virile qualities" of courage and leadership which were a necessary condition for the progress of the race. After quoting General Storey, General von Moltke, Renan, and William James on war's supposedly beneficial results in bringing forth manly qualities in its participants (which Jesse admitted), he went on to give a devastingly sarcastic analysis of what might be done in terms of conflict at home to bring out these same qualities. If this was the only way to do it, he said, the leaders of the nation ought to be consistent and promote armed conflict within the United States as regularly as they held national elections. State could be pitted against state, county against county, or city against city. And it might be possible to use baseball parks for a revival of the old gladiatorial contests; even the prize ring could be used, with "no molly coddle rules" about gloves, etc. The great advantage of this domestic strife, as compared with foreign wars, was that the foreign enemy would not benefit by developing its own manly qualities; all the virtues of courage, self-sacrifice, and leadership would stay at home.

But there was a better way, said Jesse: The pacifist "actively and concretely believes," that peace is the condition which "develops the highest type of humanity. . . ." He believes that "[peace] is the health of society, and war is social disease. . . ." Social health, of course, was a condition of the mind — a belief in "the fundamental goodness of man, sympathy and understanding for his ignorance, his prejudices and his passions, and a fraternal willingness to overlook his mistakes. . . ." The pacifist, Jesse said, believed that, on the whole, "if you 'trust men they will be true to you,' 'treat them greatly and they will show themselves great.' . . ."

This was idealistic doctrine, to be sure. But Jesse showed that he understood the psychology of war when he wrote that "it is the spirit of suspicion, hatred, panic and fear that makes [war] inevitable. . . ." The pacifist, on the other hand, would spend his time trying to remove that spirit, rather than in preparing for war. And, repeating a fundamental premise of all pacifists, Jesse said that "Such preparation may be . . . left to those who believe in it, since it is their belief in it which makes it necessary. . . ." But the war-planners were wrong, he thought, if they assumed that God was "on the side of the strongest battalions, [or] that the strongest battalions were on the side of God. . . ." Far better to use these armies and navies as an international police force for an international league of nations bent on preserving the peace of the world; this was far better than to use such troops to enforce the will of the strongest nation or group of nations. This was a fundamental idea; but, returning to an earlier thesis, Jesse held that the more fundamental project was to destroy the spirit behind the killing contest — it was "to create the condition of mind which would make killing contests absurd and impossible. . . ."

Of course it took courage to be a pacifist, or a pacifist nation, in an aggressive, chancy world. Jesse likened a nation trying to protect itself against the world's dangers to the man who, before going out on the street for a drive, tried to make himself bulletproof with steel armor, an armored carriage, and arms and defenses all around. "Most of us," said Jesse, "put on a summer suit and face our dangerous world with a smile. We know it will kill us sometime, but after taking a few precautions as to actual known dangers, we run the risks of the merely possible ones. *Life is too short to waste in merely keeping alive* [author's italics] . . . ." The United States should face its external problems in a similar fashion, he thought. The nation had "too much to do in the conservation of national health and resources, in reforming its industrial system, in safeguarding and educating its children, in developing a real fraternal democracy, to waste its time in merely keeping alive. . . . Let [America] take her risks and do her work in the world."

And in doing such work at home and in the world, American citizens could find what William James called "the moral equivalent of war." Jesse agreed with James: the high qualities which were developed by war's extreme conditions and opportunities were "developed equally in the co-operation and mutual dependence [required of workers] in mine, factory, farm, forest, railroad and ocean steamer. Wherever men put their lives and happiness in the hands of other men the noble qualities of manhood are produced. We do not need killing contests to produce them. . . ."

Finally, Jesse put forth a powerful plea for the better use of the vast sums of money wasted on war and the preparations for the possible wars so often brought on by these preparations. Instead of spending a billion dollars (shades of 1945-1979!) in preparing for "these . . . possible perils, [the pacifist] would spend the billion in fighting disease, in developing industry, in safeguarding old age, in working out the problems of labor. . . ." And, knowing the work of

English Quakers in France, and anticipating the work of the yet-to-be-formed American Friends Service Committee, Jesse proposed that a pacifist nation "appropriate other millions to help the suffering, to rebuild ruined homes, to re-establish blighted lives. . . ." The millions thus spent would be regarded as "the greatest 'preparedness for peace' yet attempted in the world."

While Quakers were reading the Holmes article and pamphlet on pacifism, Jesse's Emergency Peace Committee was doing a lot of hard work. In the Committee's general report, given to the Philadelphia Yearly Meeting during its sessions from May 14 through May 18, 1917, Jesse told how, during the past year, they had the "closest unity" with a similar committee of the Orthodox Arch Street Friends. In fact, the work was made easier through a constant interchange of service between the two committees, a constant trading of peace literature designed for distribution, and the use of a plan of organization already worked out by the Arch Street Friends. This plan called for the appointment of subcommittees on literature, meetings for peace, publicity, churches and schools, finance, and governmental relations.

The report of the subcommittee on governmental relations was given under two headings: purposes and methods. The objectives or purposes the subcommittee hoped to achieve through their work are best listed in abbreviated form:

> Peaceful solution of the Mexican problem.
> Satisfaction of the "just claims" of Colombia.
> Adjustment of differences with Japan.
> Negotiated peace settlement between European belligerents.
> Peaceful settlement of American disputes with Great Britain and Germany.
> International arms limitation.
> Development of an international peace-keeping organization.
> Moderation of the American preparedness program.
> Substitution of physical for military training in schools and colleges.
> An end to compulsory military training for adults.
> Protection of freedom of conscience.
> Ditto for freedom of speech, press, peaceable assembly, petition, and educational campaigns for the redress of grievances — which were all threatened by the so-called "Spy Bill."

As stated in the original plan in 1916, these purposes were to be advanced during the year from the spring of 1916 to the spring of 1917 through:

> Public meetings, which were to unite in sending many resolutions or telegrams to President Wilson, Congressmen, and to individuals.
>
> The stimulation of monthly and quarterly Quaker meetings to do the same.
>
> Publishing in newspapers the notices of such meetings and proposed resolutions.
>
> Sending pamphlets relating to Mexico, Japan, and Germany to members of Congress.
>
> Personal visits to members of Congress at home or in Washington.
>
> A personal visit to President Wilson.

The subcommittee on meetings managed to do related but slightly different things. It held nine open-air meetings in New Jersey in the summer of 1916 in conjunction with the Arch Street group. A peace pageant was held on the Albertson farm near Moorestown, with about 800 people present. A fifteen-day auto tour of Chester and Delaware counties in Pennsylvania resulted in thirty-eight towns being visited, some 55,000 people being addressed, and 22,000 pieces of literature being distributed. This same traveling group of Quakers went to fairs at Byberry and Kutztown in Pennsylvania, and at Mt. Holly, New Jersey, and Wilmington, Delaware. At each of these fairs booths were set up and peace literature offered to the wandering crowd. On the whole, discounting a threatened arrest in one of these areas, there was a good response by the people. When the fair season ended a series of visits to monthly meetings in the Philadelphia area was begun, and two large joint meetings were held with the Orthodox — one at Arch Street on November 9, with Leighton Richards and Rufus Jones as speakers; the other at Race Street on February 7, with Isaac Sharpless addressing the crowd.

The subcommittee on literature reported in May, 1917, that over the past year a total of 106,000 copies of pamphlets and fliers had been printed, 45,000 of these being purchased from the "other branch." Of all the pamphlets printed, Jesse's *What Is a Pacifist?* led the list with 10,000 copies; his *Why Go To War?* was second with 6,000 copies. Charles E. Jefferson's *Do Large Armaments Prevent War?* was third with 5,000 copies, while William I. Hull's

The American Plan was valued only to the extent of 2,000 copies. All of these, we must assume, were well distributed; Jesse's *Why Go To War?*, for understandable reasons, was "widely used" by businessmen and also distributed in churches. In addition, a pamphlet on *Compulsory Military Service* (author unknown) was sent throughout thirty states of the United States, the District of Columbia, British Columbia, China, England, Eastern Canada, and Mexico. Other pamphlets on the Japanese and Mexican situations were furnished to YMCA and YWCA branches. More general outlets were found for 25,000 copies of a flier entitled "Think Straight!", and 25,000 copies of another flier urging people to "KEEP COOL!".

This "KEEP COOL!" flier, issued from Peace Headquarters, 111 S. Thirteenth Street, Philadelphia, deserves special attention. A series of subheadings in bold print posed vital questions to the people of America, alternating with positive statements of what the pacifists believed to be the facts in 1916. Starting with the question "Is There Danger of Invasion?," the flier immediately answered "America is the safest nation on earth," and buttressed this with quotations from General Weaver, chief of the coast artillery, and General Nelson A. Miles of Spanish-American War fame. And they added to this Franklin D. Roosevelt's opinion, given as assistant secretary of the Navy in 1915, that " 'if national defence applies solely to the prevention of an armed landing on our Atlantic or Pacific coasts, no navy at all is necessary.' " Then, under the subheading of "Do We Really Want to Crush Other Nations?," *The Seven Seas,* official organ of the Navy League, was quoted to the effect that it was a " 'particular duty' " of the United States " 'to expand, to found colonies, to get richer by any proper means such as armed conquest.' " The Navy League was quoted further to say that " 'World empire is the only logical and natural aim for a nation that really desires to remain a nation.' " But the flier refuted these aggressive sentiments by asserting that increased military might would only breed suspicion and hate, that the friendships of other nations were a better defense than battleships, and that live friends were better than dead enemies. The latter argument was bolstered by citing the examples of the long, undefended Canadian-American boundary line, and the good will built up with the Chinese when the United States in 1908 returned $10,000,000 of the Boxer Rebellion indemnity; it was further agreed that if the Americans had always given the Mexicans "a square deal" the need to seize Vera Cruz and to pursue Francisco Villa on Mexican soil would probably not have developed. Then the flier went on to assert that "An Ounce of Thinking is Better than a Ton of Fighting," urging statesmen to forget their outworn emphasis on military preparedness and support "a plan for world federation and the settlement of international disputes by modern and Christian methods." And this reminder of the Prince of Peace was a prelude to the flier's punch line: "We Call Jesus Master and Lord — Why Not Prepare to Do as He Said?"

This was an appeal to reason and consistency addressed to an ostensibly Christian society. The trouble was that in the psychological and social climate of 1916-1917, what was felt to be a struggle for democratic survival against the onslaught of the autocratic Hun had the effect of trampling truth and consistency underfoot. Not even Jesse Holmes' prestige, or the logic of his assertion that people should put themselves "squarely behind" any message they had to give to the world, could prevent his Emergency Peace Committee from hiding in anonymity when they issued the peace propaganda mentioned above. Expediency now prevailed; nothing sent out to the public in this critical period, it was reported, bore the name of "Friend," since "it seemed better" to have this material go out "without the stamp upon it of 'professional pacifists'. . . ."

The Quakers were not alone in the use of such surreptitious means to achieve desired ends. The National Security League, "financed largely by munitions and armor-plate interests and international bankers," also hid its sponsorship behind the undoubted Americanism of such eloquent spokesmen as "Teddy" Roosevelt and General Leonard Wood when they argued for increased national armaments. And the British, controlling the transatlantic cables, censored all news favorable to the Germans while they openly bombarded the United States with a ceaseless flow of pamphlets, posters, cartoons, and doctored documents designed to win Americans to the Allied side. These documents came to rest in public libraries, civic clubs, YMCA branches and newspaper offices. In addition, newspapers were supplied with a weekly pro-Ally review of the war. That some of these stories — notably those about the Germans crucifying a Canadian soldier, amputating the hands of Belgian babies, and cutting off the breasts of Belgian women —

were later shown to be pure fabrications did not alter the fact that at the time they exerted a powerful, if immeasurable, influence on American opinion. The British were far more skillful in the use of planted propaganda than were the Germans.

On the other hand, when Jesse's Emergency Peace Committee (through its subcommittee on publicity) tried to use these same tactics by planting peace propaganda in newspapers, they were stymied by a new American policy. George Creel, the head of the Committee on Public Information established by President Wilson's executive order only a week after the American declaration of war on Germany (April 6, 1917), had resolved that, while his Committee would carry Wilson's positive and pro-Allied democratice idealism to the citizens, the newspapers could be trusted through voluntary censorship to prevent the spread of pro-German or pacifist doctrine. And so it came to pass that, when in early April the Quaker subcommittee on publicity tried to reach the newspapers of the Philadelphia area through "plate material," their efforts were thwarted by this new policy:

> This time the services of the American Press Association, which regularly supplies local papers with plate material, were called upon. The plates, which were called 'The First Casualties of the War,' defended free speech, free press, and free assemblage, and opposed conscription. Although the plates were made and a list furnished for their distribution to 75 local papers, at the last minute, upon orders from New York, the plates were destroyed and the business refused.

This report was given to the Philadelphia Yearly Meeting of Hicksite Friends about five weeks after the American declaration of war on Germany. Anti-German and pro-Allied feeling now predominated; a war hysteria gripped the country. In the discussion which followed the report, Dr. William T. Hull, representing many peace organizations, including the Church Peace Union, said that the war was a challenge to the Society of Friends. He wondered, in a time when the majority of church people were going over to the militarists, whether the Quakers would stand firm in support of their ancient heritage of peace, entering into "a glorious struggle for the fundamental principles of democracy."

The answer to Dr. Hull's question was given on April 30, 1917, when a meeting of Quakers was held in the Young Friends building at 15th and Race Streets, Philadelphia. Working in the same spirit of close cooperation which had marked their efforts since the Winona Lake Conference, the Friends assembled there took some more important steps toward the formation of a joint committee of service. Three main groups were represented: the Philadelphia Yearly Meeting of Orthodox Friends, with Alfred G. Scattergood (serving as temporary chairman), Charles J. Rhoads, Stanley R. Yarnall, Henry W. Comfort, and Anne G. Walton; the Friends General Conference of Hicksites, with Jesse H. Holmes, Lucy Biddle Lewis, Arabella Carter, and William H. Cocks; and the Five Years Meeting of Orthodox Friends, with L. Hollingworth Wood, Homer L. Morris and Vincent D. Nicholson. Henry J. Cadbury and J. Barnard Walton were also there, but with unofficial status.

The purposes of the meeting were clear enough, and discussion centered around questions of organization to accomplish these objectives. The name "Friends' National Service Committee" was adopted as an expression of purpose (changed to "American Friends' Service Committee" on May 11 to emphasize that *all* American Friends were invited to join). The desirability of establishing a permanent national headquarters was considered, and a discussion held on the formulation of plans for future service. Thinking at this time that the exemption clause in the draft law would give Friends complete and automatic exemption from military service, the Committee was unanimous in believing that Quakers could not accept such exemption and "at the same time do nothing to express their positive faith and devotion in the great human crisis. . . ." This opinion was put into the form of a minute: " 'We are united in expressing our love for our country and our desire to serve her loyally. We offer our service to the Government of the United States in any constructive work in which we can conscientiously serve humanity.' "

Operation of the AFSC.

In subsequent sessions of the American Friends' Service Committee (henceforth abbreviated as AFSC) officers were appointed, with Rufus M. Jones becoming the first chairman, Charles F. Jenkins serving as treasurer, and Alfred G. Scattergood acting as vice-chairman and also as chairman of the finance committee. Vincent D. Nicholson became executive secretary, using one room of the Friends' Institute at 20 South Twelfth Street in Philadelphia as his office.

Nicholson lost little time in informing American Quakers of the purposes and proposed modes of operation of the newly formed AFSC. Continuing the high idealism shown in the minute of the Committee's first meeting, he used the pages of the *Friends' Intelligencer* to proclaim that, in the middle of a national crisis, it would be unthinkable that the Society of Friends as a body should be "inarticulate and passive. . . ." The problems and the responsibilities posed by the war were at once nationwide and worldwide, he thought. There was the need to join hands with English Friends in their wonderful work of relief and reconstruction in France and other parts of wartorn Europe; there was an opportunity to achieve a greater unity of purpose and effort to meet the problems peculiar to the United States now and in the future; there was a need to work hard and constructively now, so that when the war ended, Quakers would have greater influence in laying the foundations for the democratic peace of the future; and there was the job of stimulating Quakers still more to "search for truth in connection with the political and social problems of this sadly disarranged world. . . ."

These were the challenges, and it was the purpose of the AFSC to coordinate all the work of the various groups of Friends in the United States in their efforts to meet them. The AFSC would serve as a clearinghouse for information and ideas, and could also initiate plans for further service. More than that, other nonresistant groups such as the Mennonites and Dunkards, who shared the particular problems of the Quakers, were anxious to cooperate and were looking to the AFSC for leadership.

Nicholson grew quite eloquent as he asserted that the time for action was *now*, for present benefits and for the future:

We can save what we can from the wreckage of the storm, and lay the basis for the constructive work to follow the war. The opposition to our convictions that we have always had to face is the allegation that they are up in the clouds, far in the future, unrelated to the staff of work-a-day life. We now have an unusual opportunity to translate these ideals, which all hold for the future, into some part of the practical present. The thinking of the country is in a mobile, fluid state. The hard crust of custom and precedent has been broken up. On all sides is the appeal to the heroic. If we wait until the thought and practices of society have crystallized once more, our opportunity will have passed. The writer hopes he is free from any delusions as to the scope of our possible influence. The scope of our duty, however, is exactly coincident with the scope of our opportunity as it is revealed — be it large or small. The fulfillment of duty will be found in the attempt to hold fast to whatever convictions we have and may attain.

And so a relatively small group of Friends, very much convinced of the rightness of their position, pushed ahead with their wartime humanitarian projects. Even before the AFSC had actually been formed, the Young Friends Committee of the Orthodox Philadelphia Yearly Meeting had been corresponding with the London War Victims committee, and had decided to raise money and to send units of workers to France and Russia. On June 2, 1917, J. Henry Scattergood and Morris E. Leeds sailed to France with Grayson Murphy, newly appointed head of the French unit of the American Red Cross. Their mission, as advance agents for the AFSC, was to investigate opportunities for relief work and to make the necessary arrangements with the French authorities, with the English Friends already on the scene, and to work out liaison with the American Red Cross.

J. Henry Scattergood soon reported that he and Morris Leeds were planning for a union of the AFSC with the English Friends in France under the title of " *'mission de la Société des Amis.'* " This union was to work in close collaboration with the Red Cross; and a tripartite arrangement was finally worked out. But, as Scattergood said, the job ahead was a complicated problem — there were thousands of homes destroyed, sometimes whole villages. Rebuilding these in permanent form would go far beyond the $100,000,000 projected by the Red Cross, even if this money was spent only for houses. The best immediate solution was to follow the lead of the English Friends in erecting temporary housing from lumber secured from the Jura district of France.

Back home there were many other problems to be solved in pursuit of AFSC objectives. Money had to be raised, relief clothing and medical supplies accumulated and sent abroad, and workers trained to perform the most efficient service, not only in France, but in other parts of Europe affected by war's destruction. As Vincent D. Nicholson saw it in June, 1917, there was a need in the year ahead for at least $200,000 for service work in France, Russia and Serbia; and all contributions to the Red Cross should go through the AFSC. In fact, he said, at this point "The only great field of service for the majority of Friends is that of financial contribution." (No doubt the small size of the Quaker community accounted for the fact that, while the Friends contributed almost two million dollars to the AFSC in the period 1917-1926, nonFriends contributed over ten million. There was an additional contribution of almost thirteen million "in kind" — food, clothing, tools, etc. One may believe that much of this material came from Quaker sources.)

The immediate need, Nicholson said, was for $35,000, to be collected as soon as possible by the various Quaker meetings represented on the AFSC. Thus, in West Chester, Pennsylvania, members of the Chestnut Street Meeting were urged to give their contributions to Margaret S. James, who would forward it to Nicholson's office. About $1800 of the money collected by such means was used very quickly to send the first group of workers to join the English Friends in France: George V. Downing, Edith Coale, Douglas Waples, Eleanor Cary, Ernest L. Brown, Howard and Katherine Elkinton, and that so-aptly named couple, William and Mary Duguid. They sailed on June 23. In July, $13,700 was given into the hands of Lydia Lewis, Anna J. Haines, Emilie C. Bradbury, Esther White, Nancy Babb, and Amelia Farbiszewski as they sailed for their relief work in Buzuluk, Russia. Some $20,000 of the $35,000 were set aside to meet the expenses of the American Friends' Reconstruction Unit being formed for training at Haverford College.

This unit grew out of the Emergency Unit organized at Haverford shortly after war was declared by Rufus M. Jones and James A. Babbitt. Practically the entire student body and many of the faculty were in it. About $10,000 had been raised for equipment and supplies: suitable clothing for emergency field service, tents, tools, and materials. Through loans and gifts automobiles and ambulances were secured, although it soon became apparent that the difficulties of getting permits from the British War Office made work with the English Friends Ambulance Unit difficult if not impossible. And American ambulance work was to be militarized shortly. But almost any other form of volunteer service was open to them, and the boys at Haverford plunged into a period of strenuous training to "discipline and harden them" for whatever opportunity might come.

Given this running start, it was a relatively simple matter to reorganize the Emergency Unit into a more permanent and stable form as the first of two reconstruction units to train volunteers at

Haverford. One hundred men were to be trained now, and a committee composed of Rufus M. Jones, LeRoy Mercer (athletic coach at Swarthmore College), Vincent D. Nicholson, and Henry J. Cadbury was set up to determine the qualifications needed, to prepare application blanks, and to screen the candidates. The committee was almost swamped by the flood of applications. However, one hundred men were finally selected for service in Europe, among them being all types of Quakers, one Mennonite, four members of the Fellowship of Reconciliation, and some men not Friends but in sympathy with them. As one would expect, the Swarthmore people were well represented, including Jesse H. Holmes III, and William I. Hull. And George O. Holmes, of Foster, Nebraska, was also accepted.

Starting on July 17, 1917, and continuing for six weeks, these men were put through a rigorous course of training on the Haverford campus under the direction of L. Ralston Thomas, Richard Mott Gummere and Robert Brown, with James A. Babbitt becoming the director in August. They were housed mainly in Merion Hall. (A year later, however, when Unit #2 was in training at Haverford under the direction of William C. Biddle, the release of fifty-six boys from army camps caused overcrowding. The overflow of boys was transferred to a fruit farm leased near Rosedale Station in the Kennett Square area.)

The daily schedule at Haverford was not one to attract weaklings:

5:45 A.M.	— Rising, followed by ten minutes of physical exercise in front of Barclay Hall.
6:30 A.M.	— Breakfast, washing of dishes, and policing of rooms.
7:30-8:25 A.M.	— Lectures by specialists on social service, sanitation, hygiene, conditions in France, etc.
9:30-11:30 A.M.	— Study of the French language under several instructors, with President William W. Comfort as director. (Most students were totally ignorant of French.)
12:00 M.	— Dinner
12:00-2:00 P.M.	— Rest and recuperation.
2:00-5:30 P.M.	— Squad training in carpentry, masonry, agriculture, roadmaking, auto repairing, and other forms of technical skills.
6:00 P.M.	— Supper

| 7:00 P.M. | — Devotional meeting |
| 7:30 P.M. | — A lecture every other night dealing with world conditions, with special reference to France and the future work of the Unit. |

Although some of these trainees at Haverford were too young to come under the provisions of the Selective Service Act of May 18, 1917 (Jesse H. Holmes III was only seventeen), many of them fell within the twenty-one to thirty-one age brackets and had registered with their local draft boards as a simple duty of citizenship. If any of them had registered in the belief that their membership in a pacifist religious group granted them automatic exemption from military service they were soon disabused of this notion. A letter to Rufus M. Jones on June 28 from Provost Marshal General Crowder made it clear that, while such membership gave relief from combatant duty, Quakers, Mennonites and others of like stripe were still subject to the draft for noncombatant duty in the armed forces as clerks, cooks, hospital orderlies, or whatever. And, Crowder continued, if some of the Haverford trainees got permits from their local draft boards to leave the country to do the work of the AFSC, they would still need to return home upon call if their number came up in the national service lottery.

But the Selective Service Act also contained the principle that, while all males are required to serve their country in a time of national peril, some are more useful in civilian roles than as shooters of guns. Under this principle a system was worked out which permitted the relief work of the AFSC to go on in Europe. Local draft boards across the country (with one exception) granted the transfer of draftee records to similar boards in the Philadelphia area; these draft boards in turn granted permits to leave the country so that passports might be issued to those not expecting an early summons. This system finally allowed ninty-eight members of the Haverford Reconstruction Unit #1 to reach France in the fall of 1917. In subsequent months a furlough system, first applied to free regularly drafted soldiers for agricultural work on their home farms, was used to make it possible for AFSC men to pursue their work in America and Europe. Almost all of these drafted conscientious objectors took advantage of this plan; exactly two hundred men were furloughed by the time the war ended.

These men had been encouraged to take this path of duty by a letter sent out to them by the AFSC, which urged them to be guided by "the high tribunal" of their own consciences. And the Central Committee of the Philadelphia Yearly Meeting, under the chairmanship of O. Edward Janney, no doubt strengthened the resolve of some Quaker draftees to live by their inner lights when, at New Year's time in 1918, they sent out a letter to the seventy-five men then known to be in the armed forces. The letter was designed to bind them more closely to their home meetings. A calendar bearing Quaker mottoes was enclosed with the letter. In March, copies of Cyrus Pringle's *Diary,* now reprinted as *The Record of a Quaker Conscience,* with an introduction by Rufus M. Jones, were sent to Friends already in camp and to those expecting an early call. Another letter was sent to men under twenty-one, urging them to make their own decisions according to their consciences, and to make these decisions in the spirit of a religious call.

Quite predictably, the reliance on individual conscience resulted in a wide spectrum of responses to the national government's call to service, as seen in the report given to the Men's Meeting, Philadelphia Yearly Meeting of Hicksites, in May of 1918. During the past year, it was said, 118 men of draft age in that Meeting had enlisted, 22 had accepted military service under the draft, and 10 had accepted noncombatant service under draft rules. This was out of a total of 961 members of draft age, with the rest not yet summoned, or in prison for refusal to register, or in France with the Friends Reconstruction Unit, or in such other categories as being under the Canadian draft, or as conscientious objectors in unresolved cases.

Among the most extreme positions on Quaker responsibilities in the contemporary crisis — and the most consistent one, considering the traditional Quaker attitudes on peace — was voiced in 1917 by Isaac Sharpless, outgoing president of Haverford College, when he told a joint meeting of Orthodox and Hicksite Friends in New York that exemptions for conscientious objectors should not be made. Better, he thought, that " '. . . .all our young Quakers should go to jail. In this way, by making the Government feel that we are ready to suffer and die for our convictions, we may perpetuate our ideals and pass them on to future generations.' "

This intransigent attitude on living according to one's convictions, with all its dangers in the time of war's excitement, was shown by some other Friends in the United States and in England. In "an impassioned address" in June, 1917, J. Bernard Walton, executive secretary of the Advancement Committee of the AFSC, declared that 2,000 members of the Wormwood Meeting in England were being "persecuted by the British authorities because they refused to join the army and navy. 'The persecuted brethren are drilled for a long time in the manual of arms until they are absolutely exhausted,' " he said, " 'then they are cast into prison and fed on bread and water. All this is done to make the Friends say they will join the service. The Socialists likewise are being persecuted.' "

In America, as indicated above, the young Quakers reacted to the draft in various ways, each one having to balance his duty to his country against the principle of pacifism inculcated by his local meeting since his earliest childhood. Many of them, not yet a part of the Haverford AFSC training program, quickly found themselves shipped off to military camps. Here some refused to drill, while others would drill but refused to carry arms. Still others objected to the whole system of war and refused to do anything demanded of them by the military authorities.

As may well be imagined, it was this last type that suffered the most from the corporals, sergeants, and lieutenants charged with making soldiers out of them. One boy at Camp Cody refused to drill, carry arms, or salute; he even refused to wear the uniform or do substitute work. The uniform was forced on him "in a harsh manner, and afterward he was subjected to cruel and inhuman treatment . . . ." Placed in a stockade under guard, his personal belongings were confiscated, including his most intimate personal necessities. In a letter to a friend, this boy, identified only as "S.W.S.," wrote that a lieutenant had threatened him with twenty-five years in the federal prison at Leavenworth if he did not change. But he didn't change; and so, as he wrote, " 'I was stripped and scrubbed with a broom, put under a faucet with my mouth held open, had a rope [put] around my neck and pulled up choking tight for a bit, been fisted, slapped, kicked, . . .' " He was forced to carry a bag of sand and dirt until he could hardly hold it any more; he was forced to stand under a cold shower-bath spray until he was pretty well chilled.

Surprisingly enough, after about three weeks in the stockade S.W.S. was acquitted by a courts-martial. But he still refused to wear the khaki, so a corporal under a lieutenant's orders beat him, gouged his eyes with his thumbs, and knocked him down several times. Blood from his nose soiled his clothes. After several weeks his eyesight began to return to normal. (We can only hope that he was soon released to join the training unit at Haverford.)

Lest we suppose that S.W.S.'s sufferings were due only to a particularly sadistic corporal, Rufus Jones reminds us that his case was "fairly typical of the behavior and treatment" of the conscientious objector. And Paul J. Furnas, field secretary of the AFSC, found the following practices quite general in the various military camps across the United States:

> . . .the various penalties [included] stoppage of mail, both incoming and outgoing, deprivation of personal possessions, ridicule, bullying, wearying and unnecessary argument, coupled with threats of shooting or imprisonment . . . starvation — one man was kept for sixteen consecutive meals on bread and water, — and various ways of wearing a man down by physical [tasks] — prolonged standing, carrying heavy weights, throwing men into garbage wagons, etc., the military machine trying every means, physical and mental, to bring the objectors to submission.

Such practices, of course, could not long continue in a country ostensibly fighting a war to make the world safe for democracy. (And it should be added that Paul J. Furnas, in his visits to army camps, found that the higher commanding officers were usually grateful for his help in going over Secretary of War Baker's more humane rulings for the treatment of conscientious objectors; these rulings had generally escaped their notice.) Some solution, which protected both the individual conscience and the nation's needs in time of war, had to be devised. While no complete solution to this problem was ever found, the national authorities, in a series of laws and rulings, finally arrived at the furlough system described earlier. It was under this system that the AFSC carried on its work without further governmental harassment from March, 1918 to war's end and beyond.

True to the original purpose of the furlough system, many conscientious objectors found opportunities for service on farms in eastern Pennsylvania. And William B. Harvey, a Quaker leader, found a way to concentrate such farm work for the benefit of the AFSC while at the same time relieving the overcrowding at Haverford College. As mentioned earlier, a large fruit farm at Rosedale near Kennett Square was rented in the harvest season of 1918; the farmhouse and a boarding house could accommodate over 150 men. Those AFSC trainees who had the longest period to wait before going to France went to Rosedale, where in about five months' time they harvested and sold fruit, made apple butter, cut and sold firewood, and largely supported themselves in the food department. Altogether, they made some $4,000 through these efforts, while at the same time getting some foretaste of the kind of country living they might experience in France.

But this work was made more difficult when the worldwide influenza epidemic hit the United States. Some of the men at Rosedale joined Haverford volunteers in going out to hospitals and private homes to help the sick and dying. Some of these volunteers also caught the disease; none died.

All these activities were supported in spirit and in action by Quaker women. The Women's Meeting of Philadelphia Yearly Meeting [H] had a Committee on Epistles. This committee, meeting on May 15, 1917, sent out a greeting to those religious organizations which had "an outspoken abhorrence of war and its practices. . . ." Among those receiving this greeting were the Mennonites, Amish, Dunkards, Schwenkfelders, and Christadelphians. And, when the AFSC leaders appointed a women's committee, headed by Lucy Biddle Lewis (later on Rebecca Carter took charge, and then Florence P. Yarnall), to organize and direct the many activities involved in supplying European war victims with food, clothing, and expert nursing services, these same women rejoiced in the opportunity to translate their feelings into action.

In June 1917, this committee, representing both Orthodox and Hicksites, issued an urgent appeal to Quaker women, asking them to send money for the purchase of food and clothing to be sent to France and Russia, or to knit or sew garments, or to can or dry fruits and vegetables for shipment overseas. (If they needed help in canning and drying, demonstration classes and other aids were to be arranged in local neighborhoods.) In addition, there was a great need for social-service workers in France and those other parts of Europe suffering from war's devastation. These workers were to teach English to foreign mothers, to give elementary instruction to children in hospitals, and to assist in the distribution of the food and clothing in foreign areas. A training course for the teaching services was to be given under the direction of Margaret F. Morris and Mary Kelsey during the summer, while the Pennsylvania School for Social Service would provide a six-weeks course in the fall.

And so the work on the Quaker home front went on. Monetary contributions poured into the central office of the AFSC at 20 South Twelfth Street in Philadelphia, while sewing groups in nearly 300 communities in 24 states energetically and enthusiastically prepared garments for shipment abroad. These garments were sent to the Hicksite Cherry Street complex, where Mary H. Whitson and a group of volunteers sorted and repacked them for shipment via the facilities of the Red Cross. By the time the Yearly Meeting of Hicksites convened in Philadelphia in May, 1918, Jesse H. Holmes, speaking for his Committee on Peace and Emergency Service (the old Emergency Peace Committee) could report that the AFSC had shipped about 30,000 garments in 150 boxes since the last Yearly Meeting. In addition, several boxes of fruits and vegetables, canned in the summer of 1917, had been sent to Cherry Street for transshipment. By July 15, 1918, the total of garments shipped abroad was 80,748, with many of these made by the Arch Street (O) women. And by this time about $30,000 had been spent on other things to be sent to France: candy, blankets, ready-made garments, condensed milk, and drugs.

No doubt all this work was given more status or prestige when it was announced in June, 1918, that window hangers, bearing the AFSC emblem of the red-and-black star, were now ready for distribution. Each Quaker family contributing to the AFSC effort in any way was entitled to hang this emblem in a front window and inform the world that here too was a house of service. (To do this, of course, would be quite in line with the national practice of the time, when a household's contribution to the war effort was well advertised through publicly displayed seals, flags, pennants, or window hangers of various kinds. Those readers who are of retirement age may well remember "Gold Star Mothers" and the emblems they hung in their windows.)

And these Quaker families were stimulated to do still more work by a constant barrage of exhortations for AFSC support from the Quaker press — *The Friend, The American Friend,* and the *Friends' Intelligencer* —, as well as from the public magazines and newspapers. As Rufus M. Jones remembered it, these news media, particularly the Quaker magazines, "reported plans, announced each new move, issued calls for volunteers, stirred up interest, interpreted our ideals, and kept the membership informed about the new service. . . ." It was instructive to Jones to note how "action and service" had "usurped the place once occupied by problems of theology. . . ." in the pages of these periodicals.

And the idealistic crusade of the AFSC was explained and stimulated still more by itinerant lecturers — people who had returned from service work in France, such as Morris Leeds and J. Henry Scattergood; and by others who had not been to France in this work but who lent their talents, time and energy to this purpose. Isaac Sharpless did this, as well as W.W. Comfort, president of Haverford College, and Lucy Biddle Lewis. In May, 1918, Robert Tatlock, leader of the Friends' Expedition to Russia, completed a lecture tour in the United States; he was then to interview a party of English Friends who had just returned from two-years' work in Russia via Vancouver, British Columbia, just before he embarked from Vancouver to enter Russia by way of Vladivostock. And this way of stimulating interest and support for AFSC projects was still going on in October, 1919, when William Price, Swarthmore '12, told a gathering of the Friends of Swarthmore in Whittier House about the work of the Friends' Reconstruction Unit in France. (Those in attendance that night should not have been surprised to see Dr. and Mrs. Jesse H. Holmes, Mrs. Paul Pearson, Dr. and Mrs. John Miller, and Dr. and Mrs. Fussell receive the guests, nor to find William Price as the speaker. As may be remembered from previous pages, they were all part of the "gang" making Swarthmore College such a dynamic center of functional learning in those days, and the speaker was the son of Jesse Holmes' old friend, "Will" Price.)

136

8. A Friendly Service of Love, Part II

By the time the members of the first unit of workers trained at Haverford were ready for their trip to France, the national headquarters of the AFSC, directed by Vincent D. Nicholson in his role as executive secretary, was a beehive of activity. Formerly known as the Friends' Institute, with its address given as 20 South Twelfth street, its first and second floors were now crowded with desks, files, and all the paraphenalia of a busy office. Here and there on the floors were duffel bags, bedrolls, travelers' kits, while a constant stream of departing or returning workers filled the hallways. From and through this headquarters the activities of the various Friends' groups were coordinated in support of the overall objectives of the AFSC, appeals went out for money and materials, and here workers leaving for France and other parts of Europe received their last instructions and encouragements.

Service Abroad

And so it was that the members of the first Haverford Reconstruction Unit were funneled through this Friends' Institute in the late summer and fall of 1917. Leaving Philadelphia by train, they headed for the docks of the French Steamship Line in New York. Here they found the docks in a state of almost chaotic congestion due to the piling up of the many cases and crates of material, not only clothing and food, but those items purchased by the AFSC for its work abroad — tractors, plows, harrows, disc drills, reapers, binders, carpenters' tools, photographic material, medical supplies, and planing mill and sawmill machinery. They found that no one French ship could take the entire Unit as a body; they had to brave their way across the submarine-endangered Atlantic in a series of smaller contingents: 14 members leaving on August 28; 49 on September 4; 12 members on September 13; and 11 (5 of whom were women), on September 16. It was not until November 13 that the AFSC could report that all members of Unit Number 1, with the exception of 3, had arrived in France.

No doubt the experience of the largest group, the one sailing on September 4, may be taken as typical. They sailed on the *Rochambeau* for Bordeaux, entrained for Paris, and arrived September 14, hollow-eyed and weary. Going to the American Red Cross headquarters on the Place de la Concorde, which was also the central office for the AFSC in France, they were met by J. Henry Scattergood, the American Friends Commissioner, by T. Edmund Harvey, president of English work in France, and by Homer Folks, director of civil affairs for the Red Cross. These men found temporary housing for the tired travelers; and then, under the direction of Charles Evans, chief of the American field unit, the 49 were sent out to devastated areas to take up their assignments in the work of reconstruction and relief.

They were joined in this work by an ever-growing number of Quakers trained at Haverford. While the Friends could not supply all of the additional three hundred men asked for in January, 1918 by Homer Folks, Unit # 2 was being readied and would soon sail under the direction of William C. Biddle. By April 20, as Jesse Holmes was to report to his Yearly Meeting, there were 190 Friends in France and 6 in Russia; by November 21, with the shooting war ended, the French contingent had 258 men, 40 women, and 5 more in transit.

These workers, drawn from Quaker meetings stretching from Maine to California, may not have been really well prepared by their Haverford and Rosedale Farm training for the conditions of living and laboring in war torn France. In any case, one of the Quaker workers, sent out to what may have been the Verdun area, gave vent to some good-natured grumbling in " 'The Star Grouch Remarks' ":

> The stopped-up drain;
> The smoky flu;
> The inside pain;
> Too much to do.

The icy walk;
The early night;
The foreign talk;
The lack of light.

The air that's damp;
The homely daughter;
O cold hard world:
O cold hard water.

Whatever the conditions of living, the AFSC workers went out into those areas of France devastated by the advance, retreat, and trench tactics forced on the combatants by technological warfare: they went into the valleys of the Meuse, the Marne, and the Doubs; they went into Bar-le-Duc, Bettancourt, Sermaize, Eaux Bonnes, and Desancon. Here, directed from the central office in Paris, they performed what must have seemed to the French to be miracles of reconstruction and relief until April, 1920, when their work was closed.

Divided into local, self-governing units called *equipes,* the AFSC people had, by the time the work was closed in France, maintained a maternity-hospital project at Chalons-sur-Marne, constructed and equipped other hospitals, built barracks for tuberculosis patients, taken care of little children, assisted in the relief of prisoners, and took part in the care of people who had gone insane during the war. They had given relief to 1,666 French villages, assisted over 46,000 families, erected 1,388 prefabricated houses, and planted 25,000 trees. Most of these were fruit trees in the Verdun area; there were five trees per family, and many communal trees. Some of these projects, according to Jesse Herman Holmes III (Swarthmore ex-'21), were accomplished with the help of German prisoners as late as September, 1919. He wrote that the fifteen Germans assigned to his AFSC unit near Montfaucon "proved capable of doing a lot of work."

And, as an article in the *Friends' Intelligencer* pointed out, this help was not extended to French people because they begged for it; this spirit of begging was not manifested in France. But, in the destroyed areas, people could not get the necessities of life; if the AFSC could bring these to them, and encourage mutual aid on the principles of cooperation, the useful and lasting work which had been done would not be forgotten.

Indeed, as Jesse H. Holmes, chairman of the Emergency Peace

and Service Committee of the Hicksites in Philadelphia, asserted in May, 1918, all this service and construction in France was "not merely building anew the homes and lives of thousands, but is building, also, the house of brotherhood." And his argument was to be continued over a year later when, in October, 1919, the Young Friends Conference at Earlham College, Indiana, reminded Quakers that the French called the Friends "the Society of Love." "If," they said, "we are to be worthy of this new title . . . we must make ourselves the Friends of all mankind. . . ."

While all mankind could not hope to be served by Quakers in the field, at least the AFSC could strive to serve still more strongly the war victims already being taken care of by Friendly people in Russia, Germany and Austria, Poland and Serbia.

As noted earlier, in July, 1917, even before plans had been completed for the French mission, a small group of Quaker women sailed for Russia. These women — Lydia Lewis, Anna J. Haines, Emilie C. Bradbury, Esther White, Nancy Babb, and Amelia Farbiszewski — joined the English workers established at Buzuluk, Samara Province, in trying to deal with the hordes of refugees fleeing before the advancing German armies in Poland and western Russia. An abandoned manor house had been turned into a hostel for about 125 people. In outlying villages English doctors set up dispensaries and opened hospitals, trying desperately to deal with the situation in the absence of Russian doctors. One English doctor's district had 60,000 people in it, many of whom spent two days in getting to his dispensary. Often he treated 120 patients in one morning, his waiting room showing a kaleidoscopic array of ethnic strains — "Tartars, Bashkirs, Kirgheze, Ukranians, Cassacks, Bulgarians, Mordvins, Serbs, Austrians," and German prisoners. On Christmas, 1917, a "sixteen-bed hospital [was] filled with patients who had anthrax, hydatid cyst, typhus, typhoid, pneumonia, puerperal fever, diptheria, tubercular bone, frozen feet, and lunacy. . . ." No doubt the two extra American nurses called for by the English Friends in a cable to Lucy Biddle Lewis in July were there helping in this desperate situation.

In addition to working in hospitals, the six original AFSC members in the Buzuluk area also helped in the economic sphere, developing wage-employment centers, where refugee women and local peasants could earn money through spinning, weaving, knitting, and embroidery. These centers not only increased the supply of clothing but gave the Russians a measure of self respect in that they could buy food instead of relying on handouts. And, when the Bolshevik Revolution led to surrender to the Germans, releasing soliders from the front, a labor bureau was started by the Quakers to find work for them. Many of these returning soldiers, of course, were peasants so poor that they could not afford to buy the seed wheat to get their farms productive again; individual Quakers loaned them the money to do this. The Friends' unit, moreover, used money from its funds to pay bounties for many thousands of *suzlick* skins, the *suzlick* being a muskrat-type animal which devastated wheat fields by nibbling the young shoots and then the ripe grain.

Now was this the limit of Friends' service at Buzuluk. Schools were opened under trained teachers for native and refugee children, the morning sessions being devoted to academic work while the afternoon classes were of a trade-school nature. Considering the type of courses offered — carpentry, tailoring, shoemaking, bookbinding — there was small cause to wonder that this school became self-supporting.

But, after it became evident that Buzuluk would soon be in Bolshevik hands, making the transfer of funds from England and America very difficult, workers left for the more distant towns along the Trans-Siberian Railroad in October, 1918. Here, at Omsk and other places, they found conditions of disease and overcrowding under Arctic temperatures so severe that one wonders how these Quaker women were able to cope with them. "One out of every twelve persons was found acutely ill with some dangerous communicable disease. . . ." At Omsk there were 3,000 refugees living in summer barracks when the temperature fell to 71 below zero; 2,500 lived in dugouts without light or ventilation; 500 were in box cars, and 6,000 lived in a variety of other places from cattle pens to the corridors of public buildings. While it was encouraging to note that the summer barracks mentioned above were disinfected by the AFSC corps, the whole situation was very much like the legendary Augean stables. In September, 1919, the AFSC workers returned from Siberia.

(While the author has not found any direct evidence that these AFSC people came into contact with the American army in Siberia under Major General William S. Graves, the chances are very great indeed that they met somewhere along the Trans-Siberian Railroad — perhaps at Omsk, at Irkutsk, or most likely at Vladivostok. This army, "sent on a hopelessly vague assignment" by President Wilson, was in Siberia from mid-August, 1918, to April, 1920. From Soviet Moscow the American presence appeared to be in support of the White Russians then trying to reverse the Bolshevik Revolution; it was indeed a foretaste of those American interferences in Asian civil wars to come in China, 1945-1949, in Korea, and in Vietnam.)

When these AFSC workers were still in Russia, doing their work under the most adverse circumstances, Jesse Holmes could report to his Yearly Meeting that case records of families were being kept and "a scientific social study" was being made in order to lay the foundation for more extended work when the war should end. No doubt the information gained by these methods proved valuable in 1920-1921, when the Soviet government was only too glad to let Friends distribute relief supplies to famine-sticken central Russia. By May, 1921, three shipments of condensed milk, soap, fats, and medical supplies had been distributed; much of this material came to the Russians from the American Red Cross and the American Relief Administration of the federal government.

In Germany, after the Armistice, conditions were chaotic: the country became a battleground where the extreme Left struggled with more moderate elements for control. In January, 1919, a Spartacist (Communist) revolt had a brief life, but was put down by the provisional government with the help of the regular army; in April a Soviet Republic was established in Bavaria only to be overthrown almost immediately by federal troops. By August the Weimar Republic was in being, first under a coalition of Socialists and Liberals, and then, in June, 1920, under a coalition of the People's Party (liberal), Center Party, and Democrats. The fact that the Allied blockade had finally been lifted the previous July, after reducing a large part of the population to near-starvation, had been helpful factor in working toward some semblance of order. But throughout 1919 and on into the 'twenties, many people continued to stagger on the verge of starvation, particularly the children in towns and cities. The stage was set for Quaker help in the distribution of food and clothing somewhat along the lines already being pursued in France, Russia, and Poland.

The first Quakers to arrive in Germany were English — Joan M. Fry, Marion C. Fox, J. Thompson Elliott, and Max Bellows. They entered Berlin on July 6, 1919, to be joined the next day by Carolena

142

M. Wood, Jane Addams, and Dr. Alice Hamilton as representatives of the AFSC. The AFSC had appropriated $30,000 for the purchases of the "most urgently needed foods"; in addition, the Americans had some twenty-five tons of clothing ready for distribution. In all of this work the Americans cooperated closely with their English counterparts, assisted all the while by Dr. Elizabeth Rotten, a native Berliner.

While most of the administrative work of the distribution of food and clothing fell on the shoulders of Carolena Wood, Jane Addams and Dr. Hamilton made an intensive study of the food and health needs in Germany, recording their findings in Bulletin 25 of the AFSC's publications. This bulletin, widely circulated in America, may have become the major inspiration for Herbert Hoover's request in November, 1919, that the AFSC take "complete charge" of the distribution of food to save the children of Germany. Hoover was then chairman of the American Relief Administration and in charge of the European Children's Fund; this fund was being used to feed some three million children in other parts of Europe, and Hoover said that "certain moneys" not yet spent could be diverted for use in Germany.

The AFSC went to work at once to organize a larger and more definite German unit, and to raise a supplemental food fund for this purpose. Alfred G. Scattergood of Philadelphia was made its leader; eighteen other Quakers (including Jesse Holmes), from both the Orthodox and the Hicksite branches, were named to advance the cause in Germany. And at first the building of the supplemental food fund met with opposition — from Germanophobes who could not understand why the late mortal enemy should now be helped, from German people in the United States who wanted to help in their own way, and from other churches who wondered why so small a body as the Friends should be given complete charge. But, as time went on, and as it became evident that Quakers were selfless in their work, the funds came in. Also, it helped to know that the names of donors would get wide publicity.

Most of the members of the special German unit reached Berlin on January 2, 1920. But Jesse found that he couldn't join with these early Quaker adventurers; his duties at Swarthmore would hold him there until the end of the first semester of the college year. Arrangements for his service abroad, however, were soon made: he was granted a leave of absense for seven months by Swarthmore's

143

Board of Managers; and Dr. Elbert Russell, formerly head of the department of religion and philosophy at Earlham College, and now director of the Woolman School, was to take his place to teach all but the purely elective courses.

But there were other reasons for Jesse's inability to join his co-workers in Berlin at this time. While the original idea had been to divide Germany into relief districts, with Jesse and others being delegated as district directors, he very quickly found that his assignment was changed: he was now asked by the AFSC to be their first traveling commissioner, to join T. Edmund Harvey, the commissioner for English Friends, in an inspection tour of the various Quaker relief centers in Europe. Obviously, this new assignment entailed more time-consuming planning.

Arriving in Paris about the middle of February, 1920 (and suffering from a head cold), Jesse joined Harvey in the complicated task of planning for the closing of the French unit, which had been in service for over four years and had accumulated much property. Some three million francs were still available for disbursement in the general service of the Friends' mission; a large part of this was now diverted to help finish the construction of the Maternity Hospital at Chalons. Also, some fifty trucks and automobiles were to be sent to a central garage in Vienna, from which they would be dispersed to various relief centers as needed.

Since Jesse and Harvey had heard that "special difficulties" faced the Friends' unit in Serbia, they decided to make that country their next stop on their tour of inspection. This Friends' unit of about a dozen people, who had gone to Serbia in the summer of 1919, included Drew Pearson, who had just graduated from Swarthmore, and Arthur J. Rawson, son of Ed Rawson, that best friend of Jesse's. It also included Loreta Rush, "a buxom, apple-faced Indiana Friend," and a Dr. Russell, a woman from Philadelphia. In the beginning the unit's chief center was at Lescowacz (Lescovatz?), a town not far from Nish in central Serbia. Here, in an area which no doubt was typical of Serbia in general (Jesse described Serbia as "dirty, verminous . . . illiterate . . . ridden by graft, inefficiency and general bureaucracy . . ."; for generations "in war, or just out of it, or just getting into it, . . ."), the unit had used Bulgarian prisoners to rebuild some two hundred houses on the site of a large experimental farm school destroyed by the Austrians. By the time Jesse and Harvey arrived the work was practically completed and the unit was looking around for fresh opportunities for service. (Perhaps it was just as well that Jesse was not thrown into a situation demanding a lot of work at this time because he was fighting off another cold. When the commissioners and their party arrived in Nish, the rest of the group went off to "a Y.M.C.A. or to a Turkish bath," while Jesse took to his bed in his hotel room. As he wrote to Rebe, "I seem to be on the verge of taking cold all the time, and get tired very easily. But Drew and Edmund Harvey take very good care of me, . . .")

A new opportunity quickly developed in the old Turkish-Albanian city of Petch (or Ipek). The entire group was moved to the new location under the leadership of Drew Pearson, where they established an orphanage, a small hospital, and placed several hundreds of needy families on land supplied by the government. This last task involved the breaking of hundreds of acres of neglected land and the manufacture of thousands of bricks for farmers' houses.

In all of this work Drew Pearson displayed a remarkable ability in dealing with all kinds of people — an ability also seen when he was in his father's Chautauqua circuit, and in his brilliant editorship of Swarthmore's *Phoenix* in 1919. He received praise from several directions for his Serbian work: from the director of the Serbian Relief Fund of England (Major Hardwicke); and from Jesse Holmes, who wrote his wife in April, 1920, that "Drew is a favorite everywhere. He gets food from this source, and machinery from that, much of it for nothing; and he got *nothing* from Phila. from August to March! . . . He's a great boy."

Of course much of Drew's success could also be laid to the fact that he worked very hard, relieving his labors only a little with humor and social activities. He ran "a tight ship," letting nothing come ahead of his duties as director of the Friends' unit. "Night after night" he could be found in his tent, clad in his military uniform and Sam Browne belt (with appropriate identifying Red Cross and AFSC insignia), working on one troublesome detail after another. He smoked not, neither did he drink — except for a rare glass of roja, the plum brandy which ordinarily livened business deals in Serbia. But he needed help; as soon as he could, he imported Andrew Simpson, a Swarthmore classmate and electrical engineer, to help him get the local hydroelectric plant functioning again. When Simpson arrived, the two "merry Andrews" had some roja and then

145

named the unit outhouse the Phi Kappa Psi, since that Swarthmore fraternity was a rival of their own, the Kappa Sigma. Aside from this jollity, there were only two other social events to relieve the humdrum of work: a unit wedding, at which Drew served as best man, and a costume party.

While Jesse was greatly pleased with the work Drew Pearson was doing in Serbia, he was not so well pleased with the situation in Vienna, Austria, which (in October, 1920) he called "perhaps the most pathetic figure in the ruinous wake of the great war." He said that "It is the most helpless and hopeless of the wretched centers of population, and is starving in the midst of its splendid palaces." As he had observed earlier, Jesse believed that in such cases as those in Serbia or Poland, "the most primitive sections recover most rapidly. . . . of course they have not so far to go to get back to normal conditions, and they are not so much enmeshed in the complexities of more advanced civilization. . . ." But, he went on, in Vienna and Berlin there was "an exceedingly complex civilization all out of gear. It's not hard to mend a wheelbarrow, but an auto calls for experts, and is easily ruined. Austria and Germany are not being dealt with by experts."

And, as Jesse reported in several letters to Rebe, the Austrian Friends' Mission in Austria was "very Messy," some antagonism having developed between the English and Americans working in their headquarters on the third floor of a palace formerly occupied by a nobleman. Dr. Hilda Clark, head of the Mission, seemed incapable of delegating authority and interfered with the work of others. Martha Speakman, a Swarthmore member of this group, told Jesse that she was dissatisfied with her job there since she wasn't being properly used. And one American who might have clashed with Hilda Clark even more never got there at all. Mary Appel, twenty-six years old, "big and strong," and a former resident of Lancaster, Pennsylvania, "simply disappeared" en route from France. After working in the French unit for about a year she volunteered for Austrian service, sent her baggage — and was never seen again. As Jesse wrote to Rebe, it was a case for Sherlock Holmes.

(The long newsy letters Jesse sent to Rebe, full of cogent comments, also gave abundant evidence of his continuing love affair with her. Fifty-six years old in 1920, he still saluted her as "My beloved" or "My dear," in many cases following these openings with well-drawn sketches of a jenny wren in various attitudes of action or repose. In the letter from Vienna, April 9, 1920, he wrote near his drawing, "Rather a fat J.W. this time, eh? Is my absence affecting thee this way?" He signed this letter "Thine lovingly" and drew a sketch of a rather subdued blue jay. And then, in a postscript, he urged Rebe to join him in England when he was to attend the London Yearly Meeting about the middle of May. "Please!", he added. Some two weeks later, perhaps still feeling miserable from his cold, he wrote from Metrovitza, Serbia: "I love thee, and long to have thee with me. Let's get together. I'm sure I can make it interesting for thee, & perhaps . . . make thee forget how troublesome I have been.")

While the administration of relief activities was probably less efficient than it could have been, the workers faced a herculean task. When Hilda Clark first led her English Friends into Vienna, in May 1919, she found that babies were being wrapped in paper and older boys and girls wore potato-bag burlap suits. Sixty per cent of the children had severe rickets, with hardly one free in slighter degree. The threat of tuberculosis was ever present. With the help of the AFSC, the English spent an initial $25,000 in buying nourishing foods, set up a system of home visitations to find and care for children in need, and planned a chain of infant welfare relief centers. The city authorities were persuaded to bring some 300 cows into the city, where Friends fed them linseed-oil cake imported from America, took care of them otherwise, and distributed the milk. It wasn't long before some 50,000 of these children were being fed and clothed, and some thousands of university students were fed as well. And beyond all these more desperate cases were the 300,000 school children being given one meal a day by the American Relief Association from kitchens in the palaces formerly occupied by the old emperor and the murdered crown prince.

But such handouts were expedients to relieve the immediate and desperate needs of the moment. In Vienna, as was true of other areas served by the Friends, the most promising plans for long-lasting benefits were those involving ways to get the people to help themselves. The food shortage would be relieved if, as was planned by the Friends' unit, city dwellers were given small allotments of land outside Vienna where they might plant peas, beans and potatoes a la the war gardens in England and the United States. And, as both Jesse Holmes and Hilda Clark observed, ways had to be found to revive the highly skilled technical and artistic crafts for which Vienna had long been famous. A beginning along this line had been made early in October, 1919, when clothing specialists were given cloth to turn out badly needed items; by the middle of March, 1920, they had made some 40,000 garments of thirteen different kinds. The only difficulty was in getting the raw materials — materials for lingerie, leather for shoes, and the copper, meerschaum, ivory, and mother-of-pearl for more luxurious products. There was a call for these things, Hilda Clark said, and she reminded Americans that Vienna was a "fertile field for investment."

Leaving Vienna for Paris, Jesse wrote to Rebe from the Hotel Brittanique on April 16, 1920, that, while some of the things he had done in Austria and Serbia were perhaps not very welcome (especially to Hilda Clark), he felt that his work as commissioner had been "much needed." He hoped that, although his successor as commissioner was arriving on that very day, he would be allowed to complete "the circuit of the field, if only to have some one see it as a whole, ..." (And, since Rebe had written that, in view of her duties at home in Swarthmore, she felt it best not to join him in England later on, he replied that "I feel more than I can say the need of thy presence to make life worth the living, . . ." "But, of course," he went on, ". . .it doesn't have to be well worth the living all the time, and I can be content to give these months to service, — at least I can be content part of the time and endure the rest of the time. . . .")

Jesse's hope that he might be instructed to complete the circuit of his inspection tour was realized soon after he wrote this letter to Rebe. He left Paris for Germany, going to Mayence, Frankfort, and Berlin by train. He arrived in Berlin about April 24, and went directly to the Friends' Mission Headquarters. Here he met Harold Evans, "who looked good, even if he is an 'orthodox'. . . ." Jesse also quickly located Alfred Scattergood, head of the American group, who briefed him on the situation there and then led the way to a long series of committee meetings and conferences with Germans, American workers, and with Quakers of the English mission. Joan Fry was the head of this latter group; Jesse found her "a sharp-featured, gray-haired woman with a cast in one eye, — not handsome but rather striking. . . ." Said to be primarily a preacher, she was surrounded by a group of argumentative idealists who were not doing an efficient job under her dictatorial direction. Very "tense and intense," she had worked herself into such an illness that there was talk of sending her home to England for a rest — "and to get her out of the way while the work is reorganized. . . ." Miss Fry *did* return to England, but when Carolena Wood stepped in to try to reorganize the work Jesse also found her "very dictatorial."

Perhaps such dictatorial methods were needed; in any case, after serving German children their first meal under Quaker-mission auspices on February 26, the work went on apace. One day, after visiting tourist attractions in Berlin, and after "a brief nap," Jesse visited one of the AFSC feeding centers. About 200 children were being fed here, the work of serving all being done by German women.

> The children were lined up and marched into the school house where the plates were already filled. . . . Some who were in very bad condition had to have very small helps [sic] at first, because their stomachs couldn't manage a square meal. One poor little girl couldn't eat at all, and wept bitterly. . . . One of the women took her on her lap and coaxed her a bit, . . .The little girl was very thin and pale, as indeed a large proportion of them were. . . .

This same sort of scene was being repeated all over Germany in the period February-May, 1920. As Jesse reported out of his experience as traveling and inspecting commissioner for the AFSC, some 700,000 children were given a daily meal during this period, and probably half a million would be fed during the winter of 1920-21 out of the supplies coming in through Hamburg.

The anticipation of so much need for food in 1920-21, not only in Germany but throughout Central Europe, must have been very much on Herbert Hoover's mind when he appeared before several hundred people at Haverford, Pennsylvania in December, 1920, to launch an appeal for $33,000,000 for European children. ". . .take as many of these invisible guests into your heart as your means can afford," he urged his Main Line audience. He went on:

> Within sixty days, if America does not furnish the money, three and one-half million children will be turned into the streets of Europe, to hunt, beg or steal food; the American flag will be taken down from 17,000 institutions and torn out of the hearts of millions of children. When they grow up, those who do survive, — our sons and daughters must deal with them. I tell you [that] to maintain the affection of those children is a greater protection than all the ships we have on the sea! *Peace is not made by documents, but in the hearts of men!* [author's italics]

Hoover's friends at Haverford followed this perfervid and prophetic appeal by asking that Friends give these ideas as much publicity as possible; also, that they should send their contributions to the AFSC headquarters at 20 South Twelfth Street, where they would be counted toward Hoover's goal of $33,000,000.

And this appeal brought results. By the time of the Philadelphia Yearly Meeting of Hicksites, May 9-13, Hannah Clothier Hull and William C. Biddle could report that, in Germany, "736,000 children were being given one supplemental meal each day before Easter," and that "plans were being completed for increasing this to 1,000,000 by the middle of May. . . ." Only the most nourishing foods were being sent: ". . .rice, peas, beans, flour, sugar, lard, cocoa, condensed and evaporated milk. In addition . . . , other things sent over included clothing and 153 barrels of cod-liver oil." (It must have embarrassed the American Quakers handing out these supplies to learn that a German woman, outside of the relief program, bought two cans of American pork and beans, only to find that no pork was to be found therein. She went to the AFSC headquarters in Berlin to find out "what we were going to do about it!") Still, this program went on so well that in July, 1922 it was handed over to the D.Z.A. (*Deutsche Zentval Ausschuss fur die Ausland's Hilfe*) for purely Germanic administration. But something must have gone wrong, because in 1923-1924 childfeeding was resumed under the direct care of the AFSC, with Henry Tatnall Brown and D. Robert Yarnall as successive directors.

While conditions in Germany were bad enough, they were even worse in Poland in the postwar years. Contesting armies had surged back and forth over parts of the land, opening the way for disease and laying waste the agricultural base in these areas. In early March, 1920, even before he visited Poland, Jesse reviewed the situation from reports he had received in his job as commissioner. He was "in full accord" with James Norton, the AFSC's on-the-spot supervisor, when Norton wrote that the situations in East Galicia and in the Lublin area were extremely precarious — typhus being epidemic in the first area and utter devastation prevailing in the second. And Norton, with Jesse's approval, called for more medical and agricultural help; the "grave immediate agricultural needs," according to Norton, would require a grant of thirty thousand dollars. A main task in this instance was to get the peasant farmers back into production. Tractors from the Friends' pool then in

France were put into service; and "the Polish Government. . .turned over 100 army horses as a loan for every square mile of land that [the farmers] were able to put under cultivation. . . ." with the help of AFSC agricultural experts. Here too the AFSC's aim was to stimulate recovery through self-help.

In addition, there was a great demand for trained social workers and nurses in Poland, particularly after the American Red Cross turned over the institutional and orphanage work to the Friends. Typhus was not the only disease threatening the population, we may be sure; and thousands of homeless children were in need of care. The AFSC organized a Health and Rehabilitation Unit of twenty-five workers, who, through rigid supervision of sanitation, were able to eradicate typhus in at least one town, although typhus claimed two of their group in the process. Rebecca Janney, Rebe Holmes' niece, and now a registered nurse and social worker, joined this unit, being responsible for a study of the needs of refugee children in orphanages and temporary shelters. Her report became a basis for the formation of mayors' committees in a number of towns to cooperate with the AFSC in child relief.

During her stay in Poland Rebecca Janney met Harry G. Timbres, a Haverford graduate also serving with the AFSC. Romance blossomed and they were married in 1922 in Warsaw under the oversight of English Quakers. Their honeymoon was spent, at least in part, in Russia, where from May to October, 1922 they joined the Famine Relief Unit then struggling not only with hunger but with the control of cholera. Here they organized districts into health areas to prevent cholera's spread, secured medical workers for these areas, supervised these workers, and allocated the necessary medical supplies.

And, as if Poland had not been afflicted enough by World War I, there was still another war going on by the time Jesse and T. Edmund Harvey visited that benighted country in May, 1920. Now the Polish Army, with French support, was battling the Bolsheviks for control of the Ukraine — a war which lasted from April 25 to October 12, and which made a large part of Poland still another war zone when the Russians counterattacked. Jesse and Harvey found travel difficult because the Polish Army used the best railroad equipment. In their travels they saw "hundreds of prisoners, trainloads of wounded, and thousands of refugees. . . ." Many refugees lived in abandoned railroad cars; everywhere were "ruined houses, homeless and starving children, broken and helpless old folk. . . ." As Jesse put it, "These are some of the details of the process of making the world safe for — whom?"

Lenin's cohorts, of course, were saying that it should be made safe for the Bolsheviks; and, when Jesse and Harvey arrived in Warsaw early in May they saw a "great 'Red' procession," along with some rioting and street fighting. ". . .there is electricity in the air. . . . ," Jesse wrote to his friends in America, "No one can say when or where there may be outbreaks of one kind or another."

After a few weeks in Poland, Jesse and Harvey went to Vienna to attend a general conference of all the Friends' missions in Europe. Here, from June 3rd to June 5th they joined in discussions of the general policies of their relief work, as well as the special problems and difficulties they had encountered. Leaving Vienna, Jesse and Harvey wound up their work as commissioners by opening an office at Frankfort-on-the-Main for the use of their successors. In this office the details of the purchase of supplies and the allocation of personnel would be attended to; it would also serve as a general clearinghouse for information for all the missions.

Having completed his tour of duty, Jesse returned to Swarthmore in the early summer of 1920. (His previous plans to attend the London Yearly Meeting had been changed by this Meeting's postponement to August; in any case he felt a financial-and-psychological urge to do some Chautauqua lecturing that summer.) He had done a fine job abroad, inspiring young people there just as he had done at home. Somehow his life style had effects as much on those young men who went into the army as on those conscientious objectors who formed the corps of workers for the AFSC. This is not to say that one type cancelled out the other, leaving Jesse with no balance of influence; it is to say that the members of each group found something in his teachings, his work and his example, which bolstered them in their own course of action. Those who knew Jesse Holmes had small cause to wonder why Owen Stephens dedicated his book *With Quakers in France* to him. Idealism has many faces.

Service in America

The work of the AFSC went on. Missions continued to serve in Europe and Asia wherever and whenever those outbreaks of trouble that Jesse Holmes had feared seemed to warrant the special talents and energies of Quaker workers. But, in the 1920s and 1930s it became apparent that there were also great fields for service back home on the American continent — areas where helpless victims of "man's inhumanity to man" were crying out with almost equal anguish for the alleviation of suffering and the redress of wrongs. In April, 1920, a Home Service Committee was added to the AFSC staff, and a call went out to young Friends across the United States to volunteer for at least one year of service before starting their life careers or businesses. Indeed, it was hoped that many qualified people would make public or community service their permanent careers.

On April 29, 1920, when there were rumors that American intervention in Mexico would endanger Mexican citizens' rights to their own oil — and because of the notoriously sad condition of Mexican peons — the AFSC decided to send representatives to Mexico in the interests of peace between the two nations. A Friends' mission was established at Tamaulipas, and a crate of thoroughbred poultry was sent to it, with eggs for hatching to be sent later. Also, there was some thought being given to the sending of thoroughbred and immunized cattle and hogs. For a while Douglas L. Parker and his wife were the AFSC representatives in Mexico City when he was a professor in the Union Theological Seminary there. The Parkers tried to get visiting Americans in touch with leaders of Mexico thought and influence for purposes of mutual understanding and trust between Mexican and Americans; they also studied local problems such as the gangs of orphan boys living on the streets. When Parker left Mexico in 1924 his replacement was Annie P. Carlysle, who continued the job until the Mexican work was closed in 1926.

In the meantime the Home Service Committee had found a fertile field for work in the bituminous-coal areas of West Virginia and western Pennsylvania, where the United Mine Workers were attempting to win union recognition and favorable contracts from 1919 through the 'twenties and into the period of the Depression. Strikes, bloody conflict, unemployment and economic distress were both epidemic and endemic, with the usual effects on wives and children. In April, 1922, the Committee decided to undertake relief work in West Virginia after hearing a report of conditions there from Walter Abell and Drew Pearson. And, although there were criticisms at first that these Quakers were interfering with "natural industrial adjustments," this relief work in West Virginia was but the beginning of a long series of similar relief missions, not only in this state but in western Pennsylvania, and in Kentucky, Tennessee, and Illinois. A child-feeding program was launched in West Virginia and Pennsylvania in 1922; in 1928 food and clothing were being distributed to miners' families in Barnesboro, Pennsylvania, with 750 children being fed daily; in 1931 AFSC officials met with President Hoover to discuss financing the coal-region relief project, as a result of which $225,000 of government funds were spent for food and clothing to be distributed in all the states mentioned above. In 1933 Clarence Pickett, executive secretary of the AFSC since 1929, announced a five-point program for the winter of 1933-1934 in the coal fields: (1) child feeding, (2) health, (3) training miners for new skills, (4) Quaker advisers for conflict situations, (5) providing leaders for subsistence homestead colonies. An agency of the federal government would assist in the last two programs.

Due no doubt to the implementation of Point 3 above, many unemployed miners began to make furniture to be offered for sale through the good offices of the AFSC. Thus, in 1933 plans were on foot to have Edith T. Maul exhibit these articles of furniture in New England and at the two Philadelphia Yearly Meetings. Even before this furniture program started — as early as the coal strikes of the 1920s — some miners built coffins and offered them for sale in their immediate neighborhoods. Jesse Holmes, visiting one of these areas in West Virginia with an AFSC group, let his impulsive good nature exceed his better judgment — he bought a coffin and had it shipped home to Swarthmore without informing Rebe that it was on its way. When the expressman deposited it on the front porch of the Holmes' resident on Whittier Place she was quite understandably startled. "What's this?" she asked. "Dr. Holmes' coffin," was the reply. It proved to be too large to be taken through the cellar door, so it was deposited in the basement of the Meeting House across the way, remaining there for years to the discomfort of more than one janitor. Jesse offered it to several of his elderly friends, but apparently no one could be found to fit it. (And, when Jesse and Rebe died, coffins were used only as carrying devices; they were cremated.)

Such humanitarian projects as retraining in productive skills, and child feeding, were as we have seen, the responsibilities of the Home Service Committee. This committee, with J. Barnard Walton as chairman, was one of the four parts into which the AFSC was

154

reorganized in 1925. William Eves, III, chaired the Foreign Section then; Raymond Bye headed the Interracial Section; and Vincent D. Nicholson was chairman of the Peace Section. From that time on to the present (with the Home Service Committee renamed the Social Order Section and then again changed to Social-Industrial Section), these sections and other special groups have served America and the world in a multitude of ways designed to lift the spiritual, moral, educational, and physical welfare of man. While the main office remained in Philadelphia, regional centers were established across the land from Massachusetts to California, with some gaps in the Deep South, the high arid plains beyond Colorado, and the tier of states bordering Canada. From the main office, and from these regional centers, plans were implemented for service in Japan and China, interracial and peace conferences were directed in such places as Haverford and Swarthmore Colleges, and peace caravans manned by college students were sent out across the land. Hardly a social or economic problem was neglected; helping people solve their problems became a voluntary religious duty.

In the areas of service described above the impact of the AFSC has been, in the strictest sense of the word, inestimable. Who can measure the sense of joy, relief, and security engendered by the appearance of the red-and-black star of the AFSC in the stricken areas of the world since 1917? Who can say how much the conscientious objectors were bolstered in their stand by the support of this organization, or how much peace-and-interracial projects have been advanced by its sponsorship? What instruments can tell us to what extent the peoples of the world appreciated the fact that AFSC projects were in the spirit of Christian democracy?

Only one estimate of the AFSC's impact can be made with a large degree of confidence in its accuracy — that the founding and operation of this Quaker institution had a great deal to do with unifying the Friends since the days of the German Kaiser. Henry Ferris, editor of the Hicksite *Friends' Intelligencer* in 1916, lamented the fact that up to that time liberal Quakers had disclaimed their responsibility for the *lack* of unity among Friends. " 'It is not *our* fault,' " he reported them as saying, " 'We are quite willing and should be glad to have unity. The trouble is with Orthodox Friends. You will not find *them* wanting to unite with us.' " But, as we have seen, when both liberal and conservative Friends were faced with a common enemy they joined hands and created the AFSC as a common achievement. Rufus Jones, leader of the Orthodox in 1919, recalled how, in 1917,

> . . .The call for relief, and the opportunity to serve which was now opened to Friends made a profound appeal to all the members everywhere. Divisions were disregarded and separations overlooked. . . . Nothing was said about unity. No labored efforts were made to heal breaches. Friends spontaneously *acted* together. . . . They simply found themselves working together in a great cause.

On the other side of the aisle in this newly created fellowship, Jesse H. Holmes in 1919 already a strong leader of the Hicksites, agreed with Rufus Jones about the AFSC's unifying effect in those years and added a thought about its possible effects in the future:

> . . .We have supplied many *individuals* to the great Christian causes, — free religion, free speech, the humane treatment of prisoners, temperance, the abolition of slavery, the emancipation of women, and many others; but our *Society* has never fully and officially accepted such duties to mankind as an essential part of the recognition of a universal brotherhood of men. We have lacked the form of organization which is necessary to open the way of service to our young folk of each generation. . . .
>
> . . .The American Friends' Service Committee, if continued, can be for our young members just that guiding and directing influence which we need for starting them aright and in the right spirit, into their 'reasonable service'. . . .

This vision of a better Quaker future was reinforced four years later by Hannah Clothier Hull and William C. Biddle when, as representatives of the AFSC, they reported on its recent activities to the Philadelphia Yearly Meeting of Hicksites. The report concluded with an exhortation addressed mainly to the young people who would carry the AFSC's banner in the future: "This work for humanity in time of peace calls for as much devotion and loyalty as is required of the soldier in time of war." Further, they implied that Quakers could hardly call themselves "Friends" unless they continued to show that same "splendid spirit of co-operation and harmony between workers" which had characterized Quakerism at home and abroad since the founding of the Committee. They went on:

> . . .If, in spite of our past differences, we can demonstrate to the world that in matters of common and vital interest we can work together in effective co-operation, we will have justified our assertion that it is possible for peoples of differing beliefs and national affiliations to join in the worth-while things of life. Unless we are

able to do this it is useless for us to undertake to bring the message of peace and good will to the contending forces of Europe.

This was written in 1923. The record of the AFSC since that time has shown that, on the whole, the idealistic conceptions of the Ferrises, the Joneses, the Holmeses, the Hulls and the Biddles have produced fine fruits, not only in America but in Europe and in the nations of the Third World. Perhaps it is not too much to say that one of those fruits was the more secular Peace Corps starting out so bravely in the Kennedy administration; at least the AFSC, in company with the missionary societies of other churches, was a suggestive predecessor in voluntary world service — and one which continues to carry on the good work.

Jesse and Rebe about 1922
Medium File Portraits, Friends Historical Library,
Swarthmore College.

The autobiographical rug — Jesse R. Holmes
Photograph by the author; courtesy Grace R. Holmes

9. High Tide in Swarthmore's Aydelotte Years

About a year after Jesse returned from his AFSC adventures in Europe a new spirit and a new force began to quicken the life of Swarthmore College. That force and spirit was Frank Aydelotte, A.B., Indiana University, 1900; A.M., Harvard, 1903; and the proud possessor of a B.Litt. earned as a Rhodes Scholar at Oxford in 1908. In most recent years he had been making the study of English literature an exciting thing at the Massachusetts Institute of Technology; now, in 1921, he accepted the all-Quaker Board of Manager's offer to become president.

When Aydelotte accepted this offer the Swarthmore catalog showed an enrollment of 510 students, the 10 being thought to provide enough margin over 500 to allow for what the dean called "shrinkage." Less than a fourth of these students came from Quaker families, and the proportion of Friends on the faculty of forty-seven was even smaller. Nor was Aydelotte a Friend, although during his nineteen-year tenure as president he often took his place on the facing benches in the meeting house on the edge of the campus and contributed his thoughts to the meeting's discussions. In spite of his obvious empathy with Quakers and their principles he would not join the group officially until he had given up the presidency. His reasons — given no doubt with a twinkle in his blue eyes — were that by remaining the non-Quaker president of a Quaker school he could show the Friends' broad-mindedness, and that this outside position would make it less painful to all concerned if he wanted something the Board of Managers opposed.

The college he was to direct had reached very respectable academic standing under President Joseph Swain. Its curriculum was like that prevailing in other fine church-related liberal arts colleges. The first two years were given over to basic courses in religion, foreign languages, English, mathematics, a laboratory science, and one of the social sciences; the last two years were open to the pursuit of a speciality or specialties. As was also true of some other liberal-arts colleges such as Lafayette, a bow was made to the practical or vocational through courses in the training of teachers and engineers. Altogether, Aydelotte thought, the Swarthmore curriculum was not outstanding, but it did offer a firm basis for what he wanted to accomplish.

And what he wanted to accomplish was given in broad outline in his inaugural address on October 22, 1921. Perhaps, as he strode up to the lectern on that beautiful fall day, his audience was not initially impressed by this little man with the bald head and the large gnomelike ears. But, as he got into his speech, it became apparent that here was a warm and sincere man — and a man possessed by a Big Idea of tremendous import to Swarthmore and to American higher education in general.

The Early Honors System under Aydelotte

The Big Idea was not his alone, nor was it new. It was, reduced to its core, a plan to so order the education of American youth that the potential leaders of society would be stimulated to educate themselves more thoroughly under the guidance of wise and able teachers; those who were not so well-endowed mentally, or who had a less urgent inherent drive toward leadership, were also to have their standards of accomplishment raised above the levels commonly accepted in the ordinary college. He was to call this plan the "honors system," and it called for the general uplift and stimulation of both potential leaders and their informed followers; it was a compromise between quantity and quality, with the emphasis on the latter; and it aimed to liberate higher education, at least in part, from that academic bookkeeping of credit-and-quality points which Aydelotte found so abhorrent. He wished to break the "academic lockstep" of programmed progress toward a degree, which so often left the thinking element of the student body feeling frustrated and unsatisfied. And, since the ideal of a liberal education which fitted a man or a woman for all the higher duties of life in a democracy was one America could not afford to lose, he asserted that it was more important to teach people how to live than to teach them how to make a living. Fundamentally, his aim was to rescue democracy from materialistic mediocrity by making education not only a compromise between opposites — quality and quantity, choice and compulsion, a curriculum too narrow or too broad, the individual and the mass —, but by making learning an active and positive process very different from the passive "soak-it-up" methods relying on textbooks, lectures, and recitations.

The major ways to accomplish what Aydelotte had in mind had been suggested well before his appearance at Swarthmore in 1921. Socrates, speaking through Plato's *Republic,* had proposed a weeding-out process of state education leading to the eventual selection of philosopher-kings to govern Athens. Thomas Jefferson, well-read in the classics, proposed a similar plan for public education which would, under conditions of equal opportunity, lead to the governing of Virginia by an aristocracy of proven talent. And, in the era of John Dewey's progressive education, with its emphasis on the experimental cultivation of individuals who would lead other citizens to an idealistic reconstruction of society, there was small doubt among Swarthmore's leading professors that Aydelotte's suggested "new" program was the plan to guide them to an educational heaven.

Aydelotte brought to Swarthmore ideas he had picked up when he was in one of the earliest groups of American Rhodes Scholars at Oxford University. Here he lived in a small residential college where the individual student was stimulated by his tutors to thorough, independent study, the results of which were finally tested in a comprehensive set of examinations. Under this method of study the student could develop his interest more intensely in a given area of learning, could see the range of relationships of parts within that area, and the relationships between that area and other areas. It developed a feeling of responsibility in the student for his own education, and it opened up to him methods of research and thinking which carried over into life beyond the halls of ivy in later years.

Since the same and similar advantages could be expected to flow from the transplating of the Oxford system to Swarthmore, many of the faculty members were eager to begin the experiment. The inauguration ceremony in which Aydelotte had explained the general nature of the honors system was hardly over when he was asked by a group of faculty, "When do we begin?" He immediately appointed a committee to develop plans for the initiation of the program the following September. This committee labored long and hard to integrate the new program with the ongoing Swarthmore system, its work not being easier by the fact that instructors undertaking to engage in it would still have to meet their regular classes and would not get an extra salary. Aydelotte hoped that they would volunteer and think of the work as a privileged opportunity.

And those two "irrepressible lively" teachers — Jesse Holmes in philosophy, and R.C. Brooks in political science — helped the cause along by jumping the gun. They would not wait until next September; they decided to make trial runs the very next semester with two small senior classes. Hearing that the honors students would meet in small groups like graduate seminars, they organized their groups to meet once a week, when the students would report on their semiguided reading since the last meeting, and when probing discussions examined the meaning and significance of what they had read. Since both Holmes and Brooks were experts at leading discussions, the trial runs proved to be excellent advertisements for the honors program. When the plans for the following year were explained in *The Phoenix*, the writer of the article pointed out that the honors technique was already functioning with great success. " 'The higher value of the new plan,' " he wrote, " 'as estimated by students who are studying under both the old and new systems, promises well of any arrangement that may be made to extend this program.' "

With this auspicious beginning, an extended program was begun in the fall of 1922. Honors courses were offered in two areas or divisions: English Literature, drawing on English, history, and philosophy professors for expert guidance; and the Social Sciences, entailing political science, economics, history, and philosophy. The presence of history and philosophy in both of these major areas reflected the belief of the planners in the bridging and unifying powers of these studies, serving to bind all other subjects together.

In that first year four teachers devoted their outstanding talents to the continuing success of the honors program: Jesse Holmes, Robert C. Brooks, William I Hull, and Harold Clarke Goddard. Passing over Ducky Holmes for the moment, special notice should be taken of R.C. Brooks since he was to become the honors program's chief enthusiast, promoter, and first historian. By 1929 he had taken enough time from his manifold activities as head of the department of political science, and from his very active membership in the American Political Science Association and the Social Science Research Council, to write *Reading for Honors at Swarthmore* (1927), and a chapter on honors work in Robert Kelly's *The Effective College* (1928). William I. Hull, Quaker pacifist whose courses in history were beamed toward internationalism with a Friendly flavor, drove his car to his appointed classes with a majestic disregard for the safety of passengers or pedestrians. Harold Clarke Goddard, "perceptive and subtle" professor of English, loved good music, Henry Thoreau, and Russian novels.

The work of these four men, plus the other professors soon to be drawn into the honors plan, was coordinated by Raymond Walters, who had been appointed dean in 1921. Walters had come to Swarthmore from his post as registrar of Lehigh University, where he was noted, among other things, for his work with the Bach Choir. Under his understanding direction not only was the honors system extended in those departments already mentioned but carried over into the sciences, foreign languages, and engineering.

Although a variety of honors methods came to be used to meet the special need of various fields of learning, an overall pattern of principles and methods emerged quite early. Only juniors and seniors would take honors, their programs taking the place of the five regular three-credit courses constituting a semester's work. Now the emphasis was on topics or subjects such as "Pragmatism" rather than on courses, and a student focused his reading on these and related topics in the original sources from bibliographies provided by his instructor. After a seminar got started, often involving only three-to-six students, the weekly three-hour meetings would be given over to the reading of student-research essays on aspects of the general topic, followed by close analysis and criticism by the students' peers and by the professor. The Holmes-Brooks experiment had helped set this pattern, as well as the practice (abandoned later on) of having professors drop in on each others' seminars to help along in the discussions in the spirit of interdepartmental unity. And this "dropping in" was made easier and more pleasant by the practice of conducting seminars in the professors' homes, with their wives serving tea, cookies, and other such refreshments about halfway through each session. Sometimes the sessions were stimulated still more by the presence of outstanding visitors to the campus, as in the time Langston Hughes, a rising young Negro poet, attended a seminar conducted by Professor Brooks.

After two years of this sort of intensive reading, writing, discussion, and cookie-crunching, the honors candidates were called to account by a system of examinations such as those given at Oxford. This involved the use of professors from other institutions — called the "external examiners" — to set both written and oral examinations in the interests of objectivity. These examiners, after studying the seminar syllabus and other descriptions of the work covered, sent their questions to the department head involved, who had the responsibility to see that they were not too broad nor too narrow, that they were on the topics studied, and that there was some choice as to which questions might be answered. Two weeks in the spring of the senior year were set aside to allow for as much time as possible between each of the eight written examinations each student took. The writing of the papers was done under the supervision of proctors, and three-and-a-quarter hours were allowed for each test. At the end of each test the proctor delivered the papers to the dean's office for immediate mailing to the examiners.

Having read the students' papers, the examiners then visited the Swarthmore campus, the last two-or-three days of the two weeks' period being given over to oral examinations. Each examiner had read one or more papers written by the student he was interviewing; it was considered important to be able to judge to what extent the student was able to discuss intelligently what he had written. His ability to show, both in writing and orally, that the knowledge he had gained was a vital and integrated part of his intellectual equipment, was then made the basis of the rating he was given by his examiners — Highest Honors, High Honors, and Honors. Two other ratings were also available: Pass or Fail.

These ratings were relayed to the faculty and to the students almost immediately, since the interest in the results was very keen. Indeed, the two-weeks honors examination period generated a tension and an excitement on the Swarthmore campus usually seen only on football weekends at some other schools. The proud payoff, of course, came in June, when the commencement program identified those earning the various degrees of honors; and in the times when the honors' ratings helped students earn graduate fellowships.

In the beginning of the program, to ease the transition from the customary local-faculty testing to the new outside-examiner system, a compromise was made. Of the three examiners chosen to test three seniors in 1923, one, Harry A. Overstreet, popular professor of philosophy at City College in New York, was strictly unconnected with Swarthmore. (But, Aydelotte was pleased to know, Overstreet had studied at Balliol in Oxford.) J. Russell Smith, professor of economic geography at Columbia, lived on the edge of the campus and was one of the outstanding members of Swarthmore Meeting. And R.C. Brooks, that ardent advocate of honors, not only read student papers and conducted oral examinations, but served as the on-the-scene coordinator for the examination procedures. The results of the testing by these three gave no candidate the highest ranking: two seniors were thought to deserve second honors, and one placed third.

After this trial run the honors examiners were chosen exclusively from other colleges and universities. In 1926, for instance, Dumas Malone of the University of Virginia joined Professor Turner of Johns Hopkins in examining students in history; Moreland King of Lafayette and O.W. Eshbach of Lehigh tested engineers; and Harry Overstreet and Robert M. Scoon (Princeton) probed the minds of honors candidates in philosophy. Of the other examiners, all were from colleges and universities within a radius of one hundred and fifty miles from Swarthmore, except Miss Helen Darbishire of Somerville College, Oxford.

And it was this Miss Darbishire, a former colleague of Frank Aydelotte's at Oxford, who precipitated a crisis in the honors program and caused the Swarthmore authorities to reexamine their teaching methods. She was the leading examiner of a field of twelve candidates in English literature — students who had looked forward to being tested by an Oxford don. They did not find her unusually difficult in the written examinations, and thought that she had been skillful and friendly in the orals. So it came as a shock to the Swarthmore community to discover that only five out of the twelve students were judged by Miss Darbishire to deserve honors at any level; six were recommended for simple pass degrees, and one failed entirely.

Subsequent interviews with Miss Darbishire, plus some agonizing self-analyses by the honors staff at Swarthmore, finally led to the conclusion that, in the seminars that had been held to date, too much play had been given to personal opinions by both teachers and students about controversial topics — and at the expense of a body of central knowledge in general fields of learning. While this incident might have dealt a lethal blow to the Swarthmore program, it served instead as a healthy corrective, and as a spur to future success.

Indeed, the program had been successful enough under American examiners to spark a lot of interest among those who had the wherewithal to subsidize its continuance. On February 28, 1925, President Aydelotte announced at a meeting of the Swarthmore Club that the General Education Board of the Rockefeller Foundation had awarded the college a series of appropriations on a yearly basis which would total $240,000 by 1930 if the honors system proved to be a continuing success. Aydelotte, as a matter of course, used this announcement as the springboard for a continuing appeal for more endowment funds from other supporters of the Swarthmore experiment in the cultivation of academic excellence.

The help of the Rockefeller Foundation, plus endowments from other sources, encouraged Aydelotte to increase and strengthen his faculty in 1925. Brand Blanshard, Rhodes Scholar, and then assistant professor of philosophy at the University of Michigan, was hired on a permanent basis to help along with the chores in the department of philosophy; he was to take charge of the department while Jesse Holmes was away on a sabbatical-year's journey. Blanshard's wife Frances would also do some teaching in philosophy, and would later on become an effective dean of women. Everett L. Hunt, for some years professor of public speaking at Cornell, was hired to replace Hoyt H. Hudson, who had gone on to fulfill a professorship in English at the University of Pittsburgh. As Professor Hudson said, the college was very lucky to get Everett Hunt; he not only taught public speaking and coached the debating squad with great success, but went on to lend the position of dean of men at Swarthmore an unusual air of academic distinction. In addition, Frederick J. Manning, then an instructor at Yale, was taken on to help William I. Hull in history. His wife, Helen Taft Manning, was the daughter of William Howard Taft, former President of the United States, and had already won her standing in the scholastic world through her job as dean of Bryn Mawr College. (In 1929, when her husband's car, a 1918-model "livid-green" Franklin, was wrecked in a newly constructed road near Bryn Mawr, the Swarthmore *Phoenix* bemoaned the passing of "a real, valued friend" — that Franklin which had made "the campus brighter by its coming. . . .")

Of all these changes in faculty personnel, perhaps the one that affected Jesse Holmes the most was the hiring of Brand Blanshard as assistant professor of philosophy. Jesse was then in his sixty-first year, was not greatly interested in speculative philosophy, and was glad to get the help of Blanshard both for the regular courses and the growing number of honors seminars. Holmes was, as we have seen, an idealistic pragmatist interested in applying scientific method to philosophy and religion; Blanshard was inclined toward a more purely idealistic position in philosophy, and had been brought to Swarthmore by Aydelotte not only because of his general scholarship but because of his expertise in seminar honors work. The two made a fine team, attending philosophical meetings together, and in 1927 collaborated in helping to work out a college-wide system of trial examinations for honors students. In this system, which was undoubtedly a reaction to the poor showing made when Miss Darbishire was on campus the year before, Holmes would give oral quizzes to Blanshard's students, while Blanshard would do the same to the honors people taught by Holmes. In this way they hoped to stimulate their students to get ready for the unknown modes of questioning that the external examiners might use. In 1928 they worked up a seminar for honors students in the physical sciences to be conducted jointly under the title of "Logic and Scientific Methods." Charles C. Price, '34, who was to go on to become chairman of the chemistry department at the University of Pennsylvania, wrote enthusiastically of what this course, or variations of it, had meant to him. In the hands of Blanshard and Holmes, the study of logic and philosophy in relation to science ". . . inspired a view of science beyond the . . . technical and set science in a perspective of the total human endeavor which has been an important characteristic of my career as a scientist."

Altogether, the Homes-Blanshard relationship was a most cordial one. In the honors-examination period late in May of 1927, Jesse and Rebe entertained the Blanshards at dinner, the occasion serving also to make Professors Piccard and Scoon, as outside examiners, feel more at home in the Swarthmore family. And, when Blanshard succeeded Holmes as head of the department in 1928, Blanshard never got "one bitter word or sullen look or grudging gesture; never anything but a good will that was whole-hearted and even gay. . . ."

This attitude, of course, made the older man's conquest of his lieutenant complete. Blanshard "vowed that any request from Jesse Holmes should be a command."

Jesse's part in the honors program, and his effect on students, is well illustrated by the experiences of three people taking a philosophy seminar with him in their junior year (1928). Beth Harbold was in it, and Ruth Cleaver and Harold Carter. (The latter two helped build the reputation of Swarthmore as "the little Quaker matchbox" — they started a romance here lasting for some forty years.) As Harold Carter and his wife remembered it, this seminar started out as a "traumatic experience." The group met in the Holmes' living room. Jesse came in, greeted them, and then asked whether they had purchased the syllabus for the course. Beth Harbold had done so, but Harold was then asked to get two copies — one for himself and one for Ruth.

The seminar began with a brief description of its purposes and the methods to be used. In succeeding sessions, held once a week in the afternoon, these young people learned what it meant to come up against a first-class mind. On one occasion Harold procrastinated in the writing of the weekly research paper expected of all students; his paper was hurriedly thrown together in the morning for that afternoon's seminar. As Harold read his paper Jesse nodded, smiled — and then began to frown. When Harold had finished Jesse said, "Harold, thee did well, *as far as thee went.*" And Ruth thought that he was a genius in getting students to do their own thinking. This prodding, of course, upset many people — especially religious people — who could not stand a questioning of their convictions. But, Ruth and Harold agreed, Jesse simply played the part of the devil's advocate in these seminar discussions: whenever he found that a student took a positive position on a given issue, he took an opposite stance to force the student to defend his position with facts and logic. Seldom did Jesse give a hint as to what his own actual position was on any given topic or issue.

And this seminar group found out that the whole process was suffused with a kindly encouragement. When, in one seminar meeting, Jesse seemed to favor the Russian system of state-run nurseries for the care of the children of working mothers, Ruth thought that this was absolutely wrong. Family life was needed. When she was unable to muster adequate counter arguments she burst into tears. This emotional outburst rather effectively ended the seminar session. But Ruth was not allowed to leave before Jesse put an arm around her shoulders and said, "Don't get upset; next time I'll take the other side." About a year later, when Harold was to be orally examined by Dr. Scoon of Princeton in Whittier House, he could see Jesse, in his flowing cape and blowing white hair, coming to meet him. Jesse said, "Harold, if thee have no objections, I'd like to sit in on your session with Dr. Scoon." Harold did *not* want him sitting there, "like a cat watching a bird," but couldn't prevent it. Dr. Scoon and Harold "went at it" for some forty minutes: whenever Harold saw a philosophical or logical trap coming up he reverted to basic points. Finally Dr. Scoon said, with a smile, "That will be all, Harold. Good luck!" (Harold wasn't at all sure whether this was a way of softening a failure; as it turned out, Dr. Scoon thought he had passed with ease.) After the ordeal was over, Jesse came up to Harold from his position in the hall where Harold hadn't been able to see him, threw his arm around his shoulders, and said, "Harold, thee did well." (This personal concern for a student's welfare, added to other Holmesian qualities, led Harold to vote for Jesse when he ran as Socialist candidate for governor of Pennsylvania later on. As Harold said, with a chuckle, "I was probably the only member of the Philadelphia Union League to vote for him.")

Elizabeth Harbold, the third member of this seminar, agreed with "Nick" Carter and Ruth Cleaver on Jesse's qualities as a friendly mentor. On a wet, blustery day she arrived at the Holmes' residence with soaked shoes. Jesse immediately gave her his wool bedroom slippers and put her shoes to dry on the kitchen stove. And, while she was laboring on her written honors examination in 1929, Jesse stopped at her table to read some of what she had written. Although he was honorbound not to speak to her, his encouraging smile boosted her "weary spirit."

George W. Stewart, who was to make his mark as a writer and book editor, studied philosophy with Jesse for two years. He was "tremendously" impressed with his wide range of interests and knowledge, and Jesse's way of cultivating the open mind, which he called "the divine state of uncertainty." To Stewart he was "a special person" — one with "the emotional discipline of the Friends, the objective discipline of good science, and the ready warmth of humanism. . . ." And, as Stewart and others in his classes and seminars testified, he influenced their thinking and behavior for the rest of their lives by engendering a respect for truth arrived at through research and discussion, and a feeling of responsibility to apply these truths in community service.

These values were of course also developed by other members of the growing department of philosophy. Perhaps some of the new members to be added in Jesse's time were among those present at the Christmas-holiday meeting of the Eastern division of the American Philosophical Association in 1925, when seventy philosophers were right royally entertained at Swarthmore by President Aydelotte, by Charles F. Jenkins (vice-president, Board of Managers), and by Jesse Holmes as local organizer. Dr. Alexander Meiklejohn, retiring president of the Association, used the occasion of their banquet to urge American thinkers to become involved in public life, "to write the program of future democracy. . . ."

No doubt stimulated by this call to action in the exciting intellectual atmosphere of Aydelotte's Swarthmore, five philosophy instructors joined the staff as the need developed and finances permitted. Brand Blanshard, as we have seen, brought his talents; his wife Frances not only taught philosophy briefly, but, even as a busy dean of women, was able to continue her writing. Among other things she wrote an article, "Socrates as a Quaker," in which she thought that "If the Society of Friends should undertake to find a patron saint among the ancients, the natural choice would be Socrates. . . ." Not for his philosophy, certainly, but for "his simplicity, love of people, courage and mysticism. . ." (She was to go on to write a definitive biography of Frank Aydelotte, about equal in adulation with the Swarthmore Faculty's *An Adventure in Education.*)

A year or so after the Blanshards had established themselves at Swarthmore, G.F. Thomas joined the staff, not only hired because he was a Rhodes Scholar with a doctorate from Harvard, but because he was an expert in ethics and metaphysics. Later on he was to become professor at Dartmouth and then head of the department of religion at Princeton. Soon John W. Nason joined them; he was to succeed Aydelotte as president at Swarthmore and became head of the United Nations Association. Then Maurice H. Mandelbaum taught for a period before he went on to Dartmouth, Johns Hopkins, and to the presidency of the American Philosophical Association. The latter honor also was earned by Professor Brandt, who, after teaching for a while at Swarthmore, became chairman of philosophy at Michigan.

Academic Excellence Extended and Tested.

These scholars fitted very well into a faculty distinguished not only by their learning and educational leadership but by their research and scholarly writing. John A. Miller, long head of the department of mathematics and astronomy, continued to lead one astronomical expedition after another, and, with the approval of Aydelotte, instituted a limited program of postgraduate studies in Sproul Observatory. When he retired, Arnold Dresden became head of the Division of Mathematics and Natural Science, and served as president of the Mathematical Association of America in 1934. Alan Valentine, Rhodes Scholar and assistant professor of English, became dean of men in 1929, succeeding Detlev W. Bronk, who had pursued his studies in physiology so well that he was offered the directorship of the Johnson Foundation for Medical Research at the University of Pennsylvania. (Dr. Bronk went on to become "the father of American biophysics" and the president of both Johns Hopkins and Rockefeller University. While heading the National Academy of Sciences from 1950 to 1962 he was science adviser to Presidents Truman, Eisenhower, and Kennedy. When Sputnik I was launched in 1957 he sent out a cold-war warning, telling Americans to eschew short work weeks and long coffee breaks.) At the Founders' Day exercises in 1927 it was announced that Dr. W.F.G. Swann, director of the Bartol Laboratories of the Franklin Institute, was bringing the Bartol Laboratories to the Swarthmore campus, opening up still more opportunities for research in physics. Research in the sciences had been going on at Swarthmore for sometime; indeed, it had been done so well that in 1923 Swarthmore became the only small college to win a chapter in Sigma Xi, the national science society hitherto restricted to the larger colleges and universities. Sigma Xi has continued to function, as it did in 1928, when Dr. Robert E. Rose, of the chemical research staff of the DuPont Corporation, addressed its meeting on "The Economics of Research."

And research was done in other areas as well. John W. Graham, an English Friend, was the first occupant of the Howard M. Jenkins Chair of Quaker History and Research. By 1930 William I. Hull held this chair, working in that wing of the newly constructed college library to be called the Friends' Historical Library. Certainly

171

the general college library furnished material for many other research professors, as it did for Brand Blanshard when he worked on his book, *The Nature of Thought* (1935). And no doubt Clair Wilcox, an economist also interested in crime prevention, used the library to gather ammunition for his study on the parole system in Pennsylvania. In 1930 he became a member of the Wickersham Commission appointed by President Hoover to study law enforcement in the United States; in 1934 he was made one of the four members of the General Code Authority of the NRA.

With such people on its faculty, and with an honors program being increasingly imitated by other colleges such as Haverford, it was not surprising that in its annual report in 1927 the Carnegie Foundation for the Advancement of Teaching included Swarthmore with Harvard and Toronto as the Big Three in American education. Things seemed to be going very well; the fruits of Aydelotte's seeds were apparently in robust health, offering all who came to Swarthmore in search of educational sustenance an excellent and well-balanced fare.

But there were several worms in the apple. Not all of these distinguished faculty people had great teaching skill; indeed, Richard G. Hubler, who was to dedicate his first book to Jesse (it was on Lou Gehrig — "Not exactly a book on philosophy but at least one I wrote"), said later that Jesse was the only professor whose lectures and seminars he really enjoyed during his stay at Swarthmore from 1930 to 1934. Other faculty members, through their assignments, "often interfered with the research I wanted to do on my own. . . ." Hubler and other students (particularly those not in the honors program, which included the freshmen and sophomores), also resented the closing of the library stacks to all except professors and honors students. While a general student could gain access to the stacks for a specific and limited time upon presentation of a written request from his professor, it *was* for a limited and specific time only, and few students took the time and trouble to secure the written permission. This "reserved-stacks" rule was such a constant source of irritation to students like Hubler that in 1934 the stacks were opened again to all students.

This concession did not heal the rift which had been growing between honors students and regular classroom students. As an editorial in *The Phoenix* put it as early as 1928, there was an increasing "mutual contempt" between the two elements; student body unity was being destroyed. So level-headed a person as James Michener, while reading for honors with Dr. Goddard in 1928, thought that he had spotted at least "three dozen" self-proclaimed and "misunderstood" geniuses on the campus, people who, by their airs and actions, gave the impression that they were superior to others. And the Aydelotte administration stood accused of selecting entering freshmen, not with an eye to developing the all-round person, or to bolster athletic teams, but to favor those who might become honors candidates. And there was some truth to this charge: certainly the system of Open Scholarships, ostensibly open to all types of students, placed the emphasis on scholarly achievement; and the various fellowships for graduate study — such as the Lippincott, the Hannah A. Leedom, and the Lucretia Mott — went to those who had demonstrated superior ability in their classes and seminars. The charge that the Swarthmore system was producing intellectual snobs grew so loud that in 1937 a two-hour student forum was held in the Bond Memorial Hall to give students a chance to air their opinions and suggest ways to improve the system. Professor Everett L. Hunt presided, and the meeting quickly heard criticisms not only of the honors program, but of the new Aydelotte four-course plan for general students. The claim was made that the old five-course plan had given them a broader liberal education and had allowed them, as freshmen and sophomores, to fulfill the prerequisities for their majors and minors more easily. A former student, hearing of the argument at his alma mater, wrote to *The Phoenix* that, on the whole, he believed that the college should stop applying the Aydelotte principle of concentrated excellence to the first two years; he advocated a return to the old five-course plan. He thought that "most people still . . . go to college for a liberal and a fairly broad cultural education rather than for a specialized . . . training."

So both sides to the general education-honors issue were heard and ably defended in the years 1921-1939. There was no doubt that life at Swarthmore was not the academic paradise that its proponents sometimes pictured in their many books, articles, and speeches. Still, Aydelotte's record by 1939, when he resigned to head the Institute for Advanced Study at Princeton, was an enviable one. Under his leadership the college had become a national and international symbol for excellence in education. Jesse Holmes, so much like Aydelotte in so many ways, counted himself fortunate that the high tide of his career had come in a time when Swarthmore College had demonstrated that learning can be an exciting adventure.

And, as we shall see, this excitement was felt not only in classes and seminars, but in the many and everchanging activities on the campus.

Jesse's son, Jesse H. Holmes III, holding up the composite portrait of The Ancestor, William Holmes.
Artist — Rae Zilboorg
Courtesy Mr. & Mrs. Jesse H. Holmes III, Washington, D.C.
Photograph by the author, 1973.

10. A Rich Campus Life

In 1927 Swarthmore College had 561 students; by 1936, despite
Frank Aydelotte's wish to retain an ideal size of 500, the student
population had risen to 706, with men and women in exactly equal
proportions.

These students, and their faculty friends, were in a position to
take advantage of the rich smorgasbord of educational and cultural
opportunities afforded by Philadelphia, its environs, and by their
own campus. In Philadelphia, only a short distance away, they
could attend symphony concerts and see traveling operas; they
could visit museums, libraries and art exhibits. At home, in the
Swarthmore atmosphere, they were impelled to attend, or take part
in, so many artistic, scientific, or mixed extracurricular activities
that one girl student became worried. After all, she told her friends,
"our parents sent us here to study."

While Swarthmore probably would have had to plead guilty —
along with many other American colleges — to the charge that it
was overorganized, this girl somehow missed the main point. The
main point was that, although no one really denied the values of
concentrated study, the extracurricular activities at Swarthmore
offered opportunities to round out what was learned in the
classroom: to learn social graces, to develop other skills, and to keep
abreast of the best and latest developments in music, art, literature,
science, and all the other aspirations of the human spirit.

And this point was made most effectively in *The Phoenix* on
March 13, 1928. The writer of the article reminded his readers that
many of the cultural opportunities at Swarthmore had been
provided through the Cooper Foundation. This foundation had been
established through the generosity of William J. Cooper of

Haverford, who wanted to see lecturers and musical artists of the highest caliber enrich the life of Swarthmore. The writer also extolled the cultural benefits to be derived from attendance and membership in the many clubs at Swarthmore — the Sigma Xi, the Philosophy Club, the Engineers' Club, the English Club, and the Trotter Biological Society. These were given only as examples; the list of other clubs and opportunities for personal enrichment outside of the classroom would have been much longer.

All of these extracurricular activities, for both students and faculty, refreshed the spirit of those interested in the search for truth — that search which was the hallmark of the Swarthmore experiment in higher education. We may well believe that, when couples strolled hand-in-hand down the wooded slopes leading to the Scott Outdoor Auditorium on a beautiful spring or fall day, they were engaged in a search for truth. And we may believe that, when Dean Walter and his wife served as chaperons for the leap-year dance held in the Somerville Hall gymnasium in 1925, this ideal was held inviolate. ("The men could only attend when invited by the women, and the 'stag' line was replaced by the 'doe' line.") Three years later the Blanshards served as chaperons at a costume dance held in the same hall, with music by the Garnet Serenaders, the local college dance band. (Ruth Cleaver, '30, and William Poole, '30, won the prizes for their Russian peasant costumes.) There were, to be sure, more formal dances, as in the time the sophomore class held its annual affair in the men's gymnasium, with huge silver '38s against a background of blue. Paul Bird's Orchestra furnished the music, and coffee was served in activity centers before the dance.

The faculty, of course, had its own social life, a social life often connected with professional concerns. As we have seen, there was a lot of informal entertaining in faculty homes; there were also opportunities for women, including faculty wives, to become involved in the meetings of the Somerville Society and the American Association of University Women. Their husbands, still operating in a male-dominated society, found congeniality in the Men's Faculty Club, which met periodically in its clubhouse on Walnut Lane until that was sacrificed as a dormitory for women students. But there were other outlets for faculty social energies, as seen in the meeting of the Fullerton Club of Philadelphia, held in Pottstown, Pennsylvania on May 11, 1929, when Jesse Holmes, and Brand and Frances Blanshard, joined other professors from the leading colleges in the Philadelphia area at dinner to discuss their common problems.

There were some national Greek-letter social "fraternities" at Swarthmore by 1930: seven for the women, and six for the men. Although President Aydelotte had been a fraternity man at Indiana University, he could now see that what might be desirable for a large state university in the way of such elitist social clubs was not equally desirable in a small college where daily contacts between students was inevitable. Under such a realization, fraternity houses for men did not exist; the men lived in Wharton Hall, and their fraternity groups were restricted to meeting in special lodges set aside for their social purposes on the edge of the campus. And the mere existence of the women's "fraternities" had been a bone of contention since 1911; it was felt that they constituted a threat to the working out of the democratic principle at Swarthmore. Finally, after "a long and tiresome conflict," in 1933 a poll of the women in Collection resulted in the abolition of women's fraternities by a vote of 168 to 109.

There were, of course, other possibilities open to Swarthmore women. Those who "just had to get away from it all" after the strain of midyear examination could go to Skytop in the Poconos for a weekend of skiing, skating, toboganning, and dancing in the company of young men. This weekend house party between semesters had become something of a tradition by 1937; the wintertime frolic in that year was to be the ninth annual trip for the Skytop Club. And in 1939 still another possibility for the release of nervous tension was being considered by the Women's Athletic Association: the erection of a small cabin about twenty miles from Swarthmore to serve as a hideaway for individuals and small groups. This cabin was to have a living room with a fireplace, double bunks around the walls and a kitchen. Swimming and skating would be afforded by a small creek, and neighboring hills offered skiing. These plans were drawn up by Norris Jones, part-time instructor in mechanical drawing, and by Carl Delmuth, owner of the property. (Whether this hideaway dream was realized the author isn't sure; probably not, since the Second World War disrupted the American scene soon after these plans were made.)

Sports.

On October 1, 1921, a motor cavalcade of Swarthmore faculty

177

members, organized by the Faculty Club, set out on a trip to Princeton to watch the annual football game between the "Little Quakers" and the Tigers. Dean Walters was in the party, as were Jesse Holmes, Robert Spiller, and Professors Hicks, Brooks, Palmer, Roberts, Myers, and Marriott. One can see them now — rolling along on this beautiful fall day, telling jokes and stories, and anticipating the vicarious thrills of spectators at the modern American equivalent of the medieval tournament.

But the days devoted to this sort of a junket under the old system of varsity sports were numbered at Swarthmore. Aydelotte had taken the presidency with the Board of Managers' promise that subsidies to athletes would be banned. Now, after he settled down in his new job, he began to enforce his conviction that sports should be for everyone. His idea was that sports should be for fun and exercise, and should include training and practice in those games which could be enjoyed in the more mature years after the students' graduation. The ideal student at Swarthmore would be one similar to a Rhodes Scholar — physically vigorous, skilled in sports, but also with demonstrated intellectual vigor combined with the forces of character and leadership. And Aydalotte soon found a wealthy "friend of the college" who was willing to help find such students through a system of "Open Scholarships." These scholarships, open to everyone (girls as well as boys, eventually), would provide five people with a yearly stipend of $500 for each of the four years of college. Many of the alumni, reared in a system of competitive varsity sports, were skeptical; they would wait for their final judgment until the new plan produced the correct proportion of athletic victories over other colleges.

These alumni, still dreaming of the "good old days" when Swarthmore was able to down mighty Pennsylvania in football, and meet other members of the Ivy League on a more-or-less equal basis, generally withheld their fire until 1935. Then, in a document sent to the Board of Managers, they not only complained about the lack of vocational emphasis at Swarthmore, and the lack of communication between Aydelotte and the alumni, but asserted that, under Aydelotte's administration, half the boys in the freshman class wore eyeglasses; they implied that such boys were " 'dippy dudes,' ' not the desired brawny "he-man" type.

By this time Charles F. Jenkins, noted for his "hearty good sense and humor," was president of the Board. In answering the criticisms about the physical quality of the freshman men, he proposed that a permanent secretary be appointed to "assist in filling up the coming freshman class with brawny students, none under six feet, all over 200 pounds with brain cavities in proportion . . . and not a spectacle among them!" And *The Phoenix* backed up Jenkins with its own brand of satire, publishing a "poem" under the title of:

> The Horn-Rim Boys Reply
>
> The Horn-Rim Boys they make no noise,
>   When piling up their knowledge,
> But call them out and hear them shout
>   On campus or in college: —
>
> The Greeks of old we're often told
>   Were men of mighty muscle;
> But Swarthmore's men, nine out of ten,
>   Could make those old Greeks hustle!

Given such support, Aydelotte's athletic policy continued to be effective. While the old college bell, now housed in the tower of the botany building, continued to celebrate Swarthmore victories over rival colleges in all athletic contests, such contests were usually with colleges of similar size and/or persuasion. It pealed out a victory over the Johns Hopkins football team in 1935, and rang again when Swarthmore's soccer team defeated Haverford in that same year. And we may suppose it rang many times the following year, when the Garnet took on Lehigh in lacrosse and track, Muhlenburg in tennis, and the University of Delaware in golf. And the girls played hockey with Ursinus and other colleges.

But the kind of athletic activity closest to Frank Aydelotte's heart was that program of intramural team sports, and the individual sports, listed in *The Phoenix* on November 24, 1936. According to this list, the Interfraternity League would sponsor basketball games in the Hall Gymnasium, and touch football in the field house. The tennis facilities in the field house would be open on certain days for men and women, students and faculty alike. Swimming, wrestling, fencing and badminton schedules were posted, and handball facilities would be open at certain hours for men students and faculty men. Bowling was not mentioned, although we may be sure that some students indulged in this sport on off-campus lanes.

Music and the Literary Arts

According to one student writing a letter to the editor of *The Phoenix* in 1932, music at Swarthmore was a "minus element." He cited other letters and recent editorials to the effect that the small music department headed by Dr. Alfred J. Swann was not developing the student potential for fine performances. The main reason, it seemed, was that the orchestra and chorus attempting to put on such shows as the recent performances of *Hugh the Drover* and *Sadko* simply didn't have their hearts in their work; what they were trying to do was too ambitious; and it certainly was over the heads of the audience. What students *did* want, and would respond to both as performers and as audience, would be a Gilbert and Sullivan operetta now and then — "something with a little dash, variety, spirit and humour. . . . "

There was little doubt but that some of Dr. Swann's programs were a bit too esoteric for the average student. At one point he seemed to have the conviction that what the Swarthmore student body needed was an exposure to Russian or Byzantine music. On April 8, 1932 the Mixed Chorus and Orchestra put on a concert in Clothier Memorial, with a member of the Kedroff Male Quartet as a soloist. A little later the same groups and their guest would repeat their performance at the Chalfont-Haddon Hall in Atlantic City. In 1936 Dr. Swann appeared in the Friends' Meeting House on campus, this time telling of Byzantine music's relation to the Russian Orthodox Church, and playing accompaniments as Madame Kurenko, soprano, sang Slavic and Byzantine chants.

But Professor Swann's department tried to offer what might be called the best in music through the Cooper Foundation. Walter Damrosch gave a lecture-recital in 1926, marred to some extent by unseemly student behavior such as whispering and giggling. (An editorial in *The Phoenix* held that if Damrosch were as temperamental as Paderewski the performance would have been cut short.) In 1931, however, the audience in Clotheir Memorial was much more appreciative of Marian Anderson's efforts, especially when she sang Negro spirituals in her inimitable style. And at least part of the college community looked forward to the concert to be given in 1937 by Joseph Szigeti, world-famous Hungarian violinist; those who missed his concert, in which he gave three encores, could probably find many of his selections in the Cutting Record Collection, open at stated times for prearranged programs.

Given the hectic pace of life on the Swarthmore campus, with so very many things to do and see and hear, it was not surprising that the vespers program started in 1931 also drew many students and faculty. Going to Clothier Memorial late on a Sunday afternoon, they could look forward to a restful half-hour of music by the pipe organ, or to recitals by student musical groups, or by church choirs. Sometimes there were talks by faculty members, or by imported speaking talent. Jesse Holmes spoke on the history of the Quakers and their beliefs and practices in November, 1931; his talk was followed by the playing of hymn tunes on the organ by Professor Shero. The following Sunday there would be a concert by the Swarthmore Chorus. In 1932, Jesse's friend Norman Thomas addressed the vespers crowd on the clash between the ideals of living engendered by college life and the realities of modern life beyond the ivory towers. Either these ideals should be abandoned, he said, or students should go out into the field, and, in a "high action of mind, heart, and spirit," try to remake the world to conform to these ideals. They could not isolate or insulate idealism from reality; they could not be like the opposing sides on the Italian front during World War I, who, during a lull in the fighting, set up altars in the field and conducted prayers for victory. "No ethical, no religious ideals, can endure such strife," said Mr. Thomas.

Two years later a student-faculty committee on vespers, with Jesse's colleague Dr. Nason as the faculty representative, planned a series of programs, again mixing music and sober thought. Organ recitals and student musicals were to alternate with talks by faculty members on the subject, "What I Believe In."

Brand Blanshard led off this series of faculty talks with a brief review of the history of Christianity. Based on the doctrines handed down to them from the Middle Ages and the Reformation, he said, most nineteenth-century Americans believed in the sacredness of the Bible as the Word of God, and that Christ had come to shoulder the sins of all those people who believed in him. But, in the late nineteenth century, and through the twentieth, three lines of attack had seriously undermined this set of basic beliefs. The first of these was the assertion, based on scholarly research and logic, that the authorship of the books of the Bible was in doubt in many cases; there were also disputes as to just what should be included in this Book of Books. The second line of attack came after Darwin's *Origin of Species* and *The Descent of Man*, which led many to doubt the origin of man as set forth in Genesis. The third wave of criticism came from Freud, the social scientists, and the liberal theologians. These asserted that the moral ideal of the Bible was no longer sufficient; there ought to be a supplementary morality based on the study of individual and social man himself. "Many thought that the Bible didn't stress sufficiently the importance of knowledge, beauty, or politics." (Nor, we might add, did it recognize the ecological doctrine that man and nature must be partners. Instead, in Genesis man is enjoined to dominate the earth and the beasts of the field.) Blanshard went on to state that true religion "entails a feeling of humility and trust, is not made up of pure reason nor of pure feeling, and involves worship. . . ." His own religion, he said, followed Platonic philosophy, and was based on four propositions. All of us, he thought, have intrinsic absolute values such as truth, beauty, and goodness. Second, these standards are the same for everyone regardless of any outward differences. Third, that these standards are the bench marks of our appreciation of reality, not just subjective ways of thinking. And fourth, that religion consists of applying these standards so as to make ourselves more like the Diety which is composed of them.

Given such Platonic abstractions, it was not surprising that students had a number of questions for Blanshard when he finished his lecture.

When Everett L. Hunt, professor of English, spoke about his beliefs, he confessed that he could not offer his audience a complete world view or an integrated philosophy. What he had to offer was "a group of fragments" of the beliefs he had developed over an active life. He stated his belief in the value of the old Greek virtues: "courage, temperance, justice, and high-mindedness," the practice of which had been a good thing since the days of Plato. He added to these his belief in the Christian doctrines of faith, hope, and love; the practice of these had produced healthy, happy people across the centuries. Pressed for explanations during the question period that followed his talk, he admitted that he had no faith in the idea of progress — certainly not in the realm of ethics or morality. The idea of progress, he said, "is a comparatively modern superstition; I don't believe that there is any more virtue in the world today than there has ever been."

What seems so remarkable about all this is that these men would consent to reexamine their own positions on this sensitive issue of personal belief, and then state them to the outside world. This may seem especially true of the three people who followed Everett Hunt in this phase of the vespers program. Dr. Winthrop R. Wright, chairman of the physics department, believed in "a personal God as an idealization of the human attributes of wisdom, understanding, and love, . . ." But, he admitted, his beliefs, like scientific theories, were "continually changing in a living process" as new data were revealed about the cosmos, and men's relations to it and to each other. The same attitude was most probably taken by Dr. Arnold Dresden, head of the department of mathematics, although we have no direct evidence of his position. But Gilbert H. Barnes, visiting professor of economics from Ohio Wesleyan, agreed with Dr. Wright — he had no consistent system of philosophy, his basic traditional position being constantly modified by a changing environment, and by his own shifting interests.

While these Sunday vespers programs were calm and reflective interludes in a busy campus life, the pace invariably picked up again in each succeeding week. There were many other possibilities for the expression of musical tastes and talents beyond the heavy and esoteric programs sometimes provided by Dr. Swann. The Men's Glee Club gave periodic concerts; and, on at least one occasion joined with an instrumental club of twenty students, and an eight-man jazz band, to make their concert the immediate preliminary to the annual prom. A somewhat similar Mixed Chorus and Orchestra gave a concert in the Grand Foyer of the Hotel Traymore in Atlantic City one Saturday night, the whole group being guests of the hotel for dinner and overnight. Back home in Swarthmore, in October, 1931, the Mixed Chorus gave a free concert in Clothier Memorial, its membership including such faculty people as Mr. and Mrs. Clair Wilcox and Everett L. Hunt. And in 1934, instead of opposing Princeton in Tiger Stadium, Swarthmore combined its Glee Club with that of Princeton to give a joint concert; the same thing had been done with Haverford the year before. Three years later another effective way had been found to stimulate interest and attendance at musical affairs — a weekend house party was to be held at the Hotel Morton, Atlantica City, in connection with the Glee Club concert to be given there of a Saturday evening. Professor and Mrs. Everett L. Hunt were to be the chaperons.

Philadelphia, of course, provided all sorts of opportunities to lovers of music and the arts. In 1928 *The Phoenix* told students that those who wished to attend an "open" concert of the Philadelphia Orchestra should apply to James Michener for tickets at a nominal price — an arrangement made through the courtesy of Dr. Swann. Earlier, *The Phoenix,* in a racier mood, had praised "Artists and Models," then playing at the Shubert Theatre, as a "Display of Beauty." Although the show was said to be occasionally "quite daring, sometimes vulgar. . . ," the director had added "much to the wardrobe" and omitted a good deal from the lines of the comedians to accommodate the "respectability of Philadelphia audiences. . . ."

While the Hamburg Show (origin of the name unknown to the writer) put on each year at Swarthmore also had its actresses and actors adequately clothed and speaking acceptable lines, it nevertheless was in the irreverent tradition of the Hasty-Pudding and Mask-and-Wig productions so pleasing to the undergraduates at Harvard and Penn. Year after year the Hamburg Show presented satirical reveues of the passing scene, combining vaudeville, theater, and music in many hilarious skits. In the 1928 show Lily Tily, daughter of the Dr. Herbert J. Tily who presented Clothier Memorial with its wonderful pipe organ, joined Caroline Robison to put on a well-executed dance. After a skit in which members of "Gwimp," the women's honorary athletic society, parodied the dress and behavior of the members of "Kwink," the men's society, the Garnet Serenaders presented a group of original arrangements "worthy of a Whiteman, a Lewis or a Waring. . . ." A group of freshmen women then put on "A Track Meet in the Gay Nineties," which the audience found amusing. Among many other skits, James Michener and Edward Dawes presented an act entitled "The Hero," which, in its depictions of love and hate, peace and war, and cowardice and bravery in World War I, proved to be one of the hits of the evening. Then a group of senior men, dressed as women, brought down the house with a high-kicking dance which would have done credit to the Ziegfield Follies. The grand finale was a combined affair — the men's chorus and the women's chorus joined to bring to a close one of the better versions of the Hamburg Show. In 1934 the proceeds of the show were to go to the Athletic Association to help maintain the college band.

In slightly more serious moments the people of the Swarthmore community attended the performances put on by the Little Theatre Club in Collection Hall or in Clothier Memorial. Wishing to elevate the caliber of these performances, *The Phoenix* opened up a Dramatic Criticism Department, with Gregory Zilboorg, Jesse Holmes' old friend, leading off a series of critical reviews in 1922. Zilboorg had staged a number of plays in New York; out of his experience he now urged the Swarthmore group to be aware of its responsibilities as a vanguard of the American Theatre to come. Broadway productions should not be its models; instead, it should choose plays of real substance and engage in some experimentation.

Zilboorg's advice produced mixed results. In general, the plays put on after 1922 were comedies with a Broadway flavor. Thus, in 1924, "To the Ladies," by George S. Kaufman and Marc Connelly, titillated the audience in Collection Hall; in 1927 Shaw's "Arms and the Man," familiar to operetta goers as "The Chocolate Soldier," again proved a success. In 1937 a double bill — "Waiting for Lefty," by Clifford Odets, and "Trial by Jury," by Gilbert and Sullivan — graced the boards in Clothier Hall. Since this bill was not part of the regular Little Theater schedule of plays, an admission fee of twenty-five cents was charged.

Any students anxious to see more professional productions found it easy to go to the Hedgerow Theatre in the nearby Moylan-Rose Valley area, where, by showing their Swarthmore identification card, they were admitted in 1936 for only 75 cents instead of having to pay the regular charge of $1.65. In the fall of that year the schedule at the Hedgerow included Bernard Shaw's "Candida" and "Saint Joan," and "One Way to Heaven," by Countee Cullen.

On campus the Somerville Literary Society continued to function, not only as a group devoted to art and literature, but serving women — alumnae, faculty wives, and undergraduates — as a forum for the discussion of politics and other public issues. Named for Mary Somerville, Scottish scholar (Somerville College at Oxford was one of her monuments), the Swarthmore group had been formed not long after the college's founding in 1864. Swarthmore women who had been members across the years began to gather for annual reunions in the early spring of each year; these gatherings were so small at first that they met in Jesse Holmes' classroom (Room 31) on the third floor of Parrish. As time went on these reunions became part of Somerville Day, the climax of a given year's series of meetings. On such a day there would be touches of a regular meeting, with literary readings and musical selections; but there were also reports of scholarships awarded, and, as in 1927, reports of the activities of a related organization, the American Association of University Women.

Whether brought by the Somerville Society, or through the Cooper Foundation, or a combination of these, some outstanding literary figures made occasional appearances on campus. In 1926, using Jesse's classroom as his lecture hall, Dr. Felix E. Schelling, professor of English at the University of Pennsylvania, spoke on "Shakespeare in His Age." As would be expected, he spoke of the Bard's universal appeal, and his "borrowings" from other writers; a large part of his lecture dealt with Shakespeare's contemporaries — Marlowe, Dekker, Heywood, and Lily. Schelling was followed by other figures gaining fame in the 'twenties and 'thirties, notably Vachel Lindsay, Walter P. Eaton, and Walter Yust. In 1929 Robert Frost gave an interpretive reading of some of his poems in Collection Hall; in 1934 Archibald MacLeish, sponsored by the Somerville Society, told his audience in the Friends' Meeting House that "A poem should not mean, but be, . . ." — a line from one of the poems he read that night. Giving his audience a series of word paintings in such poems as "Cinema of Man" and "Conquistador." he found them sympathetic to his mood and ideas.

The Life of the Mind.

Although there is abundant evidence that many Swarthmore graduates did not pursue intellectually oriented vocations, there is also a great deal of evidence to show that the students and faculty alike were stimulated to cultivate those habits of study and reflection which Frank Aydelotte believed should be part of the equipment of anyone who would call himself educated. As it was also being developed in other fine colleges, the process of an individual's self-education at Swarthmore could be described as an "inward-to-outward" progression of a series of engagements with the great minds of the past and the present — a process leading the student from his study out into the field and involving, for the active, inquiring mind, a series of mental feedbacks causing some thinking when facts and opinions clashed.

The "inward" part of the process lay in the constant encouragements, via regular classes and honors seminars, to read and study and reflect in the privacy of one's own room. The accumulation of a fine personal library was hailed as an achievement. In fact, in February, 1926, Dean Walters announced in Collection that W.W.

Thayer, of Concord, New Hampshire, had offered a prize of fifty dollars to the student with "the best collection of books and the most knowledge about it. . . ." The prize would not necessarily be given to the largest collection; the judges, it was said, might prefer a group of five books to one of five hundred if the books were significant and the owner knew what was in them. On or about June 1, the judges would call on each competitor, view his books, and question him about them. After completing their round the judges would announce the winner.

We don't know who won the prize that year; and perhaps the subjective difficulties of deciding on a winner caused the project to lapse after a year or two. But in 1930 the idea was picked up again, this time through an endowment by A. Edward Newton, of Daylesford, Pennsylvania, "famous" writer and bibliophile. Three judges — Dr. Spiller, Mr. Shaw, and Dr. Albertson — braved the dangers of picking the student best qualified to receive the fifty-dollar prize in 1931. Although it must have seemed important to Harry E. Sprogell, '32, that he won the prize, it was even more important that this whole idea of discriminating selection for one's personal library stimulated more interest in books and led to the development of a new section in *The Phoenix*. Entitled "Book-Chat," this section provided brief reviews of books recently published, or volumes newly added to the college library. When a study of unemployment in 1929-30 was made at Swarthmore by Professor Paul H. Douglas, working under a grant from an anonymous friend of the college, the resulting report — *The Problem of Unemployment* (1931) — was widely read by students and given a long and able review in "Book-Chat". Aydelotte was not only very much pleased that Swarthmore had been the center for this important special study, but immensely gratified at the great interest in it shown by the students.

And we may be sure that he was gratified in 1926 when he learned that students and professors were holding informal discussions in the newly decorated basement of Section D, Wharton Hall. Officially named the Senior-Faculty Commons, it was comfortably furnished with oriental rugs, deep armchairs and sofas, and was a very pleasant place in which to exchange ideas. Only student irreverence could account for the fact that it quickly became known as "The Pit"; when *The Phoenix* told its readers that Dr. Brand Blanshard had discussed "Belief, Religious and Secular" with a small group of interested students in "The Pit" on a Sunday evening, everyone knew where the discussion had been held. As *The Phoenix* reported, the students taking part in it felt well rewarded, not only because of the ideas they exchanged with Dr. Blanshard and with each other, but because they had learned to know him better in this informal atmosphere. In March, 1926, with Dr. R. C. Brooks as their guest, the students covered a wide range of topics such as the opportunities in college teaching, modern tendencies in married life, the value of college activities, and the worth of informal discussion. With Dr. Brooks there, one may suppose that all this talk rose above the level of a bull session.

Forward-looking students of this type, particularly those already thinking of what their life's work might be, found opportunities to attend professional conferences. In the Christmas holiday period of 1927 five honors students in the Social Science Division journeyed to Washington, D.C., to go to meetings of the American Historical Association and the American Political Science Association, each according to his interest. The previous October an industrial conference had been held at Swarthmore to which seventy-five students, men and women, were invited on the basis of the fact that they had worked with their hands the summer before or at least at some time in their lives. The idea was to discuss industrial problems in the light of their personal experiences. Presided over by A.J. Muste, dean of Brookwood Labor College, the students could also meet and talk with such noted industrial-labor men as Henry Tatnall Brown, Norman Thomas, Powers Hapgood, and Israel Mufson. This conference did not lack sponsors: the National Student Councils of the YMCA and the YWCA, the American Friends Service Committee, and six other organizations of a similar liberal or idealist coloration.

While such conference opportunities were sometime things, the institution of the Collection, or student assembly, was a weekly presence. Aydelotte usually presided; many faculty also attended, flanking the president on the platform. On one of these occasions Aydelotte outlined his conception of the purposes of Collection: it was to serve as a unification process for the College; it was a place where College ideals and the means to achieve them could be discussed. And, speaking in concert with his friend Jesse Holmes, he said that such a program was " 'essentially religious,' his test of religion being not dogma, but deeds."

This definition of the purposes of Collection was so broad that almost anything of a worthy nature might be heard from that platform on the second floor of Parrish Hall. In 1922, during a shortened week of sessions, and when daily attendance was compulsory, the students heard Dr. Miller speak on new astronomical theories; this was followed by Aydelotte's discussion of the relations between art and science; the next day (a Thursday) Dean Walters gave "a pleasing talk" on habits and the principles of learning. On Friday Gregory Zilboorg was there to talk about Kerensky, saying that Kerensky's political weakness in Bolshevist Russia lay in his respect for human life and freedom of speech. (When Kerensky visited Swarthmore in this period, Jesse and Rebe entertained him in their home.)

Several methods were used to try to stimulate more interest and improve attendance in Collection. One was to have Ducky Holmes, one of the most popular professors, appear as a speaker now and then; in 1930, after two previous appearances, he gave the assembled students a "pep talk" on the advantages of attending these weekly get-togethers in the right spirit. In 1936 he spoke in behalf of the [United] Chest Fund Drive, sharing the platform with two student leaders for this purpose. Three years earlier he had made the Thanksgiving address, telling the students to avoid sentimentality in general, but particularly that form of "pharisaical thankfulness for privileges not granted to others. . . ." which was so likely to crop up on this holiday. Unfortunately, this thankfulness for "small favors" and the custom of "waiting for God to do things" had been greatly fostered by the Christian church. And, in this time when lemming-like hordes of people were rushing this way and that way in Europe, following leaders more because of animal-like hates, fears and instincts than through the use of thought, he urged students to spend at least part of their Thanksgiving in a meditative, intelligent effort to be human. If civilization were to endure, he said in the time of Hitler, people must decide to join the "man-pack" rather than the lemming-pack or the wolf-pack.

There were still other ways of attracting students and faculty to Collection. One way which proved very popular indeed was to invite such groups as the Hampton Quartette to entertain; in 1934 they were "encored repeatedly" and sang "Waterboy" as a special number. Another way was to invite such famous people as Jane Addams, one of the founders of Hull House in Chicago, to discuss

189

her favorite work — social service. (In 1931, when she appeared in Collection, Hull House was in its forty-first year.) And a third way to quicken interest was to have some prominent intellectual or research worker give students an insight into certain very special fields of human endeavor. This was the case when Dr. Thomas Johnson of the Bartol Foundation discussed the reasons for expending money and men in the study of cosmic rays. There was little practical value in terms of dollars and cents, he said; what was of infinitely more value in such a "pure science" project, he said, was "the mental satisfaction [derived] by the partial solving of questions which have always been considered fundamental to the understanding of the world and the history of man. . . ."

Many other virtuosi of Dr. Johnson's caliber were brought to the campus, usually for evening programs through the Cooper Foundation. Bertrand Russell, hailed by Will Durant as one of the three topmost scholars and philosophers of his day, spoke on "Science and Civilization" in October, 1927. Addressing a capacity crowd in Collection Hall, Russell correctly prophesied that the United States, Russia and China would emerge as the world powers of the future, and that, if science were on the side of the offensive in the next war, it would make World War I seem a gentle one. But he held up a vision of a world government to come, which, being based on scientific knowledge, would make the world a better, calmer place in which to live.

Other aspects of man's life on earth were explored and explained by such people as Dr. William Beebe, the famous zoologist and author, who gave an illustrated lecture in 1928 on the topic "Beneath Tropic Seas." A month later Felix Adler, critic of Freudian dream analysis, told his audience that since " 'all the problems of life are social affairs'. . . .," parents had a great responsibility to develop in their children "a 'social feeling', i.e., an ability to work with one's fellow beings, . . ." In 1929, during the commencement season, Dr. Ernest Hocking, philosopher from Harvard, delivered the annual Phi Beta Kappa address in the Meeting House. Speaking to that group of scholars, he asserted that there were signs that there was a "Treason of the Intellectuals" — a growing tendency for intellectuals to repudiate their responsibilities to society as leaders for effective action. Any long-range effective action, he asserted, depended upon a thorough examination of the premises upon which such action would be based. Right here, he said, lay the major fault of intellectuals, the real treason. They were deserting their true business of testing premises for validity; they were not testing, for example, the fundamental premise of democratic theory that there was a natural, God-given equality of man under the manifest inequalities shown by men in everyday life. Unless philosophers in a democracy took up their true job, unless they gave the public rational interpretations and corrections of such real or apparent contradictions, there would be "no choice but to go back to autocracy. . . ."

Hocking's challenge to philosophers to do their job had deep, wide, and spreading implications in the horrendous decade of the 'thirties. when capitalism's free-enterprise system broke down, and when theories of racial inequality were gaining favor across the world. Here indeed were premises to be tested, and new ones to be proposed if they were found wanting.

And this is exactly what happened at Swarthmore in the 'thirties. Now Dr. Otto Klineberg told an audience in the Meeting House that Hitler's Nordic hypothesis was "anthropological nonsense"; now Margaret Mead pointed out to a Swarthmore audience that the "human part of our human nature depends on the cultural environment that produces us" — that "being human" was at least half a matter of cultural conditioning, which might produce behavior entirely "right" in Pago-Pago but entirely "wrong" if tried in Peoria. But the major trouble in Peoria was economic; as the Great Depression deepened, the Cooper Foundation director thought it wise to conduct a forum on national economic planning, so that the premises, means, and goals of this alternative to private-enterprise planning might be examined. Dr. Joseph H. Willits, '14, professor of industry at Penn, presided at the meeting in March, 1932; Dr. Lewis L. Lorwin, of the Brookings Institute in Washington, gave the case for public economic planning, while Dr. Alvin H. Hansen, of the University of Minnesota, defended free-enterprise, individual-thinking capitalism. Needless to say, no conclusion on the issue was reached, although Dr. Lorwin admitted that the country was not yet ready for general economic planning. In 1935, with the depression still unsolved, the Swarthmore Social Science Division brought Jacob Billikopf, of the National Labor Relations Board, to the Meeting House for a discussion of how the Board tried to settle labor disputes.

These were matters of grave social concern. But Swarthmore

people were also listening to other lecturers who brought to them portends of a new age of science, an age in which, for good or for evil, the terms "atom," "isotope," and "reactor" would increasingly become household words. In 1934, Dr. Robert E. Steiger, of the Pasteur Institute, used the main chemistry lecture room to explain the structure of atoms by means of models. Nine months later, in March, 1935, Dr. and Mrs. Jean Piccard told of their balloon ascent to the stratosphere in a lecture entitled "Ten Miles Above the Clouds." (At the time of this lecture Dr. Piccard was doing research in physical and organic chemistry at the Bartol Foundation on campus, where the cosmic-ray instruments used on the stratosphere flight had been constructed.) And in April, 1937, Dr. Harold C. Urey, of Columbia University, spoke on "The Separation of Isotopes" in this same chemistry lecture hall. The time of "heavy water" and the "Manhattan Project" was drawing closer.

The Swarthmore community was of course very glad to have the opportunities to hear such intellectual giants. The trouble was, they were birds of passage; most of them were here today and gone tomorrow. Frank Aydelotte wanted to correct this condition; he wanted to establish a lectureship which would bring such distinguished people to the campus for a month, during which time they could take part in classes and seminars, and meet students and faculty on an informal basis. And the Cooper Foundation was to make this possible.

The first resident lecturer was A.D. Lindsay, master of Balliol College, Oxford, who gave a series of lectures on the "Essentials of Democracy." This series was published as the first volume of the Cooper Foundation Lectures, and quite appropriately included a section on the democracy of the Quakers. According to reports, Lindsay stimulated the students in just the way Aydelotte had hoped he would; and the same stimulation, we may believe, was in effect when Don Salvador de Madariaga, philosopher and head of the World Foundation, agreed to live on campus for a period in 1937. The World Foundation was dedicated to the "intelligent organization of life on this planet," and was formed because of the weakness and failure of the League of Nations, to which Madariaga had been the delegate for Republican Spain. During his stay at Swarthmore he would presumably explore with the students the ways to organize life on earth in an intelligent way.

Since the presence of such noted outside scholars on the campus *did* stimulate thought and discussion, Aydelotte's plan was generally approved by Swarthmoreans. Still, we believe, there were also people on the campus who wondered why it was all that necessary to import intellectual stars when Swarthmore had luminaries of its own willing and able to shed light on complex problems outside of their classrooms. Indeed, as the record shows, they had been doing just this throughout Aydelotte's administration.

Among those leading off in this process of extra-classroom elucidation of problems and values was Paul M. Pearson. In 1922 he spoke most eloquently to a Meeting-House audience about the qualities to be looked for in that "improved individual" considered to be so essential for the development of a new world by Lord Bryce of England. Full of homilies about courage, cooperation, and the like, Pearson's talk also had within it the modern psycho-sociological insight that "a man will live up to what the world thinks and expects of him. . . ." Patrick Malin, Quaker member of the economics department, and a personal friend of both Pearson and Jesse Holmes, had much to say about modern social problems in his speech before the joint meeting of the YMCA and YWCA in Whittier House on November 15, 1925. Among the many points he developed he asserted that, considering the low condition of many worthy laboring people, "some system must be worked out whereby each and every man, regardless of social rank, is given the fullest possible opportunity to develop the talents which he possesses. . . ." (This was sound Jeffersonian doctrine, realized to an imperfect degree in the post-World War II period of federal support of veterans' education.) His ideas were supported by Jesse, we have no doubt. And Jesse too was drawn into the act of making many a speech in support of Swarthmore's idealistic program — "drawn" most willingly, one knows by his record. Indeed, in 1936, after twenty-six years at Swarthmore, he was becoming a legend in his own time, the students remembering not only his unorthodox views, but also that German cape he sported in the wintertime. When he was tapped by Aydelotte to give the Founders' Day address in that year, the student newspaper noted that he "honored his address . . . by wearing a tux. He does look more natural in his storm cape. Even in spite of this handicap he gave a good lecture."

Wearing neither a tux nor a cape, Jesse led off a series of lectures on evolution to be given by the philosophy staff in the winter of

1928, the object of which was, according to him, to "clear up the remarkably common, and altogether unnecessary conflict . . . between science and religion. . . ." (It seemed to many in the period just after the Scopes "monkey trial" in Tennessee, that this was a necessary series of lectures.) Speaking from the platform of Whittier House, Jesse said that evolution in general was "progressive change according to some sort of order and following the impulse of resident forces, . . ." Taking his audience back to the time when, as he said, nothing existed except unbounded "nebulous masses" of matter, he outlined certain processes which then began to organize these nebulous bits into more definite inorganic and organic forms. These processes were manifestations of energy at work — "contraction, affinity, revolution, and heat. . . ." And these processes went on for eons of time before man appeared. Indeed, he said, to properly appreciate the meaning of evolution it was necessary for man to stand aside, as it were, and view the process as an objective observer without interjecting personal standards into the observation.

A week later (these lectures were Monday night affairs) Jesse lectured on organic evolution, starting out with the comment that evolution in general — organic and inorganic — was an "historic statement" rather than an "explanation." (What he meant by "explanation" the record doesn't show; knowing his view about religion, one suspects that he meant that evolution was not an explanation of God's will.) This "historic statement" was a fact, Jesse implied; and he went on to outline some theories as to how this fact had been accomplished in the world of living things. He reviewed Jean Lamarck's theory of acquired characteristics, which held that changes brought about in bodies by living in a certain environment could be passed on to succeeding generations through the germ plasm. This would explain the gradual darkening of the skin of people living in that belt of countries running southward from Scandinavia to the jungles of Africa, regions subject to increasing exposure to the sun from north to south. (An embarassing contradiction to Lamarckian theory was the fact that girl babies in Mandarin China continued to be born with big feet.) And then Jesse of course examined the Darwinian theory of the survival of the fittest — which bad spellers in his classes (as happened in mine) may have rendered as survival of the "fetus." While Darwin's theory still depended on the force of the changing environment, as did Lamarck's, environment was now a *selective* force to wipe out the unfit, so that those living things not well adapted to living under certain conditions would not pass on their characteristics. Those well adapted, of course, would pass on any changing body structure to their children and give rise to new species. While Darwin did not know just why or how some animals or plants were able to adapt to changing environments, the answer was given later on by De Vries, a Dutch scientist, who postulated that accidental changes or mutations in the genes and chromosomes of reproductive cells could indeed bring these new species into being under Mendelian laws of inheritance.

This series of lectures was continued when Brand Blanshard spoke on the evolution of the mind. Refusing to dichotomize the mind and the body, he defined the mind as "the mass of our experiences . . . the sum total of the feelings, willings, emotions, and desires which go to make up our consciousness." He saw three stages in mental evolution: the sensory stage, possessed by all animals (and, as research demonstrated, by plants) as their way of adjusting to the world about them on a rudimentary level; the perceptual stage, which enabled animals to use a previously learned experience for the solution of present problems; and the abstract-thought stage, which differentiated man from lower animals, and which enabled man to form algebraic ideas, concepts of a god or gods, and concepts of such human necessities as justice and liberty.

Blanshard spoke again a week later on moral evolution, pointing out that two stages of response to outside stimuli by animals — the reflexive and the instinctive — were only preparatory evolutionary phases of the final stage, the development of a moral code of thinking human beings. And then, making a bow toward Jesse Holmes' pragmatism, Blanshard said that the only acceptable standard of morals would be made possible by "an intellectual working out of the consequences of actions. . . ."

In succeeding lectures other members of the philosophy department developed other aspects of evolution such as the evolution of religion. The accent was always on change — and the necessity to adapt to change in the physical, social, and intellectual affairs of men. There was no escaping certain truths about nature, or man's place in it; men and women had to try to adapt to changing circumstances, even if some thought that circumstances might be changed by men. (See chapter 16 below, where some people, labeled

"Reform Darwinists," are described as believing that Darwinism might be stood on its head for the benefit of mankind.)

This type of intellectual across-the-campus discussion continued with Aydelotte's enthusiastic support. Starting in January, 1929, and running through April, Professors Manning (history) and Wilcox (economics) teamed up to give a series of fourteen lectures on "Social Institutions." Using the chemistry lecture room from 11:15 A.M. to 12:15 on Fridays, and inviting anyone who cared to listen, they alternated in analyzing such topics as "The Concept of Society," "The Status of Women," "The State," "Business," and "Social Change."

In the spring semester of 1931, the philosophy department explored "Some Leaders of Contemporary Thought" in a series of Sunday evening lectures in the Meeting House. Jesse Holmes started the series by talking about Einstein, first describing the man, his physical appearance and his social sympathies, and then getting into an explanation of the broad meaning of Einstein's theory of relativity. (Holmes mentioned that only a dozen men in all the world held "the key" to an understanding of relativity's technicalities, and that Swarthmore's John A. Miller was one of them.) To give the proper background to Einstein's theory, Jesse traced the evolution of other theories about the nature of the physical universe, showing how the work of Copernicus, Galileo and Newton gradually built up a picture of cosmic order. But there were certain phenomena such as magnetism and the nature and speed of light which could not be well explained by the old theories. And, Jesse said, Einstein's ideas about the relative nature of physical measurements, his concept of curved space, and the idea that matter and energy are different manifestations of the same thing all helped to fill in these gaps in man's understanding of the world in which he lived. After a few questions and answers on technical points, the meeting broke up. However, anyone who had brought to this meeting ideas of a tidy universe of fixed points of measurement, a machine running according to absolute time schedules in a world of straight lines, must have had his mind opened a little wider to the nature of ultimate reality. Indeed, as his audience drifted homeward, perhaps some of them were reminded of the fact that the wider implications of relativity were already being developed in the social sciences.

If there were some on campus who thought that Jesse Holmes

should stick to his last as philosopher and religious teacher, and not play around with science in this way, the same charge might well have been leveled at other people — the Mannings, the Wilcoxes and the Nasons — in these lecture series becoming an evermore prominent part of the Swarthmore scene. Certainly Brand Blanshard seemed to be "guilty" of this sort of thing when, in the second of the philosophy-lecture series that spring, he brought all his learning to an analysis of the theories of Freudian psychoanalysis. But, as he talked of dreams, the libido, and complexes, it became evident that no philosopher — and no ordinary citizen, for that matter — could afford to neglect any clues to the understanding of man's behavior, nor neglect any effort to work out some system of thought to govern or direct wise living. Blanshard found some useful items in Freud's system; he also said that "the depths of irrationality involved in the self as conceived by Freud were intolerable to a philosopher. . . ."

A week later George E. Thomas rounded out this particular series of lectures with a discussion of Henri Bergson's belief in intuition and the existence of an *elan vital* or life force which had "duration" from one generation to another by way of developed individual organisms. Although Thomas did a good job of explaining how Bergson was reacting against the dogmatic naturalism, mechanism, and materialism gripping the period 1850-1900, it is uncertain just how much Bergsonian metaphysics meant to the Meeting House audience that night in April, 1931.

The point was, of course, that these professors were giving of their time and energy, without special monetary compensation, so that people who were not specialists in philosophy, or science, or French, or English — the generality of the Swarthmore community — might have the opportunity to round out their general education in a pleasant manner by hearing specialists in those fields. And it is a measure of the liberality and intellectual interests of the Swarthmore Quakers that Whittier House and the Meeting House, although privately owned by Swarthmore Meeting, was so often made available for these public-service lecture sessions.

These sessions must have been popular and successful because the pages of *The Phoenix* record many lecture series of this kind from 1931 to the end of Aydelotte's administration (1939). While the departments of French, English, and economics were active in this work, it seemed that the philosophy department felt most keenly Ernest Hocking's injunction to examine the premises and the systems of thought guiding human affairs.

In the fall of 1931, when Jesse Holmes started out a series of lectures on pragmatism, behaviorism and humanism by the philosophy department, he addressed an audience well-filled with off-campus people. Perhaps Jesse's popularity as a lecturer had attracted them; or perhaps the word had gotten around that Brand Blanshard, of a different philosophical persuasion, would be there to offer rebuttal to Jesse's assertations. Jesse began his speech on pragmatism by admitting that this uniquely American philosophy was nevertheless a hybrid having elements of empiricism and rationalism in it. Ticking off the several ways of knowing "truth" — by authority, mysticism, and pragmatism — he said that the pragmatic method of determining the truth of an idea was the best. You put the idea to work, and if it produced satisfying results it was true to the extent of the satisfaction derived. He admitted that since this involved a lot of trial, and a lot of error, it was somewhat "slip-shod." Still, since the world of man was constantly throwing out new ideas to be tested for truth, there seemed no better way of determining what should be believed. And, he said, "Believing is betting at least a part of one's life on what is going to happen."

Having said this, he should have been prepared for Blanshard's comments on his pragmatism. Jesse had hardly taken his seat at the conclusion of his speech before Blanshard rose to take exception to some of his statements. Blanshard disagreed that satisfaction alone is a test of truth; he said that pragmatism was "theoretically false and practically dangerous." (E.g., if a certain method of robbing a bank produces the desired results, that method is "truth.") As the student reporter for *The Phoenix* put it, "Dr. Holmes [then] dodged the issues . . . ," contenting himself with some *non sequitur* remark about rationalists wanting to reduce everything to one thing, and that satisfaction might reside in that one thing.

(If the student reporter was accurate here, Jesse's behavior on that evening was, to say the least, uncharacteristic. The record shows that he was not given to dodging issues; indeed, his personality and training led him to meet issues head on, and to actively seek or even create them. Nor was he guilty of *non sequiturs;* his mind was too logical for such departures from the joys of fruitful discussion. The writer would sooner think that Jesse did not want to start an extended discussion with Blanshard because of the lateness of the hour, or for some other reason not apparent to the student reporter. And perhaps what seemed a *non sequitur* to the reporter was due to the fact that he missed some link or connection in the brief exchange between Jesse and Blanshard.)

In any case the exchange between Jesse and Brand Blanshard was about the meaning and validity of thought systems; there was no personal rancor between them. And we may be sure that Jesse was in the Meeting House the following Sunday night when Blanshard spoke about Dr. John B. Watson's behaviorism. Since Jesse agreed with Blanshard on this doctrine we may be sure that he nodded and smiled many times as Blanshard "disposed of Behaviorism with the devastating logic that characteriz [ed] all his discussions on philosophical problems." Blanshard called behaviorism a "pseudo-science," and denied that anyone with common sense could agree with Watson that human consciousness was an illusion, or that human life was a mechanistic chain of causes and effects from which there was no escape.

A week later John W. Nason, newly added member of the philosophy department, brought this particular series of lectures to a close with a talk on humanism. At the outset Nason said that he would not talk about humanism as a philosophic aspect of pragmatism — and this omission would of course make it difficult for Jesse, who was undoubtedly there, to respond in defense of this line of thought. He would not speak of humanism as it applied to the Renaissance; he would not discuss it as a modern theory of literary criticism. What he *would* discuss was humanism as a modern substitute for religion.

And in this substitute for religion man was the measure of all things, Nason said. If humanists had a creed, its first article would be "I believe in Man" — in individual men, and in that society which these individual men, through the use of human will and human reason, were trying to build cooperatively into a kingdom of heaven on earth. Convinced that in the past this effort toward perfection had been thrwarted by the orthodox churches playing on an ignorant population's blind faith in supernatural powers, humanists put their trust in education and the use of the scientific method to attain the New Eden. But, Nason asserted, in this effort to elevate human values and satisfy human desires, they forgot or did not recognize that "religious needs are more than desires for cake rather than bread, for a Lincoln rather than a Ford. . . . They are something

199

over and [beyond] the individual human being's whim. . . ." Nason did not define precisely just what these religious needs were; his implications were that they were deeply psychological, and that inner peace could not be found simply through materialistic or strictly logical means.

In this speech Nason had come close to outlining Jesse Holmes' position as a humanist. And, as Jesse explained a year later in his part of a new series of philosophical talks on "Factors in the Good Life," religion was important. The Quaker's "inner light" was a religious "inner spur" — a constant stimulation toward the social duty to make human life what it ought to be. He agreed with previous speakers in this series that the exercise of conscience was part of the good life; the values of the good life, however, could best be realized if people planned cooperatively to attain them. He defined "Social Duty," the subject of his talk, as "intelligent planning for an intelligent future, . . ."

And he had much more to say on this subject of intelligence, its application to education, and its desirability in the modern industrial state. Defining intelligence as not only the ability to profit by experience, but that "ability to see further and live ahead of the present. . . . ," he said that it ought to be applied more to the nation's educational institutions. Schools should provide opportunities to develop one's powers, to open up ways to enjoy the good life in a remade world; they should be places where one would learn to discard blind prejudices to attain clarity of vision, and to instill in the individual the realization that no one can ever say that his education is finished. He made a powerful pitch for adult education as a way of keeping up one's interests in the world's affairs; he bemoaned the fact that, as people got older, their minds narrowed, so that they no longer played with ideas in conversation, but had to play games.

Since he had the floor that Sunday evening in 1932, and since he was talking about social duty and intelligence, Jesse could not resist interjecting his socialist ideas into his speech. What we all want, he said, is a "well-ordered society, in which everyone has all that he needs and opportunities for education, travel, and all the other things that people want. . . ." But we had not yet learned how to manage our society; all manner of things were piling up and rotting because Americans had not yet brought their best intelligence to bear on the problem. The bad citizen, Jesse said, was not only an Al Capone, but a person who would not think, who was driven by impulse rather than by an intelligent foresight of ends and means. He believed that America needed more theorists to think out principles applicable to planning for the future.

And so Jesse and his colleagues continued in their unpaid efforts to share with the Swarthmore community the mansions of Western culture. They felt a sense of *noblesse oblige* — that, as members of the American aristocracy of learning, it was their duty to open up the doors to what great minds had said, or were saying, about the problems of man in the past and in the present. This sense of obligation underlay Jesse's speech on "The Heritage of the Frontier" in February, 1933, when he pointed out that many of the values and institutions of pioneers were still in society (i.e., the relatively unchecked ownership and use of guns), but were now hindrances to progress. And the same sense of obligation prevailed a year later when the philosophy department launched a series of talks about the effects of changing modes of social behavior on Christianity: Holmes on "Christianity and Changing Science"; Blanshard on "Christianity and Changing Morals"; Nason on "New Movements in Christian Thought." The series was to end with John Dewey's views on "The Emancipation of Religion," with the Columbia experimentalist himself appearing on campus for this event.

Public Issues and Student Involvement.

It seemed particularly appropriate to many that John Dewey should appear at Swarthmore in 1934 since his ideas of active, experimentally oriented education, involving the greatest possible student participation in campus and public affairs, were then approaching a climax under Aydelotte's administration. Perhaps again the picture of student involvement is intensified too much by the telescoping of events into an historical narrative, squeezing many events across time into a few pages of a book. Nevertheless, the total impression one gets is that of a superactive campus program keeping the students so busy that one wonders when they had time to study. And the emphasis always seemed to be on student involvement in controversial issues; if nothing suitable seemed to offer from the world of public affairs or the substantive life of the campus, the students searched for an issue to stir their juices, even descending to the absurdity of " 'Should we show school spirit at the Haverford football game?' "

Some of these activities, of course, predated Aydelotte's time at Swarthmore. When James Michener delivered the Ivy Oration in the commencement-week exercises of 1929, he was speaking from a post of long tradition. The same was true for the debating squad, whose members, however, occasionally departed from the traditional American system of having a team entirely on the affirmative or the negative side by using the Oxford system of split teams. (This system made debates "a pursuit of pleasure and not a cultivation of discipline. Speakers might speak on both sides of a question in the same debate. Or the members of a team might support or oppose a cause for entirely different reasons.") Swarthmore used this method in a debate with the British Speaking Union in 1927 and with Duke University in 1928.

In the Boom-and-Bust period (1921-1929) the Swarthmore debaters, coached by Dr. Everett Lee Hunt, had no difficulty in finding topics on which to engage teams from such colleges as Haverford, Villanova, and Union. In 1929 they debated a team from Hillsdale College, Michigan, on the question: "Resolved: That the United States Government should retain and develop the water power it now owns." Clark Kerr, '32, led the Swarthmore contingent in advocating the system of individual or corporate ownership then prevailing, advancing cogent arguments against the type of government-power development seen later in the T.V.A. *The Phoenix* reported that Kerr's "directness of delivery and force of argument" were exceptional.

Kerr continued to be the leader of his group, even daring to take on Norman Thomas (with the help of Harry Sprogell) in a debate on "Capitalism" one Sunday night in the Meeting House. Jesse Holmes presided, and, after introducing the speakers, pointed out that this would be more of a question-and-answer discussion than a formal debate. Both Kerr and Sprogell addressed long, well-reasoned "interrogations" to Thomas, requiring him to explain how socialism would correct the admitted social, economic, and political ills of the capitalist system. While it would be fruitless to rehearse all that Thomas had to say, he had several points which found a welcome in some restless Swarthmore breasts. He claimed that, while socialism was not a panacea, it offered " 'a basis, a plan, and a hope' " for the gradual correction of many of society's ills.

And, he said, the time had come for people to take sides in the capitalism-versus-socialism battle; the impartial opinions of yesterday had no place in the days of the New Deal.

The Thomas injunction to debate this issue was given in February, 1932, and it was not long in being obeyed. In March the Swarthmore women's debating team played host to the ladies' team of the University of Pittsburgh, taking the negative side of the question:"Resolved: that collective ownership and operation of the means of production and distribution is preferable to private ownership. . . ." A month later the same team was to match wits with the Ursinus team on the same topic. (Given the winds of doctrine blowing over the campus at this time, one wonders what logical and philosophical conflicts may have lurked in the minds of the Swarthmore women when they praised the rewards coming to capitalists through the use of competition and the profit system.)

In November, 1934, the capitalist-socialist debate was continued by the men in some of its tangential or side-issue phases. Taking the negative side of the issue as to whether peace is impossible under capitalism, Swarthmore's team confronted a delegation from the University of Georgia through the facilities provided by radio station WDEL, Wilmington, Delaware. A month later the team journeyed to Villanova to advance arguments that the international trade in arms and ammunition should be abolished by mutual agreement among the nations. And, in this same spirit of idealism, the Debate Forum in Bond Memorial considered the advisability of continuing the Federal Emergency Relief Administration (FERA) at Swarthmore. Under this system sixty men and women had received federal monies for doing odd jobs about the college. But now some students questioned the fairness of this system, claiming that it drained away money from those outside people much more in need of relief. The question was debated in Bond, and there was so much student concensus on the unfairness of FERA that it was dropped as a way of helping those students who needed money. Its place was taken by CERA, the College Emergency Relief Association, which was to pay cash from private funds for the same sort of odd-job work done previously, but also for woodcutting, tutoring in the local high school, assisting in kindergartens, and doing social-welfare work in Philadelphia and the Swarthmore area.

Although it was less urgent then, somewhat similar social-welfare work had been carried on by Swarthmore women in the 'twenties.

American colleges had formed the Intercollegiate Community Service Association; now, in 1926, the Swarthmore chapter sent out students to contribute their talents to this purpose. In February a group of women was to go to the Sleighton Farm School, a reformatory for girls near Swarthmore, to put on a vaudeville entertainment for the inmates. (One wonders how effective this was in helping to reform those wayward girls.) This was a one-shot affair; much more in the spirit of Jane Addams' Hull House was the continuing service of the ICSA in Philadelphia settlement houses to show the "other half" that somebody cared. Backed by a donation from College Chest funds, sixteen women were giving an afternoon each week to serve at the House of Industry in South Philadelphia, and in the College Settlement in the same area. These Swarthmoreans conducted classes in cooking and dramatics, did office work, opened up a library for neighborhood children, and taught boys and girls something about handicrafts and gardening. Altogether, the Swarthmore group opened up a vista of middle-class skills and values to people living in an area where the street markets sold "pickles and blankets . . . to fat women in boudoir caps and rundown heels. . . ."

To those women more concerned with service on the campus there were many opportunities. One such opportunity lay in joining the staff of *The Phoenix*, that ever-growing campus paper providing a continuing news service and public forum to the Swarthmore community. Indeed, in 1928 so many co-eds were interested in doing this sort of work that they formed a chapter of Coranto, the national women's honorary journalistic "fraternity" started at Wisconsin in 1923. Mary Sullivan, '28, editor of *The Phoenix* in 1928, was promptly made president of the Swarthmore Coranto; Elizabeth Harbold, '29, still had enough energy left after studying in Jesse Holmes' philosophy seminar to take on the job of corresponding secretary.

The Phoenix had a long history of service to Swarthmore. From its origin in 1881 it not only provided Swarthmoreans with the news vital to their effectiveness, but opened its pages to all those shades of opinion inherent in a liberal-arts college — to all those students and professors who "thought otherwise." In 1931, when it was celebrating its fiftieth anniversary, *The Phoenix* took time out to publish a review of its life and to review the careers of its former editors. As would be expected from the editors of a liberal

204

newspaper in a liberal-arts college, these careers had little surface relation to their work on *The Phoenix* — with some notable exceptions, of course. From the fifty editors of the period 1881-1931 had grown "five lawyers, four writers, four professors, eleven . . . in the business world, three engineers, two scientists, a clergyman, a horticulturist, a contractor, a secretary, a politician, a librarian, and one dean." (And the writer knows from personal experience that one of those professors, starting out so bravely as an editor of *The Phoenix,* ended his life as a basely political opportunist drinking his lunches at the bar of a hotel in West Chester, Pennsylvania.)

In spite of this regrettable variation from an approved pattern, the list of editors was impressive. To cull only a few: William Sproul, 'Ol, became governor of Pennsylvania; Lloyd Lewis, '13, wrote "Myths After Lincoln" and then went on to become dramatic editor of the *Chicago Daily News;* Drew Pearson, too well known for his "peep-hole" and "now-it-can-be-revealed" journalism to require further comment, had been editor in 1919; and Alan Valentine, '21, Rhodes Scholar and dean of men at Swarthmore, had gone on to become president of the University of Rochester. (And, if the time-span for this list of editors had been extended to 1934, it would have included the name of Richard Hubler, who not only dedicated his first book to Jesse Holmes, but made Holmes the imaginative model for the leading character in a novel he wrote about his college days.)

To such students as Hubler, interested in creative writing, there was also an opportunity to develop skills by contributing to the *Manuscript.* This was at first a literary magazine devoted to publishing student essays, stories, poetry, and their critical review of new books. Occasionally, of course, other material crept into its pages, as in 1932, when "The Seminar-Goers Guide" offered semi-comic assistance to those wishing to penetrate the fog of rumors about the various seminars offered to honors students. By 1935 the *Manuscript* had expanded to include articles by the faculty, once again demonstrating that shoulder-to-shoulder assault on ignorance characterizing the Swarthmore experiment in education. Nor was it purely a literary magazine now: the faculty contributed analytical articles such as Troyer Anderson's "Failure as a Factor in Modern History," and Everett L. Hunt's essay "On Rising to Point Out." Guided and advised by Dr. Spiller of the English department, student editors such as Joseph Selligman and William Whyte prepared the various editions of the *Manuscript,* sometimes meeting in the Spiller home to plan or review their work.

Aside from such opportunities for self-expression as those offered by the *Manuscript* and *The Phoenix,* students found other outlets for their energies and desires in the many, many clubs on campus. Those with a technical interest could join the Radio Club, which operated a radio station (call letters W3AJ) on the top floor of Hicks Hall. Others found the social life of Kwink and Gwimp, the men's and women's athletic clubs, more fun: e.g., in October, 1936, the Gwimp members had supper together. The Sketch and Crafts clubs met regularly, as did the German Club and the Classical and Chemistry societies. One of the most active groups was the Trotter Biological Society, which imported such speakers as Professor E. Newton Harvey of Princeton (his topic was "Animal Light" in 1927), and Dr. Detlev Bronk, who spoke on "The Role of Electricity in the Biological and Medical Sciences" in 1932. The Philosophy Club heard Jesse's friend Dr. Gregory Zilboorg talk about the contributions of psychology to the understanding of philosophy in February, 1928; club members may not have been so pleased to hear him say that, whereas philosophy formerly stimulated the search for knowledge, "psychology had now supplanted it, bearing the same relation to it as bacteriology does to medicine." A month later the intellectual fare was more palatable when Professor Joshi, an Indian Hindu, addressed the club in Jesse's home on his religion and on the relation of Buddhism to Christianity. (Also palatable were the refreshments served by Rebe; in fact, *The Phoenix* reporter called them "delightful.") By 1933 the need to give more coherence to the group of honors students in philosophy had led to the formation of a special Round Table Club. Jesse attended its meetings and took part in the discussions; in 1935, however, this group was supplanted by a reorganized Philosophy Club designed now to form a liaison between the students in honors seminars and those in regular classrooms.

Ten years before the Philosophy Club was reorganized R.C. Brooks and Jesse Holmes had been sponsoring regular meetings of the Polity Club, which, by its very name, signified their concern about the formulation of wise social policy. In 1925, for instance, this club held a meeting in Parrish Hall to debate the advisability of a child-labor amendment to the Federal Constitution. Albert Maris, Philadelphia lawyer and chairman of the Delaware County Democratic Committee, was there to support the idea from the humanitarian point of view, pointing out the ways in which the states had been lax in this regard. His opponent was another Philadelphia attorney, Donald Lee McCuen, who held that a national amendment would build up too much of a bureaucracy, and that child labor was indeed a local question to be solved by local means. In the discussion which followed, Brooks and Holmes, as could have been predicted, "championed the principles of humanity and democracy . . . ."

Aside from the Polity Club, most of the other clubs served special departmental concerns, leaving those interested in broader social problems and public affairs pretty much in limbo. At least this was the feeling of a small group of students, who, in October, 1929, in a letter to the editor of *The Phoenix*, announced their intention of correcting this situation. What they proposed was the formation of a Liberal Club; and they showed that they had done a lot of thinking about it:

> The purpose of this club is to serve as a center for undergraduate discussion; to focus the attention of the community upon local, national, and international questions; and to take definite stands on such problems when we think them to be of sufficient importance. From time to time leaders of repute will be invited to present points of view which are of vital interest. We sincerely hope that opinion both conservative and radical will be advanced and considered.

The letter was signed by five students serving as the temporary organizing committee: Kenneth Meiklejohn, Peter Nehemkis, Rosamund Walling, Howard Westwood, and Elizabeth Ward.

With the help of the Cooper Foundation, this newly formed Liberal Club lost little time in getting started. Less than a month from the time the club was first proposed Kenneth Meiklejohn, serving as chairman, introduced his father, Dr. Alexander Meiklejohn, as the first distinguished speaker in its projected series of meetings. Dr. Meiklejohn was then head of the Experimental College at the University of Wisconsin, and came to Swarthmore with a national reputation as a progressive educator. Education, he said, must be functional; people must be doing something with the facts and ideas they learned in a school. Learning for the love of learning was not enough in an aspiring democracy — a democracy in which the gospel of education promoted freedom, insight, and self-direction among its votaries. He defined democracy as "the mad determination to believe in people as though they were what one wants them to be." He understood democrats to say, " 'We don't care what your father was. Born on east side or west side, every person has an equal chance to become great.' "

After this inspirational message the Liberal Club held meetings and heard speakers on topics designed to show how democratic theory was working out in specific fields of public affairs and social policy. Their next speaker, James Maurer, of Reading, Pennsylvania, had risen from wielding a pick in the coal mines to a position of leadership in the Socialist Party, running for the Vice-Presidency of the United States in the campaign of 1928. He had been president of the Pennsylvania Federation of Labor for fourteen years, a representative to the Pennsylvania Assembly, and was then, at the time of his speech, a member of the Socialist administration of the municipal government of Reading. Addressing his audience in "a delightful Scotch burr," he first outlined the historical evolution of industrial man. He said that in the present age the increasing use of tireless machines and efficiency experts, always speeding up production, operated to burn out a laboring man by the time he was "45 or 50 years old, leaving him without a job, and unwanted." Those not yet burned out were being displaced by machines installed by capitalists increasingly bringing the wealth of the nation into fewer hands through mergers and monopolies. This was exploitation of the common man; surely there must be better ways to operate science and industry for man's benefit. Such ways, of course, were offered by the trade unions and by socialism.

While the Liberal Club's attention was briefly diverted from American socio-economic problems when its members attended a luncheon meeting of the Foreign Policy Association in Philadelphia (subject: "The Problem in Palestine") on November 16, the Club soon returned to topics and projects which won the enthusiastic approval of James Maurer and Jesse Holmes. Swarthmore idealists, along with many other college students across the nation, had been outraged by what they had heard or read about the Marion Manufacturing Company of North Carolina. In 1929, when "bulls" were still gambling for fortunes in the New York Stock Exchange, this company was running twelve-hour shifts and paying its workers an average of eleven dollars a week. When seven hundred workers went on strike in July, the company terrorized the strikers

208

and brought in troops to control them. After nine weeks a settlement was reached giving the workers a slight reduction in hours and a promise not to discriminate against union members. But the picture as a whole was revolting — so much so that the Liberal Club resolved to present a proposal to a meeting of Eastern-college delegates in the offices of the League for Industrial Democracy in New York on November 30. This proposal, which won the approval of Paul Porter, the League's field secretary, and Harry Laidler and Norman Thomas, its patron saints, was to form "a national intercollegiate committee to study further the economic and labor problems of the textile industry and to protest the unjust convictions and the tragic massacre of the Marion workers."

The Liberal Club's suggestion to form an intercollegiate committee bore fruit in the development of the Intercollegiate Student Council, composed of representatives from over sixty colleges and universities in the Eastern part of the United States. In the fall of 1930 this Council was planning to hold undergraduate conferences on current problems in various colleges, each conference to be arranged by student leadership with the advice and support of the faculty and administration.

At Swarthmore, a two-day conference in November on the problems of the bituminous coal industry was sponsored by the Liberal Club, the Cooper Foundation, and the Division of the Social Sciences. Peter Nehemkis, '31, president of the Liberal Club, was the general chairman for the conference, ably assisted by Walter Robinson and Robert Kintner, both '31. Their planning was helped along by an advisory committee composed of Professors Joseph Willets and Waldo E. Fisher of the University of Pennsylvania; and by local professors Clair Wilcox, Herbert Fraser, Roland Pennock, Frederick Manning, Jesse Holmes, Alan Valentine, Mrs. Chester Roberts, and Philip Hicks.

The general subject of the conference was "Mines, Miners, and the Public." This title reflected not only the Liberal Club's desire to give all parties to a dispute a hearing, but Swarthmore College's policy of providing a public forum for urgent social issues. The opening session considered the theme, "An Industry in Chaos." F.G. Tryon of the United States Bureau of Mines was to have spoken on the harsh competitive conditions in the industry; he became ill, however, so his place had to be taken by Professor Willets. Alan H. Willet, secretary of the National Coal Association, then spoke on "What's Wrong with Coal — As the Operator Sees It." The trouble was, he said, that the industry as then organized did not provide "a fair return to the operator for his investment and his trouble. . . ." The labor side was then heard, with Van A. Bittner, of the United Mine Workers, claiming that competitive price reductions were generally made by cutting miners' wages. His solutions: reducing the industry's working force, a joint-wage agreement between miners and operators, and the establishment of a coal commission similar to the Interstate Commerce Commission.

The second session was concerned with industrial relations. Carter Goodrich, professor of economics at Michigan, in effect called down a plague upon both houses in the capital-labor conflict. He said that the operators had tried to shatter the unions, had made little use of known principles of personnel management, or even of scientific management of their own part of the industry. The unions, on the other hand, had failed to educate or organize the Southern workers in the broader values of unionism; they were too much concerned with "merely pressing claims for higher wages." This position was given oblique support by Henry N. Taylor, president of the Sheridan-Wyoming Coal Company, who bemoaned the lack of faith the miners and operators had in each other. He called for "a two-party conference" like the one held in 1897, which settled for a time somewhat similar problems. He also bemoaned the competition of Russian coal, mined by conscript labor getting seventeen cents a day, and sold in the United States a dollar a ton cheaper than American coal. Oscar Ameringer, editor of the *Illinois Mine Workers,* then spoke on "Unionism Today and Tomorrow." He said that the trouble with the miners' union lay in its aggressive attitude toward the operators. The owners of the mines were thought of as people living in territory to be invaded and devastated; the industry was an operators' industry from which miners should try to get all that could be gotten. But, Ameringer said, in the union of the future the workers must become an integral part of the industry, must have some voice in management, and have a financial interest in it. The ultimate aim was to develop "an organic union between capital and labor" such as had been achieved in the Amalgamated Clothing Workers of America.

The conference continued with a consideration of "Civil Liberties and the Company Town." Roger N. Baldwin, director of the American Civil Liberties Union, described the relationships between the operators and the workers living in the company towns as "very nearly" like those existing in the Middle Ages between feudal lord and vassal. Workers were compelled to rent company houses, buy their necessities at company stores, and were not allowed to organize for a redress of their grievances. Labor organizers were not even permitted to enter company towns. Altogether, Baldwin concluded, civil liberties did not exist in the coal fields. The president of the Boone County Coal Company of West Virginia, W.J. Clothier, responded to Baldwin by admitting the truth of some of these charges, but asserted that more and more operators were trying to correct conditions out of an enlightened self-interest. Eventually, he thought, the operators would rid the company town of the objections raised against it. But the next two speakers — John A. Fitch, of the New York School for Social Work, and Arthur Garfield Hays, counsel for the American Civil Liberties Union — were not so optimistic, and they addressed themselves to present conditions. Fitch called the ameliorative efforts of some operators "benevolent despotism" and said that life in even the better company towns was destructive of human democratic values — it "tended to kill initiative among the inhabitants, created a fearful citizenship, and denied freedom of the press. . . ." This same line of argument was followed by Arthur Garfield Hays, who was particularly critical of the way company police denied a town's citizens the right to hold a public meeting if the purpose of the meeting was opposed to operators' policy. He advocated that such company police should be abandoned and police be hired by public authorities and paid by public funds.

The drift of the conference was quite obviously toward the protection of American constitutional rights through collective action. And this drift became stronger in the last session of the conference, chaired by E.M. Patterson, president of the Academy of Political and Social Science. He introduced George J. Anderson, president of the Consolidation Coal Company (a Rockefeller holding), who also admitted many of the charges against the operators, but held that since they knew the coal industry better than anyone else they could be depended upon to run the coal fields for the greater public good. Professor H.S. Raushenbush, of Dartmouth, was of a different opinion; he advocated a sort of half-way nationalization of the coal industry along the lines developed in Great Britain. No essential change in ownership of the mines was called for, but a central coal board, with representatives from all groups affected, would buy coal from the most efficient mines and sell it to retailers. This plan, which was working out successfully in Britain, would smooth out the hills and valleys of coal production, as well as the fluctuations in price. Since the wholesaler would be a public agency at least one middleman was eliminated; prices would be lower, almost at the cost of production.

Norman Thomas brought the conference to a close. He found the Raushenbush plan important mainly because it offered an indirect method of avoiding legal obstacles such as constitutional change. On the other hand he would not retreat from his fundamental socialist position: he still advocated complete nationalization of the coal mines because in no other way could a sick industry be made to serve the interests of all the people.

If the exercise of free speech in this conference alarmed some of the capitalistic conservatives in the area, causing them to wonder what was going on at Swarthmore, a crystal-ball view of coming events would have given them still more cause for anxiety. In February, 1932, the Liberal Club heard Paul Porter, of the League for Industrial Democracy, assert that, in a time when over ten million people were out of work, "starving" while western farmers burned wheat, some sort of revolution was called for. " . . . it can be peaceful, but it must be immediate. . . . ," he said. Two months later twenty students formed the Swarthmore chapter of this League; in October, when other students and faculty were eagerly forming Hoover and Roosevelt clubs, these twenty formed the nucleus of the Norman Thomas Club, and enlisted faculty support for his presidental aspirations. Brand Blanshard helped them along with a speech before the Club, refuting the leading arguments against socialism with statistics and his usual devastating logic. His brother Paul was to speak in Clothier Memorial a few days later, following a short skit entitled "School for Candidates," to be presented by budding socialist talent. On Sunday, October 23, Patrick Malin, of the economics department, addressed a socialist group in the Meeting House on "International Finance." The Thomas Club members were there to hear him, of course; and they told of how they had been campaigning for Thomas in Delaware. And students were "especially urged" to campaign in the local Congressional district on behalf of Jesse Holmes' candidacy on the Socialist ticket for a seat in the House.

212

Jesse, of course, had no real hope of winning; his appearance on the ticket was simply his way of supporting the Socialist cause and getting the issues before the public. But there were other and related issues in those troubled years, all demanding the right to be discussed and solved through American constitutional means. One was the peace-versus-war issue, always present in Quaker assemblies. In 1928, when Jesse's colleague, Dr. William I. Hull, attacked the Big Navy Bill then before Congress, the Veterans of Foreign Wars heard Congressman Updike of Indiana call him "a dangerous propagandist, and a high-salaried tool of pacifists who would leave the country stripped of defense, . . . " And Mrs. William S. Walker, vice-president of the Daughters of the American Revolution, recommended that Hull be discharged from the Swarthmore faculty and sent to any foreign country which would take him. Though the students were divided on the merits of the bill, they were united in supporting Dr. Hull's right to say what he wished on this question, since he had spent a lifetime studying it and since free speech was at stake. A mass meeting of students passed a resolution which deplored the stand of the DAR official and expressed admiration for Hull. And a *Phoenix* editorial, "Shall We Deport Him?," castigated his critics and asserted that they were violating "the fundamental laws of the American Constituion which they pretend to uphold."

Neither Hull nor any other convinced pacifist at Swarthmore was deterred by conservative opposition. As chairman of the National Committee for Total Disarmament he continued to give speeches before many civic groups, and in 1932 he was even granted a semester's leave of absence by the Swarthmore Board of Managers so that he might attend the International Disarmament Conference held in Geneva in February. In October of that year, after his pacifist friend Jane Addams had finished her Founders' Day address at Swarthmore, Hull surprised the audience by presenting her to President Aydelotte for the honorary degree of Doctor of Laws, saying that Miss Addams' life exemplified the ideals for which the College stood. And in 1934, when a best-selling book, *Merchants of Death*, was blaming munitions manufacturers for World War I, he was proud to introduce Senator Gerald P. Nye, chairman of the Munitions Investigation Committee, to a Clothier Memorial audience. Nye recommended two remedies for war to Americans: nationalization of the arms industry; and, if this proved impossible, extremely high income taxes for those profiting from war. (His plan was to double the tax rate on incomes up to $10,000, and to levy a 98% or 99% tax on all income above this figure.)

Later on, however, when Senator Nye, out of his Midwestern isolationist conviction, voted against the United States joining the World Court, Hull, Jesse Holmes, and Brand Blanshard felt betrayed. The depth of their feeling was shown in Blanshard's open letter to him via the pages of the *Friends Intelligencer,* February 9, 1935: He called Nye a "lost leader" who, when the chips were down, "stood with the worst . . . munitions makers . . . , [and] with the Coughlins and Huey Longs and Hearsts. . . ."

> We shall march prospering, — not
>   thro' his presence;
> Songs may inspirit us, — not
>   from his lyre;
> Deeds will be done, — while he boasts
>   his quiescence,
> Still bidding crouch whom
>   the rest bade aspire.

The Senate vote rejecting membership in the World Court was taken January 29, 1935. Exactly two months later Jesse Holmes and William Hull, wearing antiwar placards, took part in a peace demonstration in Philadelphia, being the principal speakers at a mass meeting in Reyburn Plaza. They minced no words in their condemnation of the utter folly of abandoning the World Court idea in favor of the tragic illusion that peace had ever been gained, or could be gained, by preparing for war. Two weeks later, Friday, April 12, another peace demonstration was to be held, this time on the campus at Swarthmore. Through the work of the student Peace Action group, with the cooperation of the College authorities, classes would be suspended at nine o'clock that morning so that demonstrators might hear Dorothy Detzer, national secretary of the Women's International League for Peace and Freedom. Representatives from the Mary Lyon School and Swarthmore High School were to attend; indeed, the local "strike" was but one part of the national and international demonstration against war by youth on that particular day.

Was Swarthmore College Radical?

Shortly after the Hull-Holmes speeches in Reyburn Plaza, Judge Harry McDevitt of Philadelphia addressed the Kiwanis Club in Atlantic City. In the course of this speech he charged Temple University, Dartmouth, and Swarthmore with harboring radicalism — a charge which an editorial in *The Phoenix* admitted was often levelled against Swarthmore, especially by those who knew little about the school. Perhaps Judge McDevitt could be forgiven on the score of ignorance, but when he went on to call the College "a Red menace" it was time to explain the Swarthmore position.

And this position was masterfully explained by the editorial writer (initials I.S.S.). "If," he said, "radicalism means having a well-rounded faculty to acquaint students with various sides of questions of opinion, if it means having a student body free to express whatever opinions it may form on any topics, then Swarthmore must harbor . . . radicalism if it is to remain an educational institution. We are taught many solutions for the problems of society in order that we may choose intelligently the correct one. . . ." Judge McDevitt's kind of "education," which would allow students to hear only approved facts and opinions, was nothing but propaganda. So, the writer went on, by charging these liberal colleges with a radicalism which provoked thoughtful and uncoerced decisions based on knowledge instead of ignorance, Judge McDevitt was "unwittingly paying them a great compliment."

But to say that Swarthmore was a Red menace was the unforgivable sin. McDevitt had said that the Reyburn Plaza affair was "a purely Communistic effort to stir up discontent. . . ." Quite otherwise, the editorial writer said: "Swarthmore cooperated in the peace demonstration because of a sincere desire to end all wars unconditionally and permanently. This desire cannot be reconciled with Communism, a movement which would attain its goals by means of class wars. . . ." Jesse Holmes and William Hull were honest pacificists; they were not advocating class warfare, nor any other kind.

And then the editorial put the capstone on its argument. "What [such men as Holmes and Hull] may state publicly or privately as personal opinion does not become the opinion of Swarthmore College just because these men happen to be members of its faculty. . . ." (Or, to put another way, these men did not lose their citizens' rights of free expression by being Swarthmore professors.) And again to the contrary: Swarthmore had on its faculty devotees of each of the three "major" parties in America — Republicans, Democrats, and Socialists. The College was in itself not bound to any one of these parties, and, while it would "tolerate freedom of opinion on the faculty, it [would] allow no faculty member to force his views on his students. . . ." And, since Swarthmore had sent both professors and graduates to serve the United States in the nation's capitol, the editorial went on, "We cannot accept silently Judge McDevitt's charge that Swarthmore is a menace to America."

Jesse Holmes was undoubtedly proud of the quality of this student editorial. He might have added that Swarthmore's policy and action in the time of Frank Aydelotte summarized what America was all about — that the nation was founded on dissent, became consolidated as a planned (though limited) democratic society, and grew through the pragmatic testing of various alternative ways to the Good Life.

11. Life With a Wonderful Sparring Partner

While life on the Swarthmore campus in the time of Frank Aydelotte and Joseph Swain was intellectually exciting and richly rewarding in many ways, it was enriched still more for Jesse, Rebe, and their children by the general atmosphere of fun, challenge, and inquiry which pervaded their homes, first at Whittier Place, later on at 602 Elm Avenue, and then at Moylan, Pennsylvania.

A Loving but Competitive Team.

The tone was set by the parents. Jesse, as we have seen, was full of fun, challenged almost every social convention or practice, and constantly urged people to inquire into the reasons for their actions. And Rebe, although somewhat limited by her roles as wife and mother in her time at Swarthmore, nevertheless proved to be a wonderful sparring partner for her brilliant husband. Wise, witty, and vivacious, she was, as Grace R. Holmes said, "a perfect foil for Jesse." But more than that, they were a team, each helping and stimulating the other toward greater achievement in their manifold activities.

Once in a while, it is true, Rebe grew a bit petulant with a husband who seemed to be constantly dashing about the world, making speeches and meeting interesting people while she was housebound in Swarthmore. On one occasion, after attending a "very stupid" faculty tea in the afternoon, she returned to the house feeling "very tired." Jesse was there, having just returned from a speaking engagement in Washington, D.C. That evening she exploded in her diary that Jesse had had "a fine time. . . .!!" On another occasion, this time feeling ill and with "a lot of pain all day," she wrote that she quarreled with Jesse, not giving any other particular reasons. And, when Jesse was in Paris in 1920, trying to do his job as traveling inspector or commissioner for the AFSC, she wrote to him of her unhappiness back home and said that she couldn't possibly join him in Europe or England as he had wished. Jesse replied in a long and agonized letter which seems worthy of extended quotation:

> ... I do hope thee will give thyself as much pleasure as thee can. I cannot tell how much I sympathise [sic] with thee in the situation. Travel about a bit, go to see thy friends, and find some variety. And try to believe a little in thy old J over here, and don't try to find things to say against him. Dear lady, I am not having an easy time, and no one can really be a companion to me but thee. . . . Please get ready a welcome for me when I get the long job done, . . . the best thing will be getting back to thee, — if thee can only find it in thy heart to be glad to see me. . . . Please!

To placate Rebe still more, Jesse wrote that he was sending her two presents by way of Dorothy Jones, an AFSC worker returning to the United States the following week. There would be two fox skins from Serbia, plus "a beautiful piece of hand work of the Paisley shawl order" that he had picked up in an antique shop in Paris. "It is old and has some holes," Jesse wrote, "but it is exquisite. . . ." He added a postscript to the effect that "Herman needn't worry about the 'vamp'. I saw her [in Paris] for a few minutes after Meeting; my only interest in her was to hear about him, and I haven't seen her since — some 5 weeks. . . ."

There was more than a hint of petulance in Rebe's reaction to the luxurious-traveling style of the J. Russell Smiths when the Smiths and the Holmeses met in Ceylon in the course of their sabbatical-leave trips in 1925-1926. By this time Smith's textbooks in geography were selling like hot cakes; the royalties were rolling in. Rebe wrote to her son Robert in February, 1926, that the Smiths were travelling with fourteen pieces of luggage, and that they had acquired a guide to show them through India. ". . . & they travel first class! We felt very plebian — no servant and travelling *second*! Their trip must be costing a fortune, but J.R.S. is evidently coining money by his books — if I were thee I'd write popular textbooks!!. . . " She added that Colombo was full of beautiful things from all over the Orient. "I'd like to spend hundreds of dollars right here on brass, & ivory — & sandal wood — & tortoise shell — & precious & semi-precious stones. . . ."

But such reactions to the life that Rebe and Jesse shared were but occasional and temporary aberrations. In general, they were a loving but competitive team. Ruth Holmes Dryden, Jesse's niece, told how, after being separated for some time, they met again at a seashore resort. Jesse raced over the sand dunes, Rebe ran to meet him halfway, and they fell into each other's arms. Rebecca Timbres Clark, Rebe's niece, said that Jesse "adored the ground she walked on." And they shared a dislike of dullness and the politely conventional. On one occasion, when they were seated at the speakers' table during a Swarthmore alumni banquet, the main speaker proved to be so very dull that they felt compelled to entertain themselves. As the speaker ploughed through his tedious periods, Jesse and Rebe were observed nodding and smiling to each other, apparently engaged in the most fascinating conversation. When the banquet was finally ended, the toastmaster asked Jesse and Rebe what could have proved so interesting to a couple married for so long a time. Jesse and Rebe replied in wide-eyed innocence that they were merely reciting the alphabet in turns — "A, B, C! (nod and smile), D, E, F! (nod and smile), . . ."

Friends, relatives, and colleagues agreed that Rebe was a vital person with a delightful sense of humor. (And, as Eleanor Stabler Clarke commented, "perhaps she needed that sense of humor to live with Ducky.") When some one asked her how she felt when people rushed to congratulate her after one of her husband's brilliant speeches, she replied, "Oh, I just act wren-like." She had many opportunities to act like a wren when she accompanied Jesse through fourteen summers of Chautauqua touring, on political-campaign trips when he was a candidate for national, state, and local offices on the Socialist ticket, and when he toured various states speaking for the League for Industrial Democracy. More than that, she was usually there when he lectured at most of the Friends' centers in the United States, and when he addressed every Friends' General Conference [Hicksite] from 1897 to 1937. Given all this traveling, it was fortunate that she was "a tough old nut," as she admitted in a letter to Herman in 1925.

And there were many other facets to Rebe's character. That she was a vital and very feminine person was shown very vividly when she reported to her son Robert that, while attending a party given by the wife of the "Governor General of the Madras Presidency" during the Holmes' visit to India in 1926, she was impressed by the

219

colorful costumes of the jewelled women she met there. She burst out: "O Bob, I wish I had several lives to live — there are so many interesting things to do in the world. . . ." She was a liberal, and a practical joker to the point of voting for Earl Browder in a national election — a vote designed only to go her Socialist Jesse one better, and to set old ladies' tongues clacking in suburban Swarthmore. While giving the conservative element in society its just due, her whole life style was experimental, daring, and forward looking. She disliked getting "sot" in any given groove (she even sampled beer in Europe).

And she believed in euthanasia. In a letter to Robert she wrote of her concern that "the Coulter boy" of Swarthmore, apparently stricken with a terminal illness, could not "be chloroformed into a better world. I'd like to do quite a bit of chloroforming & relieve several people of useless burdens — but alas, custom forbids. . . ." This concern for human suffering, and her unorthodox way of treating it, was also shown in the technique she used to treat Herman for a bad case of hiccoughs in the Moylan home after Jesse had retired from active service at Swarthmore College. Herman had tried all the established home remedies to no avail. Finally he decided to take a cold shower in the hope that the shock of cold water would effect a cure. He went to the bathroom, disrobed, and was about to step under the shower when he heard a piercing scream and a loud thump from the stair landing outside the bathroom. He rushed out in the "altogether" to find his mother lying on the floor. He stopped to pick her up; as he carried her away she murmured, "How are thy hiccoughs, Herman?" This shock treatment worked — Herman was cured.

But long before this episode Rebe and Jesse had demonstrated another facet of their characters. Deeply attached to Ruth Holmes Dryden, they invited her to stay in their home while she attended Swarthmore. While Ruth found that there was some tension in the Holmes' family, she stayed for two years before transferring to Nebraska to get her degree. This same generosity was extended to Ruth's daughter, Helen Kendall, when family finances during the Depression threatened to end her attendance at Nebraska Wesleyan in her third year. Jesse and Rebe heard of this situation and "put up" the money to enable Helen to finish her university course. Not only did they do these nice things for relatives; they also made a sort of foster child out of Margaret Byrd while she was a student at

Swarthmore. She spent a lot of time in their home, saying later that "If Quakers had godparents and you could choose your own, they would have been mine." In the course of a visit of the Ed Rawsons to the Holmeses, Margaret was introduced to Ed's son Arthur. A romance developed to the point that Margaret and Arthur were married in the Holmes' home.

A Life Style in the Home.

This marriage occurred at 5 Whittier Place, in a time when the phone number, 39-J, still reflected a relatively uncomplicated way of life. But by April, 1927 the signs of a new and more involved campus life were seen when an article in *The Phoenix* stated that, in the fall term, fifteen junior girls would use the house formerly used by Jesse, Rebe, and their children. By the time the girls were to occupy the Whittier Place home, the Holmes family would have moved to a new house being built in the "Crum Woods back of the College." This plan was abandoned, however; during the summer the old Holmes' homestead, rented from the College, was overhauled and redecorated for the use of the Neffs, Dr. Neff being a new professor in the economics department. In November, the Holmes family was to move into one of the new homes being built by the College on the south side of Elm Avenue below Walnut Lane; their immediate neighbors were to be the Blanshards, the Hunts and the Dresdens.

The Holmes' new home was 602 Elm Avenue, and when Rebe inspected it on August 22 she called it "nice." She had left the old house "without tears;" now, while they stored their regular household furniture in a Swarthmore garage and took a room "at Abby's" [Abby Mary Hall Roberts], she went on a series of shopping trips to Philadelphia — to Wanamaker's, Strawbridge and Clothier, and Van Sciver's — looking for new furniture and drapes for the windows. While one of these trips made her "awfully tired", she had enough energy left to go to Pittsburgh on October 9 with a Mrs. Coates to attend a "Federation" meeting (of women's clubs?). She stayed in Pittsburgh almost a week, driving back to Swarthmore only to find that Jesse had moved their things into the new house during her absence, and then escaped to Washington, D.C. for reasons of his own. While Rebe found that the moving of all this furniture had left their new home in "an awful mess," she was nevertheless glad to join Jesse on October 16 "at Emma's" for supper, and then go "home" with him to their room at Abby's. On October 22 they finally moved into their new house, well ahead of the moving time projected by *The Phoenix* reporter in September.

In this new home, as was true of their other homes at Whittier Place, the furnishings and decorations represented the Holmes' life style — a life style perhaps best described as a combination of a decent respect for the past (particularly for distinguished ancestors and the artifacts they had left behind), a feeling for middle-class expressions of the fleeting present and hopes for the future, and a great interest in those Oriental cultures which seemed to fuse past, present, and future in lasting philosophies and religions. The furnishings and decorations had been accumulated over the years as wedding presents, through timely purchases in the current market, through the Holmes' travels across the world, and through the special interests and creations of Jesse and Rebe. (In one of the Whittier Place houses one could see a grandfather's clock in the hallway at the base of the stairs, a position which did not render it immune to the dangers of being upset by the feet of young boys sliding down the stairway banister. Herman recalled that when he upset it on one such occasion, his father and mother did not register undue "impatience".) Tables and chairs from Philadelphia department and furniture stores provided elegance and comfort; on the tables were brass bowls, elaborate candlesticks, mahagony cigarette-and-jewelry boxes, and a samovar — all intricately decorated by the Middle Eastern and Oriental craftsmen who had made them. In the Elm Street and Moylan homes the Holmeses were proud to display an oil painting of a Chautauqua-tent scene which had been given to them by the Pearsons when they moved to the Virgin Islands. Elsewhere in these homes were Oriental tapestries and the rugs Jesse had created whenever he found the time to pursue rug-making as a hobby. These rugs are beautifully colored and full of the symbols of various Oriental religions.

Undoubtedly his greatest achievement in this form of art was the creation of an autobiographical rug in the period between World War I and the end of his Chautauqua activities. Marking his design figures on a canvas base bought in Scotland, Jesse spent some six-and-a-half years trying sixty-five thousand knots in the woolen fibers to complete the picture. This picture was a series of symbols or figures representing the high points of his life and those of his family. On the upper left-hand margin was the figure of a deer, standing for the Jesse-Rebe courtship pursued so avidly in the Philadelphia zoo (as indicated earlier, Jesse often said that his life "never really began" until he had captured Rebe). To the upper right of the deer, inside the crenelated inner border, stands a sturdy oak for Jesse and a slender elm for Rebe, with their branches intertwined. To the right is the Capitol in Washington, D.C., invoking fond memories of Jesse's first teaching job at the Sidwell Friends' School and the first years of their married life. The "choo-choo train" is taking them back to Nebraska (corn) for a visit with Jesse's relatives; on the left two wavy lines represent a boat trip from Philadelphia to Washington; on the right there is the pet flying squirrel which lived in Jesse's coat pocket; and a Ferris wheel representing the Holmes' visit to the World's Fair in Chicago, 1893. The swastika, that ancient symbol for good luck and well-being, may have stood for Elizabeth's conception during the George School period; the red building beneath it and the flask to the right stand for George School and the chemistry Jesse taught there. The symbol for waves, and the bean pot under it, are reminders of the boat trips to Boston on the way to summer vacations at Carter Hill, Maine. The five-windowed house with a red rose to its right, and a dog beneath the rose, represent the home at George School, the birth of Elizabeth, and her collie dog Bruce. Then, on the left, is the steamer which carried Jesse to England and Oxford in 1899, while Rebe remained at Carter Hill (pictured as a wren flying in the blue above the barn). The star and crescent, and the mosque, represent Jesse's extension of his Oxford studies into Egypt and the Near East. The white symbol, which looks like a pair of waterwings united by a bubble, indicates his interest in philosophy, as the fish represents Christianity; both of these symbols point, as it were to the figure of Parrish Hall, Swarthmore College, where he was to teach philosophy and religion for thirty-seven years. Under the "water wings" stands Elizabeth, with a thistle for Herman on her right, and a thistle for Robert on her left. A blue band over the circus tent perhaps represented blue sky — or it may have stood, in Jesse's mind, as a symbol of depression following Elizabeth's death in 1912. The large circus tent, of course, is a reminder of the many years spent in Chautauqua work, while the representation of the boot of Italy, and the four figures to its left, were meant to show the family trip to Europe in 1914. The beer mug indicates that part of this trip was through Germany; the teapot indicates England. And then came the explosion of World War I, indicated on the rug by that chaotic and colorful symbol to the right of the Chautauqua tent. The cross and the question mark in the lower right-hand section indicate Jesse's concern as to the future of Christian culture after World War I. The figure of the blue jay, representing Jesse, is a wee bit hunched, rather unlike the upright, confident and aggressive picture of him we have from many pre-1914 photographs and descriptions.

That the blue jay had a vein of humility and uncertainty in his makeup, covered over most of the time by his cheerful, confident manner, was shown as early as January, 1900, when, writing, to Rebe from Oxford, he confessed that "A sense of rawness & newness lingers about me when I hob-nob with the inhabitants of this home of my ancestors . . . ." He admitted that he didn't know a thing about his ancestors beyond his grandparents, and had "a sneaking conviction that everyone knows that I've always lived in wooden houses. I put a bold face on it but I'm timidity itself within. . . ."

This feeling of inadequacy was not improved by the fact that Rebe had for years hung a portrait of her grandmother, Rebecca Sinclair Turner (traceable back to Rosslyn Castle, Scotland), over the fireplace in the Holmes' living room. At the other end of the room a boyhood portrait of Rebe's father gazed down on the many social gatherings which enjoyed Holmes' hospitality. Finally, the long-suffering Jesse burst out — "I need an ancestor too!" He spent quite a bit of time researching his lineage, drew a genealogical chart in his resource book, and wrote a description of William Holmes of Olde England, the husband of Margaret Fell, and the man he wanted portrayed as his ancestor. And now, as he looked around for an artist to paint the portrait of William Holmes, some of the bread he had cast upon the waters came back to him as pure gold. Rae Zilboorg, the artist wife of psychiatrist Gregoy Zilboorg, whom Jesse and Rebe had befriended when he was a rootless and penniless Russian refugee from Bolshevik terror, offered to do the job. Jesse gave her his description of William Holmes, and some photographs of his parents and grandparents, plus some of his own. Rae Zilboorg went to work. The end result is a brilliant composite which suggests some Holmes' traits and yet is different enough to be taken as a genuine ancestor. The portrait was nicely framed and hung in the dining room so that one could see it through an archway from the living room. Jesse had a lot of fun showing off his illustrious ancestor; his "blue eyes twinkled as he described his august relative...."

And the Dead Should Not Burden the Living.

No doubt Rebe was amused at Jesse's effort to assert his distinguished lineage; we are not so sure that she was always amused at Jesse's concern with death and the proper way to conduct a funeral. There is a hint of impatience in a diary note in 1927, when she wrote that she and Jesse spent "all day burying Mrs. Fraser's father. . . . J. did a brilliant job as a funeral director." But she most probably nodded her head in agreement when Jesse, speaking at the funeral of Catherine Rawson, said that "We have to get used to dying, just as we get used to living"; dying, according to him, was but part of living. And Rebe agreed completely with Jesse and other Friends when they tried to do something about the monetary waste and the "tom-tom beating that goes on around the American Way of Death. . . ." Jesse and his old friend Ed Rawson developed a plan to defeat the extravagant fees charged by undertakers for coffins and funerals. (Rawson, after retiring from his regular duties as an educator, taught elementary shop classes in the Rose Valley School for seventeen years and practiced carpentry as an avocation.) In the plan he and Jesse worked up, he would make coffins in plywood sections, these sections to be stored as a package for each coffin and screwed together when the need arose. Both families — the Rawsons and the Holmeses — kept such coffin-packages in their cellars, not only for their own possible use, but as a convenience for their friends. (In later years, when his reputation as something of an eccentric was in full bloom, a rumor circulated on the Swarthmore campus that Jesse kept a coffin in his living room and frequently slept in it.)

But the Holmes-Rawson scheme for cheaper burials was essentially an individual effort by pioneer spirits. What was needed was organized group activity along this line. In March, 1930, when he was sixty-six, Jesse launched such a program. He rose to speak in Swarthmore Monthly Meeting to express a concern about the high cost of funerals, and suggested that a small committee be appointed to consider the matter and perhaps work out a helpful plan. As so often happens, the originator of the idea soon found himself appointed to such a committee by the Monthly Meeting; the committee was instructed not only to guide Friends in the matter of simpler and less-expensive funerals, but to spread the word among those "not members of Society."

This Committee on Funerals, as we may call it, labored on its task until October, 1930. Its report to the Monthly Meeting in that month included the following points: That a proper study of the whole situation was being made, and that the Committee was ready to help anyone in conducting cheaper funerals; that the Meeting had available lots in nearby Eastlawn Cemetery; that a small standard stone marker be used by all Meeting members; and that "wherever possible," Friends make use of cremation. The Meeting "united with these recommendations," and the Committee was continued.

And Jesse Holmes remained steadfast in this protest against wasteful funeral expenses. He continued his crusade in an article in the *Friends' Intelligencer* in 1933, using this means to probe current beliefs and practices still more deeply, and to advance reasoned arguments for more logical changes. He started by stating that, since death was needed and inevitable, a sensible person should plan for it "with as little inconvenience" as possible. He went on:

> Fortunately our age has outgrown the terror of death, which went with the medieval superstitions of angry god, of fiery hell, of everlasting misery. Some of the phrases remain, but the active belief and fear of it have disappeared. Death now takes its place as one of the orderly processes of life, normally terminating a period of growth and development, and perhaps opening the way to another such period. I say 'perhaps' because it is a matter about which we have no certain knowledge, as is also true of most of the great human values. These are the domain, not of knowledge, but of faith — unless and until ways of knowing appear. Our faith has nothing to do with details, but depends on an inner certainty that life is not a failure but leads to greater ends, that its values are real and permanent, that past and present are way and gateway to a greater future.

But, as Jesse wrote, his main purpose in this article was to urge the development of "a more natural and a more wholesome attitude to the fact of bodily death. . . ." A major obstacle to the development of such an attitude, he thought, was that people hadn't planned for death. This "lack of orderly prearrangement," plus the grief and worry associated with the passing of a loved relative, allowed the services of the undertaker "to become exceedingly

226

burdensome, the helplessness of the bereaved family making them an easy mark for all sorts of unnecessary and undesirable rituals and expenses. . . ."

Jesse called on his readers to face the facts. "Death leaves us, for speedy disposal, bodies which have been the abiding place [s] of loved ones and are no more." The most desirable way of disposal, it seemed to him, was cremation. Ordinary cemeteries were "hideous affairs," soon became heavy burdens on the community through the expenses of maintenance, and drew from productive use the land which that expanding community could put to better purposes. "The custom of preserving dead bodies is a relic of barbarism, . . . having to do in some vague fashion with the old and meaningless doctrine of the resurrection of the body." As Jesse thought, any sensible person living in the Age of Science could see that cremation was the only real solution to the disposal of dead bodies.

(No doubt Jesse's position as a thinking Friend, plus his training in chemistry and physics, had led him to this conclusion. He probably would have agreed with a fisherman friend of the author that cremation is also the quickest way to discharge a body's debt to the universe — the quickest way to send the elements formerly locked up in a body back into that endless recycling of atoms and molecules into new, and yet old, combinations, which keeps the organic-inorganic cosmos a going concern. The fisherman friend, we might add, would have his ashes strewn over his favorite stream, sparing his relatives the expense of maintaining a niche in an elaborate mausoleum.)

Jesse of course knew that the "hard cake of custom" was not so easily broken; he therefore recommended a middle course. Since the customary conduct of funeral services led to "a maximum of suffering" for the family and friends of the deceased, and "a maximum of unwholesome emotion for the public," he proposed a scheme to be followed by Quakers:

> . . . The legal requirements — a doctor's certificate of death, and some form of license for cremation or burial — being attended to, an inexpensive and unornamented wooden chest should be provided and the body tenderly laid in it — without flowers and without silks and satins. After no less than twenty-four hours . . . the body should be privately taken to the crematory or burial ground and privately disposed of, some friend . . . of the immediate family accompanying it. . . . There should be no display of the body, no procession, no ritual. At an appropriate time soon after, a memorial

service may be held, whether in a private home or at a meeting house.

While the services of a professional undertaker might be necessary or desirable "in most cases," the casket should not be purchased through him or from him. "A chest appropriate for the purpose may be made by any carpenter for $5 to $10 [in 1933!]." And Jesse reminded his readers that one of the industries fostered by the American Friends Service Committee in West Virginia in those depression years made coffins for a price of "$10 to $15," and "the freight charges amount to about $3. . . ." Furthermore, a fund left by Anna Jeanes would pay for all the "costs of cremation ($35 to $50) on application. . . ." The reader was urged to see the advertisement in the *Friends Intelligencer* for the details of the cremation offer.

And so Jesse's crusade against the mindless and superstitious ways of handling the dead continued. As he said in 1933, "Only a rather sickly sentimentality desires the hideous formal funeral service commonly employed. A really servicable   friendship . . . should protect bereaved families from the strain and burden which bad custom has made common." In 1938, only four years from his own death, he was still serving on the Swarthmore Monthly Meeting's Committee for Funerals and Interments, undoubtedly still preaching his Jeffersonian doctrine that the dead should not impose a heavy burden on the living.

In these arguments Jesse had rather boldly faced the issue of whether there was a life after death, and a heaven in the usual sense. He had been just as bold and forthright on an earlier occasion. Brand Blanshard remembers how Jesse led off the Swarthmore Meeting for Worship on Easter Sunday in 1925 by stating in a loud and clarion voice "that it was foolish to order one's life in view of a life to come; we should struggle to enrich the here and now, for we should be a long time dead. . . ."

A Pattern of Family Living.

And Jesse and Rebe practiced what they preached: it was their joint effort to enrich the here-and-now which made life in their home so exciting, and their companionship at parties and other social events so rewarding. More than that, their belief that life is an opportunity for service to others led them to work in Swarthmore community affairs, and to make countless trips to distant places to take part in conferences, give lectures and radio talks, and to help organize projects for human uplift.

Their several houses at Swarthmore served, of course, as bases of operations for these many activities. Here, in the intervals between excursions, they developed a pattern of home life conditioned not only by their special interests as reformers, but by the ordinary routines of eating and washing dishes, sleeping and making beds, shopping for food and clothes, and doing the laundry. While Rebe's family inheritance, plus Jesse's salary and lecture fees, made it possible to hire cooks and maids, there were times when they had to do their own household work. Herman remembers how, at Whittier Place, his father sometimes whisked his plate from under his nose as he was taking his last bite so that he (Jesse) might get to the dishwashing sooner. The maids generally made the beds and cleaned the house, although Rebe, at least on one occasion, cleaned closets; on another occasion, on a "rainy queer" day, she cleaned six bureau drawers. And Herman also remembers how his father, when maid service was not available, would do the laundry in the basement of 5 Whittier Place, pushing the handle of one of those washing machines considered to be an epitome of mechanical culture in the early twentieth century. (One wonders whether Jesse had Rebe in mind when he recorded a humorous story in his Resource Book B: "What I want," said the lady, "is a handyman who will do odd jobs about the house, run errands, never answer back, & is always ready to do what I want." "Ah no," said the seedy individual, edging toward the door, "it's a husband you're looking for, ma'am.")

Other aspects of family life were to some extent compromises between the ideal and the actual — between the absolute prohibition of those practices Jesse considered to be mindless conventions and relics of medieval superstitions (voicing prayers before meals, giving wedding presents and Christmas presents), and the necessity of obeying some of those customs to some extent lest one be ostracized as just "too queer." So the Holmes family, like many other Protestant families, observed a brief period of silent prayer or meditation before meals. This led to some embarrassment when Jesse brought a Methodist minister home one day. The minister asked a blessing before they ate; the holiness of his utterance was destroyed, however, by the unseemly tittering of the two small boys — Herman and Robert — seated at the table. When Rebe rebuked the boys later for this display of impoliteness, one of them said, " 'But, Mother, that man talked all through silence.' " And we may recall how Jesse was somewhat abashed by the superfluity of presents at his own wedding. His essential position here was reported by Margaret B. Rawson: " 'What are weddings anyway? They are just excuses for the silver companies to sell wedding presents.' " Indeed, as Margaret thought, it was entirely possible that Jesse would not have given his best friend a wedding present. The matter of Christmas presents was in even worse case: Why, asked Jesse, should people wait until Christmas to give gifts to people they liked or admired; why should they succumb to that rampant spirit of commercialism so different from Christ's spirit; why should they honor the memory of those "three wise men" from the East whose very existence and actions at the time of Christ's birth were in historical doubt? Jesse even carried his doubtful attitude on Christmas presents into his ethics class at Swarthmore, one student remembering that he told a story there about the mindless Christmas shopping of one old lady in Maine who spent many hours going through gift shops, her shopping list in her hand. But she went overboard: when she put her presents on her bed and put tags on them. she found that she had thirty-nine gifts, but only thirty-eight people to whom she had planned to give them. So she gave the remaining gift — a pink-sachet pincushion — to an old Maine guide in her neighborhood, a man who always seemed to have a streak of tobacco juice running down his beard.

Rebe was of a more compromising persuasion. In 1927, she started her Christmas shopping on Friday, December 23 (bless her heart, she was not yet impelled by Macy's parade, or by other importunities, to get the Christmas spirit as early as Thanksgiving Day). The next day, December 24, she shopped some more, and then spent Christmas Eve listening to "lovely radio music" in company with her son Robert.

On other evenings, when she was home alone because Jesse was off somewhere giving a speech, or because he had gone to bed to unwind by reading those detective stories that cluttered his bedside table, Rebe might be reading poetry. Some of these poems, particularly those from L.C. Allen's "Long Cabinet," she copied on notepaper, possibly for use when she attended meetings of the Emerson Club. And on one occasion she or Jesse clipped a poem from the rotogravure section of a Sunday newspaper to keep among their collection of other poems. While it isn't Shakespeare or Wordsworth, this work by Kalfus Kurtz, entitled "Winter", seems worthy of duplication here if only to show what caught the Holmes' eye:

> The lovely days of winter come,
> The wind is like a muffled drum.
> I did not miss this pastel sky
> When summer roses bloomed near by;
> I did not know that on this hill
> There was such beauty, chaste and still;
> That mirrored ice in frozen stream
> Could catch and hold a vagrant dream;
> That tall bare trees so hard and brown
> Could sing though leaves had fluttered down
> But now with new-found joy I see
> All that summer hid from me.

If Rebe did nothing more strenuous in the way of exercise than walk to the village market, attend her many meetings, or drive the family car, Jesse found frequent opportunities to indulge his liking for sports and games. He kept Indian clubs in the house, had fun with archery in the summertime, and took on Ed Rawson in many a fencing match. About 1938, when both men were in their seventies, Jesse and Ed put on a fencing exhibition for the children at Rose Valley School, their masks, foils and stylized postures perhaps evoking a romantic picture of the duelists of old in the minds of the students. And back home Jesse and Rebe might spend a rare evening hunched over the Ouija board as part of their continuing interest in psychic phenomena.

And this was an "interest" rather than a belief; such things as spiritualism were phenomena to be studied through action, through participation in seances. It was in this spirit of scientific investigation that Jesse and Rebe, via a friend, invited a medium to conduct a seance in their home. The medium proved to be a young, rather coarse-looking woman, arriving in Philadelphia on the noon train from Chicago. Herman met her at the Swarthmore station that afternoon with the family car, and was convinced that her late arrival, plus the fact that she had no advance notice of the seance, precluded any research into the family histories of the Holmes-Webb-Price clan. The medium was greeted at the house by a group of the Holmes' friends called up on short notice for the proceedings — J. Russell Hayes (the college librarian), Dr. and Mrs. William I.

Hull, and Dr. O. Edward Janney and his wife. Living room chairs were set in a circle, all the people in the circle held hands, and the lights were turned low. Dr. Janney insisted on holding the medium's wrist to measure her pulse all through the seance, later on reporting that the beat went down almost to zero during the session. And it was a remarkable session, as Herman remembers it: all those present got messages from departed relatives in accents they recognized. But the most astounding message was from "Uncle Will" Price, the famous architect who had given up his drawing board years ago. Uncle Will had a most peculiar laugh — "a series of chuckles like a waterfall;" this laugh now came through the medium as Will answered Jesse's questions. "Will, can you name anything in this room that belonged to you?" Will: "Yes, there's a fireplace there, and on the mantle are . . . ," naming a number of things Jesse and Rebe had been given after his death. Jesse: "Is there anything in the hallway which used to belong to you?" Will: "Yes, there's a little table and a picture there." In the post mortem following the departure of the medium, the assembled intellectuals simply could not explain what had happened. But they did enjoy, we may be sure, the refreshments served by Rebe, that ever-charming hostess.

Rebe opened her house to many people on less eerie occasions, playing hostess to an almost endless round of luncheon and dinner guests, spontaneous social events, and more carefully planned parties. She and Jesse belonged to a group of colleagues and friends who met more-or-less regularly in each others' homes for dinners and charades. One year, when it was their turn, they decided to hold a barn party in the old-time tradition. The first floor of the house was transformed into a barn in a most realistic way — bales of hay were strewn about, and live chickens, ducks, and a pony greeted the guests with cackles, quacks, and whatever it is that a pony does. There was no liquor, but no doubt sweet cider quenched their thirst. In any case it was great fun; this party was talked about for years in the circle of that dinner club.

Since she and Jesse were so often responsible for planning social events, it must have pleased them when the Swarthmore Society of Friends began to hold annual suppers, followed by entertainment, at Whittier House on the campus. But even here they found themselves involved in the work — Rebe as one of the Quaker ladies serving the "ample supper" to the men, and Jesse as one of the speakers following the banquet. On one such occasion he spoke on

"Words", giving this topic, as we may believe, the same inimitable treatment he gave to any subject he chose to address. Other speakers included George A. Hadley, formerly head of the physics department, who spoke on something "Brewed Forty Years Ago"; J. Russell Hayes, who recited poems and sang a ballad called "Killaloe"; and Edward A. Jenkins, '91, who told humorous stories. The evening concluded with charades directed by William Price, the son of the architect.

In March, 1925, when this Quaker supper was held, Jesse and Rebe could feed pride in the fact that their two sons, Herman and Robert, were now well launched on their careers. Herman had attended Swarthmore Preparatory School and Swarthmore College; he then transferred to Antioch College, where he was about to receive his A.B. degree. Following a year of teaching mathematics in the Pape School, Savannah, Georgia, he married Eloise Moore, a co-ed he had met at Antioch. (Rebe called her "a dear girl" in a letter she sent to Robert in 1925). In succeeding years Herman earned a Master of Arts degree from Columbia University (1927), taught in the Orchard School in Indianapolis, and became the proud father of Jesse Herman Holmes the Fourth, who was to grow up to be a very handsome young man and the father of four of Jesse's and Rebe's ten great-grandchildren.

Robert, Herman's younger brother, attended Oberlin College, where he met his wife-to-be, Grace Darling Randall, a music major from Easton, Pennsylvania. Transfering to Swarthmore, he earned membership in Phi Beta Kappa, became a second-string All-American in lacrosse, and graduated with an A.B. in 1923. A period of study at the Harvard Graduate School of Business furthered his chances for a scholarship at some prestigious university; this ambition was realized in April, 1925, when he was awarded the Harrison Fellowship in Economics at the University of Pennsylvania.

Sabbatical Leave and a World Trip.

April of 1925 was a month not soon forgotten by Rebe and Jesse. Not only did Robert get the Fellowship, but in that month the Board of Managers of Swarthmore granted Jesse a sabbatical leave for the academic year 1925-1926. Earlier the Board of Managers had voted to grant him a half-year leave of absence after he had served Swarthmore for twenty-five years; perhaps their more generous

233

move now was influenced by the fact that Dr. Sherwood Eddy had invited Jesse to join a select group of one hundred teachers and editors to travel with him through England and Europe to study institutions, examine educational problems, and to meet the leading intellectual figures and statesmen in the several countries on their itinerary. After the Eddy tour had been completed, the Holmeses now decided, they would go on to India and return home by way of China and Japan. (When they returned to Swarthmore their passports carried visas from England, France, Germany, Austria, Hungary, Czecho-Slovakia, and Greece, as well as from countries in the Orient.)

When Jesse and Rebe were getting ready to go on this world trip they found out that others in their circle of friends would also be traveling abroad. J. Russell Smith and his wife Henrietta would make a somewhat similar journey, while John A. Miller and his Mary were to lead an expedition of astronomers and mathematicians to Sumatra in order to study the total eclipse of the sun scheduled to take place there in January.

The preparations for these trips must have been lightened considerably by the expressions of good will coming from the Friends of Swarthmore Monthly Meeting. On April 21 the Meeting "enthusiastically united with" a declaration of interest in "the work" of the travelers-to-be, offered prayers for their success and well-being, and wished them a safe return. And this declaration noted particularly that the Holmeses and the Smiths were "expecting to spend the coming year ... working toward the establishment of better understanding among Peoples; ... " This message of "loving interest" was sent to the parties named.

But more was needed: these travelers should have letters of introduction to smooth their way in foreign parts. And so that peculiarly Quaker document — the "travelers' Minute" — was composed for Jesse and Rebe, approved by the Meeting, and given to them for their use abroad:

Sixth Month 23rd, 1925

Dear Friends:

Swarthmore Monthly Meeting of the Religious Society of Friends desires to extend to you through its valued members, Jesse H. and Rebecca W. Holmes, most cordial greetings. These Friends are planning to travel and sojourn in other lands, working toward the establishment of better understanding among peoples. They have the concern to visit meetings of the Society of

234

Friends in China, Japan . . . , and [in] other lands, and our Meeting rejoices in this opportunity of entering through them into spiritual fellowship with you.

On behalf of Swarthmore Monthly Meeting,

Sincerely your friend,

(Signed) Abby Mary Hall Roberts, Clerk

A similar Minute was composed for the Smiths and given to them.

And so, heartened by the good will of their Meeting, Jesse and Rebe set out on their world trip. (They had no compunctions about leaving Robert in residence at 5 Whittier Place since he could easily commute from there to his Fellowship duties in Philadelphia; in addition, Robert would have some companionship there of an evening because the house had been rented to the Blanshards when they arrived in Swarthmore for their first year on the campus.) They went to England, and then to Rotterdam via the Hook of Holland. Here, breaking away from most of the Eddy party, they went to The Hague and to Delft, returning to Rotterdam on a little canal boat. "A lovely day," Rebe reported.

On to Berlin, where President Hindenburg received a delegation from the Eddy group, and where Hans Luther, minister of finance, addressed the whole Eddy party through an interpreter. Other notables — professors and statesmen — spoke to the visitors; Rebe thought that they were "a very sane & reasonable lot of men. . . ." After being driven to see the royal palaces at Potsdam, the group was taken to a restaurant, where four leaders of the Youth Movement addressed them after "a very good dinner." While the good dinner and the songs they sang made this a "very nice . . . sociable," the student meeting they attended later at the Berlin Opera House proved "fearfully solemn," in spite of the group singing and fine orchestral music. (Perhaps it was on this evening that she drank a glass of beer in the spirit of investigation; she found it "horrid" and didn't want any more.)

Since Rebe found Berlin expensive, she exulted in the hotel room she and Jesse occupied in Prague: "big and airy — & running water (!!!) and . . . only $1.80 a day for it — for both of us!" The Holmeses found the food in Prague equally good and equally inexpensive: while they were entertained in their hotel by a lively band playing jazz they had chicken and duck dinners — complete with potato, lettuce salad, and vanilla ice cream — for only 75¢ apiece.

After Prague, Rebe and Jesse were to go on to Dresden to see the

Sistine Madonna, to Chemnitz so that Jesse could meet with a group of Quakers, and then on to Geneva to join the main tour-party and to listen to many notable speakers. From Geneva they were to go to Paris, where Jesse wanted to attend a peace conference; then on to Vienna for a Fellowship of Reconciliation conference; then on to Cologne, Frankfort, and back to England and Oxford.

In view of all this traveling, it was not surprising that Rebe should report to Herman that Jesse had suffered two bad colds since they landed in Europe; she was glad that they hadn't put off this trip any longer since Jesse apparently couldn't stand the fatigue of a long journey "any too well, . . ." As for herself, she assured Herman, "I am feeling fine & enjoying everything very much. I guess it was a good thing for me to be pulled up by the roots & dragged off on this journey — perhaps I was getting too sot. . . ."

In Geneva they found the meetings of the League of Nations "on a high level" of method and purpose; and they were right royally entertained by Count Nisoba of Japan and his charming Quaker wife in their villa overlooking Lake Geneva, with snow-capped Mount Blanc visible in the distance across the lake. The next day the Holmeses made a pilgrimage to the monument erected for Michael Servetus, who had been burned at the stake through Calvinistic intolerance; these liberals also payed homage to Rousseau by visiting the site of his birth, and looked at the house once used by George Eliot.

Arriving in Paris on a Saturday night, they found themselves "badly stung" in their hotel arrangements; so, after attending a Quaker meeting on Sunday morning they scouted around and found a large, pleasant room with all the amenities and facilities for the "magnificent sum of $1.40 a day for the two of us. . . ." Although the street outside was filled with "enormous market trucks" in the early morning (were they near Les Halles?), there was a restaurant just around the corner, the Seine was only a block away, and Notre Dame, the Louvre, and the Sorbonne were within easy walking distance.

Jesse and Rebe joined the Eddy group in attending lectures at the Sorbonne; the lecturers, however, seemed "rather narrow & petty in their outlook"; this even was true of Stephen Lausaune, the editor of *Le Matin.* Nor did the party given in the *Le Matin* headquarters (where the wine was left almost untouched by the Eddy people) serve to change Jesse's opinion about Lausaune's pettiness.

The rest of their stay in Paris was more pleasurable. They visited Notre Dame, Cluny Museum, the Latin Quarter, had a frivolous hour at the "Folies Bergires," and were entertained as guests of the National Exposition of Decorative Arts. On this latter occasion Count Fleury was their host, taking them around to various buildings and winding it all up with "an elaborate tea" — no tea, however, but wine, lemonade, orangeade, and "cakes galore." And somewhere along the line they ran into Rae Zilboorg, who painted the composite portrait of Jesse's ancestor; she was then at the American School of Art at Fontainebleau. Rebe invited her to come to Paris, have lunch with them, attend a matinee, and then have dinner.

The Eddy party and the Holmeses were now at the permanent parting of their ways: the main group to go on a three-weeks trip to the Balkans (Rebe wished she and Jesse could have joined them), while the Holmeses were to stay in Paris a little while longer, go to Vienna for that meeting of the Fellowship of Reconciliation, and then spend some time in Germany. The main reason for not going on the Balkan trip was Jesse's "desire to please Pres. Aydelotte by going back to Oxford for October. . . ." (We may believe that Frank Aydelotte hoped that while at Oxford Jesse would absorb more of the spirit and method of the honors program which Aydelotte had brought from Oxford to Swarthmore.)

But Oxford was still in the future. Jesse and Rebe went to Austria; then they hurried to Nürnberg, where, as Rebe wrote to Robert, they were met by Frau Friedrich, "a sort of keeper of the Friends here. . . ." Frau Friedrich got them settled in a "Christlicher Hospice," which Rebe called "very nice indeed." The usual feather bed coverings were there, but in addition, there was a lighter covering. Since these September nights were cold, Rebe said that she did "not abhor this German way of dressing a bed as much as I usually do. In Berlin it was awfully *hot* all the time . . . , and to have nothing but a feather bed as cover was fearful!!" In the several days spent here in Nürnberg they walked around as any good tourists would, being impressed, as they had been in 1914, by the wall around the city and by "the *torture* chamber with its horrible instruments, . . . " But, very much unlike the ordinary tourist, Jesse felt it to be his duty to live up to that purpose mentioned in the traveler's Minute given to the Holmeses by Swarthmore Meeting — to promote "better understanding among [the] peoples" of the world. So, he somehow arranged to address a group of Nürnbergers, principally women, on the subject of "Patriotism." His speech was to be given a running translation by an English woman who had married a German; this interpretation didn't go very well, so Jesse attempted to translate for himself, the audience joining in with suggested words and phrases. Rebe thought that "it was really rather nice. . . ." But the speech given the following evening, in a hot and humid room packed with working people, was in a different case: Rebe, in a masterpiece of understatement, reported that it didn't go "particularly well," in spite of the fact that this time Herr Friedrich did a fine job of translating. Jesse's topic was "Race Questions," his idea being to criticize "in the largest sense" the efforts by the white race to dominate the yellow, brown, and black peoples of the world. As Rebe watched the faces of Jesse's audience — people still struggling to emerge from the economic chaos following World War I — she could see that it seemed to them a supererogation (she spelled it "superorragtion") on an American's part to speak to them in this lofty fashion. And, when Jesse touched on the Jewish question "one woman got quite excited & said, 'was it not written in the Scriptures that the Chosen People should devour all the other peoples' — & for her part she didn't want to be devoured by the Jews, so the only thing was to get rid of them. . . ."

After such an experience Jesse and Rebe were glad enough to move to London, where they made the Lincoln Hall Hotel, Russell Square, their base of operations. Since Jesse was absent so much of the time, giving speeches in London and observing the academic scene in Oxford, Rebe filled in her lonely days by taking walks, going to movies and art galleries, by reading, and by writing long letters to her sons. In one such letter to Robert, starting out "My beloved Baby," she described the hotel she was in, using the hotel stationery. This stationery carried photographs of interior aspects of the hotel on the left-hand margin, plus a picture of the adjacent Turkish bath. Rebe scribbled comments alongside each picture: Dining Room — "No one speaks above a whisper & I'd hate to eat celery here"; Smoking Room — "I sit here by the hour when I'm not in my room — one does not *have* to smoke!"; Billiards Room — "No one to play with, alas!"; Turkish Baths — "I have not tried these." Of necessity, she had tried the Lyons Corner House Restaurants in the neighborhood — "five restaurants on five floors, each one holding hundreds of people & each one with a good orchestra. . . ."

But now, late in October, she was getting tired of restaurant food and bored with life in Jesse's absence. Perhaps it was time that Jesse returned, for Rebe admitted to Robert that she was "down in the smoking room again & there is a nice middle-aged man here too, the only other occupant. I really ought to begin a flirtation with him, but I don't know just how to begin."

When Jesse returned for a very brief stay in London he took Rebe to see Charlie Chaplin in "The Gold Rush," which Rebe thought had "a few laughs," but was not "very good." And they tried to get tickets to "No, No, Nanette" without success.

Other interests and duties now led them to go to Oxford, where they stayed in Ruskin College with thirty-five young men and women of the laboring class. Here, living with these young people, all of them on "some sort of scholarship, but also work [ing] at the college to pay [their] way, waiting on table, etc. . . .", Rebe had her eyes opened. She wrote to Robert that "One girl, who is said to be very keen mentally, goes out scrubbing for 2 hrs. every morning & she gets 1 shilling for the 2 hrs. — isn't that a crime? . . ." The meals they had at Ruskin College were well cooked, "but the table linen was awful — I don't see why people do not use oil cloth, which can be kept clean, if they can't afford to have *clean* table linen. . . ."

Rebe's middle-class proclivities for cleanliness and order were much better satisfied when she and Jesse had lunch with a "nice young English Friend" in his sitting room on the top floor of Queen's College, Oxford. The food, as she reported, was "plain but good, served by his *scout*. . . ." And they also met several boys, formerly students at Swarthmore, and "Kappa Sigs," who were then attending the London School of Economics and Oxford University. One of these, Rebe told Robert, had been so disgusted at the fraternity hazing practiced at Swarthmore that he had transferred to Haverford.

Leaving London on October 29, they crossed the Strait of Dover to Ostend, where they boarded a train for Constantinople — this train taking them through Vienna, Buda-Pesth, Sofia, and Belgrade. In Buda-Pesth a layover of several hours gave them an opportunity to have breakfast in a restaurant and take an hour's drive around the city. In that time of currency inflation in Europe the breakfast cost them 6,000 kronen and the drive 60,000.

Jesse and Rebe found Constantinople "interesting, picturesque, and in some aspects beautiful beyond telling. . . ." They spent ten days there, indulging themselves in "an orgy of mosques, bazaars and above all the ever-changing street crowds. . . ." After settling into a comfortable hotel, they thought that here they were far removed from any friends or acquaintances. But no — an English Friend called, accompanied by a member of the New York Yearly Meeting; "Pussyfoot" Johnson, the famous prohibitionist and old college friend, dropped in on them before breakfast one morning; and "a couple of Swarthmore neighbors [the J. Russell Smiths?] called us up and invited us to lunch. . . ." Perhaps it was through the good offices of such friends that they visited the Constantinople College for Women, and Roberts College; perhaps also these friends arranged for the addresses Jesse gave at the American Women's Club ("True and False Patriotism"), at the Women's College ("Cost of War"), and at Roberts College ("Creative Vision").

During his stay in Constantinople Jesse was greatly impressed by the new spirit of enthusiastic nationalism engendered through the leadership of Mustapha Kemal. Relics of the old sultanic culture, such as the veil for women and the fez for men, were now banned by dictatorial decree. The fez had been banished only a few days before the Holmeses arrived; Jesse rather regretted the absence of that picturesque element of the native costume on the streets, and he was amused to see a tall, stately, bearded Turk wearing a small child's hat because there had been no time to find other headgear. While Jesse found the Kemal government "very assured," he also noted that it was "very militaristic in spirit and probably quite as intolerant as the old despotism. . . ." And then he couldn't resist taking a swipe at the European Christian community: "In view of the experience of the Turks with the European nations this is not surprising. If Christianity is to be interpreted in terms of the dealing of 'Christian' nations with Turkey I should say almost any paganism is preferable."

They had an "interesting" week in Greece, doing the usual tourist rounds, including visits to the ruins of Micenae and Piraeus. During this time Jesse and Rebe met Professor J.T. Shotwell, the well-known protagonist of the League of Nations, and joined forces with him and his wife in several expeditions.

Somewhere in these travels they had boarded the P.&O. ship *Mooltan,* probably in Constantinople. Now, after Greece, they were carried to Cairo, where, after doing the usual tourist round, Jesse gave his "Cost of War" address to an Egyptian audience, interpreted sentence by sentence into Arabic. Here again they found friends, and joined some two hundred Americans in a Thanksgiving dinner on the YMCA premises. As Jesse recalled it in a report via the *Friends' Intelligencer,* "Our 'Thanksgiving' included the usual Turkey [*sic*] dinner, an address by the American Minister, and some musical and other fun."

(It should be added that this account of the Thanksgiving in Cairo was in one of ten reports of the Holmes' tour sent back to Philadelphia and published in the *Friends' Intelligencer,* February through July, 1926. This series of reports, not always appearing in the *Intelligencer* according to the correct time-sequence of the Holmes' trip, bore the general title of "Carrying the Quaker Message Around the World"; the separate places visited were sometimes noted in subheadings such as "Allahabad," "A Day in an Indian Mud-Village," etc.)

Leaving Cairo, they went to Port Said, steamed through the Suez Canal, and headed into the Red Sea bound for Aden. As they cruised along Rebe wrote to her son Robert about their experiences since leaving Port Said. (She said that at Aden they would transfer to the *Raznuk,* since the *Mooltan* was bound for Australia.) Altogether, she thought, they would be glad to get off the *Mooltan,* because, as second-class passengers, she and Jesse had not been able to get a cabin together. Jesse had been forced to share a three-berth cabin with two young Catholics, Spanish priests who were "*most* devout in the early morning hours, or as J. says, 'Doing a grovel to God' about 6 A.M. . . ." Rebe also had two roommates — a young Spanish trapeze performer on her way to Australia and a young woman with a fifteen-months old baby. The baby was teething, very fretful, and cried a lot at night. But the worst thing was the heat in their cabin, made still worse by the young mother's refusal to allow the two electric fans to operate for fear her baby would catch cold. The rest of their experience on board the *Mooltan* was a mixture of the pleasant and unpleasant, the interesting and the uninteresting. While Rebe found the dining room attractive, the food was only "fair — . . . but that's the English of it. . . ." And their table companions were "dull." Going out on deck, however, was pleasant because the deck space was ample, and the reclining chairs comfortable. Every night between nine and eleven the ship's "band" (orchestra?) played on deck, the musicians being placed at the gate which divided the first- from the second-class cabins, so that both classes could dance to the

241

same music. (Rebe didn't say whether she and Jesse danced on these occasions; we can, however, conjure up a picture of them leaning over the ship's rail, gazing at the moon's reflection on the placid waters of the Red Sea, while the band played airs from "No, No, Nanette.")

As their ship entered beautiful Bombay harbor on December 11, Jesse and Rebe looked forward to ten weeks in India, which Jesse considered to be "by far the most fascinating country in the world. . . ." They found their room at the Majestic Hotel very comfortable, with ". . . a great big bathroom that was a scream. . . ." Rebe felt it necessary to scrub the tub and washstand before using them; then, however, she enjoyed "a nice warm bath, . . ." But when she drew the stopper she was horrified to see the water flooding the floor; a hasty check showed that this was meant to be, the floor being tiled and sloping to a drain.

The meals were "very good & served in style. . . ." The guests were all British, Rebe thought, and the young men would come to breakfast and lunch "in funny little Khaki shorts, shirt open at the neck, & some loose coat. . . ." But they dressed for dinner, the men being "immaculate in dinner coat & the women in low neck & no sleeves. . . ."

Although Jesse wasn't feeling very well in this Indian heat, they "did" Bombay. Rebe was particularly intrigued by the people they saw on the crowded streets — the upper-caste Hindu women in their graceful saris of many colors, the men in their awkward-looking dhobis and long shirt tails.

In spite of the heat and humidity (and Jesse's malaise) these indefatigable good-will ambassadors left the comfort of their Bombay hotel to go south to Poona, where Jesse wanted to visit a number of colleges. Jesse had already met some students from the engineering college at Poona when he addressed a small group at one of the Bombay colleges; now, however, his interest was in Ferguson College, which, in spite of its name, was "one of the few entirely native colleges in India. . . ." The Ferguson president introduced them to other men, who in turn invited the Holmeses to visit a woman's college and have a social afternoon. Rebe found this college to be of less than collegiate grade, with many of its students being child brides — even widows aged six-to-ten years; Jesse reported, however, that, in addition to the woman's college, there were more elementary schools for the much-abused widows and even for a few low-caste girls. He thought that through such colleges and schools, thousands of women were being reached to work for their own emancipation. Certainly these was a need for such education, "for a more enslaved, ignorant, and stupid life than that of the Indian women in general would be hard to imagine. . . ."

After a long inspection of the various colleges (which Rebe found "tedious") a ceremonious convocation, and a late tea, Jesse and Rebe boarded a train in Poona for Bombay, arriving there at 5:25 a.m. And it was on this train ride that Rebe had another of those small but humorous adventures which seemed to be her lot on this world trip. When they bought their tickets they had no idea what the sleeping accommodations would be like, so they simply engaged two lower births. Rebe was amused and somewhat titillated by what they found — one large room with five berths, the upper three being occupied by "very dark Indian gentlemen. . . ." There was a lavatory connected with the room, but there was not a curtain in the place. Further, no bedding was provided, the Indian practice being to carry great bedding rolls on a trip and spread them out wherever needed. While the Indians "undressed quite fully," Rebe didn't even take off her shoes; she lay down in her berth, turned her back, and "everybody was happy! . . . ."

In Bombay they called on Mrs. Sarojini Naidu, "poet, politician, and philanthropist, recognized universally as the greatest woman of India. . . ." Accepting her invitation to attend the Fortieth Indian National Congress to meet in Cawnpore, December 26-28, Jesse and Rebe journeyed northward to Baroda and Agra. In Baroda they stopped to see the "magnificent modern palace of the Goekwar, and his very unmodern stable of elephants. . . ." They had a few days at Agra, viewing the Taj Mahal by daylight and by moonlight before pushing on to Cawnpore. They arrived on Christmas Eve.

Since Cawnpore lacked the facilities to accommodate all the delegates to the Congress, an enormous *pandal* or tent, capable of sheltering some fifteen thousand, had been erected about two miles from the city. And around this tent another "city" sprang up almost overnight. As Jesse and Rebe approached this area in the forenoon of December 26 on their two-wheeled *tonga* they passed through an outer ring of roadside vendors holding up their wares with thin brown arms; then they came to a ring of "amusements, restaurants, wax works, snake charmers, bazaars and crowds upon crowds of people . . . ." These milling thousands produced that potpourri of odors, sounds, and colors to be found only in the India of that time. Leaving their cart at the gate of an enclosed section, they passed into narrow streets lined on both sides with shops or bazaars of every kind and description, selling everything from patent medicines and American bicycles to figures of Hindu gods. Another enclosed section had a display of native manufactures, including, of course, that *kheddar,* or homespun cloth, then being promoted through Gandhi's resistance to English imports. And, closer to the great *pandal,* was a collection of small tents and little reed huts which served as dwelling places for the delegates or visitors to the Congress.

Whether through Mrs. Naidu, or through the influence of the English Quaker C.F. Andrews — "greatly loved" by Gandhi's followers — Jesse was invited to meet Gandhi. Jesse found Gandhi lodged in a large brick house near the Congress tent on that memorable morning of December 26, 1925. Having passed the inspection of guards at the entrance, Jesse and Rebe sent in their cards. After a period of waiting, a uniformed nurse — English or Anglo-Indian — appeared to tell them that Gandhi had been in committee meeting all morning, and that, since he had been running a fever, she doubted that a meeting was possible. Still, she asked them to wait. Presently, having taken Gandhi's temperature and consulted with him, the nurse appeared to say that they would be received — "but only for a few minutes and only for greeting: he must not talk too much. . . ." They did meet Gandhi, in the full splendor of his ninety pounds and Indian loin cloth, setting cross-legged on a yard-high brick platform at one end of a large bare room. Invited to sit on the edge of the platform, Jesse told this "bright-eyed little man" of the Quakers' sympathy in his leadership, "and especially in his demonstration of the power of a demand for justice unsupported by bayonets. . . ." Gandhi responded that he knew about the Friends and was glad to hear directly from them. And then, after five minutes of this sort of polite conversation, the nurse appeared to say that the interview was over. Still, it was indicative of the modern democratic spirit that an Iowa farm boy, and the daughter of a Philadelphia druggist, should have this much time with the sainted leader of India's millions.

As Jesse reported, the Congress convened that afternoon, the delegates sitting cross-legged on mats or canvass ground coverings in that great tent, leaving their shoes in the aisles. The president

244

and other dignitaries also sat cross-legged on a raised platform, while the featured speakers mounted a high stand by a flight of steps. Gandhi, of course, made one of the early addresses, "presenting the case of the South African Indians, who [were] experiencing the usual dealings of the white men when property interests were involved. . . ." And Jesse couldn't resist reporting that "when Gandhi made his way into the tent the whole 15,000 rose to greet him. As he sat in his place men came quietly along the aisle to gaze at him. They brought their children in their arms and lifted them to gaze at him. . . ."

And then came the moment which Jesse and Rebe counted as one of the high spots in their lives: Mrs. Naidu, in her capacity as president, invited Jesse to address the Congress "as an American sympathizer with its plans and methods." He climbed up to the speakers' rostrum and started his speech by saying that, while he could not speak for all of America, he could express the interest of the Society of Friends in Gandhi's nonviolent campaign to gain freedom and self-government for India. As he spoke at some length of the admiration and sympathy many Americans had for the Mahatma and his methods, he was interrupted by enthusiastic applause whenever he mentioned Gandhi's name. Furthermore, Jesse told his audience, until the Hindus and the Moslems could bury their differences and put a united India into the campaign, they could not succeed in their struggle for independence. " 'When you are united you can get anything you want,' " he assured the delegates. (Later on Jesse took great pride in the fact that he was the only Westerner to address that particular Congress.)

During the meetings of the Congress, as Jesse noted, some of its Moslem delegates *were* in sympathy with its general aims of unity and independence. For a time it seemed that Gandhi had succeeded in bringing the Hindus and Moslems together in a common move for freedom from British control. But the old hostilities and mutual distrust were still there, fostered by the British policy of giving the Moslems a disproportionately large share of elective and appointive offices. A genuine national unity seemed all but impossible.

After Cawnpore the Holmeses went to Alligarh, the seat of a great Mohammedan university. They had been invited by the registrar to attend the University Jubilee, but arrived too late for its early meetings. They were, however, able to attend sessions of the Moslem League, the leading Mohammedan political organization.

Jesse found the principles of the League to be similar to those of the Gandhi party in demanding independence and self-government; they did not believe, however, that the way to achieve independence was through noncooperation and civil disobedience. And the sessions of the League, also held in a large *pandal*, revealed a much more conservative attitude on the position of women: it required the storming of the speakers' rostrum by a group of women, and an impassioned speech by one of them, before these ladies were allowed to take part in the deliberations. Even then they were required to hold themselves generally apart from the men in a remote and screened-off section of the tent.

From Alligarh Jesse and Rebe went on to Delhi on an afternoon train. Hundreds of delegates from the Moslem convention were taking the same train, and the struggle to get seats reminded Jesse of a football scrimmage. But, as "an old footballer," he played the game successfully, winning two seats and places for their baggage. The car was soon crammed to capacity, with baggage piled to the ceiling and people sitting on boxes and baggage in the aisle. Having settled down, the Holmeses made friends and the rest of the four-hour ride was of "intense interest." Two lawyers from Peshawar, near the Khyber Pass, proved to be cultured men, interested in education, and widely traveled. A delicate-featured fine-looking scholar was wedged in among a group of turbaned, heavily bearded countrymen. "All were interested in Americans and anxious to understand why we [had] passed the offensive laws against Asiatics, to know how Prohibition is working, and what America thinks of the Nationalist movement. . . ." They explained why Americans were mistaken about the Moslem attitude on polygamy; this in turn led to an interesting discussion on the position of women in world society, the lawyers tending to side with the Western view. By the time they detrained at Delhi the Holmeses had an invitation to visit Peshawar, and were even offered a position in the university there.

Such friendly contacts with Indians added to the touristic pleasures Jesse and Rebe experienced in Delhi; these contacts also showed the way to promote that "better understanding among peoples" mentioned in their Minute. Among the many friends they had made at the Cawnpore Congress was S.R. Sharma — a "farmer," as he called himself —, who sat next to Jesse on the floor of the tent just under the speakers' stand. Dressed in white homespun, he told Jesse and Rebe that he was a graduate of an

Indian university, had been an editor of a Nationalist newspaper, and also the principal of a large city high school. But, said Sharma, speaking from his boyhood experiences in an Indian mud-village, no visitor could claim that he had "seen" India until he had spent some time inspecting some of those villages inhabited by three-quarters of India's millions.

Sharma invited Jesse and Rebe to visit his own village, where he lived on a part-time basis trying to improve the practice of agriculture by introducing new crops and new methods. The Holmeses accepted his invitation. They took a sleeping car from Delhi, and arriving eventually at the station nearest the village. Met there by a large delegation of villagers, they and their bags were loaded on a heavy bullock-cart and jolted across the trackless fields past villages and over irrigation ditches, all the while hunched up in a kind of howdah, their legs tucked under them, and the big wheels "threatening" them. At Sharma's village they were taken at once to a small tent erected for their benefit, and furnished with string beds, two chairs (which Jesse thought had been borrowed from the railroad station), and a table holding copies of the *Literary Digest, Nature,* "*The Geographical Magazine,*" and *Sport.* The Holmeses were hardly settled before the leading men of the village, plus delegations from other villages, entered their tent "in groups of three and four to a dozen. At times a score were sitting cross-legged or standing about, asking all sorts of questions about America in general and ourselves in particular. . . ." Mr. Sharma, of course, acted as their interpreter.

As this interview went on, the Holmeses fanning themselves in the great heat, they could look outside their tent to a grove of plantains and fields of rice and other crops. Nearby was a well from which a pair of oxen were pulling up water in a large leather bucket to be poured into the sluiceways leading to irrigation ditches.

After a while Jesse and Rebe were served a lunch prepared by Sharma's mother. Consisting of tea and "some unknown vegetables" served on plantain-leaf platters, the Holmeses had some difficulty eating it until their kindly host provided them with spoons. Two hours later a Hindu-type vegetarian dinner was served: rice in bowls, other vegetables, various types of fried bread, some sticky sweets, and preserved fruits. While they consumed this meal they were watched by the dozen-or-so people they had been talking with earlier. Although Hindu custom called for the breaking of the earthenware bowls after guests had finished with them, Jesse and Rebe begged to be allowed to keep them intact as momentoes of the occasion. The request was granted, and the natives were amused as these Westerners wrapped the bowls in paper and packed them in their luggage.

After dinner Jesse and Rebe rested for a few hours while their hosts went off for *their* dinner. Then, after the heat of the day had abated somewhat, they were escorted through the village. Rebe was allowed to visit Sharma's mother in her home, although Jesse, "as a mere man," had to remain in the narrow alley between mud walls which was the village's only street. Like the other houses, the house Rebe entered was composed of mud plastered over reeds; it was built around a court open to the sky, and here Rebe found the women of the household spinning the cotton thread destined to be woven into *kheddar*. Around the court was a series of open stalls used as store rooms, sleeping rooms, and for cooking. Although this was a home of the better sort, it contained only the barest necessities. Water, of course, had to be carried from the nearby well; there was no drainage system for wastes. To complete the picture, the family's buffalo cow was tied to an entrance post, and her manger and feeding place were not far away.

Leaving this house, the Homeses were shown something of the economic life of the village. The local industries were handicraft (quite literally "manufactures") — the potter turning out clay pots, bowls, and bottles on a large stone wheel spun by hand; the shoemaker, tanner, and tailor also used only the simplest tools. The worn-out fields about the village were leased from a landlord by the leading men of the village and worked for wages by those still poorer. The yield was small, the wages low, and the landlord got a very large share of the profits. He, in turn, had to pay about half of the rent to the government as a land tax. Sharma told Jesse that although he had tried to improve the ways of farming, he thought that the [British] government did not encourage this for fear that a prosperous and enlightened peasantry would be hard to control. And there were no schools or temples; the special religious needs of the village were served by a priest from a neighboring town.

Although they were invited to stay overnight, shoot crocodiles, and go for an elephant ride, Jesse and Rebe had other engagements making a longer stay impossible. So photographs were taken in various groups, the bullock carts were loaded, and they were on their way. Just before they climbed on their cart their foreheads were marked with yellow ochre as a sign of special friendship, and a number of villagers walked with them to the railroad station.

(Sharma and Jesse continued their friendship through correspondence at least until 1930. And the Holmeses must have told the Hulls and a Miss White of Swarthmore about conditions in Sharma's village, for in a letter to Jesse he thanked the four of them for sending a $50 check by registered mail. This money, Sharma wrote, would enable his elder brother to distribute a good deal of free medicine from the local dispensary. In another letter Sharma said that the dispensary had been named in the Holmes' honor.)

When Jesse and Rebe waved good-bye to Sharma they were on the first leg of a long series of visits to centers of Indian culture in northeastern India and then on down through India's southeastern flank toward Ceylon. They went first to Allahabad, where they were shown about the university grounds and the principal college. Attending a class in the history of philosophy, Jesse found it using the same textbook he had been using in his classes at Swarthmore. In Benares they watched Hindu pilgrims go down the *ghat* (flights of steps) to bathe in the sacred Ganges. In Bengal they spent four days at Santiniketan, where the venerable poet-philosopher Rabindranath Tagore had established Pagores College. Here they met Tagore — tall, light-skinned, with long white hair, and a white beard falling almost to his waist. An ardent supporter of Gandhi, Tagore was very critical of the British, claiming that in two hundred years of their rule they had not broken the caste system, had not improved agriculture or sanitation, and certainly had not given India a system of general education. When Jesse and Rebe visited college classes, usually held in the shade of trees scattered about the campus, they found a geometry teacher using a slate rock as a blackboard, and an English class reading *The Merchant of Venice*. Jesse held a discussion on ethics with five students on an arcaded porch just outside the library; the discussion soon turned to the problems of prohibition in America. As the class dispersed Jesse noticed that someone had used chalk to write on the wall of the arcade: " 'Yes, we have no bananas!' "

The next stop on the Holmes' trip was Calcutta, where they again watched devout Hindus descend the *ghat* to bathe in the Ganges, its waters being dedicated to the goddess Kali, wife of Siva (hence *Kali-Ghat*). But watching the more superstitious elements of the Hindu population in action was not the Holmes' mission here; what Jesse wanted was to meet the leaders of Calcutta's intellectual and religious communities. He had his wish: he met "men of fine scholarship, widely read and widely travelled. . . ." He found a fine medical school, "with a great stone hospital" associated with the "great University, all of the students and most of the faculty being Indians. . . ." A professor of philosophy introduced him to an Indian audience in the hall of the YMCA, where he spoke on "An International Religion." And some Buddhist students he had met at Tagore's school arranged a meeting in a Buddhist temple distinguished by the fact that it sheltered one of Buddha's teeth. No doubt Jesse found this rather amusing; he thought, however, that before Christians smiled too much about Buddhist holy relics they should remember the multitude of shrines in Europe, so many of them "sanctified by various fragments of various saints. . . ." The Buddhist priests in this temple were "simple, kindly souls . . . very glad to find points of contact with faiths of other lands; and these are not few. . . ." Jesse held Buddhism to be a "very noble faith, which has produced great saints and noble lives. . . ." and he believed Friends could very easily develop mutually helpful relationships with its members.

Always critical of imperialistic abuses, Jesse could not help commenting on the fact that the British had made Calcutta "very largely a European city, with great stone business blocks, fine hotels, government buildings, parks, monuments, and the like. . . ." The costs of maintaining all this splendor were "borne by the poverty-stricken people. . . ." He was particularly incensed by the Victoria Memorial — "a great uninspired lump of a marble building, set in a beautiful park, and having no apparent purpose or meaning. . . ." While it had cost the Indian people millions, it was "the more exasperating because it was *said* to [have been] paid for by voluntary contributions, — and after a century and a half of occupation, no system of education for the general public!"

Traveling southwestward from Calcutta (at times sharing their six-berth railway compartment with Indians) the Holmeses noticed that the population grew darker in color, and they got the impression that there was "increasing superstition, and a generally lower standard of life and culture. . . ." This applied mainly to the east coast, however, as seen by Jesse and Rebe in the great cities of Madras and Madura. Even so, each of these cities had "considerable groups of marked ability and intelligence. . . ."

In Madras they were met by a Mr. Dana, the secretary of the YMCA, and taken to the room he had reserved for them in his establishment. Jesse hardly had time to get washed up and seek refreshment before he was asked to address the International Fellowship meeting on the YMCA's large front piazza. Following the address the principal of a school asked Jesse to repeat the speech before his eight hundred students, and two college students requested Jesse's presence at a meeting of their Philosophical Association.

Jesse and Rebe were pleasantly surprised in Madras when they ran into their old friends, the J. Russell Smiths. The Smiths promptly changed their travel plans so that they might have an extra day with the Holmses. But duty still called for both scholars: while Jesse gave his two speeches Smith went to a library to look over photographs for possible use in a new textbook in geography. (The Smiths, with their son Newlin, had been having a fine time on their sabbatical-leave trip. As they told Jesse and Rebe, they were granted an interview with Governor-General Wood of the Philippines, had dined with Senator Osias, leader of the independence movement among Filipinos, and had taken tea with the civil governor of Fukien, a province in South China.)

After the Smiths had gone Rebe was treated to an experience she would not soon forget: two women connected with the YMCA and the YWCA took her to a party given by Lady Goochen, wife of the local British governor. The party was mainly for Indian upper-caste women in *purdah* (in seclusion from all men except their husbands), and was held on the beautiful and spacious grounds of Government House. A fine band played "good music all afternoon, but they had to play up on a balcony, behind screens, so that by no chance could they catch a glimpse of these Indian houris! . . ." Rebe wrote to Robert that there must have been three or four hundred women there, all dressed in their best. " . . . the costumes of the Indians were perfectly *gorgeous*, & *such* jewels! Diamond bracelets, ear rings, nose rings, rubies & pearls — they were wonderful! . . ." After the women had "paraded around," looked at the large rooms, and had "eats," a movie was shown in the ballroom — Jackie Coogan in "My Boy."

While Rebe enjoyed this party, she also enjoyed the visit she and Jesse made to the Theosophist center at Adyar, a few miles from

Madras. Theosophy — described by Jesse as "a kind of Occidental-ized Buddhism, retaining the Buddhist doctrines of Karma and Reincarnation, but combining them in rather uncertain fashion with European (or Christian) ideas of the value [s] . . . of life. . . ." — had been founded "by Madame Blavatsky, a brilliant Russian woman, and Colonel Olcott, an Englishman. . . ." The head of the Theosophi-cal Society at Adyar when the Holmeses were there was Anna Besant, who, as a constant worker for the common people, had helped to write the Indian National Constitution. Under her leader-ship the Theosophical Society, functioning in its many buildings at Adyar, maintained a well-run progressive school; it had also played host in the winter of 1925-1926 to a convention of converts from many parts of the world. Indeed, as Jesse informed his readers in the *Friends Intelligencer,* almost every great city in Europe and America had its Theosophical Society, usually rather small and making little noise. "The Philadelphia branch," he thought, "would undoubtedly make welcome any interested visitor. . . ."

When Rebe wrote to Robert about the visit to see the Theoso-phists at work at Adyar she also revealed a good deal about herself. She said it was "a beautiful place" where "many learned scholars come and go — it would be fine to spend a month or two there, & get at Theosophy. Then I'd like to spend a month or so at Santiniketan, Tagore's school, another centre for [the] intellectual exchange of ideas. . . ." As she looked back on her own life she wished she "hand't wasted so much time — there is such an awful lot of things to learn, & it must be fun to know a lot about so many things! . . ." And she urged Bob to stick to his scholarly last — *"Don't let thyself be too comfortable & be lazy about knowledge. . . ."* And, no doubt thinking of Newlin Smith's wonderful experiences on *his* world trip, she urged Bob to travel for a year before settling down to a steady job. She suggested that he might finish his fellowship at the University of Pennsylvania, go to Harvard for his Ph.D., and then set out on his *Wanderjahr.* She thought he might stay in Toynbee Hall in London (a Fabian Socialist institution) for a time, then go on to Tagore's school, and "touch Indian life & thought in various places. . . ." There was a Scottish university in Calcutta, she wrote, where "thee might get an opportunity to teach economics, & thee need only promise to stay *one* year. . . ." And, if Robert could not find such jobs for self-support, Rebe thought that she and Jesse could finance him for a year at travel; she was "sure it would be a splendid preparation for teaching economics."

A day's journey westward from Madras brought Jesse and Rebe to the province of Mysore, a high tableland subject to an enlightened prince who was a patron of education, maintaining colleges for both men and women. The rajah and some higher-education authorities expected them, for Jesse had "written in advance to Mysore University of [his] coming, informing them in diplomatic fashion that it [was to be] an important event. . . ." And Jesse and Rebe's coming was indeed regarded as important: they were met at the railroad station by a representative of the University with one of the rajah's carriages drawn by a pair of white horses, taken to the best suite of rooms in a hotel, and then, after a period of rest, driven through the city of Mysore, being saluted along the way by every policeman. They spent an hour in the rajah's zoo — Jesse admitted to Robert that "I haven't lost zest for zoos" —, and then had "a glorious spin around this beautiful city as the sun went down: temples, palaces, gardens, with natural scenery in the way of lakes, forests and mountains. . . ."

Several days later, after interviews with the vice-chancellor and the registrar of the University, Jesse was to lecture on "Internationalism" and "Modern Tendencies in Philosophy." And, on one of these days, he was shown through University buildings, especially libraries and museums. In one of these musems he was particularly taken by a display of Hindu manuscripts; he persuaded the friendly curator to arrange the purchase of some of them. A day or so later, before breakfast, a little native boy appeared at the door of the Holmes' hotel suite, presented some books to Jesse, and then departed. Where or whom they came from, Jesse never found out.

These "books", as Jesse discovered, were invaluable manuscript copies of two volumes without which no Westerner could really understand Indian history or Indian religion. One was the *Ramayana*, the Indian national epic, corresponding to the *Odyssey* of the Greeks. The other was the *Brahmana*, a commentary on the religion of the Hindus. Encased by wooden covers, the palmleaf pages of these books were inscribed by a difficult graphiting process: first the characters of the language were scratched on the leaves with a stylus, then a coat of graphite was placed over the surface. When this coat was wiped off, the graphite had filled the scratched Sanskrit symbols, producing clear black "letters" of an enduring quality. Indeed, as Jesse found out, these books were some three-to-four hundred years old.

(Almost ten years later, after Jesse had placed these manuscript books in his private collection of "foreign oddities," he was asked, via a letter from the Library of Congress, to send an account of all the Hindu books he might have in his library. He sent a description of his books; a representative of the Library of Congress soon arrived to examine them, and Jesse for the first time learned of their great value. It turned out that he held two of the ten palmleaf Sanskrit books on Indian culture whose presence was known in the United States at that time. Later on he bequeathed these books, and all such religious-and-Oriental "oddities", to Swarthmore College, which in turn gave them to his son Herman after Jesse's death. Herman, in his turn, gave the "whole kit & caboodle" to the Archeological Museum of the University of Pennsylvania in 1973.)

Leaving Mysore, the Holmeses returned to Madras and then went south to Madura. While they had hoped to spend a lot of time here inspecting the details of the great Hindu temple, with its intricately carved religious symbols and its great collection of priceless jewels, they found that their host, an American missionary, had planned their schedule so tightly that there was little time left to see what they wanted to see. Mr. Saunders, the missionary, "coolly told" them what to do, and they acquiesced — "inwardly fuming at being taken to see ever so many missionary schools & being sent to church *twice* on Sunday. . . ." Rebe wrote that they didn't like to stay with missionaries; Mr. Saunders, in particular, was "perfectly horrid. . . ."

There was, however, one aspect of their stay with Mr. and Mrs. Saunders which fascinated and surprised Rebe — the enormous pool of cheap manpower from which to draw household servants. Mrs. Saunders "had seven servants — & she paid *all seven* less than half what I paid Sarah! Her seven cost about $25 *per month*, & they feed themselves! . . ." The service was constant, and Rebe said that, "to tell the truth," she didn't care for so much of it. "One isn't supposed to do anything for one's self — there is always a 'boy' around to open a door or lift a chair, etc. . . ." And perhaps all this service, all this bowing and scraping, was beginning to get to Jesse too, for Rebe reported that he was getting restless and talking of how nice it would be to get back to the United States.

By this time, of course, Rebe and Jesse had reached certain conclusions about India and Indian culture, particularly in the areas of education and religion. Jesse found education in India "decidedly top-heavy," since it provided much more fully for colleges than for elementary and secondary schools. Lacking a sound base of preparatory schools, the colleges themselves could not demand very high standards; indeed, many of them were "not much more than good high schools. . . ." Another weakness was the small amount spent for teaching the sciences and for technical education, although Jesse could see some improvement in this field for the future. And the thought undoubtedly crossed his mind, although not specifically recorded in his letters or articles, that if the Indians had spent less on their religious temples, and all the jewelry within them, they would have had much more money to spend on all levels of education.

Everywhere Jesse went he found that the Indians had a very keen interest in religion and philosophy. When he was at Allahabad he was asked to lecture to Hindu and Moslem students on the relationships between science and religion. Speaking as a Quaker, he quoted John William Graham as saying "that of all the religions Quakerism had least to fear from the development of the sciences. . . ." He presented this side of the religion of Friends, and then tried to show the points of unity among the faiths of Quakers, Hindus, and Moslems. He couldn't avoid the points of difference, of course; but, as he said, these were "to be found mostly in the popular forms of these religious rather than in the faith of the educated and thoughtful. . . ." After the lecture there was a "brisk" discussion of the points Jesse had made — an experience repeated many times as he lectured his way through India. The students, teachers and educated people generally were eager for a "simple, straightforward discussion" of religion; they wanted to hear about a religion of experience — a religion of the spirit rather than a religious of authority a la the Christian missionaries. Jesse had found a very widespread prejudice against the professional missionary, who preached his sectarian Christiam dogmas while other Christians plundered and destroyed in peace as well as in war. Indeed, in practical, applied Christianity — in the exercise of the Social Gospel — Jesse thought that India, though not Christian in name, was "far more Christian than England or America. . . ." And since Friends had practiced the Social Gospel from the time of their founding, and had no creed to present by authority, the Quaker worker in India had an "unlimited advantage" over other

Christians; he soon came into a warm welcome and unity, finding a "prompt recognition of the divine indwelling, similar the world over though with a diversity of names."

And so, looking back over their experiences, Jesse and Rebe could feel proud of their ministry. Rebe certainly was proud of him, writing to Robert that he had done a good piece of work in India — lecturing many times, holding discussions, and writing articles for the newspapers. Jesse's "absolute sincerity & frankness" in talking over Indian problems had done much to reduce some of that hatred Indians felt for Christian foreigners. "I am sure," she wrote, "[that] America has gained by his stay here."

But one more tour was necessary before they left this part of the Orient — a trip to Ceylon, which Jesse thought was "probably not exceeded in beauty by any other place on earth." The Holmeses traveled from Madura to the southern tip of the Indian triangle, were ferried across to a railroad terminal on Ceylon's northern shore, and then entrained for Colombo, the capital city. In Colombo they hired richshaws to see the sights, haggled with merchants in the bazaars (Jesse bought a pongee suit and Rebe three silk dresses — "awfully cheap"), and visited a Buddhist college. And, given Jesse's great interest in Buddhism, they took a four-hour train ride to Kandy, the religious capital of southern Ceylon, crossing great rivers and going through magnificent groves of cocoanut trees. In Kandy they visited still another Temple of the Tooth (Jesse wondered whether it was "a canine or a molar"), and were taken on "a glorious ride" to the botanical gardens by the wife of a Ceylon gentleman in her Fiat. Rebe grew ecstatic in her letter to Robert: "Ceylon is . . . the garden spot of the world — does thee know the old hymn —

> Old Ocean's spicy breeses
> Blow soft o'er Ceylon's isle,
> Where every prospect pleases,
> And only man is vile.

Although she didn't find any vile men on this ride she was led to make a comment about Ceylonese life by the prefusion of good things they saw growing along the way: ". . . coffee, tea, rice, coconuts, cocoa, pepper, nutmegs, bamboo, etc., etc. . . . All the . . . people need to do is to stand around & wait for the fruits to drop into their mouths — really, they get a living *too* easily! . . ."

Aside from this expression of the work-ethic implicit in her

Quaker culture, Rebe found only good things to report to Robert about Ceylon and its people. And her visit there, added to her experiences in India, had changed her attitude toward people of color. In Kandy Jesse had been invited to speak on "The True Patriotism" to the older boys at a Buddhist school run by a native who had married an Englishwoman. Rebe met their two little sons, and the mother, a Cambridge graduage, said in a jocular way, " 'you see, they are cafe au lait,' which they certainly were. The father is quite dark. . . ." And then Rebe confessed that she had "entirely lost all [her] American prejudices against dark skins. I think the brown skins are really very nice, & many of the Indian & Singalese [sic] are very handsome. The *pink* Englishman looks absurd to me now, kind of raw & naked."

Since China was in a state of flux in 1926, and Jesse was eager to return home, the rest of the Holmes' trip was given less attention. They sailed from Ceylon to Shanghai on the *Hekusan Maru*, went on to Japan, and then, on May 4, boarded the Dollar Line *President Pierce* in Yokahama for Honolulu and Los Angeles. In Los Angeles they would pause to visit Jesse's half-sister, Lizzie Townsend, and then take a Pullman to Kearney, Nebraska to see the Drydens. Arrival in Swarthmore was scheduled for early June.

Jesse and Rebe arrived in Swarthmore on June 2, reorganized themselves, and then set out on a Chautauqua circuit "to get some money ahead," as Jesse put it. And in September they were pleased to learn that they would be invited to a welcome-home party — along with John and Mary Miller, J. Russell and Henrietta Smith, and Walter Ross Marriott — to be given to returned travellers on October 1 by the Service Committee of the Swarthmore Monthly Meeting. This party, according to the Monthly Meeting Minutes, would be "a rare opportunity to hear through these our own members, observations and reflections that will help and strengthen our zeal and labors for peace and good will for all mankind." In view of such sentiments, Jesse and Rebe undoubtedly felt that they were indeed home again.

*Jesse and Rebe on their round-the-world trip,
1925-26. (Note Jesse's new German cloak.)
Courtesy Mr. & Mrs. Jesse H. Holmes III,
Washington, D.C.*

12. A Continuing Service

After the welcome-home party Jesse and Rebe plunged into that incessant round of activities which was their life in Swarthmore. While they generally derived personal pleasure (and occasional profit) through working with people on local committees, in conferences, and through meetings in more distant places, they regarded such work as their duty — their obligation — as Friends and as citizens of a community, to get involved in a life of service to others. If they had skills, ideas, or unusual experiences to share with other people, they should do so, even at the cost, sometimes, of fatigue, illness, and perhaps a momentary distemper.

And so Jesse spent many hours in the fall of 1926 jotting down the impressions and memories he had of his trip around the world. On one such occasion, grabbing a handful of his wife's stationery, he worked up the rough draft of a speech on India. Not long afterward he gave this speech before the Germantown Friends' Association. One can see him now, standing among the high benches of the Germantown Meeting House — his shock of grey hair in some disarray, his goatee, and his flaming tie only partly hidden by a bulging vest. "There is a country far, far away," he started out, "that is permeated with the romanticism of the old folklore, the old religious myths and stories. . . ." Yes, he said, "East is East, and West is West," and "God forbid that it should be otherwise. . . ." But as Tagore believed, the twain could be brought together in amity and peace; their meeting would be the richer because of the differences.

As his speech progressed he proposed trying to understand India through the lives and works of three of its "strongest and most outstanding personalities . . . those rarely beautiful souls" known to the world as Sarojini Naidu, Rabindranath Tagore, and Mahatma Gandhi. Jesse described how Mrs. Naidu had presided over the Indian National Congress with "a gracious dignity" which was amazing in consideration of the fact that Indian women were generally restricted to the narrow confines of the home. He foreshadowed Dr. Martin Luther King and Women's Lib when he said that Mrs. Naidu was "bearing the torch of Freedom to light all the women . . . as they follow [ed] the dark trail . . . to the mountaintop of Opportunity — opportunity for education, opportunity for enlarging . . . life in the home, opportunity for public affairs. . . ." It seemed to Jesse that Indian national independence could not be obtained until women were able to work side-by-side with their men.

Mrs. Naidu, Jesse told his audience, had been sent to England by her father when she was only fifteen; in England she studied at Girton School, and at King's College, London. Showing an early talent for poetry, she had been advised by Edmund Gosse to make her poems tell of Indian culture, its passions and aspirations. These poems, Jesse thought, were "as luminous in lighting up the dark places of the East as any contributions of scholar or historian. . . ." He read several of her poems: "Bangli Sellers" (bangli being the decorative bracelets women wore); "Ecstasy" — "an exquisite rhapsody of the approach of spring"; and then the "Song of Radha the Milkmaid," who carried her goatsmilk to the temple to sell, and then, when her brass pots were empty, carried them to the river to be washed. Although Mrs. Naidu was a high-caste Hindu, she wrote "The Prayer of Islam," into which she wove some of the "99 beautiful Arabic names of God" as used by followers of Islam. The closing stanza of this poem, as recited by Jesse, gave the Germantown Friends the flavor:

> We are the shadows of thy Light,
> We are the secrets of thy might,
> The visions of thy primal dream,
> Ja Rahman! Ja Raheem!

Jesse then turned to Tagore — poet, author of many plays, essayist — who was "loved by the people of India and . . . by the cultured of the whole world." He reminded his listeners that Tagore had received the Nobel Prize in 1913 for "Idealistic Literature" — a fact which Jesse thought should lead Westerners to inquire more closely into what men of the East had to say. Indeed, if the goal of world peace was ever to be attained, it would have to be based on a mutual appreciation of the literature, arts, and ideals of the East and the West; it would have to be reached on "the path of cultural concourse between the Orient and the Occident that would lead to the realization of the fundamental unity of the human race. . . ." After describing how Tagore had started his school in Bengal in 1902 in order to put Indian boys and girls on this "path of cultural concourse, "Jesse read the poet's statement of his life and teaching — what Jesse called Tagore's "motif":

> Be not ashamed, my brothers, to stand
>> before the proud and powerful
> With your white robes of simpleness.
> Let your crown be of humility, your freedom
>> the freedom of the soul.
> Build God's throne daily upon the
>> ample awareness of your poverty —
> And know that what is *huge* is not
>> *great,* and pride is not everlasting.

Jesse, ever mindful of the need for dramatic and memorable endings to his public addresses, now paid a fervent tribute to the greatest of the Indian triumvirate: Gandhi. "You may have been told," Jesse said, "that his day is done, that he is a song no longer sung. . . ." But this was not true, he told the Germantown Friends. At the Indian Congress fathers brought their children to gaze upon him so that they could tell their children and grandchildren that they had seen the Leader. Men prostrated themselves before him, "almost worshipping this simple, unpretentious man who loves his countrymen with a love that sometimes passes all understanding. . . ." Men all over India spoke of him as " 'Mahatma' — a term of deepest veneration. . . ." Jesse ventured to predict that after Gandhi had passed on Indians would "almost deify him. His is the soul of the martyr, gladly moved to die if India might live a united and independent country." He closed his speech with a poem, "Mahatma Gandhi," by Ellen Chater:

> If I could scrawl a great zig-zag of stars
>> Against the dark, I would write 'Gandhi.' Then
> We might look up where like young Avatars
> About our dust bright planets sing to men
> Words written plainly on our own hearts' pages —
>
>> . . . .
> 'He counts the vilest brother. He is meek.

His patience sets men's thoughts where things abide.
He seeks no praise.' Thus stars and prophets speak.
There I'd put Gandhi's name, and with the faint,
Sweet Pleiades for letters I'd add 'Saint'.

Rebe — "I Want to Work!!"

Rebe waited some months before she was ready to give the
feminine side of their Indian experiences; perhaps she was waiting
for the women's costumes and costume jewelry she had bought in
the bazaars to arrive by mail or by American Express. In any case,
she did not begin her talks until Saturday, March 5, 1927, when she
entertained the Swarthmore Alumnae Club of Philadelphia at its
meeting held in the Women's City Club. More than fifty women
attended the lecture and the tea that followed, including Mrs. Frank
Aydelotte, the president of the City Club. After disposing of some
Alumnae business, the program got under way. Emma Jane Wilson,
'07, introduced Elizabeth Barth, '21, who sang some Oriental songs
to set the mood for Rebe's talk. Rebe then appeared in the full
splendor of an Indian woman's costume, wearing "every type of
jewelry common to the women there except noserings. . . ." She told
of their experiences at the National Congress at Cawnpore, and gave
an amusing account of their visit to Sharma's mud village. Her talk
at this point was illustrated by rustic souvenirs, no doubt including
those earthenware bowls that their Indian hosts had wanted to
break after the main meal.

While Rebe enjoyed giving this talk in Philadelphia, there are
indications that she enjoyed herself even more when she gave a
similar performance before a meeting of the New Century Club in
West Chester two weeks later. Edna Pearson drove her to West
Chester; they had lunch with a Mrs. Webb, and then drove to the
clubhouse to decorate its stage with Oriental rugs and shawls. And,
since Edna was to model a costume different from the one Rebe was
to wear, they could now help each other with their costumes before
the show began.

Rebe's entrance on to this exotic stage was heralded by "the
tinkling of scores of tiny silver bells" attached to the bracelets and
anklets she wore, these anklets being just barely visible under the
lowest part of her costume. Indeed, Rebe appeared "swathed in
many yards of thin gray material, gold bordered, which formed not
only her dress, but also the head covering. . . ." As she explained, all

262

this was normally held together only by draping, not with the help of buttons, snaps, pins, or hooks and eyes. But, she admitted, she wasn't skillful enough to do it as did the Indian women; she had cheated a little with pins. And then, calling to Edna to walk on the stage in her costume, amply fortified with jewelry, Rebe explained why Indian women wore all these gold-and-silver gadgets. The explanation lay, she said, in the fact that husbands had "an incurable suspicion" of banks; therefore each husband made his wife his walking bank.

As had proved to be the case in Philadelphia, the most amusing part of her talk was her account of the visit she and Jesse had made to Sharma's mud village. She described how, when their train stopped at the railroad station in the middle of the night, their host shouted to them to get off in a hurry; how they were obliged to tumble out of their sleeping-car berths, grab their luggage, and stumble out upon the platform "just as they were, in kimono, pajamas, and general dishabille. . . ." Taken to the village, they were treated as "a god and goddess," being given the best the village afforded. But, said Rebe, "as I looked at [our] appearance, I could see nothing in the least godlike about either of us."

As Rebe wrote in her Diary for 1927, her West Chester talk went "very well." And now it was time to bring her talents to the Swarthmore audience provided by the regular April meeting of the Somerville Open Forum on the College campus. Henrietta S. Smith preceded her on this program with a talk on Korea; then Rebe appeared, clad in the same costume she had shown in West Chester, and with the same jewelry. She also told the same stories about India, this time emphasizing the extreme politeness and hospitality of the Indian people in general.

At some point in early 1927 Rebe decided to capitalize on the interest she had created in Oriental culture by selling Indian and Chinese artifacts, the profits to be used to help pay the expenses of some foreign student at Swarthmore. Although she offered for sale some of the things she had brought back from the Orient, most of the objects — brass lamps, brass bowls, scarves, costume jewelry, etc. — sold at women's club meetings, church gatherings, and campus functions were sent to her from an import house in Baltimore. There are no precise records on the size of the scholarship fund she was able to build up through these sales; perhaps we may judge her success, however, through two entries she made in her Diary: on Saturday, May 27, she "sold 5 scarfs at $3" to the ladies attending an Alumnae Club meeting at Whittier House; on Friday, November 25, she held a sale of Chinese things in her own home and served tea. But, as she sadly recorded, she "Didn't make much money."

Such money-making projects, of course, had to be fitted into Rebe's extremely busy schedule as a campus wife, civic leader, and patron of the arts. A typical week, as recorded in her Diary for 1927, does much to tell the story:

> Monday, January 17 — Poetry Circle at Mrs. Potter's — Emily Dickinson. Then called on Lillian. Called on Johnsons' in evening.
>
> Tuesday, January 18 — Went to Current Events Class led by Henrietta S. In afternoon went to Emerson Club, then met J. and went to a movie, "Stranded in Paris."
>
> Wednesday, January 19 — Went to see Lillian & then to Dorothy Ashbon's Tea — & home.
>
> Thursday, January 20 — Went to village to market. After lunch visited Lillian. Had Louis & Caroline Robinson & H. & Russell Smith to a waffle supper. Nice time.
>
> Friday, January 21 — Went to city; . . . to lecture by Prof. Moley on "crime" — then lunched with Jessie M. at Art Alliance, then wandered about ending up with dentist at 4 — home on 5:10. Quiet evening.
>
> Saturday, January 22 — Went to Phila. to see "What Every Woman Knows." To Rittenhouse for dinner & then home on 7:30 train.
>
> Sunday, January 23 — Had two lady friends in to dinner and then went to Whittier House in the evening to hear an American Indian. Not so hot.

And so this "tough old nut," as Rebe had called herself on a previous occasion, went on and on, planting many a fertile seed in the social and intellectual fields of the Swarthmore-Philadelphia area. She collected books to help start the Swarthmore Public Library and was a member of its first board of directors. In early January 1927, she had been asked to deliver a speech on a Philadelphia radio program featuring a session of the Emerson Club; the broadcast in the afternoon of January 13 "went off quite well," she thought. About a month later she spent most of a day getting ready for a late-afternoon tea in honor of some of Jesse's students. With the help of Edna Pearson and Abby Roberts, the tea was quite a success; Rebe felt repaid for her time and trouble.

But Rebe's social and personal life did not always go so smoothly or pleasantly. One Sunday, after Jesse and "a Mr. Ellis" had spoken at Meeting, the Hulls, Smiths, and Pearsons had supper in the Holmes' home. That evening, after the guests had departed, Rebe recorded "Not so good" in her Diary — not specifying whether the speeches in Meeting had been productive of irritation or whether the after-dinner talk at home had been less than satisfying. And, two days after the tea for students she fell ill with "la grippe"; she spent the day in bed and called in a Dr. McGreton to give her an osteopathic treatment. In late March she must have strained her back while unpacking and lifting a heavy brass samovar because she developed lumbago. "*Damn!*" was her reaction then; the next day, however, "suffering but bravely conceal [ing] it," she went to Philadelphia with Jesse and two women friends to see a movie and have dinner at the Walton Hotel. Perhaps she was ill and irritable again in early June when she attended a City Club luncheon at Mrs. Aydelotte's for she confided to her Diary that the women she met there were "a set of snobs!!"

Generally speaking, however, Rebe had a better opinion of the ladies she worked with, and they in turn regarded her as one of their leaders. On March 5, 1927, the Swarthmore Alumnae Club of Philadelphia appointed her its delegate to attend the convention of the American Association of University Women to be held in Washington, D.C. from March 30 through April 2. And on April 11 she was elected to be president of the Swarthmore Women's Club, an office she was to hold from 1927 to 1931, and again from 1933 to 1935. A week after her election she was inaugurated at a Club luncheon, the occasion being brightened by the flowers sent by Paul Pearson and a "Mrs. Fuller." Her first experience as presiding officer of the Women's Club at its regular meeting in May was apparently not too frightening because she reported that it was a "good mtg." And it couldn't have tired her very much since she journeyed to Glenolden to speak on India that same evening. And three days later, apparently freshly impressed with a woman's civic duties, she took a morning train to Philadelphia, had lunch alone in her City Club, and then went to the afternoon meeting of the American Academy of Political Science. She met Jesse there and took him to the City Club for dinner. They both attended the evening session.

Having accomplished so much in recent months, Rebe looked forward to the summer of 1927 as a pleasant vacation interlude. As was expected of a faculty wife, she took part in the commencement festivities at Swarthmore College in June, serving, among other ways as a hostess at a "Phi Delt Tea". Such duties over, she and Eileen Harris drove to Buck Hill Falls in the Poconos, a favorite Quaker haunt, where sister Lizzie had established vacation headquarters for the Webb-Holmes clan. She spent only two days there this time — time enough, however, to visit with Lizzie, hear a lecture on India, attend a concert, and listen to a Negro speaker on her last evening.

On August 3 she and Jesse started on one of their typical vacation trips, this one as usual combining a Quaker ministerial function with the pleasures of tourism. They headed for Toronto, where Canadian Friends were holding a four-day conference. Their route of travel by car took them first to Muncy, Pennsylvania, where they stayed in a pleasant house; their next stop was in Clarence, New York, where they spent the night in a farmhouse not boasting a bathroom. Rebe thought the house was "queer, but the woman was nice." Arriving in Niagara Falls, they found a nice place to stay, took their meals at the YWCA cafeteria, and went to a vaudeville show in the evening. In Toronto they socialized with some other Pennsylvania Quakers, and then got set for the sessions of the conference. While Rebe thought that Jesse "spoke well" on "Education for Peace," she found the other sessions — especially the one on "Social Adjustment" — "very dull," even "deadly dull." The pageant these Quakers put on "was splendid," however.

Leaving Toronto on August 13, they drove northeastward in Ontario to Prescott and crossed the St. Lawrence to Ogdensburg, New York. Then to Albany and on to Old Chatham, the summer home of the Aydelottes. In Massachusetts they visited their son Bob at his camp in the Berkshires, and went to see the Blanshards in their "beautiful" home in Northampton. Bob went with them; they stayed overnight, played some pool after lunch, and then went on to drop Bob at Great Barrington. Jesse and Rebe got back to Swarthmore via New York City, arriving August 20.

About two weeks after returning to Swarthmore Rebe found herself temporarily at loose ends. One Sunday evening in

266

September, 1927, after a boring afternoon, she wrote in her Diary, "I want to work!!" She soon found things to do: she took a series of driving lessons (during one of these lessons she "bent Mrs. Lukens' wheel guard"), spent an entire day at meetings of the League of Women Voters, bought an Essex coupe, and after getting her driver's license, drove to a meeting of the Springfield Women's Club. In April, 1928, she was scheduled to speak to the luncheon meeting of the Pottstown Reciprocity Club on "Personal Experiences in India" for a twenty-five dollar honorarium; in March, she would address the Emerson Club on "Indian Literature."

Although she might indulge her interest in the Orient by going out on such pursuits, her position as president of the local Women's Club guaranteed that much of her time would be spent working for the ladies. In September, 1930, she joined other members of the Swarthmore Club in attending the Thirty-fifth Annual Convention of the State Federation of Pennsylvania Women in Scranton. A month later she entertained the "chairmen" of the various divisions of the Swarthmore group at a luncheon in her home, followed by a general discussion of the program for the next five months. Some idea of the need for her administrative oversight may be gained through a listing of the subdivisions or special committees within the main body of the Club: Admissions, Home, Educational, League of Women Voters, Art, Hospitality, Drama, Garden, Literature, Music, International Relations, Federation Contact, Reciprocity, Needlework Guild, Health, House, Program, Publicity, and Citizenship.

In view of so much responsibility, plus her numerous other activities, it was not surprising that Rebe announced her decision to retire as president of the local club in May, 1931, after four years of service. There was, of course, a formal meeting to mark her retirement; it was equally inevitable that she should make a retirement speech at this affair. Her friends must have been very proud of her as she said:

> I consider a Woman's Club to be an important factor in a woman's life. it is the only place where we can meet on a non-sectarian, non-partisan and wholly social basis. In the other groups . . . we hear one side of a question presented, and it is necessary for our soul's welfare that we should have opportunity to hear opinions expressed by other groups, opinions

with which we may not agree. And here we come to that most beautiful of individual traits, the spirit of tolerance. Someone has said, 'The most lovable quality that any human being can possess is Tolerance.'

While Rebe received many expressions of affection and appreciation for her work at this meeting, the other officers of the Club, and the "chairmen" of its different sections, decided that her retirement called for special treatment. They organized a luncheon meeting at the Strath Haven, one of the area's top eating places, on the theme of "I Knew Her When." Pages for a miniature newspaper were put at each place and incidents which happened during Rebe's regime were noted; these pages were then assembled into newspaper form and presented to her with much jocularity. At the close of the luncheon Rebe was also presented with a wrought-iron flower container filled with pansies.

But so valuable a member of the feminine community could not — nay, would not — be passed into limbo. In January, 1932 she appeared before the Literature Section of the Women's Club in "a beautifully embroidered Chinese costume" to give the ladies "An Afrernoon in Old China." Centering her talk on Confucius, she outlined something of his down-to-earth conservative philosophy and read some of his short poems. Those which seemed to please her audience the most were "Lazy Man " and "The Age of Obedient Ears." In May she gave a luncheon in honor of Mrs. Raymond Walters, wife of Swarthmore's dean, since Mrs. Walters would soon go to be with her husband in his new job as president of the University of Cincinnati. When October came along she journeyed to the Bellevue-Stratford Hotel in Philadelphia, along with five other delegates from the Women's Club, to attend the four-day meeting of the State Federation. And in March of 1933 Rebe found herself chairlady of the Delaware County Division of the Women's International League for Peace and Freedom. She was to be in "direct charge" of all the meetings of the League in her district.

Given all this willingness to work, it was not too surprising that Rebe accepted another call to be the president of the Women's Club in the spring of 1933. Addressing the 150 members present at her inaugural luncheon, she said that, since love was the foundation of desire to serve, she hoped that the Women's Clubhouse would continue to be the center of friendliness for the Swarthmore Community.

By this time Swarthmore, like other communities, was deeply involved in the social experimentation of Franklin D. Roosevelt's New Deal. The National Recovery Administration (NRA) was created as an experiment in planning an economy; it hoped, under the administration of Hugh S. Johnson, to end cutthroat competition, raise prices by limiting production to actual needs, and to guarantee a reasonable work week and a living wage to labor. But, as Rebe soon found out after being appointed "Woman Chairman of the local N.R.A. Movement," Swarthmore was something of a special case. As a suburban town it had very little in the way of industry which could be included under the NRA codes. When, under her direction, consumer questionnaires had to be filled out through a house-to-house canvass, her office was flooded with queries from housewives. These housewives wanted to know what the NRA rules were with regard to domestic servants. Were they included under the "reasonable work week and living wage" principles? Rebe searched the law creating the NRA and then used the local newspaper, *The Swarthmorean*, to provide the answer to this question. The answer was "No" — there was no clause in the law concerned with the hours and wages of domestic servants. (We may imagine how Jesse, that sturdy advocate of socialistic equality, snorted when he learned this fact!)

Undoubtedly Rebe carried this fault of the NRA in her mental baggage when she represented the Women's Club at the Third Annual Women's Conference on Current Problems in New York City in October, 1933. Held in the Waldorf Astoria Hotel, the two-day conference was addressed by President Roosevelt and his wife Eleanor, by the Secretary of Labor, Frances Perkins, by Walter Lippman, and by Mary E. Woolley, president of Mt. Holyoke College. Four months later Rebe again was in New York, this time to attend a dinner at the Women's University Club in honor of Eleanor Roosevelt and Mrs. T.J. Preston (formerly Mrs. Grover Cleaveland).

And so Rebe's life of service went on, year after year. In August, 1934, she entertained fifty women at a tea in her Elm Avenue home in honor of Edna Pearson, who told of the visits of President and Mrs. Roosevelt to the Virgin Islands, and of the rehabilitation work her husband Paul was doing there as governor. During the course of this tea a collection was held for the Thornton Camp for Undernourished Children. In October, Rebe, as president of the

Women's Club, was first in the receiving line at the reception marking the formal opening of the thirty-seventh season of the Club; at the business meeting following the reception she was appointed a delegate, along with Mrs. Arthur R.O. Redgrave, to the meetings of the Pennsylvania Federation of Women's Clubs to be held in Harrisburg from October 15 to October 19. While she was to relinquish her presidency of the Women's Club in 1935, she continued to be active in Swarthmore affairs for some time to come. In 1937 she was still sharing the travel experiences she and Jesse had had in their halcyon years: she told the annual meeting of the Public Library Association how, in the course of such travels, they had met Bernard Shaw and the Aldous Huxleys.

A Summer Trip with Sherwood Eddy

The meetings with these famous people were incidents in a trip Rebe and Jesse had taken, as members of still another Sherwood Eddy party, in the summer of 1929. The object of the trip was to tour European countries in order to observe their political and social conditions. As it turned out, the Eddy party went through England, France, Austria, Germany, Poland, and Russia.

(The Holmes' passports for this trip gave their foreign address as Toynbee Hall, London, England; the person to notify in case of accident or death was listed as Elizabeth Y. Webb, Buck Hill Falls, Pennsylvania.)

Leaving New York harbor on June 16, Jesse and Rebe sailed for England, where they met not only Bernard Shaw and the Aldous Huxleys, but Lloyd George and Lord and Lady Astor. There is no available record of the interesting conversations that must have taken place on these occasions; all we know is that the Eddy party went on to Paris and then to Austria. As had been true earlier, Rebe enjoyed Paris — "very entertaining & so beautiful!" —; she was less enthusiastic about Gaming, Austria, where they attended a Fellowship of Reconciliation conference.

The Eddy party now journeyed northward to Germany, where Dr. Wolfers of the Berlin School of Politics received them and eased the way toward their goal of understanding German institutions. And it was through Dr. Wolfers that Jesse and five others of the Eddy party were invited to meet Albert Einstein, then professor of mathematics at the University of Berlin. Although the Berlin city authorities had been trying to present Einstein with a fine large house in the city, there were conditions attached to the gift which he couldn't accept; he therefore lived in one of the little garden houses lining the railroad tracks outside of Berlin. But this house was much too small to accommodate Jesse and his friends, so a meeting was arranged at a beautiful villa overlooking the "Dream Lake" not far from Potsdam. The owner of the villa, a friend of Einstein's, sent a large automobile to bring Jesse and his group to the meeting. Having settled the guests on a spacious porch, from which they could look out over the lake and see the forests beyond, the host and hostess disappeared so that Einstein might have the whole stage to himself. After a few moments the great man came from the house to greet the visitors with "easy friendliness." Jesse thought that perhaps the word which best described his manner was "kindly." A "man of large frame," his "massive head" was covered with "dark graying hair drawn back from the brow, leaving it high and majestic. . . ." The complexion was "very dark, his brown eyes large and friendly, his hair fluff [ed] out in a kind of halo, and he was clean shaven except for a gray mustache. He wore a loose gray suit and carried himself with an easy courtesy. . . ." After Einstein's entrance the group settled down in a conversational setting, and a maid served tea and other refreshments on light tables set at their elbows.

Jesse and his friends had considered at some length what questions they should address to the world-renowned physicist. They quickly found out that he was "intensely interested" in international politics, being a member of the Commission for Intellectual Cooperation created by the League of Nations, along with Gilbert Murray, Madame Curie, Henri Bergson and other world figures. In answer to a question about the dictatorships so numerous in Europe, "under one or another disguise," Einstein said that he believed in democracy and was against all forms of depotism. "Russia was at first very idealistic but has used the same means as Italy though with different aims. I regret the means. . . ." He greatly admired Gandhi's nonviolent campaign for India's independence, although he thought that India should try to achieve cultural independence before trying for political freedom from Great Britain. Einstein also doubted the wisdom and practicality in Gandhi's scheme of trying to beat machine-made cloth with hand-made fabrics. As an "absolute pacifist" he had "a revulsion from murder as a means of settling human problems . . . ." He believed in the League of Nations, the World Court, the Kellogg Pact, the Young Plan, and all other reasonable agreements worked out among the nations. But these were only partial, halting steps toward the goal of a genuine world peace, as were the timidly advanced ideas of a Pan-Europe or a United States of Europe. Even the Commission for Intellectual Cooperation was ineffectual because no one knew exactly what its purposes were. Einstein thought that perhaps it might accomplish something if it were able to convince the various nations of the world to use their primary schools to teach broad human ideals instead of the narrow nationalism so often taught.

Since Einstein understood English but was more comfortable in German, the interview progressed in the latter language, with Dr. Wolfers translating whenever necessary. Once in a while there was "a pleasant little conference" as to the meaning of an English word or a German phrase.

There was a need for careful phrasing and accurate translation when the group got into a discussion of determinism. "I am a determinist," Einstein told them. "I believe in the reign of law, of cause and effect, so that such words as free will, free choice, and such distinctions as active and passive are meaningless. . . ." (At this point in his report of the interview Jesse commented parenthetically that this was ". . . especially interesting from one who [had] so modified the meaning of 'law' and 'causation' in science.") But, said Einstein, "I do not regard natural law as being merely the statistical average behavior like vital statistics in insurance, applying only to large numbers and not to individuals. . . ." On the other hand, he admitted, ". . . I cannot be sure of anything, not even of my own determinism. . . ." Like Isaac Newton, Einstein thought that we couldn't know very much about the world we live in; "the human spirit is strong enough to discover its harmonies, nothing more. . . ." Yet there was room for religion in this scientist's world; it centered around the feeling of awe and reverence one must have when regarding the order prevailing in an infinitely complex cosmos. (The author remembers that Dr. Robert Milliken, another great physicist of the 'twenties, expressed the same thought in an address before students at Lafayette College in 1930.)

No doubt it was Jesse who pressed Einstein for more of his opinions about religion. Einstein held that religion could not be based on an "irrational father-God idea — a being struggling with a world he cannot fully control for the happiness of his children. . . ." He could conceive of a deity who was " 'entirely free, who does exactly as he likes according to his own caprice'. . . ." He could also conceive of a deity of absolute and unchanged law. " 'But a God who plays at dice in his own world, not knowing how the dice will fall — that does not seem possible. . . .' " And then, responding to a question about a man-centered religion such as the Social Gospel, he said that he did " 'not find it possible to select elements for human welfare out of the world influence and sum them up into a God. . . .' " " 'That,' he said, " with a twinkle and a laugh, " 'is an American idea.' "

Near the close of the interview someone asked him about the chances of his coming to America. " 'No,' " he laughingly replied, " 'I am afraid to come. I have many friends there and my heart is weak. Your energy would probably kill me. . . .' " (A few years later, when Nazi Storm Troopers were increasingly persecuting the Jews, he found refuge in the United States.)

And so, after a few more twinkles and laughs — this time over the question of reparations and war debts — the Eddy group left Einstein in the same big car which had brought them to him. The return journey took them through country lanes, suburbs and city streets to the spacious square near the old royal palace, which they found crowded with bands, parades, red flags, and orators in one of these Communist demonstrations so frequently seen in Germany in that time. This demonstration, on August 1, was peaceful; the squads of police were not needed as they had been during the street fighting between the emerging Nazis and the Communists on May 1. Indeed, Jesse noted that many of the red banners bore in-scriptions denouncing war and calling for a better world of peace and happiness. And Jesse thought that Einstein, that "quiet, kindly thinker," probably had far more influence for good than all the bands, crowds and orators, for he knew more definitely what he wanted and tried for "a practical way of attaining it . . . ."

(Undoubtedly Jesse would have expressed himself in less idealistic-optimistic terms had he known that Hitler, at a meeting of Nazi party leaders in Munich almost a year earlier, had ". . . spoken of the 'pitiable belief in reconciliation, understanding, world peace . . . .' " No, Hitler said, " 'We destroy these ideas. There is only one right in the world and that is the right of one's own strength." And Jesse would have been outraged had he known of the secret clause in the Treaty of Rapallo (1922), in which Russia, in return for German technical assistance, agreed to put three bases at their disposal. All three bases were to be used by the Germans to rebuild their war-making capacity in violation of the Treaty of Versailles. One base was the gas-warfare school at Saratov; the second was the tank-training facility at Kazan. The third was the airplane-training center at Lipetsk, two hundred miles southeast of Moscow. Nurtured by a steady stream of trained personnel and material smuggled in through Stettin and Leningrad, this center became the birthplace of the Luftwaffe which was to terrorize Europe and England in the Second World War.)

Back in his hotel room in Berlin Jesse jotted down those notes about the interview with Einstein which were to become the basis for the article he published in the *Friends Intelligencer* in September. But, since most of the subscribers to the *Intelligencer* were Quakers not well-trained in the higher reaches of physics, he thought that perhaps he owed his readers an introduction to Einstein's impact on the modern world. In any case, he prefaced the main account of the interview with a long paragraph in which, among other things, he called Einstein ". . . certainly one of the greatest minds of our time. . . ." And then:

To a large part of the world, even of the thinking world, he is a vague figure who is believed to have introduced mysterious and unbelievable theories about lines and distances, to have challenged the sacred law of gravitation, and in general to have played havoc with all the established certainties. All this is as far as possible from the truth and I believe that in time he will take his place with the great figures of the world of philosophy, who have changed fundamentally the outlook of man-kind on his world, making it more human, more livable, more in accord with experience. As Newton and his associates freed the western world, or at least the more intelligent part of it, from the incubus of the medieval cosmos, created by caprice and for men, full of magic and miracle, irrational and subject to an imperial dictator deity, so Einstein has freed us from the depotism of the mechanical, mathematical, law-ridden world which science has built up on the Newtonian mode. Science has grown more and more dogmatic until its orthodoxy is almost as narrow as that of the medieval church, and its determinism just plain Calvinism without its God, but also without its purpose. Einstein has restored our world to man, making him as he must be, the measure of all things. Science is only one human aspect of it, and not necessarily the most important. Laws and formulas are valuable, just in so far as they are valuable, but are not to be a substitute for our actual experience, which is ultimate reality. This is the writer's statement, not Mr. Einstein's who might not approve it wholly.

From Germany the Eddy party was to travel eastward and southward, going to Russia and Poland to study conditions in those countries. There are few records extant to show the exact route of their travels; aside from the articles on Russia which Jesse published later on in the *Intelligencer* (and in which the reader must pick up some of the itinerary through inference), and one short notice in *The Phoenix,* there is but one other source of information. This is a page of doggerel, copies of which were sent to friends in Swarthmore, "with apologies from the Holmes family." Three stanzas of this "poetry" seem appropriate here:

From Berlin to Lenin, from Prussia to Russia;
   From order to chaos, from west to the east,
We pass o'er the border to dirt and disorder,
   To poverty, terror, and turmoil, — and yeast!

There is sowing and growing, there's testing and trying
   As all the world over life mingled with death,
They blunder and plunder, and many go under,
   They make and destroy and remake in a breath.

Poland is a restaurant, and fine hotel, —
Coffee good, and service good, so all is going well.
Poland is Pilsudski, a despot democrat,
And war is peace, and white is black, and
   Switzerland is flat.
Poland is YMPA (P is for Pilsudski),
   It kotos here and goosesteps there, exactly
   as it shouldski.

If Jesse found Poland worthy of only passing attention, he was intensely interested in Communist Russia, which he called "one of the world's greatest and most interesting experiments." In fact, he took copious notes as the Eddy party was shown through the Soviet Union and, after returning to Swarthmore, wrote six articles for the *Intelligencer* so that others might share what he and Rebe had seen.

Leaving Berlin for the land of the Soviets, the Eddy party experienced that transition which Jesse had mentioned in his "poem" — passing "gradually from order, cleanliness and courtesy to increasing disorder, dirt, and indifference. . . ." They traveled to Riga in a comfortable sleeping car, with a dining car attached; in Riga they transferred to an old sleeping car in which the porter, "a very stupid peasant," had provided bedding for only ten of the party of eighteen. The porter felt that it was "unreasonable for so many to want to sleep on the train at once; it [had] never happened before." As the train sped on into Lithuania, Latvia, and finally Russia, the villages became poorer and more squalid, the paved roads less frequent — and dining cars had disappeared altogether. Now the travelers had to snatch their meals at railroad lunch counters (a la American before George Pullman and the luxury dining car); by this time they had "said good-bye to good coffee and the aesthetics of eating. . . ."

Leningrad proved to be a fascinating city because of the glaring contrasts they found there: the contrasts between the relics of Czarist times and the stark realities of Communism; the contrasts between "the courtesies and the graces of life which go with wealth, leisure and assured position," and the "not very clean, dishevelled, and awkward" way of life they found in the days when Stalin was invoking the first of his Five Year Plans. Driven through "long stretches of deserted streets," the Eddy party were finally brought to the famous avenue once called "Nevski Prospect"; now it was called "The Street of October 25th." Here, however, they saw a scene reminiscent of Paris: light, life, and motion; crowded trolleys and automobiles dashed about with little regard for safety. Taken to the Hotel Europa, they found it "a marble palace, with beautiful stairways and stately suites of rooms. . . ." But it seemed rather forlorn and empty; instead of its lobbies and tables being occupied by the lords and ladies once so prominent, it now was sparsely inhabited by people "of the mechanic and peasant type, mingled with a few representing the business of all nations, and with the ever-present American tourists. . . ."

Other aspects of the Leningrad scene showed this strange juxtaposition of the old with the new. The Winter Palace of the Czars, with its furnishings, was maintained as an ever-present reminder to the proletariat of the luxurious life-style of their oppressors before 1917; here also could be seen the rooms where Kerensky and "his futile group of 'intellectuals' tried out their short-lived republic. . . ." Outside, near the railroad station, stood an

276

heroic bronze statue of Lenin — his "eager face, wide-flying coat, old cap and baggy trousers . . ." symbolizing that resurgence of life under a new system which was to make the Soviet Union such a formidable force in the world. The country houses of the old aristocracy still stood, but those who frequented them and the "woodsy walks about them " were convalescents from hospitals, orphan children, or workers on vacation. Everything was "topsy-turvy," according to Jesse; it was a disgrace to be an idler, and nothing was too good for the worker. The injured, the tired, the helpless, must have the best — unless, of course they were "remnants of the parasitic classes of Old Russia; in that case young Russia is heartless and contemptuous. The cruelties of the generations past beget new cruelties today."

But, in spite of the many interesting things to observe in Leningrad, Jesse thought that it had "a rather languid spirit" as compared with Moscow. Here, in the ancient capital of the Romanovs, he found "an atmosphere charged, and almost supercharged, with vitality and with intense and unyielding purpose. . . ." The purpose, of course, was to so direct the political, social, and economic life of the people as to make the Russian experiment in Communism a success.

If Jesse discovered vitality and unyielding purpose in Moscow, he also found living conditions to be less than desirable. Up to this point in the Russian experiment the principle of "from each according to his ability, to each according to his need" had resulted mainly in a sharing of poverty. Moscow was grossly overcrowded, families being packed into government apartment houses so that some had only one room. Rents were high, and a great deal of sickness was traceable to the human congestion. Meat was scarce; people stood for hours in meat-lines just as they did for bread. But, as Jesse said, this was an old story; the same conditions had prevailed under the Czar. Further, it had to be remembered that Russia was only "a few years removed from war, pestilence and famine which destroyed some ten million of her people, killed off most of the horses, cattle and sheep, ruined the railroad system, and threw out of gear the whole organization of society."

And that society, as was well known, had been essentially agricultural; the Russian workers of the 'twenties were deficient in those industrial skills which had built up modern Western culture. The Russia of 1929, Jesse asserted, "must be compared, not with

277

America or England, but with pre-war Russia and the Russia of the years since the war. . . ." When such comparisons were made, "all unprejudiced observers agreed," it could be seen that industrial Russia was "vigorously on the up grade, and [would] soon be able to establish herself as an efficient unit among the nations."

To achieve such efficiency, however, required the help and example of Western technology, such as that provided by the General Electric Company, by Henry Ford, and by a Mr. Hammer, who held a ten-year concession from the Soviet government for his pencil factory. In this concession, Mr. Hammer was forced to pay a twenty per cent higher wage to his seven hundred employees than was paid in two competing government factories because the workers in those factories felt that they owned them; in addition, they got more fringe benefits from the Soviet system — all kinds of insurance (including protection for old age), medical care, paid holidays, special rates for amusements, and day-care centers for working mothers. And, however dull life may have been in the provinces — or in those other less-favored areas not shown to the Eddy party — the Moscow workers had available "great pleasure parks" for recreation and the cultivation of the higher culture. The pleasure park in Moscow covered one thousand acres; it contained "reading rooms, theatres, museums, exhibits of agricultural machinery, of educational supplies, of household arts, galleries of paintings, playgrounds for children and adults — all for a very small sum within reach of most. . . ." Altogether, with Western help and their own resources, the Moscovites were well on their way toward the better life promised to them by their leaders.

In all this evaluation of Russian life Jesse would not have been true to character if he had failed to make cogent observations about the fate of religion under the Soviet system. And he did indulge this major interest in his life: he studied what had happened to religion since the days of Rasputin, that Russian Orthodox monk who had held the royal family in superstitious thrall before the October Revolution. In his report via the *Intelligencer,* he told of how the Communists, reacting to the old system of Church wealth, ritualism, corruption, and alliance with the ruling aristocracy, had confiscated the wealth of the Church and had turned some of the great cathedrals into museums in which the bones of saints and other sacred and miracle-working relics were held up to ridicule. "The venality and the immorality of the monks is brought out in picture and in caricature. The oppressive wealth and selfishness of the old order is made plain by the gorgeous vestments, jewels, and gold and silver plate, in contrast with the grinding poverty of the worshippers. . . ."

Attendance by Jesse and Rebe at a service in Moscow's Cathedral of the Saviour, plus reports from leaders of the small congregations who gathered for "genuine community worship," led to Jesse's conclusion that the Soviet government had a "contemptuous tolerance for mere ritual," while it held a deep distrust of those who held services of a more thinking nature. (It should be remembered that Russia was largely by-passed by the Renaissance, which called for an examination of the values of pagan Greece and Rome, and which led to new interpretations and values in the fields of religion, economics, politics, and art in the countries of Western Europe.) Russia felt herself "isolated, hated, a pariah among nations. Any secret movement [might] be a foreign plot. This was especially likely to be true among the religious sects which [had] relations with the sects of other nations and receive [d] help from them. . . ." The old Czarist spy system had been revived; suspicion was everywhere — and it was even dangerous to talk openly at the dinner table since the waiters were probably government spies.

Jesse's final judgment on this matter of religion and the general psychological situation regarding Russian relations with Western powers deserves to be recorded in its entirety:

> So hostility and fear beget suspicion and cruelty. I do not doubt the action of Great Britain in entering into diplomatic relations with Russia will ease up on persecution even in religion. If we would do the same it would help even more. People become irrational and cruel when they are in panic; and in the grip of panic Russia is building up her army, pushing her influence in Asia, and everywhere preparing for the invasion she believes must come. Her Boy Scouts, who number millions, use the motto, 'Be Prepared.' So here, as elsewhere in the world, distrust, fear, and preparation for hostility bring the threatening clouds of warfare and violence nearer and nearer.

While Jesse made "every effort" to understand the situation of the Russian farmers, he admitted that about all the tourist was able to see of life in the country was the fleeting glimpses of tiny villages and market towns from the speeding train, or the bearded men on station platforms or at work in the fields. What he was able to report came to him second-handed via a letter from a farming village and from official news releases of the Soviet government.

From all of these sources Jesse gathered enough data to be able to conclude that "the problem of the farmer is the most serious one the Russian government has to face ...." Numbering about 120,000,000 people — 80 per cent of the population in 1929 — these farmers were scattered over an area larger than the United States, but without the railroad-and-road system which saved the American farmer from the worst effects of rural isolation. Although released from serfdom by Czar Alexander II in 1861 (Jesse had it as 1863), the older peasants were still almost as "backward, illiterate, and superstitious" as they had been for centuries. This being the case, and knowing that "the farmers must be moved a thousand years in as many days ....," the Five-Year planners were turning to the youth of the nation to gain a greater efficiency with more modern methods.

This drive for greater efficiency took two main forms. One was the government or state farms, "not far removed," as Jesse said, from those experiment stations run by the American federal government. There were hundreds of these in various parts of Russia; one of these had 125,000 acres and used 900 tractors. Just as the Soviets made use of Western technicians to help boost their industries, so they had hired an American expert in large-scale farming to advise them on equipment and methods. Since the state farms were model farms, the individual farmers near them were encouraged to visit them for whatever ideas they might pick up in the use of farm machinery, to improve their seed grain, and to fertilize their soil.

The second type of model farm was the cooperative, in which the farmers of a given area, using modern methods, produced crops or livestock to be sold through cooperative markets. This type of farm was more numerous than the state farm; in 1929 over a million peasant cooperative families were farming over twelve million acres. In the past two years they had increased their production ten times.

And the farmers were being served in other ways, according to Jesse. Lest they begin to feel farm-bound and cut off from the cultural opportunities of urban living, "all the great cities" had established " 'peasant houses' " to which visiting farmers might go for a few days of city life at state expense. In or near these cities were farm museums or exhibition halls where the visitors could go to inspect the latest machinery, model houses and barns, high-grade seed grain and vegetables, and where they might attend lectures and demonstrations on improved farming given by experts. Returning to their homes, the peasants could avail themselves of traveling schools of instruction if they lived near railroad lines; the rural schools also supported the general uplift plan.

In spite of the admission by the farmers that under the collective-farm system they had a far higher standard of living then they had under the Czars, the older people still complained "bitterly of hard times and heavy taxes, together with occasional seizure [s] of grain by the government in times of stress. . . ." But this was perhaps to be expected from the older generation; "a new peasantry [was now] being evolved. . . . The revolution has swept over the peasant with a cyclone of new ideas and practices. . . ." While it was still too early to predict the outcome, Jesse hoped for the sake of the 150,000,000 people in Russia that this great experiment in agriculture would succeed.

As a pacifist Jesse was of course far less hopeful about the increasing size and strength of the Red Army, then the largest in the world. Trying to give a fair or objective report about it, and about the Soviet policies which directed its development, he pointed out that the job of the analyst was complicated by the fact that Russia was "a land of 'infinite contradiction.' . . ." While the Soviets claimed that their system put the interests of the common people above all other considerations, its huge military machine was at the same time preparing for another world war. But the suggestion that this preparation was for world conquest, Jesse admitted, was "only a half-truth. . . ." Preparation for defensive purposes was the other half of the truth, since the Soviet leaders "honestly believe [d] that the older 'capitalistic' governments [were] trying to attack and destroy them. . . ." So they were "feverishly, and sometimes with an element of panic, striving to be ready to 'save the revolution.' . . ." The teaching in the schools, the great effort to develop industry, and the conscription of the youth for service in the Red Army — all were directed to this end.

And the psychological buildup to defend Mother Russia and its new communism was succeeding. Not only in the schools, but through three semi-military organizations, the youth of the land were taught to march, to endure hardship, and to dedicate their lives to their country's mission. Indoctrinated with that puritanical zeal characterizing communistic dictatorships, some of the Russian youth lived in an almost monastic fashion. Jesse reported that he

281

"knew of young fellows in their later teens, who spoke scornfully of drinking, smoking, dancing, and the usual pleasures of youth. 'We aim to be communists! We must be strong!' . . ." All those who did not qualify for conscription into this army of patriots — the priests, the employers of labor, and the conscientious objectors — had to pay a heavy tax to help support the welfare services for the army personnel and for pensions for those disabled in the field.

There were several other reasons why being drafted into the army did not cause much resentment among the people of Soviet Russia. Aside from seeming "a reasonable requirement for a time of peril. . . . ," the required service was not as "severe or degrading" as in many other countries. Social distinctions between men and officers, according to Jesse, did not exist; "the abuse of a private by his superiors [was] unheard of. . . ." And the army was a school which was not "supposed" to let anyone leave its service until he had learned to read and write. It was "the greatest adult school in the world. . . ."; and also, of course, it used its every power to strengthen belief in the Soviet system.

Jesse closed this report on the Russian Army by bending over backwards in his effort to be fair to his host country. Recalling what he had written in the early part of his report about the Soviets preparing for a world conflict, he now declared that, "as far as [he] could hear, the intention of the government in developing its great army is wholly defensive, and they would welcome any international agreements which would make war less probable. . . ." He praised the efforts of the British to enter into diplomatic relations with the Soviet Union as "a great relief" and one which would "ease up their fear. . . ." He thought that similar efforts by the Americans would be "even more effective." (Jesse was right, of course. But, in the atmosphere of the late 'twenties, and throughout the 'thirties, as fear begat fear, the relations between Russia and the United States were only formally correct, not cordial. When, however, the threat of Hitler's Nazism threatened any pretensions at democracy anywhere in the world, the United States and the Soviet Union entered into a marriage of convenience, signalized most vividly by American material aid to Russia while the Soviets were battling Germans on the Eastern front.)

After a trip down the Volga the Eddy party was ready to come home. And when he got home in the late summer of 1929 Jesse sat down to write his reasoned judgment on Russia. Since the first paragraph of the report illustrates so well his life-long conviction that one ought to face facts, whether they be favorable or unfavorable to one's own position, it is given here in its entirety:

Russia is the great world problem. Nothing is more stupid than hating her, condemning her, deploring her, ignoring her. There she is: with twice and more the land area of the United States and a much greater population; probably the greatest area of undeveloped resources now on the earth; probably the most profitable region for investment of capital. The average profit of the foreign concessionaires last year is reported by one of them to be about sixty percent. Russia is three-fourths or more agricultural; she is poverty-stricken, dirty, culturally backward, hostile, and afraid. Yet she is flaunting a challenge in the face of western civilization; she is scornful of its industrial system, she condemns its capitalism as parasitic, she despises its culture as superficial and petty, she holds its religion in contempt as superstition and hypocrisy.

Given these attitudes, and the world-shaking implications of the communist set of ideas, there was small cause to wonder why people in Western countries both hated and feared Stalin's new nation. But Jesse thought that the Society of Friends, in keeping with their tradition, should make every effort "to penetrate the mass of rumor, falsehood, and hostility . . . to understand the nature of the Russian challenge. . . ." As he said, they might be right or they might be wrong; probably they were partly right and partly wrong. In any case, there were some "150,000,000 of our fellowmen struggling against an unfriendly environment, and ringed about with hostile peoples. . . ." They were "neither demons — red-handed and murderous — nor angels bringing a millenium." Reacting to centuries of oppression by the corrupt nobility and the venal Church, a fanatical communist group did become cruel, unjust, and terrible in their treatment of the aristocrats and the bourgeoisie; nothing was allowed to stand in the way of "the rule of the workers, for the workers, [and] by the workers. . . ." But this was the way of revolutionaries, whether English, American, French, or Russian; revolutions were "not rose-water affairs. . . ."

In summing up Jesse asked his readers to judge the Russians in the light of their history and their present problems, and to hold up the American experience as an auxiliary gauge for this judgment. Many people raised in democratic-capitalistic cultures seized upon the cruelty and poverty of Russian life, most of which were inherited from the old regime, as inborn characteristics of communism; this

283

was "just as unfair as to regard lynching and race prejudice, which is an inheritance from slavery days, as characteristic of democracy. . . ." Like democrats in capitalistic societies, they were trying to achieve the greatest good for the greatest number; they too were engaged in the pursuit of happiness. But, so long as they felt themselves hated by a hostile world they would react "in hatred and malignity. The only useful influence which can be brought to bear on them is friendliness and good will. . . ." This, Jesse emphasized, did not mean that Americans should approve of their methods or seek to adopt them; it did reflect "a humane desire that a great and cruelly abused people. . . ." should have their chance to make their way "toward the goals we all seek for, however blindly."

Having finished his judgment-report on Russia, and thinking back over the long European trip, Jesse amused himself by scribbling still another bit of doggerel:

> So the ills of the nations, and eke all creation
> We've studied with ardor intense;
> And now we are ready, with thanks to S. Eddy,
> To deal with 'em all, present tense.

Although he was a general reformer, one detects a self-deprecating note here; he was not prone to take himself too seriously.

13. The Way of the Reformer

By the time Jesse wrote his reports on the Russian experiment in communism his life style as a general reformer had been set. As a Hicksite Quaker he believed that it was a function of man to improve himself and the world about him. This improvement was to spring from the application of certain principles developed over the ages through the study of man and his place in nature by savants such as Socrates, Aristotle, Jefferson, Darwin and William James. These principles were to be applied until further research, experience, and thought had revealed that they had to be modified or abandoned in favor of new principles. Jesse was ever the philosopher-scientist, ever the idealistic pragmatist.

And, like Socrates, he was always the gadfly who believed that it was the greatest service to mankind to sting people to reexamine the "facts" and theories which lay behind their thoughts and actions. Every convention, custom, and habit was to be tested as to its validity and logical worth in view of the data, and in view of its potential or actual worth for mankind's welfare.

Jesse's essential position here is illustrated by what he wrote in a book review for the *Friends Intelligencer* in 1932. Pointing out that Theodore Darnell's *After Christianity — What?* undoubtedly would irritate many people, he commented, ". . . probably they are just the ones who need it. . . ."

The Principles behind Jesse's Reforms.

The principles governing Jesse's life as a reformer appear in scattered fashion in his lectures, his writings, and in the memories of his friends and relatives. Viewing these principles as a whole, we see that he was a Christian first, a Quaker second (that is, a practicing Christian), a pragmatic humanist third, and a Socialist fourth. But the ideas and modes of action in each of these categories were not really to be ranked in order of priority; they were so interwoven as to form the fabric of his intellectual life as a reformer.

And human life should be logical. It should proceed from the "truths" established by careful, unbiased research about the human condition in any field at any time — subject, of course, to the tests of further experience and further research. And these "truths," always subject to revision, should be applied in close adherence to the laws of logic laid down by scholars across the centuries. If natural law in the social world does not work out, as the Social Darwinsists claimed it did, for the greatest good of the greatest number, what is wrong? Is it the theory, the facts — or the logic? If the word "socialism" has acquired sinister meanings, raising specters of violent revolution, is it because men have failed to see that the logical first object of government and business is to give men-in-society the greatest good for the greatest number? If the English language is a living, growing museum of other languages resulting in the need for a more economical and phonetic spelling — "thru" for "through," "brot" for "brought," "tho" for "though" — is there not a place for the logical reformer here?

Since accurate definitions of the terms people used in their everyday communication were so important for logical discourse in the period just after World War I, Jesse saw a great need to define at some length those smear words current in capitalistic society. In 1919 he wrote a series of articles explaining the meaning of socialism, anarchism, and bolshevism — all of these articles aiming at the reduction of the current emotional reaction to these words to the level of calm, analytical appraisal. And these articles, of course, were but an expression of his dislike of any such labels — socialism, conservatism, radicalism, etc. — which so often substituted for thought in the constant dialogue inherent among people in modern culture. Each system of thought, Jesse always maintained, should be judged on its own merits. These "merits," of course, were in turn to be judged by the degree to which they contributed to the general welfare of the individual and society.

Jesse's whole career showed that one's life should be one of action and service to others. Instead of working constantly for his own advancement, either academically or financially, he devoted his time and energies to those projects which offered some hope of lifting mankind in general above brutish levels. As Emerson said of his friend Thoreau, Jesse was never quite happy unless he had a cause to promote, an oppressed minority (or majority — e.g., the workers in the period 1890-1940) to defend. This defense of basic human rights to life, liberty, and the pursuit of that general happiness promised by all the reformers since Jesus constituted Jesse's life. It was his duty — a thought, we may be sure, which was for him only reinforced by his friend Rabindranath Tagore:

> I slept and dreamt
> That life was joy
> I awoke and saw
> That life was duty
> I acted and behold
> Duty was joy.

This joy in duty was constantly stressed, as in the time (1917) he called for "a religion of service" — a clear call to Americans to express their Christian beliefs in concrete terms by helping the criminal find a better way, relieve the condition of women, protect working-class children, and change that system of "wage slavery" governing American life. To do these things was but clearly the religious duty of the democratic citizen. "The making over of the barbarious industrial materialism into a real democracy is just the task of the Lord's Prayer — to make the kingdom come on earth."

To those who disagreed — those who saw only a devil's world in the present conditions, in which men and women should seek only individual salvation in a life after death — Jesse said "phui!" Their attitude was only an "easy excuse" for the evasion of the responsibility to improve conditions on earth here and now. What we have now, he had asserted in 1911, is an opportunity to find truth and beauty, to find and apply the Jesus principle in our lives. "Our lives as religious beings should be experimental and we should seek to supply men with clear visions of the life they seek, so that we should not have to live doubtfully and die timidly."

The philosophy of experimental testing runs throughout the Holmes' records. In 1909 Jesse told Quakers at the Winona Lake (Indiana) Conference that " 'let us seek' " is the only appropriate answer to " 'Seek and ye shall find.' " And, Jesse said, "Inertia and passive acceptance belong with dead matter. 'Run and find out ' is the formula for those who desire to have life and to have it more abundantly." In 1925, when Calvin Collidge was saying that "the business of America is business," and when the fear of new social ideas from abroad was leading the country into a sterile and irresponsible isolation, Jesse railed against "the silly stuff that is called 100 percent Americanism, which teaches that to be loyal to one's country one must keep things as they are." Such blind adherence to the status quo was against nature's endless change, against the principles of experimentalism which had started America as a nation, and not to be borne in any aspect of human life. Finding the divine in the commonplace, men should develop their religions out of their daily lives; religion, Jesse said in 1932, was a reaction to the various environments men found themselves in as they tried to earn their livings and tried to act as civilized human beings rather than as animals tearing each other with fang and claw. If men had risen above the cruder forms of personal combat they were still trying to subject others to their will through those slaughters they called wars; they were still extolling the virtues of competition in sports, industry, and business, using stratagems and tactics which too often verged on the dishonest and criminal, and which wasted natural and human resources. In 1934 Jesse asked whether the time had not come to imitate those animals which cooperated with each other, as the bull bison formed a defensive circle to guard the cows and young within. Should not the leaders of government and business get together to institute a planned economy, just as the Founding Fathers gathered in Philadelphia in 1787 to institute a planned government? Only through such cooperative labor could each member of society give according to his ability and receive according to his needs.

To advocate such socialistic and communistic ideas was dangerous in the time of the Red Hysteria of the post-World War I era; only the First Amendment and Oliver Wendell Holmes' doctrine that no "clear and present danger" faced the country allowed people like Jesse to escape the more palpable forms of wrath vented by 100% Americans in 1919 and in the early 'twenties. Even in the days when Franklin D. Roosevelt was lashing out at "economic royalists" Jesse would have had a much more difficult time at Swarthmore, and in his lecturing and writing, if he had not been bolstered by the Quaker tradition of free speech and freedom of the press so stoutly upheld in Quaker assemblies and by the *Friends Intelligencer.*

In accordance with this tradition Jesse constantly called for the rights to unfettered investigation and the public expression of any resulting ideas, facts or unpopular modes of conduct. He reminded his colleagues that the central doctrine of the Quakers was that of the "Inward Light," which came to "every seeking soul" as a result of reading, research, discussion, and reflection. In 1912 he expressed his approval of the labors of the Young Friends Conference held in Indiana that summer; he hoped that the Young Friends would not be deterred by criticism or opposition, nor be "too much influenced by precedent. . . ." This advice was reinforced by another injunction published in the *Friends Intelligencer* a week later to the effect that people of all ages should not blindly accept authority — whether this authority came from church, or state, or from the leaders of society in any field, whether found in hitherto revered books or in the latest pronouncements from the press or the rostrum. Any principles or courses of action were to be given the pragmatic test for truth. The test was always: Did they work in practice to the greater good of individuals and society?

The Reformer's Style.

The promulgation of such ideas, plus Jesse's increasing reputation as a stimulating speaker, led to an incident in 1930 which revealed much about the temper of the times and something about Jesse too. He had accepted an invitation to give the Armistice Day address at X . . . University, a long day's train ride from Philadelphia, on the "appropriate and innocuous subject of Patriotism. . . ." But, only a few days before he was to leave for X . . . he received a "rather halting and uncertain" letter asking whether the subject might be changed to "India." Jesse found it difficult to put together a new lecture, being forced to assemble his materials on the train and after his arrival at the University. However, working on the theory that those who pay the piper are privileged to call the tune, he gave his lecture to some five or six hundred students.

While he had "thought no evil" about the change of topic except that a speech on India seemed peculiarly inappropriate on Armistice Day, he was soon to change his mind. After the lecture in the main hall he gave his original address to some fifty students and faculty members in a large rooming house occupied by campus liberals. Either before or after this address he was enlightened as to why his "Patriotism" topic had been changed to "India." But let Jesse report on this in his own words:

> ... it appeared from information given by faculty and student members that the reason was that certain faculty advisers 'got cold feet' at the idea of having a Quaker talk on patriotism, that the local American Legion (and possibly the D.A.R.) might be aroused, that wealthy friends of the University might be irritated: — that, in short, a Quaker is a dangerous prson about an institution of learning, and if he speaks it is better that he speak on something quite far away.

But the story does not end here. After the address on patriotism in the rooming house, a discussion on peace and war prolonged the whole session to about two hours. And then, after a short rest and supper, Jesse gave a radio talk sponsored by the Women's League for Peace and Freedom, "and not limited by outside pressures. . . ."

Altogether, Jesse returned to the "happy hunting grounds" of Swarthmore both exhilarated by the warm reception of the liberals at X ... University, and saddened by the "narrow-minded, conceited, and biogoted " elements in that university town. He found it sad that the efforts of those who aspired to a "nobler humanity and a happier world" should be hampered by the threatened opposition of an "organized fraction of the drafted men of 1917" — some of them unwilling successors to the Minutemen of 1776 — and by those who had acquired wealth and power under the social and industrial system which had developed since the fundamental rights of man had been written into the Amendments to the American Constitution. On the other hand, he rejoiced in the guidance given to the liberal group at X ... by the "tiny Friends' Meeting" there — a meeting with "men and women of character and ability in charge." (We may be sure that if this incident had occurred in the late 1960s or early 1970s Jesse would have been condemned by the college radicals for acquiescing so easily to a change in lecture topic; on the other hand, more thoughtful liberals might have praised him for helping to keep alive a small band of workers in the fields of social betterment when America was in one of its periods of indecision as to the relative values of the rights of man as opposed to the rights of property.)

In spite of the support of such liberals as those Jesse met at X ... University, he found that it took courage to be a reformer in the social, economic and political atmosphere of the 1920s and the 1930s. It took courage to lead a parade of unkept, bewhiskered

Socialists down one of Philadelphia's major streets, with signs aloft and banners flying. It took courage to stand before an audience, as he did in 1932, and rephrase the Twenty-third Psalm to make it read "The Lord is my dynamo, from whom comes power." It made little difference to conservatives that he was merely doing this to illustrate the divine in the commonplace, and to show that when David wrote "The Lord is my shepherd, I shall not want," it was written out of *his* experience as a shepherd, whereas an electrical engineer might with equal justice write a new version out of *his* experience. But to conservatives reared on the endless repetition of David's poetry, Jesse's bold suggestion did violence to the music of the King James version. And "The Lord is my low gear, from whom I get extra power on my up grades," was worse. Even Jesse's friends were concerned; so much so, in fact, that he felt it necessary to explain his point and his motives once more in an article in the *Friends Intelligencer.*

Several characteristics about Jesse Holmes' style as a reformer, and as a speech-maker and writer, were highlighted by this incident. One was his liking for the striking phrase, the shocking word, and the shocking idea. When he addressed the Friends General Conference at Cape May, New Jersey, in 1932 his topic was "Religion — a Sword or a Pillow?".This title was sure to wake up the somnolent and attract more people to the lecture hall. This same predeliction for the striking juxtaposition of opposing ideas is seen in his assertion that we should practice ". . . a religion of life in place of a religion of death. . . ." Similarly, in writing of Jesus, the great earth-man teacher and prophet, who suffered so much from the confused-if-sincere work of his followers, Jesse held that "So a great character and a great teacher fades into just another super-natural Being. . . ." No wonder that he asserted that "The kingdom of stupidity is within us. . . ." And no wonder that, when he viewed the antics of New York's Four Hundred, he was moved to say, " 'I [have] as much use for swell society doings as a scalded baby has for a sandpaper massage.' " This quotation appeared in one of his resource books, and we may believe he used it in some of his speeches when he lashed out at the mindless stratification of society. If conservatives urged the gradual approach to social reform too strongly, Jesse could dip into another of his resource books for rebuttal. He might quote Mr. Dooley's advice to the downtrodden minorities — " 'Don't ask for rights: take 'em. There's something the matter with a right that is handed to you.' " Or he might hurl into the teeth of rock-ribbed Republicans the words of the revered Lincoln: " 'This country with its institutions belongs to the people who inhabit it. Whenever they shall grow weary of the existing government, they can exercise their constitutional right of amending it, or their revolutionary right to dismember or overthrow it.' "

Another characteristic of Jesse's style as a lecturer was seen in his habit of speaking from a few notes scribbled on a card or slip of paper. This was his style even on those occasions when he had ample time to prepare a written speech, as was true of the many times he was scheduled to appear before the Friends General Conference. *After* the address had been given he would take the time to write the speech he had given, trusting to his notes and to his phenomenal memory to reproduce what had been said as accurately as possible for the benefit of those who subscribed to the *Friends Intelligencer* or other publications. Thus, the readers of the *Intelligencer* were given a "brief outline" of his speech on "A Christian Civilization" to the General Conference in 1928. (They did not, of course, get the benefit of those voice inflections, facial expressions and gestures which added so much meaning and interest to his oral message from the rostrum.) In the same way, those who could not attend Jesse's memorable address in the South Broad Street Theatre, Philadelphia, in 1921, had to be content with reading only part of what he said when he published his speech as "The Message of Quakerism." An editorial note under the title warned the reader that "The following draft . . . lacks much of the style of the original address, having been recast from partial stenographic notes."

And this method of speaking from rough notes, trusting that those newspapermen who heard him would report the spirit and the substance of his speech accurately, got him into trouble on the occasion of the Twenty-third Psalm speech. If he had written out his speech beforehand, and delivered it as written, he could have refuted the charges of sacrilege leveled against him much more easily simply by publishing his speech immediately after he gave it. As it was, it took him some time to consult the notes used on that occasion and to write his explanation of what he had said and what he had meant. Calling his explanatory article "Quoted Religion," he lashed out at incompetent reporters while at the same time seizing the occasion to assert once again that people should not rely on what they had only read or heard to form a religious position, but should develop a continuously growing, experimental religion out of their own life experiences.

If Jesse's methods of preparing for a speech were somewhat slipshod they can be excused by the noble aim of wishing to speak directly to his audience, his flashing blue eyes always on them and not diverted to the text of the speech. (Frank Aydelotte used the same technique, and also to the point of having a secretary take stenographic notes.) His genius lay in speech-making, and there were many opportunities for a Quaker professor with a fine platform presence to give public lectures. Audiences were hungry to hear directly from the speaker, before radio and television separated them, about the many issues agitating religious, social, economic, and political life. In the days of Mark Hanna, William Jennings Bryan, Robert LaFollette and Herbert Hoover, Jesse was at times nearly swamped by invitations to speak to women's clubs, religious groups, labor unions, college groups, civic associations, and Chautauqua circuits on an almost endless array of topics.

A few sample years from the Hoover period may serve to illustrate the range of Jesse's activities. Thus, early in June, 1928, *The Phoenix* announced that during the summer he was to lecture at the University of Iowa, at a meeting of the Epworth League at Lincoln, Nebraska, at Richmond, Indiana, at Buck Hill Falls, Pennsylvania, and at Longwood Yearly Meeting. "The rest of the vacation he will read and study." Perhaps this reading and studying was done to prepare for his speech before the Ethical Culture Society of Philadelphia, meeting in the Academy of Music the following February. Here Jesse gave the Christian viewpoint in answer to the general question "What is Human Life For?"; other speakers gave answers from the standpoint of Judaism, Hinduism, and that Ethical Culture promoted by Felix Adler. On a Friday in November, 1933, he left the Swarthmore campus to fulfill speaking engagements in New York State, stopping to visit his son Robert and his wife Grace in New York City, who had recently been transferred from a state-related post in Albany. On Sunday, at eleven o'clock, Jesse addressed the chapel-service crowd at Union College, Schenectady, on "We and Our World," broadcasting over station WGY at the same time. After lunch there was time enough to go to Troy, where Jesse spoke to the people attending the vesper service at the Emma Willard School. As late as 1938, when he was in his seventy-fourth year, he was still traveling about the country giving talks to large and enthusiastic audiences on such topics as "The Future of Religion," "Nationalism and Internationalism," labor's rights, and international peace. If his tastes had not been for general reform, giving him the incentive to work up the facts and the ideas on seemingly separated, yet integrated, topics, one finds it difficult to see how he could have accomplished as much as he did.

And Jesse might have accomplished a great deal more if he had followed more closely the example of his friends J. Russell Smith and Scott Nearing. These men, realizing quite early in their careers that the printed page has enormous advantages over the spoken word, wrote profitable textbooks and many learned articles. Not only were their fortunes increased, but their published works were relatively permanent, being available to students as a more constant means of education and persuasion. Lectures, even Jesse's lectures, tended to vanish into thin air. Even if they were written afterwards, they were likely to come to people's eyes in fragmented form, or, as we have seen, in garbled versions via newspaper reports.

Jesse's Writing.

He of course realized the power of the printed word. But somehow this energetic, extroverted man could not find the time in his most active years to write those extended, logical, sequential treatments on related subjects that we call the chapters of a book. As Eleanor Stabler Clarke said, "He was too busy getting the world settled right *now!*" Not a research scholar like Henry J. Cadbury, he was a crusader hurling his spears and arrows against wrongdoing in a series of brief but pointed articles across forty-odd years and on many topics. Hastily written, sometimes failing to observe the rules of grammar, spelling, or punctuation, they were sprinkled with the "musts" of the earnest reformer — we the people "must" do this or do that to set the world on the road to that heavenly kingdom on earth envisioned by idealists. These commands, "sometimes appeals or even satires," were issued mainly from the Quaker press, particularly the *Friends Intelligencer,* which became the official organ of the Hicksites in 1924. And it is interesting to note how one perceptive reader of the Quaker press compared Jesse's style with that of Jesse's friend Brand Blanshard. Holmes' writing, he thought, had a "dynamicism and directness" not to be found in the "more scholarly ... web-spinning" of Blanshard. But "Both are fascinating men. . . . ," Blanshard being the "better writer. . . . ."

In spite of Jesse's relative inability to settle down as a serious writer, and in spite of the surprising lack of effort by his friends and relatives to collect all that he wrote into one repository, the total mass of his writings that the author has been able to find is still impressive. Some seventy of his articles appeared in Quaker periodicals from his earliest years at Swarthmore through his retirement in the middle 'thirties. Thirty-two of these were on some aspect of religion, either on general topics relating to man's religious drive, or on such more specific topics such as the series of eleven articles he wrote on Christian doctrine in the years 1909-1912. In 1926-27 a series of articles on the people and institutions of India and Ceylon aimed to promote peace and brotherhood through understanding of these foreign cultures. And, while these articles sometimes took on the flavor of a travelogue, his series of reports on Russia in 1929 also had the objective of promoting peace through education and understanding. Jesse kept his socialist sympathies in check in these reports; indeed, he found that the Russian experiment in communism had begun to be a world problem.

Other articles were concerned with generalized treatments of the need for world peace, with being a citizen of the world, and with being a truly loyal (critical) citizen of one's own country. Several articles were written on a theme which was a life-long principle of Jesse's: that there was no necessary conflict between science and religion. Indeed, one of these articles, "To the Scientifically Minded," not only was printed in the *Friends Intelligencer*, but 20,000 copies of it were sent out in the form of a letter to people who might have found a conflict between science and their accustomed religion, and who were invited to join the Society of Friends in the hope and implied promise of resolving this conflict. Originating in the fertile brain of Jesse H. Holmes, this proselytizing venture — both the original article and the letter campaign — won the approval of the Advancement Committee of the Hicksite Friends, and produced results beyond what they might reasonably have expected. More than five hundred letters were received by the Advancement Committee asking for more information about the Quakers, many newspapers quoted from Jesse's original article, and a number of nationally circulated magazines reprinted it, including the *Atlantic, Unity, Christian Century,* and *Harpers.* Altogether, as *Time* magazine put it, Jesse's idea was "... beginning what [was] probably the most vigorous effort in more than a century for converts." And Jesse's writing had at last broken out of the round of Quaker parochialism and was commanding national attention.

Nor was this the end. In 1928 "To the Scientifically Minded" was issued in the form of a small three-page circular or pamphlet by the Advancement Committee of the Friends' General Conference. Now it was signed not only by Jesse but by Dean Roscoe Pound of the Harvard Law School; by J. Russell Smith, professor of economic geography at Columbia; by Thomas A. Jenkins, professor of the history of the French language at the University of Chicago; and by Albert T. Mills, professor of history and political science at James Milliken University. A later edition dropped Jenkins' name as signer, giving in its place that of Paul H. Douglas, professor of economics at the University of Chicago. Not only was this pamphlet available to anyone who asked for it at the Cherry Street (Philadelphia) headquarters of the Advancement Committee, but, as a Quaker reported, it was to be found, along with many other circulars or pamphlets written by Friends, "on the literature table at the back of essentially every ... meeting house during the 1940's and 50's."

With this pamphlet, as well as with his *What Is Truth? A Message to Students, Who are the Quakers?,* and *What Is a Pacifist?,* Jesse joined a distinguished set of Quaker pamphleteers. The literature tables at meeting houses would also hold Brand Blanshard's *To Prepare or Not to Prepare, The Great Commandment,* and his *Inward Light and Outward Darkness.* Rufus M. Jones, speaking for the orthodox, wrote *The Quaker's Faith.* Patrick M. Malin, professor of economics at Swarthmore, gave *One Quaker's View of the Society.* And many others, friends of Jesse and Rebe, contributed to the list of notable works given in *A Guide to Quaker Reading,* (1946 and 1957).

In Jesse's earliest years at Swarthmore, when he was trying to enhance his reputation as a sound thinker and writer, he felt it necessary to identify himself as the author of "The Attitude of Christians as to Peace and War" by signing himself to the article in the *Friends' Intelligencer* as "Jesse H. Holmes, Ph.D., Swarthmore College." Since this article did indeed help to establish his reputation as a writer, he soon found himself serving as a reviewer of religious books and magazine articles for the *Intelligencer,* a service he continued to render in later years. The *Intelligencer* and other religious periodicals apparently had worked out a system of exchanging their publications for their mutual benefit; as a result Jesse's desk was usually piled high with copies of such publications as *The Christian Century* and *Unity*. In October, 1920 he reviewed their general nature and specific traits under the title of "Current Religious Magazines." In November he started a long series of topical reviews with the general title of "Exchanges" (variations of this title: "Our Exchanges," "Some Exchanges"), each review giving him an opportunity to express his own unconventional outlook as a social gospelite, socialist, and idealistic pragmatist. In this series he reacted to other writers' views on such topics as prohibition, peace, imperialism, and world politics, and the churches' lack of appeal to the common workingman. In one of these "Exchanges" he blasted the evangelists who were predicting the second coming of Christ because this sort of thing led to a giving up of responsibility for the affairs of the world, and "devoting oneself wholly to 'otherworldliness,' which, as George Eliot says, is 'worse than thisworldliness.'. . .'"

Jesse's book reviews fell into two main categories: those dealing with books of an indisputably religious character, such as Dr. George A. Barton's *The Heart of the Christian Message*; and those treating the application (or lack of application) of the Christian ethic to world affairs. Since imperialism had manifestly been conducted very largely in an antiChristian manner, its wars of conquest being eased only slightly by attending missionaries, Jesse found particular pleasure in reviewing any book on this subject. And when Haridas T. Muzumdar published his *Gandhi Versus the Empire* in 1933, Jesse found that writing a review of this book was even more to his liking — largely because Gandhi had the courage to practice those principles of democracy and Christianity at the core of Jesse's life. According to Jesse's review, *Gandhi Versus the Empire* showed how England, that pioneer in developing democracy, probably would be compelled to grant freedom to India by the moral force emanating from one man, the Mahatma or Great Soul. The book detailed how Gandhi, "as a law student in London, 'derived inspiration not from legal tomes [,] but from the writings of Tolstoy, Ruskin and Thoreau, from the Bhagavad-Gita and from the Sermon on the Mount.' " Gandhi's passive resistance to unjust rule was explained, as well as his championship of the "untouchables." And

Jesse took particular delight in quoting Gandhi from this book on the question of the franchise: " 'I cannot possibly bear the idea that a man who has wealth should have the vote ... but that a man who works honestly by the sweat of his brow, day in and day out, should not have the vote for the crime of being a poor man.' "

Such writing, of course, did little or nothing to lift the Holmes family to the level of affluence enjoyed by the J. Russell Smiths and others in the Holmes circle of friends. Whether it was due to an effort to keep up with the Smiths, or, more likely, simply because Jesse had to have something more to do during his retirement years, the fact remains that he became a newspaper columnist in the 1930s. The Philadelphia *Public Ledger* carried his series of short "Sermons" in 1934, while *The Liberal Press* (location unknown) was happy to feature Jesse's thoughts each week under the heading of "A 'Retired' Philosopher Says ..." for more than three years. Indeed, he kept his contributions going in this sheet until his death in 1942, his last published column appearing the day *after* he died. Another column, "More Rationing," was all set up in type as he died.

Aside from these more organized efforts at authorship, Jesse was constantly sitting down to dash off material best described as "miscellaneous writings." He wrote an occasional letter to the editor of the *Friends Intelligencer* in his efforts to correct real or fancied wrongs; he described "Bicycling in Oxfordshire" for the benefit of the home folks while on his Oxford tour of preparation for the job at Swarthmore; in 1910 he wrote of his experiences connected with the international congress of religious leaders held in Berlin in 1910; and, from time to time, he described his "little journeys" as he traveled about the country to visit Friends' meetings. In 1912 he paid tribute to his departed friend Joseph Walton in a moving article; twenty-four years later he wrote what amounted to an advertisement for Longwood Yearly Meeting, a group of Joseph Walton would have enjoyed under Jesse's leadership.

And, as we have seen through examples of Jesse's doggerel rhymes, and through his *Neshaminy*, he had a feeling for poetry. In one of his resource books he had copied two poems exactly as given here:

(Patsy)

Out of the shadows

into the night

floated a maiden
vested in white.

(Ken)
Ah, nightingale in yonder tree
What message has your melody
For hapless lonely souls like me?

While these were obviously borrowed for Jesse's personal pleasure, a summer-vacation trip sometime in the late 'thirties inspired authentic Holmesian poetry in free-verse style. Two drafts of Jesse's efforts on this occasion are extant; we see the more polished second draft under the title of "Some Reflections during a Bus Ride:

Wouldn't you hate to be like the woman from Ohio —
Whom I met on a bus, going west
Through the wild, weird spaces of Wyoming —
The cliffs, all colored in most beautiful tints —
Were all about us: the little wild flowers —
Bloomed on either side,
The woman from Ohio said, with calm conviction —
'This is no place to live, give *me* Ohio!'

Wouldn't you hate to be like the woman from Minnesota —
Whom I met, on a bus, going east
Through the grand, bare country of Wyoming —
The glorious colors of the cliffs —
Cliffs of sandstone, granite, and of basalt
Were enlivened by the setting sun —
Here one could see the image of a feudal castle —
Over *there,* a Gothic cathedral with its broad facade
And flying buttresses — & sculptured figures —
All glorified by the sun's golden glow —
The magic beauty of the scene [made?] me silent —
While the bus rolled on & on —
Between wide-open spaces
Filled with soft green sage brush —
And the jewel-blossoms, — coral, blue and lavendar [*sic*]
And I heard a woman's voice exclaim
'No — there is nothing beautiful in all of this —
    for my part — give me Minnesota!'

Then the bus rolled on and on,
Thro' Nebraska's flat fields of waving yellow grain —
And straight tall stalks of corn —

The colors blinking with Dame Nature's wondrous art —
And on, thro' Iowa's
Rolling prairies — a scene of restful beauty
So lush and green — hardly another color,
To be seen — save various shades of Nature's favorite — green —
The green trees in groups, the green of grass —
And fields of wheat, and rye and oats —
A granary of our nation, It gave one
A feeling of security — grain growing —
To be used for food,
Beautiful it was — so quiet and serene —
But the woman from Arkansas —
Reared in the shadow of the Ozarks —
Used to the little mountains sending their
Long shadows over the valleys — and
With homesteads nestled cosily about —
Said, 'What an uninteresting state —
How I would hate to live here!
Give me Arkansas!'

Would you care to be like the women from Pennsylvania — [Rebe?]
Who hugged her feelings to herself and thought —
'I have seen the highest mountains in the world —
When rosy dawn turned snow capped summits
To a thousand opal tints —
I have seen the glorious sights o'er all the world —
And I thank thee, oh Lord, that I can see
Beauty and majesty wherever they may be.'
Then hung her head in shame,
As she realized how smug she was
To be so pleased that beauty in all
It's varied forms, could call to her —
And meet a glad response within her soul.
And she murmured, as the bus rolled on and on —
'The Unpardonable Sin.'

Basically, of course, neither Rebe nor Jesse felt smug or shameful about the beauty they had seen in their travels. Instead, there was simply a lifelong exultation in the wonders of nature, the sounds of music, and the beauties made visible through the graphic arts. Certainly, as Jesse settled down to do his most serious writing in the latter years of his retirement, he did not feel smug or shameful when he wrote a two-page disquisition on beauty. He wrote, among other things, that one who neglects the cultivation of the sense of the beautiful misses out on a very important element of the good life. "Let us have all we can of it," he said, "without interfering with goods better understood." But let him speak at greater length:

Man has tended to be suspicious of beauty. He has had a kind of blind and pessimistic incredulity that this apparently meaningless delight can really be enjoyed without danger; and indeed, it has its dangers. Religions have condemned it, 'practical' people have warned the world against it; but man has sought it nevertheless. No doubt it is partly this attitude which has pushed the artist and the beauty-lover into the doubtful ranks, as suspicious characters, and has even driven them into revolt against social usages. It is high time for us to accept and welcome and cherish this 'gift of God.'

And Jesse had other words of wisdom on this same subject. Beauty, he said, was like truth in that it has had many standards and tests across human history. It was best appreciated in small doses, he thought. "Landscapes, seascapes and skyscapes must be looked at in successive glances rather than continuously. The great symphonies are not very long. . . ."

Nor is his Philosophy Manuscript, which he hoped to make his *magnum opus,* a very long work. Work was begun on it about 1938, when George W. Stewart, who had studied philosophy with Jesse at Swarthmore, and who was then director of Whittlesey House, a division of McGraw-Hill, asked him to write a book giving his ideas on science, religion and philosophy for popular consumption. As Jesse wrote on the first two pages, he planned to suggest "a system of life based on the experienced fundamentals of life itself. . . ." In January, 1939, he sent Stewart thirty-seven pages of typescript, adding in a letter that "This is subject to change [,] addition or subtraction." Jesse's letter also included a tentative outline of the work:

Preface
Ourselves & Our Values
We Humans
Races
Our Equipment
Language
The Truth
    Mathematics
    Logic

Science
Natural Law
Determinism
Social Science
Education
Religion
What Next?

Although Stewart "admired Jesse tremendously" — claiming that "He had the emotional discipline of Friends, the objective discipline of good science, and the ready warmth of humanism " — he was disappointed in the quality of the thirty-seven pages of typescript. While these pages contained much of Jesse's "characteristic thinking," the work as a whole "hadn't quite jelled," being "too academically categorical. . . ." Stewart asked Jesse to recast it.

Jesse worked on it some more, changed the outline slightly, and expanded it to eighty-nine pages of typescript. Completed in August, 1941, Jesse sent the whole package (still without a title beyond Philosophy Manuscript) not to Stewart, but to his Quaker friend Erwin L. Malone, of New York City, for critical review.

Malone read Jesse a little lecture in the covering letter he sent to him with his long and careful review: "Thee has given me a task of sorts to review thy manuscript. I do not know its title; have not read its . . . preface if it is to have one; and am not all sure I know for what audience it is intended." And, Malone went on, he realized that as an engineer he had had far too little time or opportunity to delve adequately into the various social, economic, and political problems which had long interested him and Jesse. The implication was there that perhaps he was not quite qualified to review Jesse's work; he could bring to it mainly "the mind of an engineer who takes as little as possible for granted. . . ."

While Malone decided to jot down his very perceptive thoughts as he read the manuscript page by page, he also formed an opinion as to the nature of the work as a whole. He could see that "a tremendous amount of both effective living and deep thought" had gone into it; he perceived that it was a work of " 'Conclusions' " — the summing up of Jesse's lifetime principles, a project George Stewart also had in mind. After reading it, Malone believed that Jesse had meant it to be read by "mature, intelligent, well-educated persons," *not* quite the audience Stewart had in mind when he asked

Jesse to write a popularized version of his philosophy. As a result Malone feared that few publishers would be found who would print this volume at their own expense because it would have a rather limited appeal and limited sale. (He was right, of course — the Philosophy Manuscript was never printed.)

Malone took some of the sting out of his adverse report by noting that the section on "Religion" was "marvelously well written," even if it was addressed to people of "high intelligence." "Sometimes," he wrote to Jesse, "I wish that thee would gather together a score of short, meaty, mature articles, each separate and complete on a single subject, which could become the 'Quaker Bible,' a 'Quaker Concern for Life.' " He thought that "No one in the world is as well qualified to tackle this, as thee. . . ." He admitted that this would be "an awesome task . . . but I have no reason to think a volume of inspired essays from the hand of Jesse Holmes should not find its place beside or ahead of 'Emerson's Essays,' or Essays written by any other person who ever lived."

Perhaps Malone would not have chosen to include in this Quaker Bible one of the last articles Jesse wrote because parts of it were too savagely critical of organized religion. Entitled "Our 'Christianity'?", this eight-page typewritten essay, written about 1940 with all his old verve and attention-getting phraseology, was not published. But, after an opening paragraph in which he severely castigated Christian doctrine and Christian churches, Jesse indicated that he had publication in mind:

> These [castigations] are not pleasant things to say, and I have resisted for years the feeling that they must be strongly and publicly said. I regret that they will hurt or anger many for whom I have respect and affection. I ask them to believe that . . . I have tried to set down the truth as I see it; and that they answer not by epithet but in sincere effort to find and clarify the truth. If they believe the truth to be attained only by authoritative revelation I hope they will say so, and tell why they accept the authority and who is to interpret it.

Although he was then near the end of his life he was still hurling the old challenge to find the truth; he was still aiming to free people to think.

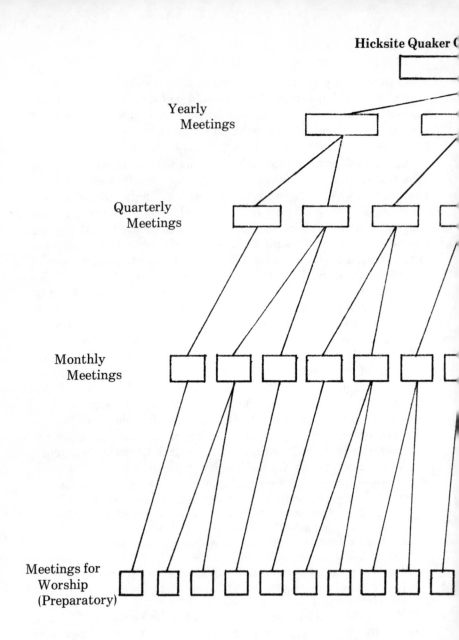

Hicksite Quaker (

Yearly
Meetings

Quarterly
Meetings

Monthly
Meetings

Meetings for
Worship
(Preparatory)

This diagram gives only the major units
shown. Also, the total number of Yearly Mee
Similarly, some quarterly and monthly me
shown here.

neral Conference

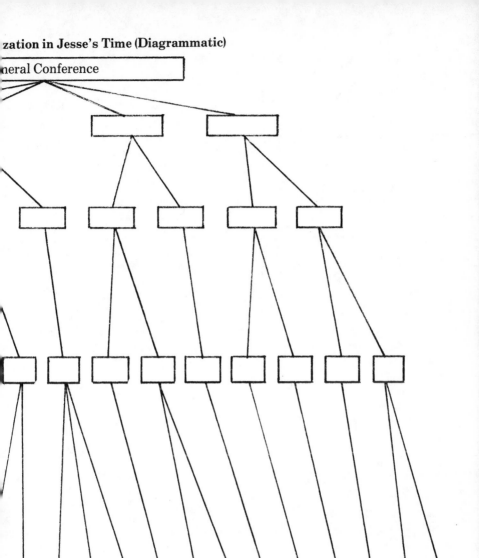

Hicksite polity. Special meetings are not
is not shown because of space limitations.
s had more subsidiary meetings than is

14. Religion As Reform

> My soul is not a palace of the past;
> A home for outworn creeds.
> The time is ripe, is over ripe for change;
> Then let it come.
>
> James Russell Lowell

While Lowell's lines were written long before Jesse penned "Our 'Christianity'?", they summed up much of that philosophy of action he had been pursuing on the religious front ever since his service at George School. Far from resisting his impulses to speak out, from the time of fundamentalist William Jennings Bryan to the heyday of existentialist Paul Tillich, he had been a constant critic of the way religious institutions, with all their apparatus for the enclosure of men's minds, had held men in thrall. He agreed most heartily with Simon Patten when, in 1911, Patten said that "So long as Mohammed, Paul, Calvin or Wesley is thought of as the true prophet who interprets religion to the less favored, tradition will control the church; servility will characterize its members." And, in 1916, from his position as a Christian, Quaker, scientist, and as a philosopher with socialistic, pragmatic leanings, Jesse told a union meeting of earnest Quakers, Episcopalians, and Dutch Reformed at Locust Valley, New York, that he disagreed most heartily with a popular conception of the function of religion. Instead of providing "a source of content and satisfaction," religion should rather be "a source of *un*content, and *un*satisfaction. . . ." A thing might be good — "uncontent would strive to make it better. . . ." Indeed, man's "main business should be in dealing with things that are *not* satisfactory. . . ."

And, since he so strongly favored interchurch unity, and since he was addressing an interdenominational meeting, he expressed pleasure at this effort to promote "unity as the basis of individualism. . . ." (Perhaps too, this Quaker, with his faith in the inner light, then expressed Paul Tillich's definition of religion — ". . . whatever concern [s] a man ultimately at the center of his existence. . . ."] Jesse's whole life, of course, was to give this definition a reformer's twist — religion was an infinite concern for the welfare of man, individually and collectively. As he told an audience in the South Broad Street Theatre in 1921, we should "be about our Father's business in this world, because it is our world; we are right here on this spinning planet. We have the task of gathering men into a great family and it is not being done. The Christian Church is responsible for the spirit of our civilization, and it is shirking its task."

Christianity's Failures.

Nineteen years later, when he wrote "Our 'Christianity'?", Jesse was still of the same mind. In spite of the liberalization and socialization of some churches due to the Social-Gospel movement, and his own valiant efforts along this line, there remained much to be condemned and much to be improved. But let him speak as only he could when he was aroused:

". . . I have been driven to the conviction that so-called Christian doctrine as now taught, and Christian churches as now organized and directed, are a handicap and a burden to our civilization. They seem to me to have lost, if they ever had it, intelligent and courageous leadership toward the great values of human life. Meaningless phrases and irrational theologies have been moulded [sic] into rigid, authoritative institutions perverting and stultifying the adventurous, creative spirit which distinguishes man from the rest of the animal kingdom. They turn his attention from the splendid possibilities of our mysterious life and toward a mythical, improbable life after death. Over all presides a despotic, unjust, and irrational deity of the medieval king type, who must be worshipped by flattery and blind obedience.

I call attention to the fact that most of the selfish love of wealth and luxury, most of the political falsehood and corruption, most of the brutal and destructive wars, most of the race and class hatreds of the world center about the parts of the world where organized Christianity is the strongest and has had the longest time in which to exert its influence. Moreover it has seldom made any considerable effort to oppose these vils, and has often supported them. Neither wealth nor political corruption nor war have or have had anything to fear from the Christian church.

While Jesse had earlier (1909-1912) written a series of eleven articles explaining Christian doctrines — e.g., the Lutheran, the Calvinist, and the Nicene and Apostles' creeds — now he felt that a restatement of orthodox Christian doctrine "in unemotional terms" was needed to try to arrive at "its actual meaning." He was willing "to try the dangers of making such a statement," and welcomed corrections:

> God is an infinite, omnipotent, omniscient, omnipresent being, wholly benevolent toward mankind [in the New Testament version], whom he has created in his own image. He consists of three 'persons' but is of one 'substance'; neither person nor substance is defined or definable. Neither of these terms, nor any hint of this doctrine [,] appears in either Old or New Testament. The [terms] turn up first in the controversies and heresies of the 2nd and 3rd centuries, and the final statement was established after bitter conflict at the Council of Nicea in 321 A.D. [by majority vote, one might add!]. The Greek words used by the Council were 'ousia' and 'hypostasis,' which were later loosely rendered into Latin as 'substantia' and 'persona,' and still later into English as 'substance' and 'person.' The original words overlap in meaning and a reversal of the translations would not have made much difference.
>
> The first 'person' of the Trinity is 'the Father Almighty, Creator of Heaven and Earth' by the creed . . . . Man was the climax of this creation, made in the Divine image by an omnicient [sic] and omnipotent being, knowing the future and able to decide it. Yet Satan, who is one of his sons, spoils his plans, and man sins by violating God's arbitrary orders. Although He is wholly benevolent toward man [,] the omnipotent being has made him so badly that he fails at the test, becomes 'deceitful and desperately wicked' [,] and passes that condition on to all his descendants. God would like to save all men, but cannot manage it; he arranges [,] however, an unjust and illogical scheme by which he can save a few, — not because they deserve it [,] but because he chooses so to do. I should hardly say 'arranges' because it was all planned out from all eternity: sin, punishment, and salvation were all exactly what he had planned, and Satan was not his enemy but his servant and ally. The scheme for the salvation of a few is an intricate mixture of rituals from various theologies, and various medieval judicial procedures, centering on the incarnation and sacrificial death of the second person of the Trinity.

And now Jesse, that Iowa farm boy and Johns Hopkins scientist, well-versed in the Oriental doctrines of the conflict between Good and Evil, and in the doctrines of a God-appointed earthly representative of the Good, turned his attention to Jesus, to whom the world owed Christian principles as a reformer in *His* time:

> The second person of the Trinity is Jesus, the son of a Jewish married woman, asserted without any evidence to have been a virgin. The creeds say that his father was the first person of the Trinity; Matthew and Luke say 'she was found with child of the Holy Ghost,' — the Third person of the Trinity; and [they] later trace his descent from David through Joseph. He was baptized by John the Baptist (or only announced by him according to the Gospel of John), and lived for a short time the life of a prophet and evangelist, various miracles accompanying his career. He was arrested and put to death by the Romans as a dangerous claimant [to] the Jewish throne. The Jewish priests and their wealthy backers had demanded his death, but the common people had accepted him as a leader and perhaps as the Messiah. His execution was a great sin although it was absolutely necessary for saving even a small group of human beings. Without the actual shedding of blood God could not, — because he would not, — save any. He remains as a remote being, unreasonable, terrible and threatening, though a loving father, while Christ sits at his right hand with no special function until the judgment day.

There is abundant evidence that Jesse believed in an earth-man Jesus — a very human and nondivine Jesus — as a great prophet and teacher, whose moral principles were too seldom obeyed or practiced by capitalistic followers of Mammon. And Jesse, like other Quakers, Unitarians, and vagrant members of more prestigious sects, cultivated the God-within, the inner light, through reading whatever promised to resolve a spiritual dilemma, not only the Bible. Then, in Quaker meeting or out, there would be meditation, resulting perhaps in the sharing of a thought or feeling through speeches and discussion. There seems to be no question but that the inner light so cultivated was culturally induced, being the reasonable product of all their upbringing as Christians, Americans, and members of a free-enterprise society. But note how different was the nebulous and illogical Holy Spirit as Jesse saw it in the generality of Christendom:

> The third person of the Trinity, — the Holy Spirit or Holy Ghost, — is abroad in the world, being that element of the Divine

being which deals with man in this world period. He takes little part in the large affairs of man, — war, pestilence, famine, poverty, — but is ready to comfort (not relieve) those who call on him. The preachers of Christianity never succeed in maintaining or understanding their own theology; their petitions are seldom addressed to the Holy Spirit but rather to the Father or to Christ, who are far more vivid and interesting.

Such petitions or prayers were of course mainly offered in Sunday-church services. But, while First-day meetings were convenient ways for Quakers to assemble, to them every day was equally holy, and every worthy deed a sacrement. If prayers were offered by Jesse in such meetings they were not supplications for God's favor but rather a means to air ways of reforming the world and wishes for the accomplishment of such reforms. But he believed that prayer had personal therapeutic value; it could result in people being their own best physicians. If a drug addict, for example, did not know the meaning of his symptoms he should consult his physician; if he did know the meaning but was powerless to break the habit on his own "he should consult his friend, his priest or preacher, and he should resort to prayer. . . ." This prayer would involve "a resolute attempt to look at his weaknesses without pretense and to follow the lines of intelligence and human dignity. . . ." Long experience, Jesse thought, had shown that "honest prayer" brought out extra powers in people; this self-examination, this introspection, resulted in a sort of self-hypnosis to do right. " 'Greater is he that ruleth his own spirit than he that taketh a city.' "

Thus spake the good Quaker. What Jesse thought of prayer as generally practiced in other churches was put down most effectively in his manuscript on philosophy, that effort which George Stewart hoped to give the world as a popularized version of Jesse's ideas a la Will Durant's *Story of Philosophy:*

> Prayer in Christian worship is a curious mixture of genuine communion [with God? with other people?], of mere quotation and formula, of flattery and servility, and of begging for favors. Only the first has any value, though it usually holds a minor place. Most absurd of all is the common practice of begging an omnipotent and loving deity to change the order of events to suit the needs of this or that group of worshippers. We have now the frequent spectacle of men and women devoting a 'day of prayer' to petitions that the war may be stopped, that we may have victory,

that drouths may be ended, that crops may be abundant. All these imply that the deity does not know what is going on and may be induced to change it if he is sufficiently urged, which is just plain nonsense.

Prayer in most churches was of course only part of that elaborate system of incantation, ritual, ceremony, genuflection, and symbolism which Friends and other plain sects had rejected in the time of their founding. As Jesse saw it, general " 'Christian' worship" had "allied itself with splendid music, architecture, and the arts generally, all of which has led it into further alliance with wealth and luxury. . . ." The Holmeses had found in the Catholic Church, both Roman and Greek Orthodox, the best examples of this. When they stopped in Vienna in the course of their world trip in 1925-1926 Rebe visited a "gloriously beautiful" cathedral. It was probably St. Stephens; and she attended a high mass there one Sunday morning. She was "simply carried away" by the sights and sounds — the dim and rosy light from the stained-glass windows, the candles, the statuary, the magnificent altar, the incense "sweet in my nostrils," and the choir's singing along with the great organ's music. After this feast of "light & color & sensuous sound, & mystery & romance" Rebe went to a little Quaker meeting in the city of the imperial Maria Theresa. Only fifteen people were there; she found small cause to wonder why the great cathedral was thronged with people while only a handful sat in silent meeting. Even though she was a Quaker, she loved the pageantry and the beauty of the service. But, as she wrote to her son Robert, "I couldn't feel it to be a *religion* for myself — . . . and of course regard it as a *show.*"

If degrees of show in their services separated the various Christian churches, many Protestant sects were guilty of the same errors as distinguished the Catholics. They too, like the earliest Christian church, started among the poor and disadvantaged; but now they tended to ally with the rich and powerful. Now the "prosperous middle-class churches [were] usually dull and dignified, but assume [d] the same irrational and irresponsible deity. . . ." And now those missions for the poor, those spontaneous revivals characterizing Christian behavior since the Reformation, had, as usual, settled "into poor relations." These people led "dull lives," but had "the longing for power felt more or less by all of us." The result: "A very low grade of preaching [,] with loud promises of glory, and of the future misery of their enemies. . . ." — always accompanied "by music of the same quality, and aims to excite the audience to noisy demonstration and to various forms of hysteria. . . ." Those converted to the "true religion" by such holy-roller tactics were not likely to be thinking Christians testing what church leaders said was the will of God by their own developed sense of right and wrong. As Jesse wrote in one of his resource books: "Converted man will hereafter do all that God commands, unless it is absolutely immoral."

And this same God, according to these holy-rollerites who believed His will was recorded in the Scriptures, had ordained that the Sabbath Day should be kept holy as a condition of entering that life-after-death heaven, always held up as the final reward for good Christians. (Jesse, as we have seen, regarded this promised heaven as improbable.) If the Sabbath was to be a foretaste of heaven, where daily cares and duties did not exist, many members of the stricter sects found to their dismay that they didn't know what to do with a Sunday afternoon in blue-law states. But to a Quaker of Jesse's persuasion, a Sunday afternoon was a wonderful opportunity to sit around with his family, friends, and neighbors, indulging in long discussions about various topics. Some of these discussions were extensions of issues raised in the morning meeting for worship. On one such occasion, John Kendall (Jesse's nephew) recalled, his father got annoyed, saying "Jesse just questions everything; is there anything that he doesn't question?" At dinner Jesse would pound the table in mock anger, and, with a twinkle in his eye, would cry out "Down with the orthodox!"

Jesse of course knew that most of the orthodox differed from liberals mainly in being more conservative, more resistant to change; certainly they were not holy-roller fundamentalists. But both conservatives and fundamentalists, he thought, stood in varying degrees across the path leading to that heaven-on-earth which could be developed by reasonable, thinking people if they joined in basing their religion on life's experience, if they thought of religion as a human experiment. But this required an open mind — a mind receptive to new facts and ideas, a mind glorying in what Jesse called " 'The divine state of uncertainty.' " John Kendall reported how Jesse thrilled the more liberal students at Muskingum College with these ideas in the early 1920s; he also recalled how a fundamentalist preacher "almost insulted" his listeners' intelligence with a "very egregious, demeaning talk" in chapel at about the same time. When Kendall, who prided himself as being something of a heretic in a United Presbyterian school, questioned some of the speaker's allegations afterward, and told him that he was a Hicksite Quaker, the speaker cried out, "Hicksites — instruments of the devil!" (As late as 1973, when the author showed one of Jesse's essays on religion to a fundamentalist in Florida, the old gentleman read it and then threw it aside, exploding with "But he's a humanist!")

The old gentleman was right, of course. Jesse *was* a humanist, and as a humanist decried the fundamentalists' excessive reliance on the historical scriptures as authority for any thought, word, or deed. Instead of standing up to be counted in support of their own messages, they practiced what Jesse called "sleight-of-tongue" by extracting whatever they needed from the pronouncements of ancient church councils, the church fathers, or the Bible itself, to support whatever *they* wanted. Thus, in spite of the fact that modern Biblical criticism had shown that the Bible was, in its two Testaments, a heterogeneous collection of Hebrew tribal history, the efforts of an agricultural and unscientific people to account for their world, plus poetry, prophesy, and the story of Christ, with all its contradictions and puzzling interpretations, these fundamentalists worshipped the Book, the most extreme among them believing in the truth of every word and passage. They found holy justification in it for war or pacificism, slavery or freedom, polygamy or monogamy; they condemned as agnostics, or athiests, or traitors to society, any persons who dared question what *they* said was Holy Intent.

And of course Jesse also played this game of quoting the Bible in support of *his* points. He quoted Amos, Isaiah, Jesus, Paul, and Jeremiah to demonstrate that these men, convinced that they were right, stood up and were counted even when this led to danger from the law and the authorities in *their* time.

> 'These were men of present valor — stalwart
> old iconoclasts
> Unconvinced by ax and gibbet, that
> all virtue was the past's'

All this raised the issue as to whether the testimony of such biblical characters should be taken without question since so many people assumed that they spoke out of a divine revelation denied to ordinary mortals. Indeed, the fundamentalists asserted that the whole Bible was the Word of God, and should therefore be the final authority. But, as Jesse reminded his fellow Quakers in 1912, one of George Fox's "earliest public challenges was that . . . he denied that the Bible should be called the Word of God. . . ." to the exclusion of other possible sources of the truth. The spirit of God, the inner light (however culturally induced), was indeed the driving force of those who wrote it, but this same spirit was, as Jesse saw it, "also back of every earnest and sincere presentation. . . ." In 1921 he told his audience in Philadelphia's South Broad Street Theatre that this spirit of God — "this power of righteousness in the life of humanity" — was experienced by everyone. God, he said, "is in the heart of a Wilson or Harding as in the heart of Joseph or Isaiah . . . . A Bible could be written about the United States or England, or France, if men wrote in the spirit of Moses . . . of Matthew. Religion has no exclusive subject matter; it is the spirit that quickeneth." In his classes at Swarthmore he was saying much the same sort of thing, according to his friend and colleague Brand Blanshard:

> . . . He was forever impressing upon his students that the Bible was the expression of the real loves and hates and aspirations of those who wrote it; that to be as good as those old writers we must be different and better [than we are now?]; that we must write our own Bible in all that we are, in the achievement of an inner light as clear and authoritative as theirs, in speech faithful to our experience, and above all in concrete errands of mercy and good will. . . .

This desire to make religion a living, evolving thing, intertwined with all other aspects of life, led Jesse to support many ideas and projects advanced by other people. He applauded Arthur C. McGiffert when he told the Friends General Conference in 1910 that revelation, far from being the importation of truth from above by a supernatural power, was ". . . the gradual awakening of the human mind to truth which it discovers for itself in the process of its development." Accepting the King James version of the Bible, with all its poetic expressions, as a record of religious experiences in the past, and well worth studying for the inspiration to be found therein, Jesse also believed that this Bible should be improved. He agreed with the *Christian Century* in 1921 that a new Bible ought to be published, chronologically arranged, and reduced to smaller dimensions by the exclusion of certain items not essential to an understanding of the Christian message. And, as noted in one of his magazine articles, Jesse would have approved the recent publication of the *Good News Bible* (1976), which turns the Scriptures into modern, everyday English. Writing about "Some Books on Humanism" in 1932, he told his more conservative readers that the main difference between the humanists and the Quakers was a "matter of vocabulary." But, more generally, modern Americans wrote and spoke from different frames of reference than those used by writers of Holy Writ or by its ancient interpreters. ". . . we are thinking different thoughts and following different paths from those who used our words before us. Certainly religion needs . . . rephrasing, and those who continue to use the wording of medieval philosophies and theologies, must do so in constant peril of being misunderstood." While a change in the wording of the King James version would cause it to lose much of its poetry, its message would be better understood; the Bible would become more useful. (And Jesse undoubtedly would have approved a recent book, *Decision Making and the Bible* (1975). In this work H. Edward Everding, Jr. and Dana W. Wilbanks use psychological and sociological techniques to show how the Bible's moral principles and historical incidents can be used to resolve some of the dilemmas and problems in the daily life of modern man. In short, the Bible is made functional.)

As we have seen, this emphasis on religious functionalism, on usefulness as tested by experience, was a major arrow in Jesse's quiver of idealistic pragmatism. It flew throughout that "Message of Quakerism" which so disturbed the conservatives in the Philadelphia of 1921. And in this speech he mentioned, either implicitly or explicitly, some major concerns of the truly religious being which had been neglected, shunned, or largely bypassed by the Christian church. The first of these was an implicit reference to the work of the Social Gospel — that reform effort to apply Christian principles to society and its institutions as well as to individuals. As Jesse told his Philadelphia audience then, "Read through the Sermon on the Mount and see if you can find anything else there but directions for serving mankind."

The second great failure of the Christian church, as Jesse saw it in 1921, was its inability to enforce the teachings of the Prince of Peace — a failure which led opposing nations in 1914 to pray to the same God for victory; a failure which still supported a spirit of conflict among nations, races, and classes of people.

Toward Religious Unity.

The third failure of Christians was their inability to unite into one effective body against all the forces of evil. Divided into hundreds of sects, they were too much concerned with "individual moralities, and local virtue," and missed "the great ideal of a world family of brothers and sisters under a father-God. . . ." And, as Jesse well knew, this ideal of a sectless religious unity was an old one; it had been given expression by many people, notably by Henry Bernard Carpenter (1840-1887) in his *Liber Amoris:*

The time will come when this, our Holy Church
Shall melt away in ever widening walls,
And be for all mankind. And in its place
Shall rise another church, whose covenant word
Shall be the act of love. Not *Credo* then
But *Amo* shall be the watchword through its gate.

Since the Society of Friends was not a church in the usual sense, not having a formal creed or posturing as "the representative or mouthpiece of God," Jesse found it very easy to play a leading role in the movement for religious unification. He was an early member of the National Federation of Religious Liberals, which had been organized at Philadelphia in 1908 by liberal Quakers, Jews, Catholics, Methodists, Presbyterians and many other groups. Its purpose was "To promote the religious life by united testimony for sincerity, freedom, and progress in religion, by social service, and a fellowship of the spirit beyond the lines of sect and creed." By 1919 this Federation had held eight congresses in Philadelphia, New York, Rochester, New York, Oakland, California, Pittsburgh, Pennsylvania, and in Boston. In 1915 Jesse became the group's president (serving until 1927), and as president saw to it that the ninth congress took place in 1919 in the Longwood Meeting House near Kennett Square, so long a mecca for those kindred spirits called the Progressive Friends. In fact, the Progressive Friends formed the greater part of the audience.

The two-day program heard at Longwood by invitation of these Progressive Friends revealed not only how the Federation hoped to achieve its goals, but also showed something about the character of its membership. Each of the morning and afternoon sessions was

315

preceded by a brief devotional service, followed by addresses dealing with some aspects of a central topic. Thus the general topic for the Saturday-morning session, May 31, was "The Supreme Loyalties." Five speakers addressed themselves to this question, Paul M. Pearson of Swarthmore leading off on loyalty "To One's Own Conscience." He was followed by Leslie Pinckney Hill, principal of the Cheyney School for [Negro] Teachers, who spoke on loyalty "To the Ideal." Perhaps Dr. Hill brought into his speech a thought appearing on the printed program: "If you cannot realize your ideal, then idealize your real" — a thought approved rather more by Booker T. Washington than by W.E.B. DuBois. This mediating posture was indeed his as he stoood before several hundred sympathetic listeners, although he still made a stirring appeal for fairness, justice, democracy and brotherhood in behalf of Americans Negroes and the dark-skinned people of the earth. "Despite 'Jim Crow' cars and lynchings," he said, "we will not be discouraged; hated, we will not hate; lynched, we will not become lynchers; persecuted, we will not become anarchists. . . ." And then, with a sly but friendly dig at Jesse Holmes, who was so active in promoting American Friends' Service Committee work in the devastated areas of Europe, he said, "Not in Belgium, Serbia or Armenia is there a field so rich for charity and service as among the ten million dark ones at home." The Reverend Samuel A. Eliot, president of the American Unitarian Association, responded to Dr. Hill's speech by saying that, bad as conditions were, the doors of opportunity for Negroes were "not altogether closed." He pointed out that, while he was the descendant of eight generations of Puritans, and Dr. Hill's ancestors were probably slaves, both of them were graduates of Harvard University. " 'He himself is the chief bright spot in the situation.' "

Anna Garlin Spencer, a vice-chairlady of the American Section of the International Committee of Women for Permanent Peace, then spoke on loyalty "To Family and Home." Her presentation was bolstered in the printed program by quotations from David Starr Jordan, Mazzini, and especially one from Lucretia Mott — "In the marriage union the independence of the husband and wife will be equal, their dependence mutual, and their obligations reciprocal." Loyalty "To the Nation" was the title of the next speech, delivered by the Reverend William Laurence Sullivan, minister, All Souls Church, New York City. His address was noted on the program sheet by a long quotation from James Russell Lowell, which, after giving excellent reasons for national patriotism, ended with these lines: "We will not dare to doubt thee, But ask whatever else, and we will dare!" (If Jesse Holmes had anything to do with developing the program at Longwood that day, as we suspect he did, he slipped a bit on the Lowell quotation: Jesse's whole life as a thinking, moralistic democrat was imbued with the idea that when the nation, through its leaders, strays from the path of right and justice, it is the duty of a citizen to doubt and speak out in the spirit of "His Majesty's Loyal Opposition." Or, we may wonder, was the Lowell quotation inserted to forestall any action by Attorney General A. Mitchell Palmer in his ongoing drive against unAmerican communists? If so, Jesse was untrue to his own ideals.) The fifth and last speaker for this session was Jesse, who considered what loyalty we owe "To the Brotherhood of Man." His speech was also accompanied by long quotations on the printed program from Emerson, Fenelon, Edwin Arnold, and Goethe — the latter to the effect that "Above all nations is Humanity."

By this time it was noon, and undoubtedly this particular segment of humanity was a bit weary of oratory, and in need of sustenance for the inner man. Luncheon was served on the grounds; after lunch these religious liberals could stretch their legs by walking about the lawn or perhaps strolling through the adjacent Longwood Cemetery.

After lunch, the reassembled liberals heard considerations of the general topic, "The National Tasks that Await Us." Reverend Frederick Lynch, editor of the *Christian Work*, believed that the war-spirit which had permeated the nation during the First World War might be replaced by ideals of social service and universal brotherhood. Then, helped along by long excerpts from Walter Rauschenbusch's *Prayers of the Social Awakening* (eg., "A Prayer for Employers"), Raymond H. Bye spoke on "Social Forces of a New World," while Emerson P. Harris explained "The Cooperative Movement." Reverend J. Clarence Lee, of the Church of the Restortion, Philadelphia, held up a vision of the religious rebirth of America, while Morris Jastrow, Jr., of the Ethical Culture Society, held forth on the League of Nations as a way for countries to live up to their international obligations.

Since the last two sessions were held on Sunday, June 1, it seemed appropriate that they be devoted more specifically to questions of what was generally thought of as religion. The Reverend Franklin C. Southworth, president of the Meadville (Pa.) Theological School, told the assembly of the nature and possibilities of interdenominational fellowship. This fellowship, he thought, must grow out of cooperation and mutual tolerance, "because it appears necessary for a variety of minds: many branches, but one stem; one body, with many members, whether Jew, Catholic, Protestant, Barbarian, Lythian, bond or free." The Reverend Southworth was followed by Charles W. Wendte, D.D., the secretary-treasurer of the Federation, with a talk on the possibility of forming a universal religion. There *was* a possibility — if people of good will would not let their petty sectarian differences stand in the way. He called for a "larger and true Catholicity" — "the universal religion of humanity." Rabbi Henry Berkowitz, Temple Rodeph Shalom, Philadelphia, was in substantial accord with him, although Berkowitz envisioned a less ambitious universality to be called the "World League of Religions."

Near the close of the meeting the Reverend Frederick A. Bisbee, of Boston, Massachusetts, mentioned a general purpose of the Federation's work by saying that the members present had been educating each other. "Education," he said, "must bring about union. . . ." On the other hand, it was "far from the [objective] of the Federation of Liberals to make Friends into Jews, Unitarians into Universalists, or Catholics into Baptists, but to cheer, strengthen and help each other in the common purpose." These remarks were supplemented by Jesse Holmes, who closed the final session "with force and spirit."

If this drive for world unity still had a long way to go, considering historically based passions and the power of institutional inertia throughout the world's religions, a more immediately feasible plan lay in pushing Social-Gospel projects. Indeed, two years before its Longwood meeting, the Federation's congress at Boston had considered what was termed a "Testimony Concerning Social Ideals." (The nation's economic and social conservatives must have shaken their heads in grave disapproval when they saw its terms; Samuel Gompers, Robert LaFollette, Sr., and Norman Thomas, on the other side, must have expressed their glee.) The records available to the author do not reveal whether the Boston congress approved and issued this "Testimony," although we suspect that it won approval since all but one of its affirmations had recently been issued in a statement by the Social Service Commission of the Federal Council of the Churches of Christ in America. These affirmations deserve a complete listing:

1. Equal rights and justice for all men in all walks of life.
2. Protection of the family by the single standard of purity, uniform divorce laws, proper regulation of marriage, proper housing.
3. The fullest possible development of every child, especially by the provision of education and recreation.
4. Abolition of child labor.
5. Such regulation of the conditions of toil for women as shall safeguard the physical and moral health of the community.
6. Abatement and prevention of poverty.
7. Protection of the individual and society from the social, economic, and moral waste of the liquor traffic.
9. Conservation of health.
9. Protection of the worker from dangerous machinery, occupational diseases, injuries and mortality.
10. Equal rights and opportunities for women as well as men in the social, economic, political, and religious world.
11. Suitable provision for the old age of the workers and for those incapacitated by injury.
12. The principle of conciliation and arbitration in industrial disputes.
13. Release from employment one day in seven.
14. Gradual and reasonable reduction of hours of labor to the lowest practicable point, and for that degree of leisure for all which is a condition of the highest human life.
15. A living wage as a minimum in every industry and the highest wage that each industry can afford.
16. The most equitable division of the product of industry that can ultimately be devised.

An explanatory note at the foot of this list, which was printed on a leaflet, indicated that "The whole statement is not intended as a social creed obligatory on the members of the National Federation, but as a presentation of the social ideals of a majority of its members, binding in part or in its entirety only those who are in accord with it."

If Jesse's presidency of the National Federation of Religious Liberals was a peak of his efforts along the line of religious unity and cooperation, it was but one aspect of his total effort. Indeed, this peak could more properly be regarded as a high plateau for the years 1915-1927, with gradually ascending and descending slopes on each side of this period. His position as a birthright Hicksite Quaker had put him on the side of the religious liberals early on; his constant speech-making and many articles since 1900 had earned him a reputation as " 'the acknowledged prophet of the Hicksite Friends.' " As a writer for *Human Life* (Boston) put it, "Fearless in the exposition of truth as he sees it, he has won through his original and striking views the attention not only of his own denomination, but of the religious world at large." Small wonder that the Hicksites chose him to represent them at the International Congress of Religious Liberals to be held in Berlin in August, 1910. Susanna Gaskill, another indefatigable worker, was to accompany him.

Although the prospectus for the American delegates, as arranged by Thomas Cook and Son, seemed to call for still another tourist junket through England, Holland, and the usual places of interest in Germany, Jesse felt his responsibilities to the folks back home. He prepared an article describing his experiences at the Congress, noting that of three important sectional meetings, the attendance at the meeting on socialism was measured in four figures, the peace meeting in three, and the temperance meeting in two. He was happy to report that the peace resolutions he proposed were adopted — perhaps mainly because he was so mercifully brief in presenting them as opposed to other long-winded speakers. He complained that other meetings in the Congress "tended toward theoretical rather than practical religion" — something almost inevitable in the country which had produced Martin Luther and Paul Tillich. And, even here, in a congress of liberals, Jesse saw evidences of "the persistence of a medieval theology, with a pagan idea of God, and of a superstitious attitude toward the Scriptures as a book of magic. . . ." These continued "to block the path of progress in religion and to cause un-Christian dissension and difference. To remove entirely these relics of . . . ignorance is one of the important tasks of our generation. . . ."

He was still pursuing religious unity in the later years of his ministry as a Quaker. In 1926, studying various religions during his sabbatical-leave trip around the world, he noted that God by whatever name — Jehovah, Allah, Great Spirit — was seen as a common source of good; the inner light also glowed to dispel ignorance among members of other faiths. Returning to Swarthmore, he soon

320

found himself again speaking on religious unity: to the World Unity Conference at the Baptist Temple in Philadelphia in September 1926; to a meeting of the Fellowship of Faiths at St. Stephen's Church in the same city in 1928; and to one of the Ethical Culture Society's series of meetings (1929) in the Academy of Music, Philadelphia. His Ethical Culture topic was "What Is Human Life For?" On this occasion he gave the viewpoint of Christianity; other speakers treated the topic from the standpoints of Judaism, Hinduism, and Ethical Culture. And in the late summer of 1933, Jesse and Rebe made a two-weeks trip to Kearney, Nebraska, to visit Jesse's sister, Mrs. J.N. Dryden. (A snapshot of Jesse taken alongside his sister's house shows that he still was portly, still had the rugged look of a mountain climber which people had remarked on during his early years at Swarthmore.) On the way back from Kearney the Holmeses stopped in Chicago, visited the World's Fair, and attended several meetings of the American Philosophical Society's convention. Jesse also somehow found the time to address a Friend's forum, going from that meeting to a session of the Fellowship of Faiths which had been holding a world-religious conference all summer. He shared a program with a Methodist bishop from Denver and a Mohammedan from India.

Reconciling Religion and Science.

If Jesse saw the need for greater unity among the world's religions, which lay side by side in a sort of horizontal series of beliefs across the globe, he also saw other dangers to human unity in their membership. Each great religion, with Christianity as perhaps its best and most familiar example, could be thought of as a vertical structure, divided within itself. At the top of the church were the educated, thinking people, who (if they were not agnostics or athiests), as priests or powerful laity regarded religion as a philosophy — as a way of finding their relationships to the World Spirit, to nature, to each other, and to lower members of the social order. Members of this upper-echelon group had defined the Apostles' Creed and the Nicene Creed, had insisted that only *their* Bible be taken as the unerring Word of God, had promulgated the virgin-birth story, and had given supernatural sanction to these and other myths, legends, and miracles as essentials of belief. They had the authority; they held the answer books to The Truth for some fifteen hundred years. Then, when a rising middle class of merchants, guildsmen, and scholars began to use their increasing education and power to challenge the Church, the Church was split, with some of the resulting segments then asserting *their* right to burn heretics to protect the purity of *their* beliefs. As time went on this middle class, now more and more directing economic and political affairs, paid lip service in church to many of the old religious doctrines, superstitions, and legends because this class could see their uses as methods of social control. The lowest social classes — the peasants and the workers in the mines and factories — were more easily controlled in their behavior if they could be led to believe that the moral code was God-given, that Heaven would be their reward if the code was obeyed, and Hell the punishment if it was violated. Events on earth were God-willed, and God would some day set all things right. Education, the means to challenge these old conceptions, was largely denied to them by design or circumstances; religion did indeed become, as Marx said, "the opiate of the people." And then, since these lowest elements had only their religious beliefs to hang on to in an increasingly educated world — a world of increasing scientific inquiry — they defended their indefensible positions with vehemence and fury, waving their Bibles against all critics of their beliefs. They were, in short, the fundamentalists, organized into many sects across America in the time of Jesse Holmes. Their leaders were such evangelists as "Billy" Sunday, Aimee Semple McPherson, and William Jennings Bryan. And, aside from their circus-tent meetings at crossroad towns, the audiences they exhorted at such places as Chautauqua, New York, or Asbury Park, New Jersey, were often members of the affluent middle class, showing that there was considerable overlap with the more elemental fundamentalists, and that they too preferred to have someone else do their thinking for them — that they too preferred emotionalism over reason, faith over experienced fact, the authority of medieval mysticism over the freedom to search for truth in the modern world. In brief, they helped to bring about what the parlance of the day termed "the conflict between religion and science" — another great failure of the church.

To Jesse Holmes, trained in both religion and science, there was no necessary conflict between the two. Such conflict as did exist lay mainly in the fact that each had tried to invade the province of the other. The church "has no business whatever in the determining of truth or falsehood," said Jesse. "It is not equipped for such determination, and has only made trouble when it has intruded upon it." If religion were defined as "enthusiasm for the good," and Christ's principles of universal friendliness followed, people could develop their own experiences because when they did right they would feel a sense of well-being; when they did wrong they would feel bad. These results could be tested in the pragmatic way by every person in his daily life. The true function of religion was to explore the world of ideals — to hold up a vision of the world that *ought* to be. As such, Christianity offered a choice in the way of life, one not to be determined by authoritative, mystical doctrines set down in the days of the Emperor Constantine, or by St. Thomas Aquinas.

So, if the old theology had to go, essential religion should not go with it. Jesse hoped to get people to bring into their own religious lives — indeed, with his brand of inquiring religion penetrating *all* phases of their lives — that same fidelity to experience, that strong sense of reality, and that honesty of utterance that he had found in science at its best. Religion would develop the goals, science would show the ways to achieve them, and private and governmental institutions would provide the means.

Jesse found two other aspects of science bearing on the issue: the famed objective attitude of scientists, and the expanded meaning given to the word "science" itself. The term "objective attitude" meant more than "honesty of utterance"; it meant also a mind-set which would not be influenced by anything but facts in developing conclusions, judgments, or opinions. As people formed opinions, "each [person] should bring the best he [had], expressed as clearly as might be, to the everlasting effort of man by discussion to find the way, the truth, and the light. . . ." No one should yield lightly "to the gusts of popular opinion"; no one should soft-pedal his convictions out of consideration for the feelings of others. Soft-pedalling would merely withhold something, perhaps, which would have helped clarify the discussion. These "others" had "no right to have 'feelings' except those of interest and inquiry. . . ."

If scientists had developed the right approach to forming and expressing opinions, there was some danger that, due to their successes in the modern world, science was itself becoming almost a new religion, with a mysticism of its own in the popular mind. The word "science" tended to mean more than knowledge gained and verified by repeated observations and correct thinking; it had, with its new priesthood in white laboratory coats, tended to expand the meaning of science "to cover," as Jesse thought, "our deeply founded intentions of human values, our ideals and the enthusiasm which drives us to spend ourselves to make those ideals and values real. . . ." But, said this Ph.D. in chemistry, science had "narrower limits" than inquiring religion; it could not "pronounce upon values." It could, however, show a method of thinking and serve as a "friendly critic" to clarify and modify "the excesses of religious enthusiasms." Indeed, he thought that science, rightly conceived and guarded against its own errors, should be "the foundation of religion"; no other attitude or mode of thought would "sustain a safe superstructure . . . ."

And indeed, in this essentially false conflict between true religion and true science, there were signs that the two, like capitalism and communism, were letting go of their more extreme positions and tending toward a common partnership, each recognizing the other's field and worth. Liberal religionists were throwing aside the incubus of medieval authority and were trying to clarify their own conceptions of values. Scientists, on the other hand, were modifying the deterministic, mechanistic world they had seen developing out of Newtonian physics and Watsonian behaviorism; now, after Einstein's relativity theory, their concepts of fixed and absolute standards and laws of nature were subject to new and changing interpretations. And now even their most careful measurements were suspect: Werner Heisenberg's Principle of Uncertainty, announced in 1927, shocked his compatriots when he said that it was impossible to determine at the same time the position and the velocity of an electron. The simple act of observation changed the behavior of the thing being observed.

So, having pointed out the limitations of both religion and science, and their worth in their own fields, Jesse called for a partnership between the two. Opening the philosophy lecture series in Whittier House at Swarthmore on a Sunday evening in 1934, he showed the need each had for the other, and their logical relationships. "Men must build from a foundation of science," he said; "ideals must guide their progress." And finally, "What limit can you conceive to what might be, with religion and science as partners? There is none."

Convinced of the correctness of his position, Jesse spent a lot of time and effort, along with other Quakers in the same camp, in informing and instructing his fellow citizens as to what their religious stance could be and should be in democratic America. He told the readers of the *Friends Intelligencer,* in an article called "The American Code," that "The real values of life are truth, beauty, friendship, love, experience. To make these accessible, and to develop our powers to use them, is the primary aim of governments and all other human institutions." In 1928, when Herbert C. Hoover, Alfred E. Smith, and Norman Thomas were asking the nation to accept their philosophies of life, Jesse told the readers of Philadelphia's *Public Ledger* that the presidential election "is not a mere conflict but a great national sacrement in which each brings and lays on the altar his best judgment as to that course which will most advance the 'Kingdom of God.' " Ever keeping in mind the need to enlighten conservatives as to God's way in nature, in 1930 he faced a capacity crowd in the Fifth Baptist Church, Philadelphia, to debate evolution with the Reverend Dr. W.B. Riley, executive secretary of the World Fundamentalist Association. We don't know how many people he pulled from Genesis to Darwinism; perhaps some were enlightened if he read to them that fine expression of a Quaker's position penned by S.S. Green some years earlier:

IMMANUEL

'Tis not alone in Him of Galilee
that Christ is manifest;

A portion of the Light divine must be
By every one possest;
And they are sons of God who own its sway
And follow where it leadeth day by day.

God thru His prophet Darwin speaks; and, lo!
Our cherished creeds are dead;
We learn to read the thoughts of God and know
A reign of Law, instead.
A pagan Hell no longer terrifies,
Nor vainly seek we Heaven in the skies.

Our seats of learning schools of prophets are,
Where earnest eager youth
Accept fair Science for their guiding star,
And for their watchword, — Truth!
While Hebrew legends, once their leading strings,

Are put away with other childish things.

God reigns, and in the majesty of Law
Doth everywhere abound.
Put off your shoes and bow your heads in awe
Ye stand on holy ground.
To you, as ne'er before to human race,
Emanu-el speaks daily face to face.

Jesse's supreme venture in the effort to bring religion and science together was addressed to an audience likely to be sympathetic to his aim. His famous letter "To the Scientifically Minded" was beamed to those members of the middle class who had received an education in the modern scientific vein, and who now found themselves, as members of churches still preaching the old theology, in an embarrassingly hypocritical position. In short, they were attending church services they regarded as full of ritualistic rubbish, and giving lip service to doctrines they did not believe. "To the Scientifically Minded" invited such people to join the Society of Friends so that they might lead a more honest and satisfactory religious life in the search for "a human society organized on a basis of good will and friendliness. . . . ," corrected as always by the methods and facts of science. This was the common purpose. Denying any conception of absolute right and wrong, Jesse told his readers that Quakers used the pragmatic test to determine these: "RIGHT is that which serves the common purpose, WRONG is that which hinders or thwarts it. It is the standard by which we undertake to test the organization of society, international policies, and indeed all human conduct and institutions. . . ." We don't know how many converts to Quakerism this appeal made; we do know, as indicated in Chapter 13, that it made quite a stir on the religious scene in 1928 and thereafter.

Jesse Attacked, Defended — and a Program for the Church.

It was but to be expected, given the excited social climate in the era of the "Monkey Trial" at Dayton, Tennessee, that the fundamentalists would attack Jesse for such ideas and his way of expressing them. In 1929 the Reverend Floyd W. Tomkins, rector of the Holy Trinity Church in Philadelphia, used the *Philadelphia Record* to call him an "atheist" and an "angostic," probably having heard one or two of the series of lectures Jesse gave on "Science and Religion" at a Friends' meeting house in that city. A short time later Jesse received two letters, one addressed to "Dr. Jessy H. Holmes, D.D.," and the other to "Mr. Holmes & Co.," which were both so illiterate, so sprinkled with expletives, as to make the interpretation of their exact meanings difficult. Difficult, that is, except that their abusive tone emerged very clearly from the scribbled, scrawled pages. The only comprehensible line found by the author is in the letter from Hurricane, West Virginia, which told Jesse that "... ADAM (like children of mankind)..., when he touched the Hot Stove, got results. ..." Another letter, this one written in a careful, scholarly script after Jesse's speech at Columbia University was interpreted by newspapers as a radical rendering of the Twenty-third Psalm, was much more sympathetic with Jesse's ideas. However, even this writer could not quite swallow Jesse's illustration about "The Lord is my dynamo." He would not, he wrote, "give up *'The Lord is my Shepherd, I shall not want'* for all the automobiles and aeroplanes and locomotives ... ever made, and humanity could better spare them than sheep."

Such reactions to Jesse's stand were, on the whole, few and sporadic. And Jesse's defenders far outnumbered his critics. When the Philadelphia minister accused him of being an agnostic and atheist, Harvey W. Watts, Philadelphia, called him "a very noted humanitarian" who taught at Swarthmore — a college which "is doing more for [the] character-building of youth than any other college I know of. ..." Beth Harbold, one of his seminar students, recalled "how proud he was to have the Philadelphia papers term him a 'radical' and advocate his dismissal from Swarthmore. His students would have rallied in anger against the Board of Managers if such a dismissal motion would have come before them." Although Eleanor Stabler Clarke remembered how the more conservative members of Swarthmore Meeting sometimes grew restive when Jesse "scolded" them for not doing this or that in reform work, the majority supported him. And the larger body of Hicksites, through its Yearly Meeting Advancement Committee, must have liked what he was saying because it issued in pamphlet form a number of his speeches and magazine articles, including "To the Scientifically Minded."

There is evidence that Jesse took *informed* criticism kindly. In 1921, when he was in the sixth year of his presidency of the National Federation of Religious Liberals, "brief extracts" of a speech about the Christian Church which he gave at the Boston congress, were published and excited "widespread criticism." (He suffered considerably from such partial quotations in the public press, usually given out of the context of the whole speech.) He admitted that much of this criticism was justified, particularly that part of it which labelled his speech as "not constructive." He therefore requested the privilege of suggesting a constructive program, and also requested "a thoughtful consideration of the same. . . ." He wished to have it understood that he spoke from the inside as one who believed in the Church, "and to himself and his own church as well as to the Church in general." The *Friends' Intelligencer* granted his request and published Jesse's ". . . Program for the Christian Church":

(1) The Church should plant itself squarely across the way leading to general military training, and all preparation for war, — whether in the way of increasing armies or increasing navies. It should show a real faith in the power of the Christ spirit by trusting it and taking the consequences.

(2) The Church should take a strong stand against the jingo talk of war with Mexico or Japan. It should make it plain that no Christian man can allow or take part in any such policy, and that the whole force of the Church will be turned against any administration that suggests it.

(3) The Church should take strong ground in combating the growing hostility between capital and labor. As it has more opportunity to deal with capitalists it is the more responsible that they should show a genuine spirit of unselfish brotherhood in approaching questions of wages, hours, etc.; but it should also seek out the laborer and show sympathetic understanding of his problems and difficulties. If this hostility grows to actual conflict we of the Christian Church are to blame.

(4) We should take the lead in a nation-wide campaign to give adequate support to the agencies which are fighting disease and starvation in Europe.

(5) We should take under our protection the millions of Negroes now oppressed, maltreated, and murdered in our midst. We should see that they have adequate schools, opportunity to develop their special powers, and fair play generally.

Jesse admitted that these propositions were not new; churches "here and there" were trying to do their work in all of these lines. "But," as he wrote,

. . . the Church as a whole everlastingly works inwards instead of

328

outwards, acting on the apparent assumption that a church exists for its members; whereas in fact is it not true that a church should be an organization by which its members act on the outside world? I believe that the church could revive, regain its power among the poor, which it certainly has not now, and be a really effective agent in making 'the kingdom come,' if it would take up such a program as that outlined above.

FAMILY TREE of QUAKER GROUPS
in the
UNITED STATES ★

1975

1955

Uniting Tendency

1940

1917

1865

Primitive Friends

1870's

Prog. Frds.

Orthodox

Hicksites

Progressive Friends (Pa.)

Controversy

Congregational

Wilburite

1861

1853

1848

1845

1836

Great Separation

1827

Free Quaker Schism

1781

1696

Keithian Schism

1692

1682   William Penn arrived in Pennsylvania

1656   First Quaker in America (Mass.)

1647   George Fox began preaching in England.

★ Based on "Family Tree of Quaker Groups in Pennsylvania," Pennsylvania Historical Survey, *Inventory of Church Archives Society of Friends in Pennsylvania* (Friends Historical 330 Association, Haverford, Pa., 1941), opposite p. 2.

15. Jesse and Rebe in the Society of Friends

The prescriptions Jesse gave for the Christian Church were of course those he had developed as a member of the Hicksite branch of the Society of Friends. George Fox had started the Quakers in protest against the high-church formalism and aristocratic flavor of the Church of England; given this original protest, it was the nature of Friendly worship to engage in many religious and social reforms, even at the cost of being imprisoned and persecuted. Some carried their message to America, where they in turn suffered at the hands of those who could not bear to be opposed — who dared not run the risk of having such democratic levellers undermine their pedestals of authority. After a while these persecutions stopped, Quakers took their places in American economic and social life, and those who had come to America to do good now did well. With increasing prosperity and safety, Quakers grew more conservative; sometimes their testimony for righteousness lost its revolutionary character and was spent instead on meliorative measures such as helping the poor with Christmas baskets or establishing schools for Negro children. Their various meetings, originally organized to facilitate democratic representation from lower (smaller) to higher (more powerful in decision-making) bodies of Quakers, were increasingly dominated by conservative elders. To Elias Hicks and his liberal followers, the original precepts of Quakerism were being sabotaged. By 1827 the situation was so bad that they broke away from the conservatives (Orthodox) to found their own version of the Society of Friends.

This fracture — "The Great Division" — was a constant pain in the side of Jesse, that Quaker so intent upon unity. His work, and that of other Quakers on both sides of the Great Division, finally healed much of the split in 1955; his wife Rebe lived to see the United Philadelphia Yearly Meeting.

The active, productive, period of their lives, however, was spent in the reformist atmosphere of the Hicksites in the period 1890-1942. During this period the Hicksites continued to use the organizational structure of the church which had been developed before the Great Division; the major difference between Hicksites and Orthodox lay in the more liberal, less formal spirit of the Hicksite administration. The entire structure resembled that of a pyramid. Forming the base of this pyramid were the local meetings for worship, each one gathering its members into a simple but substantially built meeting house, without pulpit or lectern, but with some high benches facing the more numerous benches below. The elders sat on these high benches, lending their dignity to the meeting, the silence of which was so often broken by those who felt that they had something worthwhile to say. When, in the judgment of the elders all those who wished to speak had had sufficient opportunity to express their thoughts, two of them would rise, shake hands, and the meeting was over.

First-day schools were usually associated with these local meetings; and many other activities — midweek meetings, special forums, and social affairs — were carried on at this level under the direction of the monthly meetings.

These monthly meetings were meetings for business. The more active members of the meetings for worship attended these sessions, elected a presiding clerk and recording clerk, and appointed many committees to plan and pursue those projects deemed to be the proper concern of Quakers. Bills for the operating expenses of the local meeting houses were reviewed and ordered to be paid; committees were appointed to examine applicants for membership and recommend courses of action on such applications; committees were appointed to have "oversight" of Friendly marriages; births and deaths were recorded. And, at the proper time, delegates to the quarterly meetings were appointed — meetings generally held in some distant place agreed upon by the constituent monthly meetings. These delegates were likely to be older members of the lower groups; it was their responsibility to carry such items as proposals for change in the *Book of Discipline* to this higher body, and to bring back to the lower levels any decision arrived at through discussion and what was deemed by the presiding clerk to be "the sense of the meeting." (Generally, there was no counting of "yeas" and "nays" for any proposal; the sense of the meeting was felt by the presiding clerk through a sort of intuitive process.) If the proposal for change, or for any other course of action, was so important, or so difficult to resolve, that the quarterly meeting did not feel competent to bind lower groups, the matter was passed upward to the last court of appeal, the yearly meeting.

The term "yearly meeting" had two meanings. It referred in a geographic sense to the large area in which the lower meetings were situated, and in which the decisions of the annual council had a binding effect. (Thus, the Philadelphia Yearly Meeting of Hicksites exercised control over many constituent groups in the counties of eastern Pennsylvania and southern New Jersey.) The term yearly meeting also referred to those large annual gatherings, lasting usually for a week in the spring or the fall, in which the more senior delegates from lower meetings gave committee reports, debated questions of policy, and resolved moot points by that same sense-of-the-meeting process. In Philadelphia they met in the Society's headquarters at Race and Cherry streets; the Indiana Yearly Meeting met at Earlham College, Richmond, Indiana; Baltimore and New York saw similar sessions in Hicksite headquarters there, while the Ohio Yearly Meeting held its sessions in Salem.

Some idea as to the operation of a yearly meeting may be gained through samplings of what happened in several different meetings of Hicksites. In May, 1917, the meeting for worship on First-day morning in Philadelphia was attended by more than three thousand people, filling the Cherry and Race street houses and requiring the use of the First-day school's lecture room to accommodate the overflow crowd. Keynote speeches were then made, with Isaac Wilson speaking to the Race Street crowd, and Jesse addressing the Cherry Street and overflow groups. He called upon the Quakers for action to heal social ills in the spirit of Christ and St. Paul. In doing this, he said, "We claim absolute freedom for ourselves and concede the same to others . . . ." There seems to be no record of how Jesse's call to action was received by his audiences; the silence was perhaps indicative of disapproval. Isaac Wilson's speech fared better — "The deep silence which closed the Race Street meeting was spoken of by many as being one of wonderful inspiration."

In the Philadelphia Yearly Meeting, May 12-16, 1919, the

committee having general oversight of education — Quaker schools, the activities of Quaker students in distant non-Quaker colleges, and with a collateral interest in the Young Friends' Association — made its report, telling of its work to stimulate and encourage activities by these groups. And then the Committee on Peace and Emergency Service, Jesse H. Holmes, chairman, gave its report of the work done in these fields since the last yearly meeting. Six general business or planning sessions had been held by this Committee; one other session had been prevented by the influenza epidemic in the autumn of 1918. A subcommittee on finance had served as a collection agency to receive the contributions for European reconstruction work from various monthly meetings; these contributions had been sent on to the treasurer of the American Friends Service Committee. While many public meetings had been held in the interests of reconstruction, for the League of Nations, and in the interests "of a social rebuilding in closer accord with the Christian ideal. . . . ," the report complained that their work in this regard had been hampered by the refusal to open the Race Street Meeting House for these purposes. And this refusal, the Committee complained, contravened an earlier directive from the Yearly Meeting that the "Study of the Social Order" be added to the work of the Peace and Emergency Service Committee. Surely, Jesse's Committee argued, this had been a wise directive; surely the time had come to try to understand the underlying causes of general social unrest, industrial conflict, wars and rumors of wars, class conflicts, etc.; surely the Subcommittee on the Social Order had been doing the work of the Master when it had, during the past year, encouraged and assisted study groups throughout the Yearly Meeting "by means of outlines, lectures, advice as to reading, methods of study and the like. . . ." The general session listened to these arguments, and, while the work of Jesse's subcommittee was in "large measure approved," there was enough conservative and moderate sentiment in the Yearly Meeting to rap its knuckles. "The Meeting did not approve of the implied criticism of the Property Committee of Race Street Meeting, and cautioned . . . against harsh judgments. . . . " The Meeting also cautioned Jesse's subcommittee against "the rash acceptance of social and political theories, and advised that they limit their work on this line to an effort to clearly understand the application of the principles of Jesus to the current life of our time; . . . ." Further, ". . . that they avoid any propaganda of a particular social panacea in the name of the Yearly Meeting. . . ."

Such criticism of the work of Jesse's Social Order Subcommittee was not new; the Quaker conservatives in both Hicksite and Orthodox branches had for some time feared him as "a dangerous thinker." One of these conservatives, Robert Biddle, had attacked Jesse and his committee after the Yearly Meeting of 1918; so much so, in fact, that Jesse felt it necessary to defend himself through the pages of the *Friends' Intelligencer.* He denied that his committee had "become partizans or teachers of any especial social theory. They [were] authorized to conduct a *study,* not a propaganda. They would abuse the confidence of the meeting if they should go further than this. . . ." The members of the committee, Jesse said, represented "a very wide variety of opinion," being united only "in mutual respect and tolerance" for such differences, and by "a loyal desire to see the truth and act in accordance with its dictates." A month later (March, 1919) his friend Philip W. Smith helped him, saying that "No one who knows Dr. Holmes would intimate that he desires to propagate false or evil theories. . . ." Of course, Smith went on, "The most revolutionary and unsettling propaganda of our present social order is Christ's teaching consistently and practically applied, . . ." Further, "If our Society of Friends is going to measure up to its opportunity and the need of the world today it will be because of such leaders as Jesse H. Holmes."

But the Yearly Meeting as a whole was not yet completely convinced. Although the May session (1919) continued Jesse's overall Committee, and appropriated $1500 to its use, it still denied the use of the Race Street facilities. The Yearly Meeting's message was clear: soft pedal the work of the Subcommittee on the Study of the Social Order. This subcommittee did subordinate its work in 1921-22 to the more immediate demands of the disarmament drive; however, merging with a similar committee of the Orthodox under the name of the Social Order Committee of Philadelphia Friends, it held several meetings, arranged for one public lecture in Philadelphia, and held a weekend conference in Salem, New Jersey. Also, in 1922 a course of study in international relations was being prepared, with special reference to the results of the recent war. But by 1923 interest was waning in the sort of probing for fundamental causes of conflict which the Social Order Subcommittee had fostered; only one speaker at Yearly Meeting cared to venture the opinion that "strikes are a sort of petty war and it is as much our duty to find out the causes of strikes and prevent them as to study the problems of war . . . ."

Since almost any development in human affairs was grist to the Quaker mill, and reform movements had long since been started or supported by individual Quakers, it was not surprising that yearly meetings heard many speeches on social betterment. This was certainly the case when Jesse addressed an evening session of the Baltimore Yearly Meeting, October 30, 1929, on the subject of Soviet Russia. In this speech he was not binding the Society of Friends to the advocacy of this particular social panacea as a reform reaction to the old Czarist tyranny; rather, he was speaking as a private Quaker who had recently been in Russia and could give his audience some first-hand impressions of communism in action. Still, whether out of náiveté, or his natural predisposition to see this experiment through socialist eyes, he gave a report which was on the whole favorable to Stalin's regime. He declared that Russia "was eager to avoid war, but was overcome with a fear that the whole world was against her . . . ." Great Britain, he said, was about to resume diplomatic relations with Stalin's country, and he recommended that the United States do the same. The suffering there, he said, had been very great; but now, under the Soviet plan, ". . . all the available [land] had been divided among the people and the existing wealth was evenly distributed."

Being a society of individualists organized on democratic principles, the Hicksites had found that, if they expected to get any work done by associated action they had to rely on committees. And so, like the lower meetings, the Philadelphia Yearly Meeting in 1921 appointed what might have seemed to the outside observer to be an endless number and variety of committees, generally for a term of four years. There was, of course, the Nominating Committee, charged with preparing slates of nominees for presiding clerk, for recording clerk, for treasurer, and for all the other committees. These included the Committee on Philanthropic Labor, dealing with charitable projects for human uplift; there was also the Committee on Central Bureau, and the one on the Joseph Jeanes Fund. While other groups were appointed, the one which had most to do with helping to bind together the scattered American Hicksites was the Committee of One Hundred of the Friends' General Conference.

This Committee, also called the "Central Committee," was

composed of representatives from many yearly meetings, and was charged with two duties. It met at least once a year — e.g., in August, 1903, at Salem, Ohio; in the Christmas season at Buck Hill Falls, Pennsylvania in 1932 — to air the current opinions of Friends. At the same time it served as the planning-and-program committee for those big, annual gatherings of all these yearly meetings known as the General Conferences. These Conferences were held in the summer time, and in places where the delegates could find the maximum combination of business and pleasure. Thus the General Conference for 1906 found cool air and fresh inspiration at Mountain Lake Park, Maryland; the Conference in 1912 met in the shady groves of Chautauqua, New York, where delegates could listen to Jesse's speech on "The Modern Message of Quakerism." At other times the Conference was held at Asbury Park and Cape May, New Jersey, where cooling ocean breezes dispelled midsummer heat — and where Rebe and other wives could disport themselves on the beach with their children. When Jesse retired from his professorial duties at Swarthmore College in 1937 he could boast that he had been a featured speaker at every one of these Conferences for the last forty years.

In 1902, quite early in Jesse's period of service, he reported that the Asbury Park General Conference had appointed a Committee on the Advancement of Friends' Principles "to labor as way opens in the extension of the Quaker faith outside our immediate borders. . . ." He was named secretary of this Committee then, holding the job for some years; in 1932 he was still active in this work as chairman of the Message Committee of the Friends' General Conference. A number of methods were used to spread the good word: speeches by Jesse and others were published in the *Friends Intelligencer;* some of these articles were reprinted as pamphlets available in large quantities from the Hicksite headquarters in Philadelphia; and a subcommittee of the Advancement Committee saw to it that these pamphlets and selected books on Quakerism were put into cooperating college libraries. A circulating library among scattered members of the faith was proposed; and Jesse and others of the subcommittee spent their own money to visit places where there was some hope of starting a regular Quaker group — even to the extent of holding a meeting in a Methodist church.

The Holmes' Service in Swarthmore Meeting.

Returning to Swarthmore after attending General Conferences, Jesse and Rebe took leading parts in the manifold activities of their own Meeting. Rebe had transferred her membership from the Race Street Meeting in Philadelphia in 1902, and was given a most cordial "visit of welcome" by Alice Hall Paxson and Sidney A. Durnall, who had been appointed for this purpose by Swarthmore Monthly Meeting. (Strangely enough, Jesse, and their children — Elizabeth, Herman, and Robert — were not so visited or taken into Meeting until June, 1903.) She soon found herself serving with Jesse on a committee to teach Friends' principles, served for many years on the Membership Committee of the Monthly Meeting, and was named a representative to the Quarterly Meeting to be held in Darby, October, 1906. On May 14, 1918, attending the Philadelphia Yearly Meeting with Jesse, she presided at a woman's suffrage meeting held between morning and afternoon sessions of the main body. She introduced Ruth Verlenden of Darby, who said that since 1915 some forty millions women, in England and other places, had been enfranchised. Miss Verlenden urged her audience to work for the passage of the Nineteenth Amendment, which had already been passed by the House of Representatives and was pending in the Senate. Elizabeth Powell Bond, Rebe's old friend, agreed, adding that long ago "George Fox saw that women were needed by the men to accomplish their work, and [that] the organization of the Society of Friends had been an object lesson in democratic government . . . ." (No doubt Mrs. Bond forgot that in that same Yearly Meeting the men were still meeting separately from the women, recording their deliberations as "Men's Minutes.")

In 1925 Rebe was just hitting her stride as a Friendly worker in Swarthmore Meetings. The Committee of Overseers claimed her allegiance, and again the Membership Committee. In 1929 we find her presiding at a women's luncheon party, introducing two speakers recently returned from missionary work in Poland and Syria, and, in closing remarks, giving thanks to the ladies who had planned the occasion. As Rebe said, ". . . . if they had been singers as are the men, they would have sung":

> Oh, these Quaker feeds are famous,
> And they warm us through and through;
> So here's to Edna Pearson
> And the whole Committee too.

In 1929 she was appointed to a four-year term on the Committee of

Overseers, along with E. Clayton Walton, Claude C. Smith, and Rosalie G. Roberts; and in July of that year, on an automobile trip to the Midwest, she would lend the dignity of her presence to the Friends' National Conference in Indianapolis. Two years later she presided at the Friends' Forum in Philadelphia, held in the Race Street Meeting House on a Sunday evening. In 1937, when she was in her sixties, Rebe was asked by the Monthly Meeting's Committee on Ministry and Counsel "to visit local families for the primary purpose of distributing the advance study outlines of the Friends World Conference and to ask Swarthmore Friends if they wished to have pre-conference study groups." She performed this service, was heartily commended for it, and was asked to make similar visits in 1938. Small wonder that, in view of her untiring efforts, Rebe was made a member of the Ministry and Counsel Committee. As such, her work continued into the period of World War II, although it was somewhat restricted and changed by wartime gas-and-tire rationing, as well as by the fact that young Quakers now needed to be bolstered as conscientious objectors. From May, 1941 to May, 1942, she kept office hours on Monday afternoons in Whittier House, made 39 calls on prospective members of Swarthmore Meeting, and opened her home to 98 people interested in talking about Quakerism. In addition, she had written many personal letters at the request of the Peace Committee and expected to correspond with the young men of the Meeting who were in Friends' service camps.

While Rebe was pursuing all these activities, Jesse, of course, was not idle. Although his niece Ruth Price remembered him as merely attending Swarthmore Friends' meeting at first, only "gradually" rising to give more and more of his messages, so ebullient a man could not long be restrained. In fact, in November 1901, even before he had been admitted to membership in the local group, he addressed a Philanthropic Meeting of the Swarthmore Hicksites on "The New Patriotism." The "true patriot," he said, was independent of popular political fads and moods; he was loyal not so much to individuals or parties as to "principles of right." In March, 1903, attending a session of the Young Friends' Association in the College Parlors, he was chosen to accompany a student, William Roberts, to the Central Conference of Young Friends to be held in Philadelphia later that month.

Such activities were connected with, but peripheral to, the

meetings for worship on First-days. And it was to the Quakers who normally attended these First-day sessions that Jesse addressed so many of his inspiring and thought-provoking messages. As time went on he polished his technique, gradually moving from the rehearsal of Quaker beliefs to more critical exhortations and appeals for more action, more Quaker involvement in the life of the times. On March 15, 1921, *The Phoenix* reminded students that those who had resisted the call of the outdoors the previous Sunday to go to meeting were "well rewarded." Dr. Holmes, it reported, was the speaker of the morning, prefacing his main speech with the reading of a heartening message from the All-Friends Conference held in London in the fall of 1920. Then he spoke of the purpose of a meeting for worship. "It is one hour in the week," he said, "when we may gather, not for amusement, but for quiet contemplation, for introspection, to review our fundamental ideals and our successes or failures in living up to them, to get a hold on ourselves, new inspiration and courage." Seven months later Jesse was telling the Meeting about symbolism as found in the Old Testament; what he and other speakers had to say provoked his friend, Dr. John A. Miller, to get up and quote the motto of the College: George Fox's phrase, "Mind the Light." And George Fox's message as applied to the present was the topic of Jesse's talk in meeting one Sunday in May, 1924. He deplored the fact that "mankind had deified all its greatest teachers" and urged his listeners to "consider their teachings rather than worship them as gods." "We must face religion scientifically," said he, "and experiment with it, otherwise how can we have knowledge of it?"

Experimentation with Christian principles, of course, would involve their application and testing in daily life; it would also involve telling fellow worshippers in meeting of the results to society and to individuals. Although Jesse had spoken of the nature of silence in meeting — it "could be sympathetic and receptive, or unfeeling and unresponsive" — there was altogether too much of it, in his opinion. His own example was always before the Friends: a constant rising from the benches to speak his mind whenever the occasion seemed to demand it. (Everett Lee Hunt, an old friend of Jesse's, recalled how, at a Thanksgiving meeting in Whittier House, diagonally across the street from the old football field, Jesse was holding forth in his usual energetic fashion. And then, just as he finished, a loud chant was heard from the direction of the football field — "Hold that line! Hold that line!") Certainly he wished that Frank Aydelotte would give the meeting more of his keen mind, not waiting until the end of a meeting to bring other people's ideas into unity. In 1930 Jesse called for more activism among Quakers, in meeting and out; in 1932 he railed against those Pharisees who were in the Society of Friends but not of the spirit. And very late in his life Jesse's influence along this line led the Swarthmore Monthly Meeting to express the wish that everyone might consider "the balance between meditation and the spoken word," and that "more Friends should feel the responsibility for occupying from time to time seats facing the Meeting. . . . " It was also suggested that the bulletin board carry a list of all committee chairmen and other officers so that new members might become acquainted with the possibilities for receiving and giving service within the Meeting.

One such possibility for service lay in the field of religious education, a field well cultivated by Jesse since he and Joseph Walton had launched a series of summer schools for this purpose in 1907 on the campus of George School. A year later Jesse gave an address before the Department of Universities and Colleges of the Religious Education Association, then in its annual convention in Washington, D.C. — an address which was Jesse's *tour de force* in this field, and one which could well give guidelines to religious educators then and since. Considering the end product of a program of religious education — the Christian citizen —, he said that such a person must know and love both God and man. This person must know and love God through experience in living according to Christian precepts; he must know and love humanity by being part of it, by rubbing elbows with it, and by thinking through such measures as would help man in Christ's way. Every Christian citizen must work for fair play, equality of opportunity, and the elimination of the handicaps borne by some people — "without these there can be no democracy, no Christian brotherhood. . . ." But, in its efforts to achieve these human values, America found itself "on a terribly wrong track. . . .": individuals and institutions were using "palliative charities, temporary reliefs, lacking either the intelligence or the courage [or the desire?] to meet the situation fairly and to see that deep-seated changes are necessary in our social order: . . ." Jesse held that in this social order we "kill children to pile up our bargain counters, stunt and maim and destroy men in the interests of our balance of trade, and buy and sell girls in the

341

market to gratify the lusts of men. . . . " He told of how Walter Rauschenbusch, in one of his recent books on the Social Gospel, described a test sometimes used to distinguish the sane from the insane. "The physician sets the patient to dipping water from a basin under an open faucet. The insane merely dip; the sane first turn off the flow. It is a fair question whether in its dealing with pauperism, disease and crime, our civilization is or is not sane."

And so the religious educators in Washington, D.C., were enlightened. Teachers in Sunday schools must be educated; they must use both history and science to get the message across; and, since in Jesse's view, all education was religious, they must constantly teach, in all types of schools, the love of God and of man. "Genuine democracy," he said, "is organized Christianity. Training for good citizenship means training for the lessons of experience, science and history [are both needed] to make 'the kingdom come on earth as it is in heaven'; for a kingdom which is within you is of necessity a democracy."

We may be sure that these principles, essentially Hicksite in nature, were put into action when the Friends' School for Social and Religious Education was opened near the Swarthmore College campus in January, 1915. The school was planned to run for three terms of twelve weeks each under the overall direction of Bird T. Baldwin, professor of psychology. Situated in the John Woolman Home at Eighth Avenue and Walnut Lane, with Dr. and Mrs. William I. Hull as resident host and hostess, the school was to be independent of Swarthmore College and yet cooperating with it for a common purpose. Ten hours a week would be required of its students to secure a certificate; a day's program of study would consist of devotional exercises, lectures, student conferences, round tables, and assigned library work. Its faculty would include Jesse Holmes for the history of religion and the study of Christianity, Elizabeth W. Collins and George A. Walton would direct a detailed study of the Old and New Testaments, and Edith W. Winder would give a course on the history of the Friends. The psychological aspects of religious teaching would be handled by Professor Baldwin, Paul M. Pearson would deal with public speaking, and Dr. Louis N. Robinson would give a course in social reform. Professor J. Russell Hayes was to provide the necessary guidance in the Friends' Historical Library. Altogether, the program offered considerable promise for those who wanted to do more intelligent work in First-day schools as well as in the line of social service in the community.

Jesse, of course, rejoiced in all these activities. In First-day schools, as well as in his college classes, he saw golden opportunities to get young people — the hope of America — to combine God and man, religion and science, and to work for the realization of man's best dreams. In the fall of 1901 we find him making his ten o'clock Bible class in the Meeting House "more interesting than ever" by relating Old Testament incidents to present-day moral problems. By 1912 he was so much in demand that he found it necessary to conduct two Sunday morning sessions: one for college students in his regular classroom at nine; the other, the Men's Bible Class, in Whittier House, the new addition to Swarthmore Meeting House. The topic for the year in the students' class was "The Social Teachings of Jesus"; only the words of Jesus, as most directly reported in the Gospel of Matthew, were used, carefully omitting what other commentators said of Him. In the Men's Class, which was growing all the time, "The Christian State" was the topic for the year. This study was launched by considering the principles of taxation which a Christian state would rightly use, and various experts were called in for the edification of the assembled Quakers. One of these class meetings was addressed by Judge Johnson, of Media, on the "Principles of the Protective Tariff"; another meeting heard Professor Fleischer, of the University of Pennsylvania, explain the "Principles of the Revenue Tariff"; and a subsequent session was to listen to William L. Price, Rose Valley, as he spoke on the "Principles of Free Trade." And, lest some people think that such secular topics were temporary aberrations, and not properly considered in a Bible class, Jesse followed this series of discussions with another series in 1914 on local politics. It was an election year, and, while the Philadelphia newspapers were "educating" the electorate almost *ad nauseum* on the senatorial and gubernatorial contests, very little could be found in the public press bearing on a number of minor but important offices. The question of who should be elected to represent the second district of Delaware County in the state legislature was of particular moment to Jesse and his friends because Swarthmore was in this district. The issues and the qualifications of the candidates needed to be aired. So, on Sunday morning, September 27, Dr. Robert C. Brooks, of Swarthmore's political science department, gave nonpartisan sketches of the

343

candidates, with particular attention to the records in the last legislative session of the two sitting members, the Honorable Richard J. Baldwin and the Honorable Harry Heyburn. On the following Sunday these two gentlemen appeared before Jesse's Bible class to speak and answer questions. On Sunday, October 11, the Messrs. C. Wilfred Conrad and Harvey Ogden, Fusion and No-License (Prohibition) candidates, were to present their cases. All interested citizens were invited to come to these meetings, particularly the students of Swarthmore College.

And come they did, perhaps in college youths' reaction against the type of "wishy-washy" Sunday-school teaching which they had known previously, and which Jesse had denounced as early as 1904. Although there were only sixty-four adults in the Swarthmore First-day School in 1912, Jesse's Bible class was growing through the increased attendance of younger men, many not Quakers, who were attracted by "the live discussions upon varied and important questions." By 1915 additional chairs for Whittier House were needed. A piano was to be provided, and perhaps through the Holmes' prodding, the Monthly Meeting was "willing for the Superintendent occasionally to make use of music in the closing exercises of the First-day School, but would add that the feeling of the meeting is strongly against making it a leading part of the program." This departure from the traditional stance of Quakers against music in the church was, however, a liberal step in the right direction; it helped to give a new and more attractive tone to First-day activities.

This same tone continued after World War I; indeed, Jesse's influence on the young men and women of Swarthmore grew apace. In 1919, Jesse's class in First-day School was often conducted as a discussion group led by a student. One of these students, Claude C. Smith, who was to go on to become a Philadelphia lawyer and a distinguished member of Swarthmore's Board of Managers, was so moved by "the good, live, peppy discussions" held every Sunday morning from 10:30 to 11:30, that he wrote an open letter to *The Phoenix* about them. He wrote that this meeting was "not a dry Bible class, a class of theories, or a class of creeds. It is a place to talk about those things that concern you so much that you are afraid to talk about them to anyone. They are a part of you. They are you, as you stand before the fellows, stripped of outside appearance." And, he went on, "It is a place to exchange ideas

344

about some of the things that make or unmake a healthy normal life." A list of possible discussion topics was added; two weeks later the students were told that similar lists would be posted on the bulletin board in Parrish Hall at the beginning of each week.

In the 'twenties and 'thirties Jesse continued to carry his particular brand of Quaker ministry to the young people of the College. One of these was Margaret Byrd Rawson, who recalls that at times Jesse was, like Socrates, called "a corrupter of youth." "And I," she said later on, "was one of the corrupted ones, and it was all right with me." She recalls how, after disagreeing with a part of the *Book of Discipline,* she went to the Monthly Meeting to propose a change. She rose, made her proposal, and sat down — only to have the Meeting immediately go to another matter of business. Jesse was there, and he now rose from his patriarch's seat on a facing bench to protest this cavalier treatment. "Wait a minute!", he cried out. "This young Friend has a concern and I think that we ought to take it seriously." After some discussion, the Monthly Meeting did take it seriously: Margaret's point, along with other desired changes, was sent up to Quarterly Meeting and Yearly Meeting. As a result the *Book of Discipline* was revised in such a way that she could accept the new statement of the point at issue.

This ministry to youth was carried on in varied ways. Jesse spoke in Collection on many occasions in 1931 when he again rehearsed the ideas, ideals, and practices of the Quakers. Quakers believed, he said, "that it is the work of man to wipe out all things which would hinder the development of great lives; one of these is war." Perhaps Robert J. Cadigan, '34, who was to go on to become a teacher at Friends' Central School, Philadelphia, and then editor of *Presbyterian Life,* heard Jesse's talk in vespers. In any case, "no longer sure what to believe" after being bombarded with all kinds of theories about man and God, he joined Friends' Meeting, where Jesse Holmes was saying that there was a religion " 'for the scientifically minded,' " and "one didn't have to *know* the answers, *seeking* was the thing." Cadigan went to every First-day meeting, and also "at nine a.m. every Fourth Day. Sometimes on cold winter Wednesdays, there'd be only 'Ducky' on the facing bench, facing only seeking me. At 9:15 we'd shake hands, sometimes not even breaking the silence. . . . I belonged."

Quaker teachings, plus this kind of consideration for students by Jesse and others in the Swarthmore Meeting, may have accounted for the rather startling statistics compiled by *The Phoenix* staff after a student poll on religious beliefs in 1938. According to this poll, 65 per cent of the Swarthmore seniors had changed their religious convictions since entering college; 45 per cent of the juniors, 30 per cent of the sophomores, and 20 per cent of the freshmen had done the same. Of course, these results were quite similar to those recorded by the Presbyterians. In these studies it was found that there was a close negative correlation between educational achievement and an allegiance to the church of their childhood. Jesse was right: the old Church was not doing a good job with its youth; it was not giving them a view of life they found very rewarding in the time of Roaring Twenties, the Great Depression, and Hitler's rise to power.

Applying Original Quaker Principles.

Undoubtedly one reason for the declining appeal of the old-style Church to youth lay in its tendency to formalize its system of worship, to reduce otherwise desirable ideas and events to a regular, predictable ritual. Even the Society of Friends was guilty of this type of institutionalization. Over the years the questions individual practicing Friends were to ask themselves had become "frozen" into a set of fourteen Queries designed to keep the larger body on the straight-and-sometimes-narrow path of Quakerism. This set of Queries was to be read in its entirety once a year at preparative and monthly meetings and answers formulated. These answers were then sent on up to quarterly meetings and yearly meetings. No wonder that some of the more liberal, the more active, members stayed away from monthly meetings; no wonder that in 1903 Jesse Holmes rose in Swarthmore Monthly Meeting to say that "the time had come to re-write the Discipline so that it may better present to Friends and the World what Friends stand for. . . ." Although "much Sympathy" with Jesse's proposal was expressed by the assembled Friends, the matter was left for further consideration by future meetings. In the next few months a committee was appointed to look into the matter, its membership including not only Jesse but Joseph Swain, president of Swarthmore, Hannah Clothier Hull, and other liberals. But in May, 1905 Jesse's original rather sweeping proposal to rewrite the entire Book of Discipline had been toned down to "the changing of certain Queries." Five years later he again found it necessary to rise and propose a change in the Queries, adding this time — "and in the manner of answering them. . . ." He also suggested that his proposal be sent up to the next quarterly meeting and that the necessary steps be taken to bring about such a revision. By January, 1911, Jesse had persuaded his immediate colleagues that the Queries had departed from original Quaker simplicity, that they were no longer fully adopted to the Society's needs since some of them dealt with conditions which had changed, that new conditions called for new Queries, and that the manner of presenting them was repetitious and time-wasting. The matter was referred to Concord Quarterly Meeting, and from there to Philadelphia Yearly Meeting.

Changes in the Queries were made eventually, although the road to improvement was long and tedious. Those Queries in force when Jesse grew irritated with them in 1910 were outlined in the *Rules of Discipline* for 1894:

Queries for 1894.

First Query. Are all our religious meetings for worship and for discipline regularly held? Do Friends duly attend? If the hour observed, and is the behavior of those assembled becoming?

Second Query. Are love and unity maintained amongst you? Are tale-bearing and detraction discouraged? When differences arise, are endeavors used speedily to end them?

Third Query. Do you maintain a faithful testimony in favor of a free ministry of the gospel?

Fourth Query. Do you bring up those under your care in plainness of speech, behavior, and apparel? Do you encourage them in the frequent reverent reading of the Holy Scriptures, and guard them from pernicious reading and the corrupting influences of the world? And are you, yourselves, good examples in these particulars?

Fifth Query. Are you clear of the manufacture, sale, and use of intoxicating liquors as a drink, and careful to discourage the same? Are you cautious in their use as medicine, clear of signing applications for license to make or sell them as drink, and of renting your property for these purposes? Do you avoid the unnecessary frequenting of taverns, and the attendance of places of harmful diversion? Do you maintain moderation and simplicity at marriages and funerals, and on other occasions?

Sixth Query. Do you take care of such of your members as need aid, and assist them in business if they are capable of it? Are their children freely instructed to fit them for suitable occupation and self-support? And are any of these or other Friends' children placed from amongst Friends?

Seventh Query. Are you careful to live within the bounds of your circumstances, without ostentation or vain display, and to keep to moderation in your trade or business? Are you punctual to your promises, prompt and just in the payment of your debts, and are such as give reasonable ground for concern on these accounts, seasonably advised or labored with, for their preservation or recovery?

Eighth Query. Do you take due care to treat with offenders in the spirit of meekness and love, without partiality or unnecessary delay, in order for their help, endeavoring to reach a judgment in the authority of Truth?

Ninth Query. Do you maintain a faithful testimony in favor of peace and arbitration, and against war and the preparations for and excitements to it, fraudulent or clandestine trade, oaths, and all forms of lotteries and gambling?

Tenth Query. Has due care been taken to record each birth, removal and death that has occurred among the members of your meeting during the last year? Has a duplicate or copy of each marriage certificate been carefully made and preserved? Have all disused or completed record or minute books of the meeting been deposited in a place of safety, approved by the meeting?

Eleventh Query. Are there First-day Schools held in connection with your meetings? Are they under care of committees appointed in the Preparative or Monthly Meetings, and are they conducted in accord with our principles and testimonies?

Twelfth Query. Are there schools established amongst you for the education of your children, under the charge of teachers in membership with us, and superintended by committees appointed in your business meetings? Do the teachers and pupils attend midweek meetings?

Thirteenth Query. What changes have been made in the times and places of holding your meetings, and what new meetings have been established?

Fourteenth Query. Are the several Queries regularly read and answered as directed?

By 1927 there was some easing of the burden of answering these set questions because the number of Queries had been dropped from fourteen to twelve. Further, the monthly meetings had to read only one Query each month, although the suggested schedule for doing this was awkward and confusing:

Query No. 1 in Second Month
Query No. 2 in Fourth Month
Query No. 3 in Tenth Month
Query No. 4 in Seventh Month
et cetera.

In March, 1933, the Swarthmore Monthly Meeting, following a directive from Yearly Meeting, announced a simpler pattern after reading the Fourth Query. "Hereafter," its members were told, "it is proposed that Queries follow the number of the month, the First Query being read in January, first month, etc. . . ." And by 1942. although there were still twelve Queries listed in the *Book of Discipline,* to be *considered* at least once a year by monthly and quarterly meetings, only eight of these major questions, or parts of them, had to be *answered* by monthly meetings. The Society of Friends, under the prodding of such people as Jesse Holmes, was liberalizing itself, even if the process was a slow one.

Such revision, offering a new vision of Friends' responsibilities in the modern world, was but a return to George Fox's belief that an organized religious body should be alert to any departure from the moral code — and do something about it. If other churches were willing to wink at such departures, or any interference with what might be said to be the general welfare, not so the Quakers. Or at least, not so the Quakers under Jesse's more immediate influence. In 1905, Newton P. West, a member of the Swarthmore School Board, had been convicted by the County Court of dishonest dealing in his office as Director of the Poor in Delaware County. Following this conviction, and as a result of the Monthly Meeting's investigation of the facts in West's case, the Monthly Meeting drew up a minute to be presented to the School Board requesting that West be discharged from his position as a member. In view of the strong position of Quakers in the affairs of Swarthmore Borough, there could be no question as to the outcome of this request.

The outcome of another of the Monthly Meeting's concerns in 1905 was less sure, perhaps because sports-loving Jesse Holmes had a leg on both sides of the issue. A concern had been aired: That "the excitement attending the game of football as now usually played, resulting in injury to the physical, moral and spiritual nature of many who patronize the game makes it incumbent on our Society tenderly yet earnestly to entreat our members to withhold their encouragement therefrom." Upon a suggestion from President Swain, a committee was appointed to confer with the Advisory Athletic Committee of the College on this concern. The Monthly Meeting committee did not engage in a face-to-face conference with the College committee; instead it addressed a letter to it which not only expressed the earlier sentiments but added protests that the professionalism and demoralizing practices accompanying college football made "of no avail the Testimonies of our Society against wagering, the use of alcoholic liquors and the unfair and brutal treatment of fellow-beings. . . ." The committee reminded the Athletic Council that Swarthmore had been founded primarily for the benefit of Friends' children; it asked for relief in this matter. The Athletic Council replied, with Jesse Holmes' signature heading the list of those signing the letter, that they were in "entire unity with the spirit of the protest" and were using their best efforts to correct the evils mentioned. Whether or not all these evils were corrected, we do not know. Football continued to be played at Swarthmore. (However, the author remembers a story circulating in eastern Pennsylvania in the time of Frank Aydelotte: That, if a Swarthmore football player's experiment in the chemical laboratory ran over into the time set for football practice, he finished the experiment and *then* reported to the coach.)

And so Jesse's service continued. In 1923 he was appointed to the Committee on Ministry and Counsel by Swarthmore Monthly Meeting; four years later, at a meeting of this group, he gave "a very stimulating" message about the necessity for Quakers to *practice* their principles. This speech, "so dynamic in its thought and presentation," made a deep impression on his audience. He, of course, practiced what he preached, as in the time he upheld the Quaker's right to independent judgment in marrying out of meeting. In the old days, when even Hicksites were regarding themselves as "a peculiar people" and attempting to make membership in their Society a very exclusive thing, anyone daring to marry someone not a Quaker was promptly disowned. Now, in 1930, Jesse told the Monthly Meeting that this had been a great injustice, that the Yearly Meeting had "suffered incalculable loss" by such action, and that in these cases there had been "official interference in a matter essentially and vitally personal." He suggested that a minute along these lines be sent to Quarterly Meeting, and if it was approved, from there to Yearly Meeting. The minute, including an expression of regret for this injustice, and inviting the descendants of such victims to rejoin as birthright members, was approved and directed to be sent to the ensuing Quarterly Meeting. As is so often the case, the proposer got the job of carrying the proposal: Jesse was named as one of the Meeting's representatives to the Quarterly Meeting held in Swarthmore on January 28, where we may be sure he won his case. Two months later the Swarthmore Friends expressed their appreciation for all his labors by giving a dinner for him and two colleagues in Whittier House.

But the dinner to honor Jesse and his colleagues was given not only because of their work in the inner polity of Quakerism; it was given also to honor them as men and for the many ways they had labored in the Friendly spirit. In 1912, the Philanthropic Committee of Swarthmore Meeting, of which Jesse was a member, had sent three Christmas barrels of "goodies" to the "Neighborhood Guild and Southern [Negro] Schools"; in that same Christmas period Jesse had given an illustrated talk in Whittier House to about seventy colored people from Swarthmore and Morton. Twelve years later, when the Ku Klux Klan was rampant, the Whittier House Open Forum, under Jesse's leadership, passed a resolution denouncing the Klan's aims and methods. "The hope of the future," the resolution read, "lies not in the way pointed out by organizations for the cultivation of race prejudice and hatred, religious bigotry and proscription." Instead, the Forum believed that ". . . what the world needs today is mutual sympathy, a broader tolerance, a frank expression of the ideals and purposes of all other groups." The Klan's secrecy was condemned, and the citizens of Swarthmore were asked "to stand aloof" from the efforts then being made to introduce this movement into that "borough and district." At the next Open Forum, to be held on a Sunday evening in October, 1924, Jesse had arranged for Noah Swain, of Philadelphia, to present the Republican point of view in connection with the current presidential campaign. And in ensuing years the Open Forum heard Patrick Malin, chairman of economics at Swarthmore, tell a combined meeting of YMCA and YWCA people that "The New Reformation" included not only a new theology, a new church, but also "commercialized religion" — no doubt of the

"Billy" Sunday type. In 1928, Dr. G.F. Thomas, assistant professor of philosophy, spoke on "Evolution of Religion," pressing the thought that "the ideal religion would not stress any one idea or factor too strongly, but will be one containing the best elements of them all." This spirit of selective unification prevailed when Jesse addressed a large group of Young Friends from Swarthmore, Haverford, and Philadelphia on one of his favorite topics — religion for a scientific age, a religion of the spirit versus a religion of authority.

And the application of the original Quaker principle of "seeking" continued into the 1930s. Jesse told the Forum of "Specific Ways of Creating a Better Understanding of the New World Order"; and in 1936 the economic issues of the presidential campaign were discussed by Professors Malin, Wilcox and Fraser, Professor Malin contending that he favored the gold-standard position of the "Alf" Landon Republicans because he "fear [ed] it less" than New Deal money manipulation. Indeed, 1936 was a big year in Swarthmore: Professor John W. Nason of the philosophy department, looking like a handsome combination of Ronald Coleman and Sir Anthony Eden, was to give the first of a series of lectures on "The Ideals of Life." His lecture dealt with "The Greek Ideal"; on the following Sunday evening Maurice Mandelbaum would tell of "The Medieval Ideal of Life," to be followed on other Sundays by Brand Blanshard on "The Puritan Ideal," and by Jesse on "The American Ideal." A few months later, in the dreary month of February (1937), those who attended the Forum session in the Meeting House may have been enlightened about the Soviet system when they heard Constantine A. Dumansky, counselor to the Russian Embassy in Washington, explain the new Soviet Constitution. And steady readers of *The Phoenix* must have been interested to know that in the week of September 1-8, the World Conference of Friends was to meet on the Swarthmore campus. Dormitories at Swarthmore and at Haverford were to be opened for the use of the delegates; the main meetings were to be held in Clothier Memorial Hall and in Whittier House, with discussion groups meeting in classrooms at Swarthmore and Haverford. To prepare for this conference, Swarthmore students were urged to attend special study-group meetings in Whittier House in 1936: a meeting on November 4 on "War and Peace," on November 6 on "Economic and Social Justice," on November 9 on "The Spiritual Message of the Society," on November 10 on "The

Individual Christian and the State," and on the next day, "Friends and Education."

In 1936 the forty-third anniversary of Swarthmore Meeting was celebrated in the Meeting House. Although the people at this celebration heard William I. Hull report that the most striking development since 1893 has been the Meeting's growth in membership from a very small nucleus to some seven hundred members, Jesse Holmes was not satisfied with Quaker progress. Two years later, after the current Seventh Query was read in Monthly Meeting ("Do you fulfill the responsibility of membership in your religious Society by regular attendance and support of its meetings? What are you doing to strengthen the spiritual life of the meeting and to invite others to share in its fellowship? Are you active in advancing the principles of your Society and in working for the spread of righteousness in the world?"), he "called on members to 'adopt' a nearby meeting, and to visit it at least half the time, thus strengthening neighboring meetings and building up the Society. . . ." We don't know how many people followed his suggestion; we do know that in Swarthmore itself the Meeting grew until it had 850 members in 1940. Many of these had joined while students at Swarthmore; and as Dr. Hull said at the anniversary celebration, the geographical distribution of members of the Meeting corresponded almost exactly with the distribution of graduates of the College. Indeed, Eleanor Stabler Clark, clerk of the Meeting, reported in 1940 that 45 per cent of the membership were nonresident — a fact making for loss of unity.

If local unity was threatened by this widespread membership, Jesse and his colleagues could take considerable pride in the very real gains made by the general Society of Friends since the turn of the century. Overall membership had increased, and the American Friends Service Committee had been formed as a major step in that unification drive so dear to Jesse's heart. The Queries were modernized and the manner of their administration simplified. Music now brightened First-day schools, and, due to such programs as those of the Open Forum, new and liberalizing ideas were informing the minds of even the most conservative Quakers. Due to the public speeches and articles of men like Jesse Holmes, Patrick Malin, Brand Blanshard, and Rufus Jones, the world at large was learning more and more about the Quaker point of view — a point of view which could and did show ways to live with individual and social dilemmas, and which might solve some of those social problems arising from the uneven development of men and their institutions in the modern world.

16. Reform as Religion, Part I

As we have seen, Jesse constantly tried to apply his conception of Quaker principles to the reformation of religion and religious institutions. At the same time these principles were to guide the reformation of society — a reformation conceived as a religious duty. Religion was reform, and reform was religion. The old Puritan ideal of the "city on a hill" was still alive; Jesse's generation read of it in Felix Adler's "The City of the Light":

> Have you heard the golden city
>   Mentioned in the legends old?
> Everlasting light shines o'er it,
>   Wondrous tales of it are told;
> Only righteous men and women
>   Dwell within its gleaming wall,
> Wrong is banished from its borders,
>   Justice reigns supreme o'er all.
>
> We are builders of that city,
>   All our joys and all our groans
> Help to rear its shining ramparts,
>   All our lives are building-stones;
> But the work that we have builded,
>   Oft with bleeding hands and tears,
> Oft in error and in anguish,
>   Will not perish with the years.
>
> It will be at last made perfect,
>   In the universal plan,
> It will help to crown the labors
>   Of the toiling hosts of man;
> It will last and shine transfigured

355

In the final reign of right,
It will merge into the splendors
Of the City of the Light.

Felix Adler's idealism, and that of Jesse, was exercised in the period of American history running from about 1890 through the 1930s — a time when Populists, Progressives and Socialists wrested social-reform measures from Big Business with only moderate success, a time when the battle between Big Labor and Economic Royalists caused Franklin D. Roosevelt to cry out, "A plague on both your houses!" Dollar materialism was in the saddle and riding mankind. As Scott Nearing observed:

Dollars and dimes! Dollars and dimes!
To be without money is the worst of all crimes.
To grab what you want and to keep all you can
Is the first and the last and whole duty of man.

After spending his mature years as a socialistic reformer in this competitive and acquisitive society, Nearing came to certain conclusions: That almost anyone could overload his stomach, pile up gadgets, and push himself to an eventual heart failure in affluent America — if he was willing "to make humble obeisance and kiss the big toe of the Oligarchy. . . ." But this was demeaning; he called for a more independent simplicity. One had to live; the question was: "Live where, live how, by what means, and for what purpose? . . ." Nearing noted that Buddha long ago had at least partially answered this question in his "Eightfold Path to Righteousness: 'Right livelihood consists of following a trade or occupation compatible with harmlessness, and help to all living creatures.'"

And the Progressive Friends, those general reformers to whom Nearing spoke in 1915, skirted the edges of this Buddhist sentiment in one of their morning meetings:

The cause that lacks assistance,
The wrong that needs resistance,
The future in the distance,
The good that we can do.

Sometime, somewhere, in Jesse's life he must have seen these Progressive couplets since he used them in one of his statements of the reformers' position:

With the interminable list of the causes that lack assistance and the wrongs that need resistance it is essential to recognize that the thing needed is not charity but justice — and that justice is *whatever is best,* alike for society and the individual as a member of society. Charity is the merest temporary expedient. Justice and fair play is the only solution. The freeing of every opportunity for life and labor is the central problem of the Christian religion. Only when a man is free to labor and to receive all the results of his labor *as his right,* can we have anything approaching a real equality and a real brotherhood. Brothers stand on a common land of mutual good will — not one looking down however kindly on another.

These were controversial words, and Jesse believed them. Charity *was* a mere "temporary expedient" when it came to helping those who suffered from the operation of the American System. And yet Jesse too, like so many other people of good will, engaged in "meliorism" — an effort to treat the symptoms of social illness (poverty, hunger, unemployment, inadequate housing, and inadequate clothing) by such means as the Salvation Army and other community charities. In 1934 he was the faculty chairman of the Swarthmore Chest Fund drive, urging the students in Collection to contribute liberally for the relief of the needy in that community. Some 82 percent of the students responded; they and faculty members gave a total of almost $3400 for use among tenement dwellers and other deserving poor, not only in the Swarthmore area but more widely through the United Relief Organization and the Red Cross. The American Friends Service Committee got some of this money, as did the International Student Service. The following year Jesse was again faculty chairman; this time the Chest Fund goal was $4000.

Reform Darwinists Apply the Social Gospel.

But these lapses into meliorism did not, of course, represent Jesse's true attitude about how the good society should come into being. The main thrust of his thinking lay, as he explained in his Philosophy Manuscript, in the demand for "changed conditions that will make impossible the misery, poverty, and neglect of an industrial world." He was, in short, a Reform Darwinist, deriving many of his ideas from such leaders of thought as Henry George and Lester Ward. These men had emphasized that the heart of Darwinism was continuous evolution in relation to the environment. Accepting the evolution of plants and animals, they went on to insist that the institutions of man — e.g., the church, the family, the school, and the industrial corporation — also could and should change if conditions about them changed. And, since the environment was such a powerful selective factor in Darwinian evolution, why not experiment to change it? Could not slums be cleared and better housing provided? Could not more laws be passed like the Pure Food and Drug Law? Would not the social environment be improved if corporation capitalists, themselves forming a union of stockholders, would see the justice of an industrial union of workers? If capitalism's rapaciousness, emphasizing the struggle for survival in Social Darwinism, went too far, could it not be tempered with a Christian charity and moderation? Was it not time to remind people that cooperation also had survival value in Darwin's animal world; was it not time to band together via local, state, and national laws which would set up conditions under which the lowly of the social world might have an opportunity to show that they too had something to offer to man's welfare? These Reform Darwinists were out to save society as well as individuals; they were going to apply the principles of the Social Gospel so that individuals, working as socialized Christians, would direct the institutions of man toward that greater brotherhood, that greater democracy, which reformers believed Christ had in mind.

The Drive Toward Greater Democracy.

But, as Jesse well knew, democracy was a hard-fought thing. In 1919, when his erstwhile friend and Swarthmore graduate, J. Mitchell Palmer, was running rough shod over the First and Fourth Amendments in pursuit of Reds, Jesse felt it his duty to exhort the Swarthmore student body on "Permanent Patriotism":

> It seems that the German autocracy is ended. But to end one autocracy is of little consequence if we do not end the spirit of autocracy. Already it raises its head everywhere here and abroad. . . . Autocracies of disorder and anarchy, of class and race, of wealth and poverty, of party and privilege, are not less but more dangerous than the medieval [tyrants] which were inevitably destined to fall before the onward march of the free peoples.

> May we not turn to you, the makers and masters of the next generation, for a permanent self-dedication to the struggle for human freedom, which lies, not behind us, but before us?

This apparently endless struggle for human freedom had been a daily occupation for reformers of Jesse's stripe. Well before the

358

American Civil War, the Progressive Friends, fighting alike the tyranny of institutionalized religion and the tyranny of the slaveowner's grip on the national government, had published some verse which carried a satiric message of universal force:

The Tyrant's Ancient Argument: Or, The Dangers of Thought.

> Cease your thinking, O ye people! shouts the
> Tyrant, fierce and loud,
> As with scornful eye, he glances o'er the
> slowly moving crowd;
> Ye were made for toil and labor — mark your
> hard and brawny hand!
> We are God's appointed Ruler, to obey is
> his command!
>
> Cease your thinking, lest ye fancy ye can rule
> *yourselves* by thought,
> And the world's fair peace and order to
> swift destruction brought;
> Lest, seduced by idle dreams, ye may fondly
> think there be
> Winds and souls in those rough bodies, and
> ye're men as well as we.

As Jesse achieved a more influential position as a Quaker liberal he continued this fight for the common man's freedom. In 1906, when he reviewed Henry George's book on *The Menace of Privilege*, he found a fine opportunity to express his own ideas. While he admitted that great wealth — "at least in some sense" — had been earned by the first generation of American entrepreneurs, "it rarely happens," as he said, "that its third generation shows any other industry than the pursuit of pleasure. Our aristocracy of wealth tends to be idle, extravagant and immoral. . . ." Their wealth was inherited, it was unearned by them, and it became the basis of that special privilege in society which led to more unearned wealth and power. And this special privilege was a "great menace to democracy, and, indeed, to civilization. . . ." Its holders seized control of the machinery of government, of education, and even of religion. Their henchmen in the courts of the land abused the power of injunction for their benefit; "free speech, trial by jury, and almost every cherished safeguard of liberty has been overridden by irresponsible judges in the interests of corporate wealth. . . ." Such practices, which put the chances "for life, liberty and happiness at the disposal of a small number, to give or withhold at will," were the

359

marks "not of a great nation, but of a great despotism."

Such despotism, no matter how or where it was felt, was not to be borne. In 1912, when powerful political bosses and J.P. Morgans were still largely dictating local, state and national affairs, Jesse rose in Concord Quarterly Meeting at West Chester to fulminate against them. ". . . just as the great prophets of old denounced the entrenched evils of that time," he said, "so must the prophet of today protest against the . . . tyranny which permits one man to have more power in the community than is possessed by ten thousand of his fellows." In this and other speeches and articles he was constantly holding up to his fellowmen the vision of that "real democracy" which they might achieve if they were willing to work hard and take the risks inherent in the American system of freedom. As they worked toward democracy, he told the graduating class of the Sidwell School in 1907, they should "quit" themselves "like men" in the struggles and conflicts which were a part of American life. And, like that older reformer, Wendell Phillips, Jesse urged his audiences to trust the people as they spoke out — even if they were patently wrong. "It is as important that error get into the light, as for truth to do the same. The former is fungoid in nature and dies in sunlight, where the latter flourishes. . . ." And "whenever anyone, however humble and poor, however repugnant to our ideals, is refused the public hearing which is his due. . . .," we should help him have his day in court. There should be freedom under law; this was the basic American plan. "Without free thought and speech we cannot hope to make the necessary readjustments in a changing world; and it is much more important that unpopular ideas shall have a hearing than that the customary and popular shall be restated. . . ."

The trouble was, in the minds of American isolationists living in the early 1920s, that so many of these unpopular ideas had originated in Europe. Anarchism and bolshevism were associated with Russia; socialism had seen its great bible, *Das Kapital,* emerge from the mind of a German Jew; the theory of organic evolution had been written in *The Descent of Man* and the *Origin of Species* by an Englishman; and even the League of Nations had been advocated by a man with the unAmerican name of Smuts. These ideas, it was held by tub-thumping Fourth-of-July orators, were dangerous; they were not to be entertained by "100% Americans."

This attitude, of course, enraged Jesse because it was so patently in violation of the principle of giving every idea a hearing. But more than that, it asked Americans to close their eyes to the facts of historical development; it asked them to forget the roots of their culture. And so, about 1924 Jesse sat down to develop a speech on "The Foundations of American Tradition." In his preliminary note-taking he asked himself how many ancestors America had — millions? trillions? and of what kind?: not only the physical ancestry of the Indians, Jews, Germans, English, and many other ethnic strains, each adding its flavor to the American stew in the melting pot, but also the distinctive and historic contributions of their homeland cultures. He noted six main sources of the American tradition: the Jewish concepts of religion; the Greek spirit of scientific inquiry; Roman law and forms of government; the Teutonic idea of the administration of justice via deliberative assemblies (folk moots); the Norman genius for organization and government transmuted after Magna Carta into the English system of limited monarchy; and the lessons and spirit of the Italian Renaissance — that overthrow of authority to discover anew ancient values and to examine this earth with a fresh eye. These roots, inextricably entwined in England, Holland, and France, nourished growing trees of liberty refreshed every now and then by the blood of tyrants spilled in civil revolutions. Democratic ideas and institutions were the hidden cargoes in the *Mayflower* and the *Susan Constant;* after a time France sent a lasting symbol to hold aloft the torch of liberty at the main entrance to America for foreigners and their ideas. As immigrants stood by their ships' rails, clutching their poor baggage, they were encouraged to believe that here, in America, all the best principles of mankind's age-old struggle for life, liberty and the pursuit of happiness had finally come to a focus. This was the Promised Land.

To those who had lived in this Eden for some time, and who knew that it still had some snakes in it, Jesse of course had constant words of advice and encouragement. As they tried to apply the Christian principle to the eradication of these snakes, he told them, they might get periodic inspiration or new ideas by reading not only the *Friends Intelligencer,* but such other magazines as *The Christian Register* (Unitarian) or *The World To-morrow* (Fellowship of Reconciliation). And, in a long review in 1921, he paid a special tribute to *Unity* — a weekly founded by Jenkins Lloyd Jones, and continued after his death by John Haynes Holmes and Francis

361

Neilson. "In general," Jesse wrote, ". . . it is strongly for real Democracy and the faith in the ultimate goodness of men, which is the necessary foundation of Democracy; . . ." *Unity* was strongly against "all imperialisms, whether of family, race or class; . . ." It gave "powerful expression to the demand for fair play and free speech everywhere; and . . . [was] against wars, fightings, and conflicts of hate for whatever purpose, and wherever found. . . ." Its editors and most of its correspondents believed that the love-principle would "really solve the worlds riddles, and bring order into the world chaos. That means they are willing to try it *and take the consequences.*"

And, as we have seen, Jesse had found on more than one occasion that his style of liberalism forced him to take the consequences of a stand on this or that issue. "Many people hated and feared him. If the things he stood for ever came to pass, their easy lives would become harder. . . ." Special privilege and injustice would have to go, he told them, his voice ringing and his eyes flashing. He helped to found the People's Rights Association of Delaware County, urging people to do away with corrupt leadership. Complacent audiences were shaken "when he told them that as long as they voted for a party which supported a proved criminal for office, they were themselves crooked . . . ." And these same people, sometimes even Quakers, would become uneasy when he insisted so strongly that they owed responsibilities to their brothers — that they were soldiers for human welfare. His nephew, William W. Price, said that Jesse always reminded him of the James Montgomery Flagg poster during World War I with Uncle Sam pointing straight to the observer, and saying, " 'Your government wants *you!*' "

This government — local, state, and national — was in itself deficient in some of its operations. In 1932 the Swarthmore Borough Council charged the Public Library with rent for the rooms it used in Borough Hall, thus contravening the will of the taxpayers as expressed in the last election. Jesse promptly sent a letter of protest to the editor of *The Swarthmorean.* The Commonwealth of Pennsylvania executed convicted murderers, a practice Jesse disapproved not only because of his deeply rooted faith in the goodness of man, even the erring brothers, but for other reasons. When reporters for the Philadelphia *Public Ledger* interviewed Jesse and five other prominent citizens on this subject in 1933, he gave two standard reasons for his opposition. Criminological studies had shown, he said, that the death penalty had "no effect" on the number of murders in a specific locality. Further, it sometimes happened that the state executed the wrong person. Mistakes of this kind could "be retrieved in the case of life imprisonment, but not of capital punishment. . . ." In 1926, when the United States was most definitely an empire, maintaining exploitative control over the Philippines, Hawaii, Alaska, Puerto Rico, the Canal Zone, and Nicaragua, Jesse thought that it was quite fitting to address an Armistice Day mass meeting in the Aldine Theatre, Philadelphia. Twenty-five clubs and organizations were represented in the crowd; the Lit Brothers Chorus entertained them at appropriate times. No doubt Jesse reminded his audience that in Nicaragua the United States had used military force from 1909 to the present to keep unpopular but pro-American conservative governments in power, "in defiance of the wishes of a large majority of Nicaraguans." Such practices, of course, made a mockery of any Armistice Day — the world was not yet safe for democracy, certainly not that more-equal social and *economic* democracy which Jesse believed the majority wanted in Nicaragua and other areas subject to American might.

If the principles of democracy were being subverted abroad there was a great need to reinvigorate them at home. In the schools boys and girls were pumped full of idealism in their civics courses, only to find out as they entered the workaday world that those freedoms vouchsafed in the Bill of Rights by the Founding Fathers were but permissions to stick their necks out — and to have radical labor unions or conservative Union Leaguers chop off their heads! The threat of violence by labor unions against a free-thinking or independent worker was no less effective than the employers' "blacklist." Jesse knew all this, and yet he continued his efforts to hold before Americans those civics lessons learned in school. He helped to celebrate Armistice Day as one of those holidays (holy days) like the Fourth of July, through which Americans observed their secular religion of patriotic nationalism. This religion, like any other, had its rituals, its martyrs, and its holy books. The Declaration of Independence was its Old Testament; the Constitution and its Amendments was the New. It was altogether fitting and proper that the principles of the American Democratic Faith contained therein should be rehearsed periodically in a reverent spirit. As Jesse said, "Our loyalty to that which is really our country is identical with our loyalty to our religion." What was needed was more interpretation of these principles, and some definition as to what truly constituted American patriotism. In November, 1927, just before the annual Armistice Day observance, Jesse published his contribution to this definition in the *Friends Intelligencer*. Patriotism, he wrote, is more than "taking vows of vague loyalty, . . . flag waving and flying the eagle. . . ." Our country is more than " 'rocks and rills' "; " 'Our Country' is a group of great ideals together with the institutions by which we endeavor to put them into the actual life of people. A real patriotism is loyalty to these ideals and to these institutions in so far as they efficiently serve the ideals. . . ." Loyalty was *not* owed to any political party or administration, nor to any officials, except as they faithfully discharged the purposes embodied in national principles. If they failed to do this, or hindered those who were trying to live up to these ideals, patriotism demanded that they should be opposed "even to the point of destroying them or dismissing them from public office."

Nor was it hard to find such violators of the American Dream. ". . . certain powerful but irresponsible bodies are challenging the rights of free speech and free assembly and are assuming the right, for which they have no legal basis and no fitness, to decide as to what is to be said, and as to what shall be discussed. . . ." Thus the American Legion was trying to hamper Quakers from criticizing the federal government's foreign policy of force; it was interfering with peace meetings in schools and colleges; it was trying to withhold from teachers the usual rights of citizens, or to hold opinions which its officials did not approve. Friends were being blacklisted by "100% Americans," and were being accused of taking " 'Russian gold' " for their "propaganda". And American educational institutions were "being involved by a system of . . . military training, backed by an insidious teaching of militarism by officers of the War Department detailed for this purpose . . . ."

Jesse bemoaned the fact that this invasion of the American schools by the military was a sign of the times, was indicative of the tendency of countries everywhere to fall back on force as the ultimate way of settling international disputes. True patriotism in America demanded that this drift be opposed in every possible way. If, on the other hand, it could not be slowed down or stopped at home, and in its expression in foreign imperialistic adventures, the

United States, as the world's richest and most powerful nation, would become "the chief menace to the peace of the world. . . ." Quakers, and all right-thinking citizens, had a duty to point out certain things which might reduce this danger. Among them was the concept of limited power in the American system. "The authority we delegate to our President does not extend one foot beyond American soil. The intervention of our authority in the affairs of other nations is [an] usurpation which has no possible support from our Constitution . . . ." And the doctrine that the Constitution followed the flag was a false one, and one fraught with the peril of further conflict. As Jesse said, "we would not admit it for a moment if applied to foreigners [following *their* flag] in our own country. . . ." Those who wanted to do business in such places as Nicaragua or Mexico should take their chances with the laws and conditions they found there, and not ask American Marines to risk their lives in defense of their properties.

Jesse finished his appeal for true patriotism on a lofty note. Since loyalty to American ideals was the primary mark of a good citizen, he held that "Our ultimate loyalty is due to that Brotherhood of Humanity, which is implied in the Divine Fatherhood, and that loyalty should be as nearly absolute as our human nature can make it. Our patriotism is subject to it. Our country is our great contribution to it. . . ." He called for fortitude and sacrifice in that perilous time. "Property and life are temporary affairs, — we will soon lose them in any case; shall we not spend them, if need be, worthily and for our faith? If the time comes . . . when we must suffer loss or abuse for our ideals, shall we not be worthy of those who founded our Society, and say with the prophets of old, " 'Here am I, — send me!' "

Two years later he was still of the same mind, this time speaking under the sponsorship of the Philadelphia Federation of Churches, and broadcasting his message over radio station WLIT. Once again he stressed the democratic values of free speech and a free press in the exercise of true patriotism; once again he attacked those who dared to limit these rights in the interests of a ruling group or administration.

By this time, however, the nation had experienced a rude awakening from Hoover's dream of permanent prosperity. It was the time of the Great Crash. Now the United States was to get a taste of what the other countries of the world had suffered during their post-1918 economic depression — that period of unemployment and monumental inflation which set the stage for the rise of Mussolini, Hitler, and other totalitarian regimes. As these regimes grew in power, their agents carried their ideas to America. Taking advantage of America's code of civil and political rights, which notwithstanding Jesse Holmes' strictures, were still relatively liberal, they carried on shadowy propaganda campaigns in speeches and in the press; and, when they represented Moscow, were seen on the fringes of the labor movement. Nazis held meetings in neighborhood taverns, Fritz Kuhn organized the American *Bund*, and Brown Shirts drilled and marched in a summer encampment in westcentral New Jersey. And America was beginning to develop its own *führers* — William Dudley Pelley's Silvershirt Legion was equally anti-Semitic and anti-Communist; the Reverend Gerald L.K. Smith organized the Committee of One Million against Jews, Negroes, and Communists; and the Reverend Gerald B. Winrod, of Wichita, Kansas, used familiar rivivalist tactics against Catholics as well as Jews. By 1936 people began to wonder whether Justice Holmes' times of "clear and present danger" to the nation's safety had not arrived once again: was it not time to restrict the exercise of free speech, and freedom of assembly, lest these sacred rights, used as worms, would destroy the whole apple?

Brand Blanshard addressed himself to this problem in a Sunday-night lecture in Whittier House in November of that year. As reported in a student's editorial in *The Phoenix,* he posed a dilemma for Americans: "Must an honest democracy be equally tolerant of all shades of opinion within its borders, or is it justified in suspending its toleration toward those groups within it which would deal harshly with liberalism if they came to power?" Blanshard was quoted as saying that "The choice we must make is between a temporary and local suspension of toleration, or a permanent [loss] of freedom. If we do not choose the former, we may see the latter forced upon us. We must take measures sufficiently severe to prevent dangers to liberalism, and we must resort to force if other means are not effective." (This from a nonresistant Quaker!)

But the student editor of *The Phoenix* took a somewhat different tack. Pointing to the recent election returns, he held that neither the Communist vote nor the Fascist (Union Party) vote attained the proportions of a loud threat. Indeed, the minor party vote "was hardly more than a murmur. . . ." Shrugging aside the presumed threats from the totalitarian elements, he claimed that the real threats to civil safety were coming from "the patriotic societies which, paradoxically, are prone to use undemocratic means to defend the American traditions. . . ." Those Americans who were "sincerely concerned with the preservation of the liberal philosophy would do well, now that the election is past, to shift their gaze from the . . . bugaboos of the spellbinders to the groups which are determined to preserve American ideals if they have to break every radical head in the country to do it."

But the picture changed. As the war fever mounted in Europe, with the United States more and more serving as the arsenal for democratic nations, American Communists began to foment strikes in defense plants and otherwise impaired national solidarity. Congress aimed to check such subversion by passing the Smith Act (1940), which made it unlawful for any group to advocate or teach the violent overthrow of the American system of government, or for any person to belong to such a group. In July, 1941 a special grand jury in Washington, D.C. considered the evidence against the Nazi and other fascist organizations in the United States. As a result thirty leading seditionists were indicted under the Smith Act for their alleged efforts to set up a Nazi government in this country, and for their part in inciting disloyalty among the armed forces. The trial dragged on until, for various reasons, the Washington Circuit Court of Appeals dismissed the indictment on the ground that the government's proceedings were a travesty of justice. Other cases under the Smith Act and under the Espionage Act of 1917 were also unsuccessful because the Supreme Court said that specific intent to obstruct the war effort was not shown, or that criminal intent had not been proven. After Pearl Harbor the Justice Department, working through the FBI, destroyed the German espionage and sabotage systems; there was not a single case of sabotage after December 7, 1941. But, since the United States was then at war, censorship was inevitable; again, as in the First World War, civil liberties had to be limited for the duration of the nation's peril so that democracy might resume its course once more when that peril had passed.

Education: the Means and the Goal.

As a reasonable interpretation might suggest, World War II was but an extension of World War I. After World War I had finally ground to a halt, Lloyd George made a speech in Manchester, England, in which he rehearsed the lessons democratic countries should have learned from that conflict. One great lesson, he said, was that "We must pay more attention to the school. The most formidable institution we had to fight in Germany was not the arsenals of Krupp or the yards in which they turned out submarines, but the *schools* of Germany. . . ." They had been the sources of the most fearsome competition in business before the war and the most terrible opponents during that holocaust. "An educated man is a better worker, a more formidable warrior, and a better citizen. . . ."

Jesse was in complete agreement. And he was so concerned about the poor quality of American education that he filled page after page of his resource books with notes for use in lectures and articles. He quoted the United States Commissioner of Education to the effect that while in 1914 "1 in 4 [of the draftees] in the American Army could not read or write," in the German Army the ratio was "1 in 5000." Also, that "1600 teachers gave up the business" during the war; their average salary was $500, with one state paying its teachers only $234. No wonder that Jesse and the Commissioner grew angry: "It is the world's greatest disgrace that in the richest country on the globe there is not [enough] money available to pay red-blooded men and women to teach our children. Unless we are willing to pay teachers more than scavengers or janitors the temple of freedom will be destroyed."

If conditions were so bad in the United States, and so much better in Germany, they affected the great mass of the common people primarily on the level of elementary education. But every country had its elite schools and colleges where a very small minority of students were educated far beyond elementary levels so as to become the leaders of society. These were to be the germinal thinkers in the several fields of human endeavor; it was this group which produced those who tried to enlighten the human mind. About 1930 Jesse declared that only some 100,000 such men and women stood between civilization and a throwback to the Dark Ages. "If I could choose this number carefully," he said, "and kill them all I could plunge the world back into a state of savagery from which it would emerge as slowly as it once did." This slow reemergence was predictable, Jesse thought, because in no age had "even a sizable majority of the people been interested in furthering

368

human progress, materially, spiritually, socially or biologically . . . ." This work had always been in the hands of relatively few people.

Although the honors program which Jesse so enthusiastically supported at Swarthmore College was at least partly designed to encourage the development of an educated elite, his basic hope and belief was that sound education could and should become the birthright of all classes of people. As he knew from his own experience, the common people, if they had the opportunity for a mind-stretching, horizon-lifting education, might well add to these 100,000 germinal thinkers; perhaps indeed class lines in education might be wiped out if enough financial support were given and properly administered for the right objectives.

In Pennsylvania public support for education was a mixed picture: local public schools were paid for rather meagerly by a combination of local real-estate taxes and state appropriations; on the other hand, private schools, private colleges, and other favored institutions found themselves in the early 1900s the beneficiaries of a system of political patronage engineered by bosses Matt Quay and Boise Penrose. These powerful men persuaded each state legislature to appropriate public money for these private institutions, each institution of course having the "best people" on its board of directors. Dr. Russell Conwell, of Temple University and Samaritan Hospital, was a grateful recipient of such money, as were others. (This system has continued to the present day, marking a breakdown between public and private education).

Working within this system as professor, school-board member, and as president of the Swarthmore Home and School Association (the local version of the PTA), Jesse remained true in public education to those principles he thought should apply to First-day schools and Christian education in general. Indeed, here as always, there was an interpenetration of two elements too often thought of as separate: education and his variety of religion. He thought that each should penetrate the other to produce the final product — a Christian citizen who would "help to make the righteous State." In 1910 the National Education Association agreed with him up to a point: it declared "the function of education to be 'to make a child healthy, happy and righteous, and to develop character.' . . ." But, said Jesse, the trouble here was that Americans did not quite know what kind of character to develop. Instead of exalting "the Christ

369

type as the pattern of all character ...," American society, in schools and out, "taught as an ideal a kind of conglomerate ... of irreconcilable elements — a monstrosity:

> ... a keen, successful business-like Jesus, who can lovingly down his competitors in the warfare of competition; a money-winning Christ; a friend of sinners who is never seen in bad company; a happy and comfortable bearer of the sorrows of the poor: is not this something of the combination we hold up before our children?

(In the 1920s Bruce Barton, prominent New York advertising man, wrote a book entitled *The Man Nobody Knows*. The "man" was Jesus, and Barton in effect hailed him as a good Rotarian.)

To people like Jesse, the job before American educators was to resolve this conflict between God and Mammon: the tax-paying citizens should try to rise above their own inconsistencies and see to it that the schools taught adherence to "the larger loyalties — to mankind, to truth, to harmony and beauty. . . ." This was a moral obligation, and Jesse applauded his fellow pragmatist John Dewey when Dewey said that "One of the functions of education is to equip individuals to see the moral defects of existing social arrangements and to take an active concern in bettering conditions."

Indeed, Jesse's suggestions for the conduct of the schools were largely Deweyite in nature. Like Dewey he warned against the excessive use of books in the educative process; the tyranny of the printed page should be countered by creative work in the laboratory, art and music classes, and in the manual-training shops. Learning to do by doing was a big thing. More than this, through the use of tools and equipment the child learned "to *handle himself.*" And, since American draftees in World War I had shown so many "deplorable" physical defects, Jesse called on his fellow Quakers in March, 1919, to give letter-writing support to the Bigler Bill then before the Pennsylvania Assembly. This bill provided for the general physical training of all school children over eight years of age, including classroom instruction in personal and social hygiene.

All of these aspects of the school program were to be part of that broad, general education which Jesse thought to be so necessary for effective living in modern society. History, science, English, mathematics, and other subjects were to be taught by well-trained, imaginative, and sympathetic teachers. "Narrow and specialized education tends to make narrow and specialized people; and these are necessarily low-grade citizens of the world and nation." There could be, Jesse held, ". . . no more suicidal policy than that to reduce education to the merely vocational type, or to over-specialize it, . . ." And it was just as suicidal to set apart any special segment of society to enjoy special privileges in higher education, for this would tend to keep students from close association and understanding with all classes, races, and conditions of life. "For genius and noble leadership may and do appear anywhere in the world [in any social class], and their loss or suppression is the greatest of disasters. . . ."

This concern for a mixing of all classes of people, and for what they might and could teach each other, was at the heart of Jesse's interest in adult education, an interest he was developing as early as 1899. In the fall of that year, when he was just starting his Oxford term of preparation for the Swarthmore job, he went out of his way to visit the Westminster and Bun Hill adult schools in London. He found them rather religious in tone, although one evening class was enlightened on the growing of roses by a local expert. Later on, after Frank Aydelotte came to Swarthmore, Jesse must have been vastly encouraged by Aydelotte's account of how Lord Lothian of Scotland was helping the cause. When Aydelotte was a Rhodes Scholar he had heard how Lothian proposed to give over his ancestral estate, Newbattle Abbey, as a place for adult education and for the recreation of working people in connection with the University of Edinburgh. This was to be a place where scholars and teachers could have an inexpensive vacation, and where they could mingle with each other and with working people to their mutual enrichment. Here, surrounded by beautiful furniture and works of art, there would be opportunities for working people — those who were really able and eager to learn — to get instruction during vacation periods in history, art, music, and many other subjects. A somewhat similar plan was being followed by Coley Harlech in Wales.

Undoubtedly Jesse hoped that the same sort of benefits would come out of similar ventures in America. He helped to further the movement by teaching evening classes of workers in the Ardmore and Cheltenham adult schools after his retirement. And in 1939, he expressed his concern to Swarthmore Monthly Meeting that the South Media Adult Education School might have to close because the South Media community was having difficulty in raising the three dollars a week required for janitorial services. The Monthly

Meeting agreed to pay this bill for four weeks.

The Philadelphia area teachers recognized a friend and leader when they saw Jesse in action; so much so, in fact, that in 1934 he was elected president of Local 192, the Philadelphia branch of the American Federation of Teachers. Two years later, as president, he welcomed the delegates to the Twentieth Annual Convention of the Federation, telling them that the educational situation in America was "critical." Schools were adapting themselves too "slowly, [and] imperfectly" to changing conditions of life. "We must have teachers of intelligence, initiative and courage, teachers free from the handicap of narrow-minded and stodgy stand-patters, free from corrupt politicians, . . ." "Such teachers," he said, "must be united and loyal, and must be closely allied with the rest of our citizens, who, having the same prize to gain, are willing to dedicate their lives to the creation of [the] new world." So spoke the Deweyite and the idealistic laborite. Another Friend, Dr. Jerome Davis, of the Divinity School of Yale University, spoke on "The College Teacher's Place in the Union," and conducted a section meeting limited to college delegates. He also was elected as the new president.

In 1939 Jesse Holmes was rewarded for all his good work in trying to improve conditions for instructors in the Philadelphia area by being reelected honorary president of the local branch of the Federation.

Temperance.

The gods we worship write their names on our faces.

Anon.

And mead can do more than Milton can,
To show the ways of God to man.

John Donne

If these two quotations suggest something about two points of a temperance spectrum — the bloated, veined face of the habitual drunkard, and the alcoholic happiness of people at a wedding reception — they but reinforce the fact that ever since man learned about the fermentation of nature's fruits and grains he has wanted to indulge in the product. Since overindulgence often caused problems, various authorities had tried over the centuries to ban or regulate the manufacture, sale, and consumption of alcoholic beverages. If the authority was a church, banning the use of liquor on moral or religious grounds (e.g., Mormon, Moslem), there was a considerable measure of success; if the authority was a civil one (e.g., a king, a state legislature) the effort to ban or control almost invariably resulted in failure, raising more problems than it solved. The trouble was that such a control measure was a sumptuary law — a law regulating the personal habits of people.

As a Quaker endeavoring to give the right answers to the Hicksite Query on spirituous liquors, Jesse was always consistent. We have seen how he refused to eat or drink anything with "a stick" in it while he was at George School, and how he took time out on his honeymoon to deliver a temperance talk in a small New Jersey church. In 1910 he rose in Swarthmore Monthly Meeting to call attention to the fact that liquor was being sold at a club in the neighborhood. Since this was perfectly legal, Pennsylvania not yet having even a local option law, little could be done about it except investigate; the Philanthropic Committee was given this job. Five years later he was active in Swarthmore Monthly Meeting's effort to get the Pennsylvania legislature to pass such a local option law. In 1917, when, wartime conservation measures were being used as arguments for prohibition, one can see Jesse's hand in the minute passed by the Monthly Meeting, with directions that it be sent to the President of the United States, to cabinet members, and to Swarthmore's representatives in Congress and in Harrisburg: "To help a threatened crisis in the world's food supply we urge the immediate prohibition of the use of food materials for the manufacture of alcoholic drinks." In the meantime, until national prohibition could become a reality, there was a need to protect the draftees then learning the art of war at various places throughout the country. The Women's Meeting of Philadelphia Yearly Meeting [H] saw its duty: it appointed a committee to draw up a letter to be sent to Secretary of War Baker, asking him to ban saloons near mobilization camps.

After the Eighteenth Amendment was adopted (1920), and then implemented by the Volstead Act, people like Jesse seemed to have some cause for rejoicing. In rural and predominantly Protestant areas, where public opinion generally supported enforcement measures, there probably was less drinking and a decline in the liquor traffic. In fact, prohibition brought "a sharp decline" in the more "measurable results of drinking — arrests for drunkenness and deaths from alcoholism."

In the large cities, however, both the native-born and foreign-born soon protested that they had an inalienable right to drink; as time went on this attitude spread into the suburbs and country districts, where even the "best" people proudly served their guests with the liquors supplied by bootleggers and rumrunners. Now the genius of the Americans for social invention bore fruit: "speakeasies" replaced saloons, "cocktail" parties served "bathtub" gin, and the hip flask was flashed rather openly at football games. And now there was more drinking by women in speakeasies and cocktail parties alike — another sign of their "emancipation" after 1919.

An almost inevitable result of the "noble experiment" in prohibition was the development of gangsters and racketeers fattening on the desires of people to drink *something,* even if it was declared illegal by national statute. Bootleggers organized into underworld gangs fought law enforcement officers and each other; gangsters like Al Capone, in unholy alliance with crooked politicians, threatened the very existence of democratic government in America.

Jesse found that this was just as true in Delaware County as in other places. When he attended sessions of the county court in Media, then trying a political boss notorious for his connections with bootleggers, he found that no jury would convict him. After attending another such ineffectual trial, this time against the county's leading bootlegger, Jesse told his friend Eleanor Stabler Clarke, "with eyes blazing," that he had to get up and leave in the middle of the proceedings "for fear the judge would read his mind and have him for contempt of court! . . ."

By 1927 Al Capone grossed $60,000,000 a year from his assorted houses of prostitution, his gambling establishments, and his bootlegging. In the following year Jesse Holmes sat down to take stock of the temperance movement up to that time. In an article called "Prohibition" he claimed to have been "in the midst of the temperance agitation for over half a century. . . ." As a close student of the movement he recalled that in its "earliest beginnings" (before the Civil War) it centered on moral suasion — an appeal to the conscience of the drinker to curb his "dangerous appetite." Its methods, carried over into the postwar period, were those of the old-fashioned revival meeting. Jesse remembered a protracted series of such meetings in Clinton, Iowa:

> There was congregational singing led by a skilled performer, whose function was to arouse the audience to the highest possible

pitch of excitement: there was clapping of hands to the time of the music, there were shouts and groans, there was walking up and down the aisles with cries and waving of hands. Then presently appeared the speaker — a funny story or two brought ready laughter in a crowd gathered with intent to have excitement, a few personal experiences with the suffering of those under the curse of drink, incidents, — alas, too common, — of the cruelties of drunken brutes, taken from the papers or perhaps invented for the occasion, — all these things skillfully aimed at the emotions of the crowd, and then the appeal to sign the pledge of total abstinence. Impressionable children seized pledge cards and walked the aisles looking for inviting victims. . . . Pledge signers came to the platform to the accompaniment of shouts of encouragement, and experienced a delirium of publicity that many of them could acquire in no other way.

For a time this total abstinence movement, so mistakenly called the "temperance" movement, was a considerable success. But, as Jesse said, "its very success was an invitation to those whose business was threatened to get busy and drum up trade. . . ." The saloon was made more attractive, new advertising methods were used, and even the school was invaded to get new drinkers. And, since there was a lack of enough wholesome entertainment in the small towns and cities following the Civil War, the saloon became the "people's club," with all the attractions "of music and dancing, of light and noisy fellowship, of newness and adventure."

The increasing prosperity of saloons stimulated countermeasures by the "drys." Under the prodding of the WCTU, the Anti-Saloon League, and various churches, the states entered hesitantly into a long period of experimental legislature. But, as Jesse said, "It would be hard to think of any scheme that was not tried somewhere to make the liquor business safe for democracy. . . . Here the beverage must be taken home in unbroken packages; here you must drink standing; there you must be seated to drink. . . ." One state limited the number of saloons in proportion to the population, another would try to make them respectable by charging a very high license fee. They were required to be so many feet or yards from schools or churches; they had to close at stated times; they were not allowed to be open on Sundays, election days, or holidays. But saloons "never obeyed any law for more than a very short time. . . ," and they always seemed to link up with other forms of vice and crime.

As time went on the anti-saloon people went into politics to gain their ends. Gradually the major parties were induced to add tentative prohibitionist planks to their platforms, hoping to attract temperance people without losing the saloon vote. The Prohibitionist Party, although small and noisy at first, gained strength. Starting with Kansas, state after state prohibited the manufacture and sale of liquor and beer until, by 1919, this was the law in three-fifths of them and in three-fourths of the area of the country. Jesse thought that these facts refuted the arguments of the "wets" in 1928: "Could anything be more false or stupid than the claim that Prohibition was forced through in a hurry, that people hand't a chance to make up their minds, that a small majority imposed its habits on a large minority . . . ?"

And now, Jesse reflected in 1928, although the sober prohibitionists had won their point, "the old lawless business . . . [was] still a lawless business . . . perhaps more lawless than ever. . . ." But, he added, "A generation which was taught for four long years [in the period of World War I] that all the moral laws of civilization were [to be] set aside and that killing, lying and destruction were deeds of the highest nobility, is not likely to be a very law-abiding generation . . . ." Still, to repeal prohibition under present conditions would only be "a cowardly yielding to the criminal classes . . . . To violate it secretly because of a personal appetite is the act of a sneak, not a protest against the law. Such a protest can only be made by open violation and publicly taking the consequences . . . ." Jesse found it amazing that so many otherwise good citizens were lined up with the bootleggers. He thought that anyone who dealt with such criminals was also morally implicated in their crimes and was the "most dangerous kind of a traitor to his country. Flag waving, flying the eagle, and making a noise on the 4th of July cannot make him any less a traitor."

When the Congress and the states repealed the Eighteenth Amendment in 1933, taking less than a year to do it, Jesse and his Quaker friends must have felt betrayed. Still, they continued their testimony against the excessive use of alcohol within their own ranks as well as outside. Jesse wrote in his Philosophical Manuscript of the personal dangers and the social costs of alcoholic abuse; he also touched on education as the sovereign remedy for this problem. "Some day," he wrote, "an intelligent society will . . . put an end to it, training its children to recognize it for what it is, a dangerous personal vice and a selfish unsocial practice. . . ." And he lashed out at other forms of intemperance: "Your drug addict — all the way from tea and coffee topers to drunkards — is a handicap to social progress. . . ." He had the same opinion of tobacco users — they were "anxious to have even a single inhalation at the expense of filling a car or a room with odors, and many of them are permanent centers of disgusting smells. . . ." Still, he wasn't completely rigid in his opposition to these popular practices: if tobacco, alcohol, tea, and coffee detracted from personal and social welfare they should be eschewed or indulged in only as "trifling deviations" from the main sobriety.

The members of Jesse's Monthly Meeting agreed with him in most respects. In 1934, a subcommittee of the Overseers reported that the Monthly Meeting should continue the previously appointed Committee on Temperance. And the subcommittee — Abby Mary Hall Roberts, Elliott Richardson, and Roland G.E. Ullman — went on to suggest that the Meeting should direct an educational program against intemperance, but "without bias or ascetic ardor. . . ." The knowledge gained from such a program should, they thought, provide "a foundation upon which the youth of [the] Meeting can build their own set of standards."

Five years later the flat, temperate tone of the Swarthmore Monthly Meeting's Minutes pretty well concealed the sense of outrage Friends must have felt when the Schenley Corporation used the term "Quaker" for one of its whiskies. It was reported that Friends had met with the State Liquor Control Board in Harrisburg about this invasion of institutional rights, and that a hearing would be held on this subject in the near future. Additional protest from Swarthmore by way of a "minute" must have carried weight: the "Quaker" brand of Schenley whiskey disappeared from the market.

(As time went on, and the Holmes' children and grandchildren took their places in a world not so much concerned with the temperance question, Rebe too could be persuaded to try a cocktail. In the 1950s, while visiting her son Robert and his wife Grace in their Washington home, she was delighted when her grandson J. Herman IV and some of his friends dropped in for a social call. Also present was a Mr. Teegarden, an older gentleman and a connoisseur of many things. The conversation grew lively, but Rebe didn't contribute; her daughter-in-law Grace thought that she was assessing the guests and their interests before joining in. Finally she said: " 'I don't know much about cocktails but their names sound so silly to me. Now Robert once introduced me to a Thomas Collins, [but] I never tasted a mint julep, mention of which I come across so frequently in my reading.' " Rebe's remark broke up the party in the Holmes' apartment: now nothing would do but that the whole group must go immediately to Teegarden's apartment so that all could witness "the ritual involved in the making of a proper mint julep — the right mallet, the right canvas bag, the glasses so thoroughly chilled so that they had to be held with a linen napkin." Rebe exclaimed over hers as she sipped it daintily, but when she got up to leave, and on the way to the car, it was noticed that she was weaving perceptively. Grace became alarmed because Rebe was an old lady. They got her home and placed her on the porch, feet elevated and crackers and cheese at her elbow. Half an hour later, when dinner was ready, Grace went in to escort her. The food was untouched. She sprang to her feet and "literally marched" into the dining room. Grace was astounded; her nephew J. Herman, just chuckled. " 'Won't you ever learn, Aunt Grace," he said, "what a ham actor she is?' ")

17. Reform as Religion, Part II

While temperance and sobriety were always major strands in Jesse's tapestry of reforms, his concern for a wider justice shaped the design and color of the whole fabric. This wider justice meant, among other things, equality of constitutional rights for all people, Mankind was of one species, divided into recognizable subgroups called "races"; there was no essential or important difference between the average intelligence of these races attributable to their physical inheritance. In short, there was no such thing as genetic racial superiority; whatever differences existed between races were mainly due to education, varying cultures, and the standards used to measure them. If one person was superior to another in the performance of some act it was due to his individual make up or training, not to his race. So to deny equal rights to individuals (or to groups), simply because of their color, or shape of nose or kink of hair, was utterly wrong. "Race prejudice is not only one of the meanest of human emotions," wrote Jesse in his Philosophy Manuscript, "but is one of the stupidest as well, sure to be widespread and strongest in the lowest [least educated] grade of people. . . ." He invited the reader to look himself over and grade himself on this score.

Interracial Justice.

And Jesse practiced what he preached in this matter. While many people said that they believed in racial equality on the theoretical level, he invited Negroes, Chinese, Japanese and Russians to his home — "to dinner, to spend the night, not to prove any point, but because they were friends of his. . . ." A good teacher, he was eager

379

to learn from such people, and his contacts with them gave him greater insight into their problems and a greater determination to do what he could to have society accord them a more just consideration.

His role in much of this was mainly that of the inspirational speaker, urging in his many addresses the need for greater effort and more practical solutions by other people. Thus, while Philadelphia Friends, through their Whittier Center, were putting up low-cost houses for the colored people, and supporting the National League on Urban Conditions among Negroes in other ways, Jesse was making speeches, developing programs for conferences, or serving as chairman at conferences for racial equality. In October, 1924, he presided at the All-Day Conference on Interracial Justice held at the Social Service Building on Juniper Street, Philadelphia. In 1933 he took part in the Institute of Race Relations held at Swarthmore College under the direction of Clarence E. Pickett, secretary of the AFSC, and Charles S. Johnson of Fisk University. He spoke on "We and Our World," that oft-repeated lecture of his on world unity and racial justice, sharing the platform with such notables as Dr. Herskovitz, famous anthropologist, and Dr. E.B. Reuter, president of the American Sociological Society. And in 1938, as chief program designer for the yearly meetings of the Progressive Friends, Jesse invited Dr. Leslie Pinckney Hill, of the Cheyney Teachers College, to speak on the relationships between education and Negro labor.

By this time Rebe's niece, Margaret Price, was making quite a name for herself as in inspiring elementary-school teacher and as chairlady of Swarthmore Meeting's Interracial Committee. In the latter capacity she reported in 1939 of the progress being made at the Schofield School, Aiken, South Carolina, a school encouraged by Quakers for the benefit of Negroes. An auditorium was to be added, the Albert G. and Mary H. Thatcher Auditorium. One hundred dollars was quickly appropriated from Monthly Meeting funds, and other private contributions were solicited for this purpose. It was pointed out, however, that since the auditorium and the school were to serve as a community center, the people of Aiken County were also being taught — in "typical Friendly fashion" — to carry their own fair share of this educational load.

Miss Price also reported that Swarthmore's segregated school for Negro children in the lower grades would disappear by the end of that school year. A year later she was able to report that this had indeed been accomplished.

Jesse and Rebe probably heard and approved her report that evening; they were always interested in advancing social justice. A few years later, after Roosevelt and Churchill had met in Placentia Bay to proclaim the Atlantic Charter, Jesse continued the fight, this time in favor of Chinese sailors. Writing in his *Liberal Press* column, "A 'Retired' Philosopher Says . . . ," he asked whether America's allies were equal. He was referring to a recent incident in New York harbor, when the underpaid Chinese crew of a freighter long at sea were not allowed shore leave. The Chinese tried to leave anyway, only to be forcibly restained by American authorities who killed one and injured others. Jesse grew indignant at this treatment, pointing out that the Chinese were our allies now, and suggesting that if the sailors had been British there would have been no denial of shore leave on the basis of a presumed inferiority. In a succeeding column he called for some overt expression by Americans of our appreciation of China's contributions to the war effort against Japan; he thought "a bit of loyal fellowship" here in America would help to reassure Chinese that we were really on their side. And he lashed out at the panicky action of the government in uprooting American-born Japanese from their West Coast homes and transporting them to concentration camps in desert and mountain areas. This was an outstanding case of racial prejudice, prejudging their disloyalty before any disloyalty had been shown; it was still another case of condemning people for their ancestry — this in midst of a war for the survival of freedom, equality, fraternity!

Long years later, after the shooting war was over, Margaret Price continued her interest in fostering brotherhood through elementary education. In 1972, when she was 81 (according to a feature article in the Philadelphia *Evening Bulletin*), she was still carrying a "gay plaid suitcase" into classroom after classroom in Delaware and Chester counties, picking out 14 dolls and lining them up in front of her childish audiences. There were 7 "colored" and 7 white dolls, each 14 inches tall. Some of their papier-mache heads had been made in Germany 25 years before; their bodies, and the covering dresses or suits, had been made by members of Media Fellowship House. Each doll was a good likeness of some famous person, some humanitarian who had worked very hard to elevate the human condition. Miss Price would hold up each doll in turn and tell of the life of the person so represented.

First in line was Lao-tse, the Chinese philosopher "who preached many Christian principles 600 years before Christ. . . ." Founder of Taoism, he declared that war and the death penalty for crime were evil, urged people to return love for hatred, and taught that happiness would be found in simplicity. Next came Louis Braille, who, blinded as a boy, designed in 1829 the system of raised dots on paper which has ever since enabled the sightless to read through their fingers. Harriet Tubman, the first of three black women among the dolls, came next. Born a slave, she escaped to help others to freedom via the underground railway; after the Civil War she founded a home for destitute Negroes. Mary McLeod Bethune, as a teacher in South Carolina, sold homemade sweet-potato pies to railroad workers to raise money for a school. Although the school was so poor that her first eight girls had to write on old shingles with sharpened sticks dipped in elderberry juice, it grew into Bethune-Cookman College. Marian Anderson, composer of "My Lord, What a Morning," was the third black woman in the doll group. The first Negro to sing at the Metropolitan Opera, she carried her philosophy of song to kings, queens, presidents, and prime ministers. Ralph Bunche, the 1950 Nobel Prize winner, was born in Detroit, worked his way through college, and, after helping to write the United Nations Charter, went on to become an under-secretary of the United Nations in 1955. Father Damien, the Belgian-born priest who moved to the Hawaiian leper colony on Molokai Island in 1873 to try to improve the living conditions there, fell victim to the disease.

Continuing her talk, Miss Price pointed out that Charles Drew, creator of the first blood bank in 1940, and champion of better medical care for all Americans, suffered an automobile accident and bled to death before help could reach him. The next two dolls represented Jews. The first of these was Rebecca Gratz, who some thought had been the model for the heroine in Scott's *Ivanhoe,* and who raised her voice against the treatment of Jews in Russia; in Philadelphia she founded the Hebrew Sunday School. Emma Lazarus was a New Yorker who wrote the words enscribed on the base of the Statue of Liberty: "Give me your tired, your poor . . ." And then there was Harry O. Tanner, of Pittsburgh, whose paintings of Biblical stories led to his election to the French Legion of

Honor; he had been disqualified for an art scholarship in Paris by the Philadelphia Academy of the Fine Arts because he was a Negro. He got to Paris anyway; he sold the paintings he had produced as a student so that he could pay his passage money. George Washington Carver, born a slave, went on to become a teacher, a naturalist and a chemist. By discovering how to produce more than two hundred useful products from peanuts and sweet potatoes he probably was more beneficial to the South than scores of its politicians. Mahatma Gandhi, famous for his nonviolent resistance to British rule, was "not a very beautiful child. . . ." But, Miss Price told the pupils, "he discovered [that] truth is the most beautiful thing in the world — he saw the face of God in every living thing, . . ." The last of the dolls represented Albert Schweitzer. This towering genius gave up his renowned career as an organist, composer, and religious philosopher to become a doctor, carrying modern medicine to the jungles of equtorial Africa. He was active in his hospital there until his death at the age of 90.

At the close of one of her programs — the one at the Rose Tree Elementary School — she told her fifth-grade audience that the Media Fellowship House was preparing other dolls to portray John and Robert Kennedy and Martin Luther King, Jr. She asked the class who else they thought worthy of being added to the doll collection. The suggestions ranged from Helen Keller, Jane Addams, and Booker T. Washington, down to Babe Ruth and Spiro Agnew. And then one pupil sang out — "My mother!"

Toward Social Justice.

> Civilization implies balance. How can we be civilized with this obvious lack of balance — the very poor, the unemployed, the rich and those sated with security?
>
> Leopold Stokowski.

According to Stokowski's standard the United States was by no means civilized in the days of William McKinley and "Teddy" Roosevelt. In fact, conditions were so bad that, as part of a larger series of progressive reform movements marking the period 1900-1916, a social justice movement got started to try to make the country a bit more civilized. "Social justice" meant that the tenement dwellers in the teeming cities should have cleaner, safer housing; it meant that the savage exploitation of women and children in factories, coal mines and cotton mills should cease; and it meant a general uplift for all workers, particularly in providing through state and federal laws a public system of industrial accident insurance.

Accomplishments along these lines were largely palliative: slum clearance, child-labor laws, eight-hour laws for women, minimum-wage laws for women, and those industrial accident insurance systems established in twenty states, three territories and the national government by 1916. The War against the Kaiser slowed the movement, and little was done during the Harding-Coolidge-Hoover time of Boom-and-Bust. Still, enough was done to lay the groundwork for the social justice movement people were to call the New Deal.

There were, of course, reformers who were not content with such halting steps toward social justice. Jesse Holmes knew that countries in Western Europe had gone beyond the United States in welfare measures; before the New Deal got started he said that America too should implement public schemes to insure workers against unemployment, sickness and old age. And his compatriot, John Haynes Holmes (no relation to Jesse), went even further in a speech entitled "From Absolute Monarchy to Pure Democracy in Industry." Speaking to the Progressive Friends in 1915, Holmes said that the political monarchs of Europe compared favorably with the industrial monarchs of the United States. The "Rockefeller organization of Colorado was as much an absolute monarchy in industry" as the Czar's regime or the Kaiser's. All of these were benevolent despots in one way or another. As further examples he cited the Ford empire centered at Detroit, and the National Cash Register Company in Ohio, each controlled by one man. He said that each of these monarchies made "as high as 1000 per cent per year off the labor of thousands of employees. . . ." But look, he said, at the Dennison Manufacturing Company of Framingham, Massachusetts. "Here we have an example of pure democracy in industry. The present head of the concern had turned control of the business over to the employees with the stipulation that they pay him a salary so long as they want him for manager, and that 8 per cent be paid on the preferred stock before any general distribution of the profits takes place. . . ." In short, the business belonged to the employees and they could run it with their own board of directors.

Jesse agreed with all this — and more. He was convinced that democracy was indivisible: that political democracy could not long continue if economic and social democracy were denied. "Our acquisitive society must be born again or is inevitably headed for conflict, followed by some despotism of oligarchy or dictator." This rebirth of democratic values would of course take place only if the working people — "four-fifths of our population" — were able to band together into unions to plan for an increasingly socialized state; only in this way could a working man become independent of economic dictators; only in this way could the working people break out of the ridiculous situation capitalism had produced by the 1930s, when hungry, jobless men watched wheat being burned and milk poured away so that prices for farmers might be kept high.

In the face of all this, Jesse thought, people were confused and were grabbing the package of problems by the wrong handle. "We Don't Want Work!," he wrote in an article in the *Friends Intelligencer* in 1931. "What we really want is things: food, clothing, houses, play, friendship, theatres, music, pictures, travel; and we work to get them. We desire to get what we need with the least possible work. . . ." And, since capitalism failed the common people here, "are we not intelligent enough [via socialism] to change a system which is ruinous to 'life, liberty and the pursuit of happiness'!"

But this new system, to be brought into being through labor unions and socialism, would stress moderation; it would not fall into capitalism's trap of excessive gadgetry and luxury. In 1931 Jesse told the Woman's Club of Swarthmore that "luxury becomes evil when it possesses us, . . ." He recalled that onetime when he was waiting for a young lady on whom he was calling, he counted thirty-nine "jimcracks" in the room, not counting clocks or the usual equipment of a living room. ". . . she had to play valet to all those dustable articles." But, freed from the tyranny of wanting too many material things, or not having enough for a decent livelihood, men and women [under socialism] would have the time and energy " 'to create beauty, grace, skill and power . . . , to be friends and enemies, lovers and haters, co-operators and competitors. A Utopia? Of course! Any improvement is a Utopia until we get to work on it." And further: "We'll never have a decent civilization until [we recognize] that only the people and their welfare are the real values." (Had Jesse been alive in 1973 he would have undoubtedly hailed the new economic indicator proposed by a Japanese economist as a step in the right direction. Called the "net national welfare" (NNW), it would deduct from the customary gross national product (GNP) the social costs of doing business — such items as auto accidents, traffic congestion, pollution, and run-down public facilities — so that Japan would have a better picture of whether its economy was improving the quality of Japanese life. The NNW was to go into action soon; in the United States such economic concepts were still germinating in economists' minds and had not yet entered the public forum for serious political debate.)

It was in this spirit of concern for the quality of American life that Jesse entered the labor-capital arena. In 1932 he called American civilization one still too much afflicted by "Baby Killers" — gangsters mowing down innocent children as they fled from the police in crowded cities, and employers still too little concerned with the effects of factory life on juvenile workers. In January, 1921 he had been concerned about conditions in the steel industry, when labor unions and owners were squaring off for a new conflict. He found these conditions "evil and oppressive," a situation in which "the lives and happiness of men evidently count as nothing when in competition with profits. . . ." Half the men in the steel industry worked twelve hours a day, and many of these had a seven-day week. The upper third of these, the skilled workmen, got "fair wages"; the second third got less than "a standard income" for a family of five; the lower third did not even get comfort. Men were "discharged wholesale" for joining unions, an "army of spies" kept secret watch on the doings of employees, race conflicts were encouraged, and "free speech was everywhere suppressed." Jesse wondered how the churches could stand idly by while standards of social morality and Christian brotherhood were so flagrantly violated.

Considering the ethnic diversity of the American industrial labor force, recruited from many countries where public schools were rare or nonexistent, cooperative education seemed to be the sovereign remedy for social unrest and labor's troubles. To the Polity Club, functioning on Swarthmore's campus in the early 1920s, cooperative education meant that labor leaders would come to a series of conferences on or near the campus to instruct college students on industrial problems, while at the same time getting college help for their adult classes in labor education. This help, it was hoped, would come through the training of students to serve as labor's teachers; there was talk of securing scholarships for such students so that they might train still more effectively for careers in the labor movement. And students were urged to take summer jobs in industry, wearing aprons or overalls, so that they might get a practical insight into conditions behind factory walls.

This Polity Club, under the leadership of Jesse, and with Dr. and Mrs. Harold C. Goddard serving as genial host and hostess, held its third conference at the Woolman School, April 6-8, 1923. Gathered around the conference tables were a veritable potpourri of humanity: "... alert, intelligent Russian Jews from the garment trades, lace operatives with a background of wholesome Scotch country life..., Americans and Englishmen who had woven the patterns of fine upholstery for many years, ..." There were also organizers from the American Federation of Labor, "who had swabbed the deck and polished brass on all the seven seas...." Sitting with them were students from Bryn Mawr, Haverford, Ursinus and Swarthmore, all eager to find out what these labor people thought. As discussions went on it became apparent that there was a strong opinion that education was a tool through which the labor movement might improve conditions and achieve more power.

The messages of the featured speakers were a bit more idealistic. Although John Phillips, of the Typographical Union, described the intensive education forced on printers by the need to defend their standards, Spencer Miller, of the New York Workers' Education Bureau, believed that the fundamental idea of workers' education was to give them a perspective of civilization in terms they could understand. And Walter Polakov, consulting engineer for the New York, New Haven and Hartford Railroad, thought that only rigorous thinking and the cooperation of labor, capital, management and the public would bring about utopia. (The author is reminded of the time he taught economics in high school, when the idealistic textbooks he used analyzed land, labor, capital, management and the people's government as the *partners* of production, with scarcely a hint as to the savage infighting taking place among and between the "partners.")

Before this conference ended resolutions were passed calling for permanent cooperation between the college personnel and the labor groups. Two conferences a year were planned to keep students and workers in touch with each other. In addition, a labor bureau was to be formed on Swarthmore's campus to sift information from the labor journals, and to serve as a clearhouse for such information by means of an economic newsletter to labor groups and other colleges. The bureau would also sponsor crossvisits between union meetings and the Polity Club, as well as arrange trips to industrial plants. Altogether, through the drive and enthusiasm of such students as Gertrude Knapp, Sara Bitler, Richmond Miller and Thomas Philips, the Polity Club was a successful venture in a special field of education. With the help and encouragement of Jesse, Harold Goddard, and several other faculty members, the Club was still functioning in 1925. And, perhaps inevitably, Norman Thomas, of the League for Industrial Peace, was the featured speaker at this last meeting.

Jesse's work with the Polity Club was but a continuation of his interest in labor education. Starting about 1916 he taught for many years in Philadelphia's "Labor College," holding evening classes in labor law and current events. By 1933 this college was called the Labor Institute School. Located on Locust Street, it opened its doors on Monday nights for a ten-weeks course on "Social Attitudes" to be given by Jesse. His lecture topics included "The Individual and Society," "The Basis of Human Behavior," "Primary School Attitudes," "Collective Behavior," and and "The Nature of Social Inertia." The admission fee was two dollars for the entire course; single tickets cost twenty-five cents.

In the week's interval between two of these Monday-night sessions he joined a group of lecturers making a tour of more than forty towns for the League for Industrial Democracy. Albany, Schenectady, Syracuse, Niagara Falls and Buffalo were on Jesse's schedule; in each of these cities he was to lecture on the general theme of "America and the Machine Age," involving such specific topics as "The American Scene, 1932," and "America in an International World." By 1936 he was 72 years old, but this didn't stop him from planning still another tour for the League, this time invading other areas in February for two weeks of lectures on "The White-Collar Worker Enters the Labor Movement." He was to speak in Louisville, Memphis, Chattanooga, Knoxville, Nashville, New Orleans, Houston, Austin, Dallas, Tulsa and Kansas City.

When Jesse returned from such a tour to initiate still another course of lectures at the Labor Institute, as he did from time to time, his friends in Philadelphia must have congratulated themselves on his presence. Here, they must have said, we have another Norman Thomas, another intellectual warrior in the fight for equality in the realization of those rights — economics, social, political, civil — which are at the heart of the American experiment. With such help social justice is bound to come.

A Political Moralist.

When social justice was narrowly defined to include only the efforts to alleviate living and working conditions for tenement dwellers, children and women, such reformers as Jesse objected most vehemently. To them it meant political justice too — a system of government in a democracy in which voters could make their votes count without fear of retribution if they voted against ruling powers; it meant that minorities had the right to be heard and to persuade people to become majorities; it meant freedom under law. And it meant also that every voter had a precious power in his hand, a power to be wisely and justly used if effectual self-government was ever to become more than a vague dream. More, it meant that everyone had the right and responsibility to run for public office under the sovereignty of the people. The people elevated their representatives to perform certain duties, and when their service had been completed they should then return to the ranks of the people and help to elevate others.

This democratic system, of course, could not succeed unless the people in general had a sense of the old Roman *civitas:* a "spontaneous willingness to obey the law, to respect the rights of others, to forego the temptations of private enrichment at the expense of the public weal — in short, to honor the 'city' of which one is a member."

Jesse believed all this, and other things too. For him political issues were essentially moral issues; and this morality extended far beyond the periodic chant to "Throw the rascals out!" His belief dictated that righteous citizens should publicly stand up and cry "Shame!" when their trust had been violated. This he did when he rose in Friends' meeting to denounce a Swarthmore graduate, then a state senator, who had been indicted for violation of the prohibition law. In 1928 his belief led him to proclaim that the Declaration of Independence, with its ringing assertion that all men had a natural right to compete under equal opportunity for life, liberty, and the pursuit of happiness, was on a par with the law of Moses and the Sermon on the Mount. Once again he asserted that these were the essential conditions for a great Christian family; once again he trumpeted that the "vision of Democracy is in part at least, the vision of the 'kingdom come on earth.'" And the same thought was expressed two years before, with the addition that political institutions, activated by moral, upright men, would be the means to bring all this to pass.

Jesse's essential attitude toward politics was expressed much earlier. In October, 1905, when William H. Berry had offered himself as the "Lincoln" Party's candidate for Pennsylvania state treasurer over the opposition of Republican Party bosses, Jesse felt it to be his obligation to express his thoughts and feelings in *The Swarthmorean:*

The Present Crisis

For many years Pennsylvania has been sinking deeper and deeper into the mire of partisan politics. It has seemed for a long time that her people care only for party victories and not at all for good government. We have endured the misuse of public funds for private gain, the passing of laws which could not have been passed unless purchased by the beneficiaries, the violation by legislators of their plain duty under the constitution, the shameful subservience of public officers to unworthy party leaders, and the betrayal of the public trust on the part of the people's representatives in almost every branch of public service.

The low tone of our citizenship has been displayed not so much by the character of our so-called bosses as by the apathy of the people. That offenses have come is not so disheartening as that the people did not care about them. We have not been shocked when thousands of our children have been left without proper school opportunities, when other thousands have been forced into premature labors which must stunt their bodies and minds alike, when hundreds of young girls have been sold into lives of vice and kept in such lives as actual slaves. We have not been aroused when dishonest dealing with our water supply has slain many thousands and general neglect of sanitation its thousands more.

The coming election is a testing time; not of the "organization," but of our citizenship. The "machine" has already been tried and found wanting. Its farce of reform 'within,' under the leadership of those who have degraded it, would be laughable if it had not so serious a side. But our patriotism claims the privilege of being tested once more, and the claim is allowed. The Lincoln Party offers a list of candidates whose loyalty to righteousness cannot be doubted. In many instances they are tried men who have sacrificed much for the cause of better government. They are conducting an honest campaign. They have avoided the snare of "fighting the devil with fire," knowing that the devil is more accustomed to the weapon and can use it better. They have chosen honesty as their weapon and they deserve our support. If we do not give it, it is we, not they, who have failed.

From this point on Jesse's political interests and affiliations showed a steady inclination toward those candidates and those parties which were termed "liberal" or even "radical." In October, 1912, he spoke in favor of Woodrow Wilson at political meetings held in Lansdowne, Media, Chester, Parkesburg and West Chester. Undoubtedly Jesse saw in Wilson that same streak of idealistic moralism which he himself had in such abundance. He also saw it in Robert LaFollette, who ran for President in 1924 under the Progressive Party's banner. Indeed, at this point Jesse was a Progressive, chairing a meeting of the Party at the Machinists' Temple in Philadelphia, and introducing Mrs. Robert LaFollette as the first wife of a Presidential candidate to stump for her husband. A week later he joined his friend Robert C. Brooks, professor of political science, in analyzing the "third party as a prophecy and a challenge" at the fourth industrial conference held by the Polity Club at the Woolman School. Another man, Tobert E. Lamberton, had been scheduled to represent the Republican Party's views, but was unable to be present. Even if he had been present, his forthright opponents would still have said what they did: Brooks, that the Republicans evaded the League of Nations and had granted only three of labor's fifteen demands; Holmes, that the Republicans had no constructive policy, being a wealthy class-party opposed to popular government, or, as they put it, "mob rule." Brooks believed in the Democratic Party's principles, although he thought that, since Democrats and Progressives were so much alike in their liberalism, they ought to coalesce into one party. " 'Liberals of the U.S. unite,' " he cried. " 'You have nothing to lose but the Republican Party, and you have a nation to gain.' " Holmes was not quite of the same persuasion, since a union of the two parties would have brought the windy, vacuous Bryan wing of the Democrats into the fold. Rather, he favored LaFollette for his "courageous experimental attitude," and believed that the Progressives' stand on the abolition of war would get enough support to make them a viable third party.

A few years later Jesse's language became more indignantly radical. In 1928, after the Harding scandals and the machine-dominated period of "Silent Cal" (not to speak of Democratic "bossism" in Jersey City and Boston), he wrote that "We are confronted with two utterly filthy political parties, largely officered by semicriminals, and with recent records that revolt the spirits of any decent citizen. . . ." He believed that people had taken their citizenship too lightly, demanding no more of officials "than that they avoid giving us too much trouble in the way of effort or taxes. . . ." The nation was not finished, he said; "shall we stand aside and see it ruined by triflers, self-seekers, — yes, and even by thieves and assassins?"

Given Jesse's disgust with the two-party system as it was functioning in the United States by 1928, it was entirely logical that he should become a leader of the League for Independent Political Action. In 1930 he and Rebe, in company with Paul Douglas, went to Washington, D.C., to attend the first annual dinner of the League. We don't know what was done or said at this banquet; we do know that this journey was a sign that he was edging toward that third party — the Socialist Party — which he believed held the greatest promise for the realization of the American Dream.

But such high-level activity, however important to the nation as a whole, could not cancel out Jesse's conviction that democracy begins at home — in the grass roots of one's own community. And in the early 1930s local democracy was threatened by the Republican machine in Delaware County, most notably through its control by State Senator John J. McClure and Representative Turner. It seemed to the Delaware County League of Women Voters that this situation, as well as other issues before the people in October, 1932, should be aired at what was called a "three-party rally." The rally was held at the Swarthmore Woman's Clubhouse before a large audience. The Democrats were represented by Robert C. Kitchen, a Philadelphia lawyer; the Republicans by Franklin S. Edmonds; and the Socialists by Jesse Holmes.

When the speakers got into their messages it was noted that, while Jesse found many Socialist sympathizers in the audience, the greatest amount of applause followed Edmonds' references to Hoover's program for depression relief. And then Edmonds, implicitly recognizing the moral turpitude of Senator McClure and Representative Turner, attacked Jesse by referring to the student careers of both politicians. He said that both he and Jesse had taught them at Swarthmore College. "I taught them law and I'm satisfied with the results. Dr. Holmes taught them ethics." When Jesse rose to offer his rebuttal to this remark he somehow couldn't find the right reply. He carried this forensic defeat to bed with him that night, rolled and tossed, and then, about midnight called to Rebe. "I've got it!" he cried. "I flunked John McClure in ethics." (But note the corrective applied to this rather wonderful story by Peter E. Told, former student of Jesse's and publisher of *The Swarthmorean:* "McClure never took any courses with either Edmonds or Holmes.")

A year later the scene of political involvement had moved even closer to home. Swarthmore Borough itself was in the grip of the McClure machine, making the control of local events a travesty of democracy. Now a group of college leaders under the chairmanship of Charles G. Thatcher, professor of engineering, organized "The Committee of Fifty" to take Swarthmore's government out of the hands of the Republican forces. The Committee called for a mass meeting in the high school auditorium on a Saturday night, the meeting to be chaired by Frank Aydelotte. The "Town Meeting Party" was formed; and in November of 1933, it was pleased to see many of its politically "clean" candidates elected to local office. Jesse and Rebe Holmes, it should be added, played no small part in this local revolution: they were both active as vice-chairmen of the Committee in the campaign.

An Active Socialist.

Indeed, Jesse's friends welcomed his activities in behalf of the Town Meeting Party; his reputation as a Socratic gadfly to the body politic in Pennsylvania enhanced their cause since they all knew that when he stang people into political thought with his socialist barbs he was thinking only of the public welfare and not of his own profit.

His avowed socialism had been slowed to develop. When Margaret Byrd knew him on the Swarthmore campus in the early 'twenties he was only beginning to develop that high impatience with the two major political parties which eventually caused him to join the Socialist Party. And, given his occasional adverse reception by conservatives when he spoke at Quaker functions, he was sometimes reluctant to offend his fellow seekers after truth by reference to the principles of Norman Thomas. As he wrote in a letter to an acquaintance as late as 1933, "I'm for a Socialist Society — but couldn't present that at the Friends' Meeting, I suppose."

And yet, given the definition of socialism provided by Jesse's friend, Darlington Hoopes of Reading, Pennsylvania, Jesse could scarcely avoid weaving socialist principles into almost every speech he made or every article he wrote. Hoopes said that socialism meant "the collective ownership and the *democratic management* of the socially necessary means of production, transportation and communication." Since a genuine, all-out democracy, guided by Christian values, was at the heart of Jesse's message, he could no more resist making his speeches or articles sound socialistic than he could resist breathing. If, as John W. Nason "always suspected," he had "a limited understanding of the economic and political issues involved in his socialism...," he could still take "an impish delight" in pricking stuffed shirts; he could still cry out in moral indignation for changes in the American system.

In the incubative period of his socialism Jesse probably read with great approval of the series of lectures given by Norman Thomas at Earlham College, Richmond, Indiana, in the summer of 1919. This course of lectures was heard by the General Young Friends' Conference; and it must have warmed Jesse's heart to read the student reporter's estimate of its worth: "It is an impossibility to give the spirit of the course... by Norman Thomas without knowing, working and playing with the man...." To know this spirit was a privilege reserved for those attending the Conference. Aside from the "spirit," the course had "real depth" in social meaning. (If some older Quakers were insensitive to the modern world revolution for a thoroughgoing democracy, not so the young Friends.)

By 1922 Jesse's interest in socialism was heating up to the point where he somehow arranged to have lunch with Alexander Kerensky, then a refugee from the more radical Bolshevik regime in

Moscow. Jesse invited his nephew Kenneth H. Dryden to this lunch at New York's Astor Hotel. Dryden was then a student at the Columbia Law School; he remembered that the conversation was "extremely interesting," centering on the development of socialistic ideas in Russia. A short time later Jesse arranged a Kerensky tour of the United States, accompanying him as he tried to speak in city after city. In one city they were kept out of a public hall where Kerensky was to speak; there were pickets and the hall was closed to them. The two socialists sat on a curb outside of the hall, and finally police picked them up and took Kerensky to his hotel for safe keeping. In 1927, Rebe was drawn into the act: in mid-April she wrote in her diary that she went to Philadelphia for a dress fitting and then attended a dinner at the City Club for Kerensky. That evening he went to Swarthmore with the Holmeses, stayed the night, and had breakfast with them the following morning. He spoke in Collection a few hours later, undoubtedly being invited to do so through Jesse's good offices.

And now the election year of 1928 was upon them. Swarthmore people, faculty and students alike, became politically active. "A small but enthusiastic" group of students (helped along by Jesse, we may be sure), met in October to organize the Socialist Club, electing Mary Roberts, '29, as their president, with two other girls chosen to serve as secretary and publicity manager. Similar student clubs had been formed by campus Republicans and Democrats, but the Socialist Club was to be the only campus organization able to present a candidate for the presidency as a speaker for one of its rallies. Norman Thomas was to be the headline attraction at a meeting in Collection Hall on October 16. A week later Thomas was scheduled to give a radio talk over Station WFI in Philadelphia, but due to his inability to be in two places at the same time he asked Brand Blanshard to speak for him. Brand was glad to do this service for his friend, telling his radio audience that, since the two major parties had practically identical points of view, America's voters really had only two choices — that between the Republican-Democratic stance and the Socialist position. And that position, he said, was virtually the same as that of the British Labor Party, endorsing a conservative socialism. (Three years earlier Brand Blanshard's brother Paul, then secretary of the League for International Democracy, had addressed Swarthmore's College Forum on conditions in Japan and China.)

The campaign of 1928 went on apace on Swarthmore's campus, culminating in a triangular debate in Collection Hall on November 1. Professor Brooks was to present the Democratic side; Professor Herbert Fraser would speak for Republicans; and Jesse Holmes, hailed as a "prominent Socialist worker," would give his party's views. Dean Raymond Walters would serve as chairman of debate, while Joseph Calhoun, '29, would conduct the meeting as president of the College Forum. After the speeches the meeting was to be open for general discussion, with any member of the audiences being limited to five minutes.

On the following day *The Phoenix* was to take a straw vote of faculty and students. Student leaders were confident of victory, each for his own side. Joseph Calhoun, of the Republican Club, predicted that, in spite of the favorable impression made by Norman Thomas in his recent appearance on campus, his party would get 300 out of the 500 votes expected to be cast. Meyer Cohen, of the Democratic Club, said that "Nothing less than a landslide will satisfy us. On the basis of 550 votes we predict a 400-100-50 division.

We don't know exactly what the straw-vote results were on Swarthmore's campus. We suspect, however, that they followed rather closely the pattern of results in Pennsylvania for the presidential candidates:

Hoover and Curtis — 2,055,382
Smith and Robinson — 1,067,586
Thomas and Maurer — 18,647

Perhaps Thomas and Maurer got a few more votes, considering the nature of the Swarthmore student body and the influence of resident Socialists like Holmes and Blanshard.

The poor showing of the Socialists in the election of 1928 did not discourage Jesse, nor did it dissuade him from continuing his activities in their behalf. What was needed, quite obviously, was a greater public education in Socialist principles and modes of action. So, when the American Friends' Service Committee and the YWCA's Ethical Society sponsored a "radical tour" in Philadelphia in January, 1929, he grasped this opportunity to promote greater understanding. The tour plan was to have speakers visit in turn the headquarters of the Anarchists, Communists, Socialists, and the International Workers of the World. At each headquarters the speakers would not attempt to convert anyone to a particular brand of radicalism, not to dissuade anyone from it, but "to erase some of the ignorance of the people regarding these newer movements. . . ." Jesse was to speak on " 'How Socialists will change politics, economics, commerce, industry and marketing.' "

This radical tour, plus all of his other activities, helped to establish Jesse as a leader in Pennsylvania and Philadelphia Socialist circles. After the election of 1928, he joined a group of instructors from the University of Pennsylvania in reviving the Party. Andrew J. Biemiller and his wife Hannah were in this group — indeed, Jesse knew Hannah as a member of the Morris family of Philadelphia Quakers. Casting about for more talent for this revitalization process, in 1930 they invited Franz Daniel of New York to come to Philadelphia as a Party organizer. Daniel had been a student at Union Theological Seminary, and in 1929, had helped in the campaign to elect Norman Thomas mayor of New York City. During this campaign Daniel organized the Morningside Heights branch of the Party which had, as he remarked, "a very distinguished membership. . . ." He was also active in the League for Industrial Democracy, doing a good deal of speaking for the League in the colleges along the eastern seaboard.

As Daniel said later, "Those were exciting years and all of us were very young and dedicated. We were sure of what we were doing — that we were building a new world, we thought we were living history. . . . Jesse Holmes remains a bright and distinct light in the memory of my youth."

Jesse, of course, was an exception to this youthful membership; he was then in his middle sixties. But, Daniel recalled, when Jesse sat in the councils of the Party — those "deadly serious committee meetings, . . . interminal in length" — his presence made it "a pleasure to attend them. . . ." He added wit and humor, "and he struggled to understand the heat that sometimes the debates would engender. . . ." Much of the factionalism weakening Socialism in Europe had been transmitted to America; native-born Americans developed their own factions as well. Indeed, "There was always a sense of unreality about building a Socialist party in the United States. We were laden with terminology and definitions, [and with] orthodox interpretations that were essentially unreal in our native setting. I can think now and feel how frustrated Norman must have been. . . ." But, in the midst of such "heated debates about orthodoxy" it was a relief to see Jesse Holmes sitting there — "it kept alive my faith that a native Socialist party could be established. . . ."

Indeed, in spite of such internecine bickering, conditions were favorable for the growth of socialism. The capitalistic system had collapsed; a third party offering a reasonable, nonviolent way out of economic misery stood a good chance of gaining many new members. In Philadelphia this happened, the Socialist Party growing upon the solid base of the Jewish union members in the needle trades, and on the Scotch, English and Irish workers in the textile mills in the city's northeastern section. At that time 75 per cent of the nation's full-fashioned hosiery was made in Philadelphia and, as Daniel said, "the Hosiery Workers was a fine union. . . ." In addition, as the Party grew, it attracted Jewish intellectuals, professional men and women, and idealists from the colleges and universities.

These idealists had not yet reached the conclusion developed later on by Scott Nearing — "that radical political ideas had not more chance of survival in the United States of that period than the proverbial snowball in hell. . . ." But Nearing admitted that radical or liberal party candidates could "occupy a tiny corner of the public platform as Election Day approached." So, realizing the difficulties of the job before them, and yet buoyed up by the hope that more people might be persuaded to vote Socialist, the Party decided to field some candidates for public office in the general state election of 1930. Jesse was made chairman of the election committee; he was proud to announce that while there would "not be a complete list of Socialist candidates for all of the offices, the ticket [would] be one of the largest ever backed by the party."

The results were inconsiderable, of course. But the struggle for recognition continued: Franz Daniel and others were more active than ever in the spreading of Party doctrine; and in October, 1931, Jesse spoke on "Socialism vs. Anarchy" before the Race Street Forum in Philadelphia. And, if Jesse sometimes gave the drive for a socialized society the flavor of a moral and religious crusade, he was helped along most powerfully by the *Friends Intelligencer* and the Federal Council of the Churches of Christ in America. A month or so before Jesse spoke at Race Street, on the eve of Labor Day, the *Intelligencer* carried a "Labor Sunday Message, 1931" prepared by the Council's Commission on the Church and Social Service. Asserting that economic security was "a demand of brotherhood," it bemoaned the millions of unemployed then in America, not merely "the inefficients," but chiefly "the manual and clerical workers upon whose competent labor we have all depended for the necessities of life. . . ." "Such conditions," the article went on, "have constituted a serious indictment of our economic organization both as to its efficiency and its moral character." This economic system had gone through some twenty economic dislocations since 1855, eight of which could be classed as major depressions. Two significant questions were raised: Was the country to continue indefinitely to drift into such situations through lack of adequate social planning? Was it true, as many economists believed, that a major reason for such depressions lay in the grossly unequal distribution of wealth and income — a situation in which the wages of the workers were not able to exert enough effective economic demand for all the products of industry? All this, it was held, was "peculiarly a problem of brotherhood" calling for action by those who believed in Christianity. This Federal Council statement, originally designed to be read from pulpits on Labor Sunday, "was one of the most sweeping indictments of American capitalism ever drawn by a middleclass group. . . ." And the bishops of the Protestant Episcopal Church, long defenders of the Establishment, now seconded this indictment in "a pastoral letter demanding that employers abandon the profit motive for the ideal of service to mankind."

By 1932 Jesse was so involved in the Socialist movement that one wonders how he was able to continue to meet his philosophy classes at Swarthmore. In January of that year he travelled around for the League for Industrial Democracy, giving speeches in Lynchburg, Virginia, in Richmond, in Philadelphia and Lancaster. A short time later, no doubt responding to the urging of his colleagues in the movement, he decided to run for Congress on the Socialist ticket.

His campaign was a mixture of public appearances before potential supporters of his position and organizational and ideological conferences in his own home. In the summer of 1932 he opened his house on Elm Avenue to a series of these meetings, all of them being concerned with the analyses of various current proposals to preserve capitalism and the socialist responses to them. Early in August the third of this series was addressed by Dr. Walter H. Seely on the subject of "Building a Party." The Socialist Party was the one to be built; but it could be built only on the knowledge of what the capitalists had to offer in such proposals for economic recovery as the Swope Plan — a suggestion by Gerard Swope, president of General Electric, that industrial leaders cooperate in increasing production and protect workers against poverty and unemployment. Swope's warning that the people, through their government, would surely rise to protect themselves if industry did not act wisely was repeated by Owen D. Young, banker-industrialist, and by the president of the United States Chamber of Commerce.

Although two more of these political meetings were to disturb Rebe's domestic peace at 602 Elm Avenue — one led by Dr. William Blaisdell, instructor of business administration at Temple University, and the other devoted to a discussion of taxes — Jesse spent much of his time during the fall of 1932 spreading the doctrine of socialism in distant places. On September 7 he addressed "a live and interested group" at Knauertown in Chester County, Pennsylvania, in competition with other speakers from the Republican and Democratic parties. This pattern of triangular debate also marked his appearances at Johns Hopkins University on October 30, and at Bryn Mawr on November 2. At Johns Hopkins he discussed the tariff, unemployment, and international relations. And, considering his appearances in such widely separated places, it became apparent to his friends that he was less interested in becoming the Congressman from Delaware County than in getting the Socialist views of national issues before the general public.

And he lost the election, of course. However, defeat seemed to be but another spur in his incessant round of activities. He and some other activists started a Citizens' Forum early in 1933 — a series of Monday-evening lectures and discussions held in Whittier House. Here, on February 6, Jesse told his audience that the American frontier was gone, that we were no longer a nation of free land and unlimited natural resources, and that the time had come to abandon the obsolete capitalistic "grab" technique and substitute for it the Socialistic theme of "production for use, not profit." A week later Dr. Herbert Fraser was to discuss the gold standard; and in March Paul Blanshard, co-author with Norman Thomas of "What Is the Matter with New York?," and a member of the City Affairs Commission which had led the drive to oust "Jimmy" Walker as mayor of New York, was to give his inimitable insights on the crises in

Socialist solidarity in Eastern Pennsylvania; he could expect considerable support here. He was not so well known in Western Pennsylvania, however, so he planned to drive to Pittsburgh during Swarthmore's spring vacation and address Socialist meetings there. The summer and fall were spent in barnstorming trips throughout the state, from Upper Darby through Delaware County and into central Pennsylvania and beyond. In Upper Darby he harangued the crowd on "Free Speech, Free Men and Freedom"; in Harrisburg the chief of police tried to intimidate him by forbidding him to make a speech on the street. But Jesse drove his old touring car to the designated street location, and, using his car as a platform, "spoke loudly, with much humor, and a great deal of logic, . . ." The police did not disturb him. After a three-weeks trip to Pittsburgh and its steeltown suburbs, Jesse returned to the Swarthmore area in September. Here the police *did* catch up with him at an evening Socialist meeting, arrested him for disturbing the peace, and clapped him into jail. Some hours passed before Jesse was able to get his appeal for bail money through to President Frank Aydelotte. The next morning, when Jesse marched into Aydelotte's office to thank him for bailing him out, Aydelotte said he was glad to do it. "But," said Frank, "in the future I would appreciate it if you could manage to get arrested before midnight; getting you out of jail would not disturb my sleep so much."

Undaunted by such harassment — nay, *bolstered* by this overt demonstration of the need for more of *his* kind of free political activity —, Jesse continued his campaign. In early October, he opened the Race Street Forum's fall series of public-affairs meetings with a talk on "A New Deal or a New Game." The new game he hoped might be played some day was obviously Socialism. A week later, on a Sunday evening, Warren Mullen, organizer of the Lead, Paint and Varnish Worker's Union, was to give the Forum the union side of a strike, paying special attention to the textile strike then in progress. Another meeting was to hear Professor Herbert Miller, of the department of social economy at Bryn Mawr, discuss the Tennessee Valley Authority. We may be sure that Jesse attended this last lecture, since this experiment in Socialism fitted in not only with his political-economic ideas but with his constant teaching that all life was an experiment.

Considering the total situation in the nation and in Pennsylvania, the results of the election for governor in 1934 were predictable if

public affairs at that time. He was to be followed by Dr. Walter H. Seely, former editor of the *New York World,* in a talk on "Bandits I Have Known."

By the middle of April, 1933, the "chaos and misery" endured in America since the stock market crash in 1929 was so great that liberals and radicals called for a "New Continental Congress" to meet in Washington, D.C. on May 6, 7. Over two hundred labor, farmer, and progressive political organizations had signified their eagerness to send delegates; a new American revolution was in the making, at least to the extent of developing a plan of action for economic reconstruction. Walter H. Seely and Olivia R. King were to represent the Swarthmore branch of the Socialist Party, while Jesse Holmes, and George B. Cooper of Upper Darby, were to be delegates-at-large for the Delaware County Local, Socialist Party of Pennsylvania.

This New Continental Congress met, but apparently had too varied a membership to accomplish anything; we hear nothing more about it. Back home in Delaware County, however, Socialists were more unified: they met in picnic on the nearby Longwood Meeting grounds to select a complete slate of candidates for the next county election. Jesse Holmes was nominated for prothonotary; George Cooper, a certified public accountant, for county controller; Thomas McGee, a Tinicum steel worker, for sheriff; Olivia R. King, of Swarthmore, for director of the poor; Agnes S. Barker, of Moylan, and Charles N. Young, of South Ardmore, for jury commissioners. (Because of her husband's illness Mrs. King withdrew later on and Jesse was persuaded to run in her place for director of the poor.)

The slate of candidates having been formed, the Socialists at Longwood turned their attention to the development of a program that they could carry to the people. Robert Cullum, of the Executive Committee of the United Workers' Federation of Pennsylvania, and Socialist organizer for eastern Pennsylvania, outlined a policy which went beyond the ordinary generalities of socialism. "To be a success," he said, "any organization must serve the immediate needs of the people, ..." Following some of his suggestions, the assembly drew up and approved a petition to Governor Pinchot, asking that he call an immediate special session of the legislature to consider social legislation only — laws abolishing sweatshops, fixing minimum wages and maximum hours, and to bring an old-age pension plan before the voters in November.

Much work had to be done by the candidates in getting ready for the November election; and in the meantime party solidarity and enthusiasm had to be maintained. One good way to do this was to hold another Socialist picnic, this time in August at Schentzen Park, Philadelphia. Part of the entertainment lay in the viewing of "The Strange Case of Tom Mooney," a film showing how unjustly Mooney had been treated by California police and courts for his alleged part in the bombing of the *Los Angeles Times* building. Held in prison for a long time, he was shown in the film as demanding his unconditional release or to be put to death. And no Socialist picnic was complete without a series of speeches. Now the Schentzen Park crowd heard Norman Thomas, always full of wit and humor; Leo Krzycki, former sheriff of Milwaukee, was there; Emil Reive, president of the American Federation of Full Fashioned Hosiery Workers, added his German accents to the proceedings; and Franz Daniel, organizer for the Amalgamated Clothing Workers, enlightened the assembly with his experiences. Not the least of these speakers was Frank Crosswaith, native of the Virgin Islands, and at this time an active organizer of Negro labor unions.

The November election in Delaware County showed only one Socialist candidate with any kind of a sizable vote: Jesse Holmes, running for director of the poor, received 186 votes; his Republican and Democratic opponents got 381 and 689 respectively.

Far from being discouraged by these election results, Jesse seemed to be stimulated to greater action. In the middle of February, 1934, he spent several days lecturing on socialism in North Carolina and Virginia, visiting leading cities and speaking to the student bodies at Black Mountain College, Sweetbriar College, and the Negro state college at Petersburg. Apparently the last stop on this tour was in Harrisburg, Pennsylvania, where a Sunday conference of Socialists named him their candidate for governor of the state on February 18. The final Socialist ticket for this general election included Birch Wilson, running for lieutenant governor; Franz Daniel for secretary of internal affairs; Meyer E. Maurer for judge of the superior court; James H. Maurer for the U.S. Senate; Edward B. Rawson for Congress; and for the state legislature, George B. Cooper, Richard A. Montgomery, and Thomas Reed.

Jesse lost little time in getting into his campaign. His recent election to the presidency of the Philadelphia chapter of the American Federation of Teachers (AFL) helped cement labor-

not inevitable: the New Deal put George Earle in the governor's chair. However, his mandate to lead the people of the Keystone State was weakened by his slim margin of victory over the Republican candidate, William A. Schnader, 1,476,377 to 1,410,138. Of course, if the minor parties — Socialist and Prohibition — had not polled 63,781 votes for their candidates, the Democratic vote probably would have been much larger. One other fact helping to explain the Democratic victory lay in the considerable amount of vote-switching taking place in the secrecy of the voting booth. In 1934, 63 per cent of those registered to vote were Republican; 33 per cent of those registered were Democrats; while only 1 per cent were convinced to register as Socialists or Prohibitionists. But in the election only 48 per cent voted Republican, 50 per cent voted Democratic, and 2 per cent were for minor parties.

Considering the long Republican domination of Pennsylvania — Earle being the first Democratic governor since 1890 — and the mood of conservatism this demonstrated, the vote for the Socialists was not too surprising. Miniscule in comparison with the total vote of the major parties, it still showed an advance for liberalism — a liberalism taken over in a muted form by the New Deal. Jesse garnered 26 per cent of the citizens' votes in Berks County, the home of James Maurer, and almost 5 per cent of the votes in Venango County. This was of course exceptional; other areas were not so liberal. Back home in Swarthmore, Jesse got 116 votes out of a total of 1326; 75 of these were from his own precinct.

Nor did Jesse's defeat in this election, and the defeat of the Socialist Party on the state and national level, put out his idealistic fire. He continued to run for office under the Socialist banner — for Congress in 1936, and again as a candidate for governor of Pennsylvania in 1938. His chances for election had been increased a little by the fact that he was state chairman of the Socialist Party from 1935 on. But, as Norman Thomas found out through his three unsuccessful presidential campaigns up to 1940, Socialism's time had not yet come in America.

And time was running out for Jesse Holmes. In 1940 he was in his seventy-sixth year. But there were still a few things he could do for Socialism. In that year's election campaign he was glad to serve as treasurer of "The Independent Committee for Thomas and Kruger," this Committee being centered at Socialist headquarters on Fourth Avenue in New York City. A Socialist campaign leaflet listed sixty-nine prominent American liberals as members of the Committee, including Van Wyck Brooks, John Dewey, Harold J. Faulkner, Henry Pratt Fairchild, Rabbis Sidney Goldstein and Joseph Warren, John Haynes Holmes, Sidney Hook, Alfred Kazin, Ferdinand Lundberg, Broadus Mitchell, and Richard Rovere. Philosophers, economists, and educators loomed large in the membership; and, while the Committee obviously had been organized to support Norman Thomas and Maynard Krueger as presidential and vice-presidential candidates, the leaflet emphasized that membership on the Committee or support of its aims did not involve endorsement of the full Socialist program. Neither did it mean active participation in the campaign activities, although such help, plus financial contributions, would be appreciated. This part of the leaflet's appeal ended with: "You can do your part — before it is too late."

Of course it *was* late in the day for lovers of democracy at home and abroad. Even before Hitler's invasion of Poland, these Socialists recalled, "semi-fascist electoral laws had denied to political minorities a right to appear on the ballot in many [American] states. . . ." This process, they were afraid, would be "accelerated and completed" during the world crisis unless "the genuinely democratic forces" in the country asserted themselves politically. The campaign of 1940 "must be used to bind together those men and women who are determined to make democracy — social, economic, political — work in the United States and who are eager to unite with like-minded friends of justice and sanity against the mounting tide of reaction. . . ." If this reaction, hand-in-glove with the rising armament economy riding the wave of war hysteria, could not be checked now, this might be "the last campaign for a long period to be conducted under conditions of relative freedom of speech and assemblage. (One strongly suspects that Jesse Holmes wrote this perfervid appeal for support — the phrase "to unite with" is characteristically Quaker, and all the rest is typical of his style.)

And, this Socialist campaign document continued, neither could democracy be advanced by voting for the other political parties. Certainly sane and thinking people would not be fooled by the Communist Party's antiwar policy then "in process of revision on word from Moscow . . . ." Similarly, no one would be fooled by the antiwar stance adopted by the Democratic Convention in 1940.

Hitler's successes, and the low state of the American army, had made it "impracticable" to land forces in Europe; Roosevelt was now simply trying to win the " 'peace vote' " by making a virtue out of a necessity. Far more serious was the Administration's drive to develop the armament economy and to enjoin national conscription. Having failed to solve the economic depression, the Administration was seeking "to disguise this failure and to divert public attention by hysterical militarization. . . ." Already this drive had curtailed relief measures and social services and was threatening wage-and-hour standards. All this could succeed only "in an atmosphere of fear and exaggerated nationalism. The attempt to whip up in artificial 'national unity' on this basis [meant] the suspension, perhaps the death, of democracy at home."

The Republicans, of course, were in no better case. The Socialist campaign leaflet turned their "Win with Willkie" slogan against them by putting a question mark after Willkie inside the quote marks; the leaflet charged that, while Republicans had criticized Roosevelt's war-mongering, their national convention had still gone ahead and nominated Willkie, the "only outspoken interventionist among Republican aspirants." Indeed, the GOP's campaign slogan — "Americanism, preparedness, and peace" — accented "the worst of Roosevelt's war program: the utilization of the national defense issue to evoke national hysteria and to 'put labor in its place.' . . ." The real slogan of the Republican Party, it was said, "should be 'Back to Normalcy.' Its social program is still that of the Harding-Coolidge era." The leaflet closed in typical Holmesian style:

> We believe that the Socialist Party candidates are the only ones who warrant the support of men and women who know that social justice is the only lasting foundation for political democracy. Their constructive program, their long and consistent opposition to reaction in every form, have won them the respect of thousands outside the Socialist ranks.

> Norman Thomas and Maynard Krueger will not be elected in November, but a million men and women united behind them in this campaign, registering an uncompromising opposition to the tide of reaction, alien baiting and war-hysteria now sweeping the country, will prove a powerful factor in arresting that tide and demonstrating that there is a force in this country which cannot be 'panic-ed' into a surrender of its democratic rights or fooled by glittering generalities.

This is no time for compromising with 'the lesser evil' in politics. It is a time to stand up and be counted against *all* evils, greater or lesser.

Given Jesse's incessant gadfly activities, conservatives probably agreed with the caricaturist when he gave Jesse these Mephistophelean characteristics.
Courtesy Grace R. Holmes.

18. Leader of the Progressive Friends

Although Norman Thomas and Maynard Krueger found only 100,264 people who were willing to "stand up and be counted" in the election of 1940, during the campaign Krueger had received a most courteous hearing from an organization in the rolling countryside near Kennett Square, Pennsylvania. This organization, mentioned several times in earlier pages, was the Pennsylvania Yearly Meeting of Progressive Friends, founded before the Civil War in protest against the restrictive policies of the Hicksite hierarchy of those days. Known locally as the "Longwood Friends" because their meeting house was built on a tract once part of the Longwood Farm owned by John and Hannah Cox, this group maintained a public forum for the advancement of the democratic way of life from 1853 until 1940.

Origins and Development of the Longwood Friends.

The founding of the Pennsylvania Yearly Meeting of Progressive Friends at Longwood was no isolated rebellion against particularly obdurate conservatives in Pennsylvania; it was but another expression of the general state of unrest among American Protestants in the period before the Civil War. The Protestant churches had become arenas for a most unseemly battle between those who favored progress in the spirit of Christ and those who opposed it. This contest — on questions of antislavery, women's rights, and kindred causes, as well as on points of doctrine and policy — brought on that phenomenon known as "Come-outerism." Come-outerism meant revolt and a division of churches into splinter groups, and one of its most striking examples lay in the birth of the

Progressive Friends from the body of Hicksite Quakerism. Starting in 1848, and continuing for some years thereafter, yearly meetings in some northern and midwestern states were shaken by what the *Pennsylvania Freeman* called a "moral earthquake." Rebel meetings — variously called Congregational Friends, Progressive Friends, or Friends of Human Progress — were formed in New York, Pennsylvania, Ohio, Indiana, Iowa, and Michigan. They all claimed to be throwing off the authority and formalism of superior church bodies to return to the liberty and simplicity of primitive Quakerism — and they were all condemned most vehemently by conservatives. Such reform meetings, said the elders in the Indiana Yearly Meeting, were places where progress was a "beast of many heads and horns," and where people were "heaping to themselves teachers of men's making having itching ears and clamorous tongues. . . ."

One of those teachers (and he had a "clamorous" tongue) was Joseph A. Dugdale, who had been under fire from the conservatives in Ohio for some time. He had been disowned by his yearly meeting and accused of immorality in a business deal involving Ohio Quakers; now in 1850, he and his wife Ruth decided to move to Chester County, Pennsylvania, where he believed he would find a more congenial reform climate.

Although he found many liberal Friends to help him in his reform activities here, he also found that, just as in Ohio, each local meeting was a scene of battle between the liberal element and the conservatives who advocated that Friends should "stay in the quiet" and not "mix" with non-Quakers in the reforms of the day. Each side claimed the just right to use the meeting houses for *their* activities. In the Marlborough Meeting, for example, Isaac Meredith and Vincent Barnard were accused by the conservatives of acting as clerk and doorkeeper for those holding irregular sessions "in opposition to the meeting itself." Indeed, Vincent Barnard had not only taken the keys to the meeting house but was said to have "affixed padlocks to the doors of the outbuildings with the apparent design to exercise exclusive control over their use." Needless to say, such willful resistance to the ruling powers brought the threat and actuality of disownment; by 1858, thirty-four people had been disowned by the Kennett Monthly Meeting.

But the most exciting event at Marlborough Meeting occurred in June, 1852, when Oliver Johnson, *agent provocateur* for the

410

American Anti-Slavery Society, rose to remind the Friends of their reformist tradition. Flanked by Joseph A. Dugdale and four other liberals, Johnson had barely begun his speech when one of the elders called for his forcible removal from the premises. Johnson was arrested for speaking on a reform subject in a meeting for worship; he paid his five-dollar fine without protest. However, those arrested with him — Vincent Barnard, Dr. Bartholomew Fussell, Eusebius Barnard, and William Barnard — refused to pay their fines for reasons of conscience. The latter two had recently been disowned by Kennett Monthly Meeting; now they expected to go to jail as martyrs. But even this pleasure was denied them — the prosecutors (the regular Hicksites) paid their fines for them.

And so the pressure mounted. In October, 1852, a committee of the liberal group reported to an irregular quarterly meeting in Kennett Square that they had made a fruitless appeal for relief to the Philadelphia Yearly Meeting; they now recommended that a yearly meeting be established for themselves. While this recommendation threw the assembled Quakers into "lively exercises," it also resulted in the writing and issuance of a call for a general religious conference to consider the advisability of establishing an independent body. This "Call", signed by fifty-eight of "the most . . . intelligent among the Society of Friends and others," invited all those interested in divorcing "Religion from *Technical Theology*" [sic] to gather in the Old Kennett Meeting House on May 22, 1853.

The notice of this meeting was sent out to general newspapers, reform sheets, and by way of circulars. It brought to attendance Lucretia Mott, that well-known bundle of reformist energy, Ernestine L. Rose, ardent feminist and abolitionist, and Robert Purvis, well-educated mulatto now devoting his talents to the uplift of American Negroes. Even "General" Sidney Jones and his consort Fannie Lee Townshend were allowed their day in court, although their free-love doctrines threatened to disrupt the peace of the other people jamming the Old Kennett house.

The meeting got under way through the efforts of William Barnard, temporary chairman. It soon resolved to appoint Joseph A. Dugdale as its presiding clerk or chairman, with Sidney Peirce elected to perform her duties as recording clerk. After much discussion the decision was made to form a new society and call it "The Pennsylvania Yearly Meeting of Progressive Friends." An

411

"Exposition of Sentiments," written by a committee headed by Oliver Johnson, was adopted as the official statement of the group's principles, purposes, and methods of work.

According to this Exposition there were to be no set doctrines, forms or ceremonies, and the Yearly Meeting would exercise no disciplinary authority over individual members or related associations, if such should be established. The group would not be responsible for the individual, and the individual could avoid responsibility for majority decisions by voting against them. The door to membership was to be wide open — open to "all who recognize the Equal Brotherhood of the Human Family, without regard to sex, color or condition, and who acknowledge the duty of defining and illustrating their faith in God . . . by lives of personal purity, and [by] works of beneficence and charity to mankind. . . ." Such individuals, in meeting assembled, would seek to intensify in each other a feeling of responsibility to "labor for the redemption of mankind from every form of error and sin." The Progressive platform would be as "broad as Humanity, and as comprehensive as truth. . . ." The Exposition closed with some questions: "Are these the ideas of a Church Utopian? Are we dreamers and enthusiasts? . . . Let us . . . not falter, or hesitate. What if our numbers are few, and the hosts of superstition and sin stand before us in meanacing array? . . ." The answer was clear: the people at Old Kennett were assured that "the truth we promulgate is 'a part of the celestial machinery of God,' and that 'whoso puts that machinery in gear for mankind hath the Almighty to turn his wheel.' "

Fortified by this deep sense of right, the Progressive Friends launched themselves on a career of service which was to last for eighty-seven years. Erecting their own temple of reform at nearby Longwood in 1854-55, they made this modest frame building the center of liberalism in Pennsylvania. They conducted weekly Sunday services and ran a Sunday school for some years, opened up their building for midweek community forums, and made their annual three-to-four day yearly meetings memorable opportunities for the people in the surrounding area to hear the country's leading reformers lecture on the major issues of the times. In the discussions which followed, each person had the right to speak, subject to parliamentary procedure and a ten-minute time limit. Discussions often resulted in the passage of resolutions or petitions sent to local, state, and national governmental authorities; on one occasion an appointed delegation visited President Lincoln and presented him with a petition for the immediate abolition of slavery.

Given the open invitation to all people of good will, it was not surprising that the big annual meetings, usually held late in May or in early June, took on something of a carnival atmosphere. Sutlers' wagons and other refreshment stands did a thriving business, and a veritable potpourri of humanity milled around the grounds. Sometimes the crowd outside the meeting house was so large that Progressive leaders felt impelled to mount the front steps and address the throng. Earnest-faced Quakers were there, clad in plain brown coats and broad-brimmed hats, with their women in "casing' bonnets. There were also men with beards and long hair, and bobhaired women who supported Amelia Bloomer. Altogether, there were some good reasons for the outburst of a conservative newspaper in nearby West Chester when it asserted that Longwood was a place where "long-haired men and short-haired women" plotted revolution, where crack-brained extremists threatened the stability of society. Still, as Thomas Wentworth Higginson was to say, "without a little crack somewhere, a man could hardly do his duty to the times."

Inside the temple of reform, however, the scene was more decorous. The audience, now settled on padded Quaker benches, gazed up at the featured speakers with eager anticipation and with an equally eager desire to subject whatever was said to critical analysis and discussion. Typically, the presiding clerk would step forward to the low oaken pulpit to open the meeting with a few appropriate remarks; or there might be a period of "silent waiting upon the Spirit." Then the recording clerk would read the Call for the meeting, reminding the audience of Progressive principles and purposes. Committees would be appointed to draw up "testimonies" on various reform topics, to prepare memorials for deceased members, to nominate officers for the ensuing year, and to audit the treasurer's account. The reports of these committees would be acted upon later, the testimonies and memorials sometimes undergoing considerable amendment before being approved for publication in the *Proceedings*.

Procedural matters being disposed of, the meeting turned to the more interesting business of the regular program. Now such fiery advocates of human rights as William L. Garrison, Anna E.

413

Dickinson, or Theodore Parker would be heard; now Charles C. Burleigh, a tall man with auburn curls and long beard trying his best to look like the accepted picture of Christ, would speak in a way some people thought blasphemous.

At intervals the tensions engendered by such speakers were eased with music, perhaps, as in 1861, when Larooqua, "the Jenny Lind of the Penobscot tribe," thrilled the audience with her Indian songs; perhaps as in 1855 and 1861, when the Hutchinson family, "keen-eyed and stalwart youths clustered around the one rosebud of a sister, Abby," enlivened proceedings at Longwood with their rousing campmeeting hymns and comic pieces. On occasion the audience attempted congregational singing accompanied by the organ. In 1856 it was embarassing to find that only "several Friends" were able to follow Samuel J. May's lead in the singing of a hymn. (This inability to sing, this neglect of one of the grace notes of life, had been remarked on earlier by an abolitionist newspaper, which thought that it was a sufficient commentary on that "Quaker education [which] had deprived them of all opportunity to cultivate the musical faculty, and even of testing the power of music over the higher feelings of the heart.") By 1859, however, the audience was loud in its "Hymn to Progress"; and, following the Civil War, with the meeting led by Unitarians, they sang "Songs of Natural Religion," which included a hymn expressing Longwood's open-door policy:

> Come hither all, the great, the least,
> The Heathen, Buddhist, Jew;
> Come, Christian, Moslem, Layman, Priest,
> There's room enough for you.

Such singing was encouraged by a distinguished line of presiding clerks, who, as practical psychologists, were convinced that the religious-and-reform activities carried on at Longwood should leave the participants with feelings of joy and beauty. The first of these presiding clerks, as we have seen, was Joseph A. Dugdale, who envisioned the Progressive Friends as the vanguard of a "Christian Democracy," a "Church of Humanity" destined to sweep all the hosts of conservatism before it. He served until 1860, leaning on Oliver Johnson for help from the time of the 1856 Yearly Meeting. The poor state of Dugdale's health, plus the outbreak of the Civil War, caused the cancellation of the annual convention in 1861. Yearly meetings, plus other Progressive activities, were resumed in

1862 under the leadership of Oliver Johnson, who guided Longwood's destinies as presiding clerk until 1873. Johnson had a national reputation as a professional reformer and skilled journalist, with long years of experience as Garrison's right-hand man, as editor of the *Anti-Slavery Bugle* and the *Pennsylvania Freeman* and as co-editor of the *National Anti-Slavery Standard.* A kindly person, "alert and firm," he could keep a meeting to its "best line of thought and give it animated interest . . . He knew how to conduct a meeting without its knowing that it was being led." His personal tastes, however, led him to dress in a manner quite unlike most of the regulars at Longwood. Conservative critics described his coat as "fashionable" and thought that his "dress would have done credit to a tip-top dandy, if placed upon a well-shaped person."

Johnson was succeeded as presiding clerk by three very able and very handsome Unitarians: Charles G. Ames, of Germantown, Pennsylvania (1874-1877); Charles D.B. Mills, of Syracuse, New York (1878-1884); and by Frederick A. Hinckley, of Providence, Rhode Island, and other cities in the East. Hinckley, like Johnson before him, had made religious-and-social reform his career, serving the Progressive Friends and other reform groups for over thirty years. During that time, wrote one regular attendant, "To most of us Longwood *was* Frederick A. Hinckley. . . ." When he became fatally ill in 1917, the yearly meeting suffered its second cancellation, again coincident with American involvement in war. From 1918 through 1926 the annual conventions were carried along by the local regulars and a variant succession of ministers and college professors.

Jesse as Longwood's Presiding Clerk.

In 1927, however, the regulars in search of a more permanent leader struck "pay dirt" — if that rather inelegant term may be used to describe Jesse H. Holmes. In that year he consented to become the presiding clerk of Longwood Meeting, a post he held until the group's dissolution in 1940.

Quite naturally, he meant to continue the spirit, policies and methods of his predecessors — those ideas outlined so eloquently in the "Exposition of Sentiments" of 1853. This was not a very difficult job since the Exposition's ideas were almost exactly the same as his own. And the rapport existing between the Progressive

Friends and Jesse may be judged through a part of a brief advertising notice he put into the *Friends Intelligencer* some years after he became presiding clerk:

> Longwood is one of those interesting and rather quaint institutions that spring up in communities of the original and creative type of people. It originated as a strong anti-slavery group of Friends and has continued as an alert, interested association of people who want to know what is going on in the world, and are not impressed with the idea that to be popular is to be right.
>
> Longwood has continued ... to supply a forum for idealists and for the oppressed. It has had its active part in the abolition of chattel slavery, the struggle for justice for the Negro citizen, woman suffrage, prohibition, peace, and others of the movements for social righteousness.

And "social righteousness" was spelled out more-or-less explicitly on the front page of the program folder for Jesse's first Yearly Meeting (1927): "We welcome to fellowship, all those, of whatever creed or race, who are seeking to apply the principles of Christianity to daily life and to social customs and instituions." This was a standard Progressive Friend statement, appearing in this instance over the names of Sara D. Chambers, recording clerk, and Percy V. Cope, treasurer. But on the inside page, the program listings were topped by statements obviously contributed by Jesse, and used by him as texts for his opening remarks in his capacity as chairman.

Thus the program for Saturday morning, June 11, was headed by his statement that "If there is a conflict between justice, right and humanity on the one hand [,] and patriotism on the other, patriotism must yield precedence or expand." Jesse held that such a conflict should not exist, for a country or a nation was not an end in itself, but the organization of a group of people to gain certain objectives — and those objectives were justice and the rights of people within that organization; the "means" — the government — "should never have precedence over ends. ..." He thought that the "chief peril to civilization" was the arrogance of the white race in its dealings with the colored races. The growing unrest in the British colonies, and the growing hostility to the United States by Central and South American peoples were "ominous," he feared.

Having set the stage with these remarks, Jesse then introduced the Reverend Joseph Paul Morris, curate of Prince of Peace Chapel of Holy Trinity Church, Philadelphia, who spoke on "Progress Toward Interracial Understanding." In the discussion which followed, Dr. Robert T. Kerlin, of West Chester, called attention to two recent events which showed progress toward interracial justice. One was the declaration of labor that it stood for "an absolute equality of races" in its unions; all discrimination on account of color was declared to be contrary to the basic democracy and brotherhood on which the labor movement was founded. The other event was the assurance given by Memphis delegates to a conference of social workers in Des Moines, Iowa, that if the next annual conference were held in Memphis the Negro delegates would not suffer segregated treatment during meetings or at mealtime.

The next speaker was Rossiter P. Barnes, executive secretary of the Committee on Militarism in Education, who held that the U.S. War Department and various "patriotic" or "defense" societies were "Prussianizing the Youth of America." The result of this process by 1927, he said, was to class the United States among "the most militaristic of nations, . . ."

After a brief discussion on issues raised by the Prussianization address, the morning meeting was brought to a close with some "delightful" music — the music on this occasion being supplied by two ladies from Kennett Square, who offered vocal numbers to the accompaniment of a zither.

And then, starting about 11:30 a.m., there was a period of "social worship," as the early Progressive Friends had called it, and an opportunity to refresh the inner being. Some people, as was the custom, had brought their own refreshments and formed impromptu picnic groups on the lawn; others, as the program folder had suggested, could work up their lunches from the sandwiches, coffee, pie, and ice cream offered for sale on the grounds. After lunch they could exercise a bit by strolling through the Longwood Cemetery across the street, a cemetery established in the 1850s by Joseph A. Dugdale and his friends. Here, under magnificent trees, they could gaze at the weatherbeaten tombstones marking the remains of some of the leading lights in the early history of the Progressive Friends. They could see Oliver Johnson's marker there, and J. William Thorne's modest slab, which tells all the world that "Here lies one who was not afraid to speak the truth as he believed it." (Perhaps it is indicative of the nature of American values, or of what is considered newsworthy, that Longwood Cemetery derives its greatest fame from the fact that Bayard Taylor, poet, novelist, and world traveler, now rests there under an imposing Greek altar of the Doric order.)

Reconvening in the meeting house for the afternoon session, the crowd [described as the largest in recent years] found that the program topics were listed under the statement that "Loyalty to our country is loyalty to its ideals." The first speaker was Forrest Bailey, director of the American Civil Liberties Union, who held forth on "Constitutional Liberty in the United States." He discussed the "violations and infringements, now so common," of the first ten amendments to the Constitution, popularly known as the American Bill of Rights. Then the Reverend Norman Thomas, perennial Socialist candidate for President, stirred the proceedings with his talk on "Why Freedom Matters." "Liberty," he said, "was the right to think, to know, to argue." Without this right "We cannot have real education, which is the [cultivation of] the ability to think." And any vital democracy must be based on this ability, and not on mob action. American ideas of truth, said Jesse's old friend, must come from free discussion.

The afternoon meeting concluded with the adoption of three testimonies written by a committee. These testimonies were consistent with the topics considered that day: against the military spirit threatening to Prussianize the youth, in defense of civil liberties, and a reaffirmation of support for the colored people of America in their efforts to secure these liberties. (Although the Progressive Friends did not publish their Proceedings after 1905, such testimonies, and the salient points of speeches given at annual meetings, were given faithful treatment by local newspapers. Indeed, the full texts of testimonies were usually printed.)

Since all days were equally holy, Jesse continued the Progressive practice of holding Sunday morning sessions in the same spirit and vein as had prevailed in the Saturday meetings. On this particular occasion, Sunday, June 12, he introduced Thomas O. Harrison of the American Friends' Service Committee, who addressed the group on "A Challenge to the Heroic." The youth of major countries, Harrison thought, needed an heroic spirit to resist the war-oriented pressures; he urged the followers of George Fox to continue carrying forward the banner of peace even if this might bring on persecution.

In the years that followed Jesse and the Progressive regulars labored mightily to keep Longwood a vital institution. An effort was made to attract and involve more young people, as in the Yearly Meeting for 1928, when James W. Wise, son of the renowned Rabbi Stephen S. Wise, spoke on "Youth Challenges the Churches." In the afternoon session following this speech, the meeting was conducted by young members of the two branches of the Society of Friends; young workers among the Unitarian churches in Wilmington, Germantown, and Philadelphia were also invited. In 1929, discussion leaders included Andrew J. Biemiller, instructor of history at the University of Pennsylvania, and the young George W. Cadbury. In 1932 those leading the discussion on the topic of social planning included Herman Wolf of the Social Problems Club, University of Pennsylvania, Arthur Fletcher, a graduate student at the same school, and John Snyder, Central High School, Philadelphia.

By 1932, of course, such young people were very conscious of the need to plan and to adjust to what Scott Nearing called a "social hurricane" — that series of revolutionary changes taking place in the United States and the world in the depression period 1930-1940. Like these young men, Nearing was concerned, and he gave thought to what had happened to himself and the world since the days he had studied and taught economics at the Wharton School of Business Administration. He came to the conclusion that the "masters and shapers of the world" had scattered just enough crumbs of wealth and power among the masses to "divert, deceive, and corrupt each generation," and to secure their adherence to the masters' interests. This had been the nub of the social problem — "the success of the oligarchy in brainwashing the populace to the point where they believed that what [was] best for the oligarchy [was] best for them. . . ." Under these conditions the world "was moving inexorably toward a new paroxysm of international struggle. Historians would call it World War Two. It was in fact the same old war, in a new phase."

To the Progressive Friends at Longwood, it was indeed the same old war that their kind had been waging since 1848, that memorable year of revolutions at home and abroad.

So, at Longwood, in the days of the New Deal and the rising tide of the totalitarian threats to the democratic way of life, two-to-four hundred people gathered annually to advance their belief that reasoning and reasonable human beings could in some measure

419

influence the course of events. Now Jesse and the program committee, in contrast with the general-reform, shotgun tactics of earlier program directors, organized each yearly meeting around the general theme or topic which seemed most pressing at the time. In 1932, when the nation was in the early stages of that long depression resulting from the free-wheeling excesses of free-enterprise capitalism, the annual convention considered the possibilities of social and economic planning. Dr. Alfred H. Williams, professor of industry at the University of Pennsylvania, talked on the topic "Can Capitalism Plan?" He was followed by Maynard C. Krueger, of the economics department at the University of Chicago, with a consideration of "Socialist Planning Proposals." This favorable report was reinforced by Andrew J. Biemiller, now the executive secretary of the Philadelphia chapter of the League for Industrial Democracy, who spoke on "Roads to Social Planning." And an earlier talk had been given on the "Social and Economic Accomplishments of the [Soviet] Five Year Plan."

The theme to be considered in the 1933 meeting was the conflict between dictatorship and democracy. Rudolph T. Kessemeier, of the North German Lloyd Steamship Company, spoke of "The New Era in Germany," giving his first hand impressions of Hitler's regime and its meaning to Europe and the world. Then Judge Eugene V. Allesandroni, of the Philadelphia Court of Common Pleas, and "a warm friend of Mussolini," gave a talk on Fascism. This was enough for one session. On the following day Rosa L. Hanna, the Open Road representative to Soviet Russia, spoke on "Russia in Transition: The New Ideology." And then, to provide a balance to any unduly favorable impressions about totaltarian societies which might have been given by these addresses, the program listed three other speakers: Jesse H. Holmes was to hold up the choice between "Idols or Ideals?"; his friend and colleague Patrick Malin, of the economics department at Swarthmore, would speak on "Democracy: A Warning and a Challenge"; and Harnett Hart, professor of social economy at Bryn Mawr College, was to probe "The Future of Freedom."

As the decade of the 'thirties uncoiled its troubled years the themes of the meetings at Longwood took on a more-and-more desperate tone. In 1934 the best theme that the program committee could come up with was "A World in Confusion." Dr. Frank Aydelotte had been a member of this committee, and on June 9 he found himself adressing the Longwood crowd on "International Anarchism." Warren D. Mullin, of the British Labor Party, held up for public view "The Threat of Fascism," while Walter White, executive secretary for the National Association of Colored People, spoke on "Race Conflicts." And Senator Gerald P. Nye found sympathetic ears in his audience when he told how wars are always primarily economic in origin, with the major benefits going to the munitions industry. The theme for the 1935 yearly meeting was "What Next, America?". The answer, according to Socialist Thomas R. Amlie, and member of Congress, was to form a new political third party which would truly represent the common people. Perhaps there had been adverse criticism about the constant attacks on capitalism launched from the Longwood platform, or perhaps the program committee simply tried to live up to the tradition of giving all sides a hearing; in any case the program for 1936 gave Howard E. Kershemer of Montclair, New Jersey a chance to speak "In Defense of Capitalism and the Profit System." And in 1938 Hugh Denworth, Philadelphia banker, had his opportunity to tell the Progressive Friends what to expect from business within the general theme or topic of "Whither Civilization?"

Longwood Meeting Dissolves.

By this time, however, the regular attendants were asking themselves, "Whither Longwood Meeting?" There had been signs of decline lately; the old spirit and enthusiasm were lacking. People seldom brought their own picnic lunches now, preferring to take advantage of the catering services provided by Mrs. Georges, dietitian at Cheyney Teachers College. Instead of joining in invigorating congregational singing, as of old, now they were entertained at intervals during the program by musicians such as the Cheyney Singers, or by skilled amateurs such as Everett Lee Hunt and his wife Dorothy. And now, in the late 1930s, a white-haired professor emeritus opened meetings too little refreshed by the young. And it seemed absurd to maintain a building used only two days a year. In 1939 Jesse, after due consultation with the executive board, proposed that the organization be dissolved, the property sold, and the proceeds used to set up "an endowed lectureship . . . in the Longwood tradition . . . at some such center as Lincoln University or Cheyney State Teachers College . . . ." The board of managers, with the consent of the membership, decided to follow the Holmes' suggestion and authorized the trustees to sell the property subject to their discretion as to its future use.

But, everyone agreed, there had to be one more yearly meeting before this "heart of liberalism," as one local newspaper called it, stopped its beating. Saturday, September 7, and Sunday, September 8, 1940, were chosen for a combination reform meeting and commemorative service. The advertisements for these services brought results: these two days saw Progressive Friends crowding into the old white-painted frame building, completely filling the ground floor benches, the stage, and the two balconies. The theme for the Saturday sessions was "Equality and Freedom," a theme most appropriately reminding the faithful of what Longwood had stood for since the time of its founding. In the morning there was a brief business meeting, featuring the reading of the minutes of the 1939 session by Sara Chambers, a treasurer's report by Waldo Hayes, and Jesse's outline of the plan for a Longwood Association Lectureship. Since this business was conducted by men and women sitting together, Robert Leach, of the Pendle Hill Quaker center, felt impelled to rise and comment on the fact that the Progressive-Friend movement in Ohio apparently had not liberalized the Friends there very much, for in the Ohio Yearly Meeting men and women still met separately.

After the luncheon interval the afternoon session opened with music furnished by J. Russell Hayes, that old-time fiddler, and by Vera Hagans and Jessie Smith of Kennett Square. Regina L. Smith, a singer from Cheyney, gave a "beautiful" rendition of "The Lord's Prayer," accompanied on the piano by Robert Currington.

Although the pulpit from which William Lloyd Garrison, Norman Thomas, Anna H. Shaw and other famous reformers had hurled their fiery appeals to reason was gone (having already been given to Cheyney Teachers College), the speakers for the afternoon session needed no such support. Indeed, much of the traditional Quaker flavor was there when Janet Payne Whitney, of Westtown School, with nothing to lean on, stood erect and addressed her topic, "Freedom or Voluntary Servitude." Her opinion was that, while no one was entirely free, except in the sense of being free from the involuntary servitude of the Negro slave, all people were to a degree free to choose a cause, or causes, to which they would render service. And it was entirely fitting, in view of Longwood's origin in support

422

of the antislavery movement, that the next speaker should be A. Philip Randolph, national chairman of the Union of Sleeping Car Porters. He spoke on "Industrial Slavery and Industrial Freedom." All mankind, he said, wants social improvement, and this had been realized across the centuries by changes in the social order from slavery through feudalism into the "newer and higher" forms of industrial slavery. But, even in 1940, the battle for equality and freedom, for industrial democracy, had not yet been won. "The workers still have no rights in selecting their representatives, naming their wages, hours, and hence their living conditions. . . ." He went on to explain in detail how public opinion worked unfairly against the labor unions.

The next morning, after a brief period of music, Jesse relinquished his scheduled place on the program so that Maynard C. Krueger, then professor of economics at the University of Chicago, and Socialist candidate for Vice-President, might speak about the national economic situation. Professor Krueger thought that, due to the present economic and social conditions, the greatest danger in the United States was the threat of the development of Fascism from within the country; the solution to American problems at this time, he thought, was not to assure that trains ran on time, or that all people had a job related to the defense industries, but that peace should be presented as being more desirable than war.

After Professor Krueger had made his points there was more music, and then J. Russell Hayes, "the "poet laureate" of Swarthmore College, read his poem, "Longwood's Founders:"

> Across the fields of memory they come,
>   Dim figures from a legendary day,
> To bring their greetings gracious and serene
>   To us who reverence them from far away.
>   What would those Founders say
> Could they but speak the thoughts that moved them so
>   Here 'neath this very roof so long and long ago!
>
> Great, earnest souls, they spoke their fearless minds
>   In Emersonian accents sweet and strong;
> They sought in vigorous yet peaceful ways
>   To vanquish ancient and embattled wrong;
>   And still with hymn and song
> They loved to cheer their often hopeless hours
> And strewed the weary way with sweet and fragrant flowers.

Philanthropists they were — they loved their kind
  And sought to lift the lowly and oppressed;
And if the Negro and the Indian
  Have seen their sufferings in part redressed,
    They gladly must attest
That here at our own Longwood has been sown
The seed that into untold harvests now has grown.

Love was the guiding principle that led
  Those far-off fearless friends to gather here,
To face reproach and strong hostility
  With simple earnestness and souls sincere.
    Their memory we revere —
Apostles brave of liberty and love,
Crowned now with gracious light and radiance from above.

J. Russell Hayes' poetic effort set the stage for that afternoon's mood of nostalgia and reminiscence. A group of descendants of the founders, some of them dressed in the costumes of the 1850s, now took their places on the platform, and from this vantage point recalled salient features of the history of Longwood. Mrs. Mabel Foulke, of West Chester, read a list of the reform documents placed in the cornerstone of the building in September 1854. (These included the *Proceedings* of the Pennsylvania Yearly Meeting of Progressive Friends for 1853 and 1854, the *Proceedings* of the Women's Rights Convention held in West Chester in June, 1852, and the *Five Points Monthly Record* for the Improvement and Elevation of the Ragged and Destitute Children of New York.) Mary R. DeVoe read a long account of how Isaac and Dinah Mendenhall had operated a station on the underground railroad at their home near Longwood; their names, of course, were on the list of eight-six founders and friends enscribed on a commemorative plaque to be presented to Swarthmore College. Emma L. Higgins, the niece of J. William Thorne, told how, in 1843, her uncle had led a rebellion against conservative Hicksites in Ercildoun, a small community about six miles from Kennett Square — a rebellion leading to the formation of a group, who, meeting in their own "People's Hall," were offbeat, and yet direct, progenitors of the Progressive Friends.

Josephine Pennock was there, although so advanced in age that she had to be carried to the place in the balcony where, as a child, she had peered at the famous speakers through the railings. Unable to speak, she had written her impressions of early Progressive meetings, and these were read by Jesse Holmes. Coming back to

Longwood, she said, was just like going home.

Emalea P. Warner, Sr., was also there, being well enough to mount the stage and read her free-verse tribute to the founders, entitled "The Spirit of 1853." While it overemphasized the antislavery origins of the Progressive Friends, forgetting their very active work in the many other reforms of the day, the last part of it seems worthy of inclusion here if only to give some indication of the character of these Friends, as well as to indicate something of the nostalgic mood at this last meeting:

> This, in brief, is Longwood's story;
> In those early days of struggle.
> Men and women, staunch, courageous,
> Braved its foes and opposition,
> Stong with "truth for authority",
> Spoke the voice of Saint Lucretia [Mott],
> In her vision of the future,
> So today we bow in honor,
> Grateful to our noble Founders,
> Golden deeds that shall not perish;
> They have joined the Host Triumphant,
> In the world of the Immortals.

(While the sophisticated reader may smile at such effusions, to the people attending this meeting at Longwood in September of 1940 there was little to laugh at. In the time of Hitler's madness they were not only honoring the bravery of the old Progressive Friends in their resistances to the tyrannies and injustices of *their* day, but they were mourning the passing of a dream. One young woman, greatly saddened by the news that Longwood was to close its service, offered her services in the interests of keeping it a going concern. Her thought was that, while many of the reforms that the Progressive Friends had worked for had been accomplished, a great deal remained to be done. She even offered to take the responsibility of running Longwood in the future if no one of greater stature could be found.)

The commemorative service wound down to its close. Nathan Walton, long associated with the Progressive Friends, and an old friend of Jesse's, gave him a fine testimonial for his services as presiding clerk. Jesse responded in his characteristic fashion, at once criticizing Western culture and, at the same time, holding up a standard for the future. As seemed fitting to the final ceremonies of a society which had constantly regarded general reform as a religious duty, he first looked at America and found it wanting: " 'The religion of [our country] cares little about honesty or truth,' " he said, " 'and no part of it is prepared to hasten the destruction of evil forces in this democracy, which is rapidly becoming less of a democracy.' " But, the old idealistic pragmatist told his audience, there were still functions people such as they could perform: " 'Our lives as religious beings should be experimental, and we should [try] to supply men with clear visions of the life they seek, so that we will not have to live doubtfully and die timidly.' "

And so the final song was sung, the last moment of silence observed, and Longwood Meeting came to an end. In the final moments a gentle rain began to fall, seeming to some of the old Quakers there "to be the tears of those kind spirits who had made Longwood famous and were now sad at its passing."

During the course of the last meeting Jesse had announced that there would be no public sale of the meeting-house furnishings, but that they would be allocated at a nominal price to those people who wanted them for sentimental reasons, or given to local institutions. Cheyney Teachers College, as we have seen, received the oaken pulpit; the Chester County Historical Society got a padded bench, as well as the wrought-iron hanger, complete with four kerosene lamps, which had been suspended from the ceiling since the days of Joseph A. Dugdale and Oliver Johnson.

In 1854-55, when Joseph A. Dugdale and fifty-six other Progressive Friends bought the land upon which to build their meeting house, the deed to their new property stated that the building should be used for "Religious, Moral, scientific & literary purposes. . . ." These restrictions on the building's future use most likely were the reason why the Longwood trustees had to engage in "considerable effort" to find a buyer. But, by the time of the last annual meeting, Mabel Foulke, chairlady of the trustees, had received a letter from M.P. Darlington, a West Chester attorney representing Pierre S. duPont of Wilmington, Delaware. In this letter the attorney said that duPont had authorized him to offer six thousand dollars for the property. Also, Darlington said, "Any restrictions you may care to make in the deed or otherwise prohibiting the sale of liquor on the premises, the erection of mushroom houses, or any other use of the property which you might think objectionable to neighboring land owners will be entirely satisfactory."

426

The Longwood trustees could find nothing to quibble about in these terms; in fact, they believed that the offer of six thousand dollars was more than they could have obtained at a public sale. And so the deal was consummated, the proceeds being put into a West Chester bank under a trust-fund arrangement. Just how the income from this fund would be used remained in doubt until after Jesse's death in 1942.

The old temple of reform was left to stand for a while in a woebegone and unused condition. Then, after some interior and exterior alterations, it was made available for community purposes not out of line with Progressive ideas, being used by such organizations as the Boy Scouts and Girl Scouts, garden clubs, and the Kennett Little Theatre group. To some of the old timers in the neighborhood, however, it stood as a pale reminder of those days when fiery tongued agitators mounted its stage to lift the world against the dead weight of the status quo, when "Truth for Authority, not Authority for Truth" was the slogan emblazoned on the cover pages of Longwood's *Proceedings*.

Any attempt to anlayze the reasons for Longwood's passing must of course recognize the well-known sociological and historical fact that no institution of this kind can operate successfully for very long unless the social climate favors its existence — or, to put it another way, unless there is a need and a call for its operation. In the time of its founding the Longwood group was part of a wave of general reform; it worked in a time when the eternal tension between liberty and authority caused such eminent Bostonians as Wendell Phillips, and such wealthy philanthropists as the Tappan brothers, to applaud the efforts of reformers to afflict the comfortable and comfort the afflicted. As time went on, individual members of the Progressive Friend group, and the group itself, engaged in reforms such as the abolition of slavery, the emancipation of women from the slavery of men, the labor movement, the socialization of Big Business, and the many other projects which eventually came to enrich American life.

But, in the decades of the Great Boom and the Great Depression, and in the build-up to World War II, the social climate was no longer really favorable to the successful operation of such a group as the Progressive Friends. Before 1917, as Scott Nearing noted in his *The Making of a Radical*, liberalism and radicalism were, with certain exceptions, recognized as "a normal part of public life."

Norman Thomas and other Socialists were allowed to run for public office; their articles were published; their speeches were heard. Differences of opinion were regarded as a "natural right." But, after the collapse of industry and business in 1929, and after the apparent success of totalitarian ideologies in Europe, a Great Fear swept across America — a fear that these radical ideologies, if allowed to be discussed freely, might further undermine the shaky foundations of the "democratic" free-enterprise system; there were increasing criticisms of the liberalism seen in the New Deal by predominantly conservative agencies of communication. No wonder liberal meetings came to take on a somewhat surreptitious character in some quarters. While, as we have seen, surreptitious meetings were not necessary at Swarthmore, even here middle-class conservatism at times raised its voice at liberal antics. The student body favored Landon over Roosevelt in 1936, reflecting, no doubt, the opinions of their parents and their social class. And one member of the class of '93 thought that a liberal *Phoenix* editorial in the time of the Landon-Roosevelt contest expressed ideas "utterly at variance with the principles that have guided the managers and administrators of Swarthmore College. . . ." He believed that, at Swarthmore, "we should aspire to the finest things in life and get above this criticism of the motives and the principles of the men and women who have been the leaders of our country."

So Jesse and his Progressive Friends should not have wondered too much why their meetings did not attract more young people to carry on the good work of promoting the American Democratic Faith through Longwood methods. The young people who would normally have taken part in Progressive activities were already very busy at Swarthmore and other colleges in their manifold liberal clubs; and through their meetings and publications they were doing a more effective job than was being done at Longwood. To other young people, perhaps less idealistic than their friends in the American Student Union, it had become a matter of economic survival *not* to be labelled as liberals or radicals by Big Business elements. And, by the time Longwood Meeting closed its doors the threat to national survival posed by the totalitarian dictatorships had undermined the belief that much could be done to avert disaster through intellectual discussion in a religious atmosphere. After all, these aggressive ideologies were threatening the very values which Longwood had been trying to explain and defend; it now became a matter of the utmost practicality, on all levels of the Western culture system, to resist with armed force the threats to freedom of choice, freedom of religion, the right to speak out in defense of one's beliefs — in short, all those civil and political rights for which the American experiment in self government had been launched in 1776 and 1789. Perhaps — no, certainly — the young idealists who stayed away from Progressive Friend meetings in the period 1930-1940 had a better idea of the realities of the situation than did Jesse and his elderly audiences. To these young people concerned with their future, and the future of America, the preparations against Hitler were necessary; attendance at Longwood meetings was, for the time being, a waste of time.

Still, when Hitlerite clear-and-present threats to the fundamental American value system had been thwarted, there remained a very large spectrum of unfulfilled expectations in the American dream. Many of the old Progressive Friends must have wondered whether their style of citizenship, through which the controversies of American life were filtered by close examination and reasonable discussion, would not be needed in the new world after Hitler's suicide and the tragedy of Hiroshima. The American experience since these events has provided a sufficient answer to their question.

Views of Old Kennett Meeting House
Photographs by the author.

Longwood Meeting House, with some of its leaders, in 1865. (Note William Lloyd Garrison, guest speaker, holding a bouquet of flowers in the center of the first row.)
Courtesy Chester County Historical Society, West Chester, Pa.

Last meeting of the Longwood Progressive Friends, 1940. Courtesy Friends Historical Library, Swarthmore College.

430b

"Will that help Man?" — *Jesse H. Holmes, ca. 1940.*
Courtesy of Grace R. Holmes.

19. "Retirement" — and the Afterglow.

In 1934, when Jesse still had six years to go as the leader of the Progressive Friends, he was pushed into partial retirement by Swarthmore's policy that all faculty members should retire at age seventy. The word "pushed" is appropriate, not only because he had been eligible for retirement under a Carnegie pension (TIAA) since 1929, but because he so much wanted to stay on as an active member of the Swarthmore faculty.

For Jesse this forced retirement was made a bit more palatable through the Board of Managers' decision to declare him an emeritus professor of philosophy; also, through some academic legerdemain and the help of friends in court, he was to continue on a part-time basis as an instructor, with John Nason, in a new "Social Ethics" course to be offered by the philosophy department. Added to this assignment was Jesse's part in another new course, "Introduction to Religion," in which he would join six other professors in a general survey of why and how people had sought solace and fulfillment in religious activities across the centuries.

This partial retirement from Swarthmore's classrooms was to continue until 1937, when, after thirty-seven years of service, he finally hung up his academic paraphenalia. Before he left Swarthmore, however, he gave to the College all those religious relics he had spent a lifetime in collecting — all those artifacts which used to adorn Room 31 in Parrish and which his students had studied as symbols of man's religious impulses over the ages.

He left Swarthmore quietly and rather sadly in 1937; sadly, at least in part, because he could see that his friend Frank Aydelotte also was approaching the end of his effective service at the College. But three years earlier, given the promise of half-time teaching, he

431

had not been quite so sad. During Commencement Week, when the faculty and their wives entertained the Class of '34 at an afternoon tea in Collection Hall, Rebe poured and Jesse circulated among the guests in his usual jovial fashion. That evening, as a newly proclaimed emeritus professor, he addressed the last Collection of the year in Clothier Memorial Chapel, telling the graduating class that "It's a great game — play the game!" Life's game, of course, had to be played by a double self: "the narrow self bounded by the petty affairs of the immediate world about us, and the greater self which is a creative citizen of the greater world which humanity is building." There was more in this vein, reminding some of his older listeners of the Chautauqua speeches he used to give in the 'twenties. But then he turned to the graduates and their future:

> For many years you will be returning now and then to renew old friendships and old associations. It is my hope . . . that as you return you will find yourselves year by year as alive and alert, as keen and efficient as you have been here at Swarthmore; that you will take life and its problems in the wide, wide world as you have taken college and its problems — with intelligence, with good humor and good sportsmanship.

One other event during that Commencement Week must have affected Jesse Holmes very deeply. Returning alumni had been informed that they should not miss the exhibit of newly hung portraits in the front parlors of Parrish Hall — portraits of some Swarthmore greats they had loved and honored in their undergraduate years. During the past spring, Keith Martin, a young New York artist commissioned by the Benjamin West Society, had, in an amazingly short period, painted four portraits: of Caroline Lukens, alumni recorder; of Jesse H. Holmes, professor of philosophy; of William I. Hull, professor of history; and of J. Russell Hayes, librarian of the Friends' Historical Library. These were finished in time for the exhibit in early June; during the ensuing summer Martin produced additional portraits, notably those of President and Mrs. Frank Aydelotte and Professor John A. Miller.

Hailed by his friends as "capturing his spirit so well," and being "a true image of the man," Jesse's portrait was shown in many places. After milling crowds had admired it in Parrish Hall during Commencement Week, Keith Martin got permission to put in on exhibit in Montclair and Plainfield, New Jersey. Returned to Parrish Hall, it graced the main reception room for a while, and then was placed alongside the portrait of Frank Aydelotte and his wife in the hallway facing the Parrish parlors. When the author saw it last (1976) it was hanging between two windows in one of these parlors, still looking down on students as an "Old Testament prophet with a sense of humor . . . ." (See the photograph of the portrait in the Frontierspice.)

After Commencement the Holmeses continued to live at 602 Elm Street in Swarthmore until the middle of November. ·· Then, Jesse's campaign for governor having ended, they moved to a newly purchased home at 700 Manchester Road, Moylan, Pennsylvania — a location offering easy commuting to Swarthmore by car. Jesse H. Holmes III, and his wife Eloise and son Jesse IV, accompanied them in this move.

Having "lived a life of enthusiasms," Jesse soon developed new ones at the Moylan home. Always a lover of the outdoors, he dug a terraced garden from a backyard slope and built a swimming pool with his own labor. Much interested in shrubbery and trees, he planted a dozen hazelnut trees imported from his native state of Iowa. These, together with other plantings, provided a beautiful setting for those garden picnics Jesse and Rebe enjoyed with their friends and relatives. Son Robert S. Holmes and his wife Grace were part of the festivities on one occasion: there is a snapshot of a swimming group around the pool; the snapshot is mounted on a sheet of paper and under it Jesse had written "A happy memory of our swimming party — & Grace's baked beans!" On the back of this sheet Jesse had dashed off a poem expressing his joy and pride in his garden, his home, and his friends:

> A screen of green from the busy street,
> A bush of yew where the arch comes thru,
> A shady seat in the summer's heat,
> Or a friendly room for the winter's gloom,
> With a blazing fire that flames up higher,
> If it's *you* we greet at the Holmes Retreat.
>
> The Outdoor Rooms are to the west,
> And these, perhaps, we love the best;
> A cubic mile of country air,
> Half an acre of garden there,
> A shady place that is mostly cool,
> The shine & splash of the swimming pool;
> And out beyond the horizon line,

433

Lie miles and miles of sunset shine;
Or great blue clouds & summer rain,
With rolling thunder for refrain.
All these delights & others too,
At Holmes' Retreat we'll share with you.

One fine summer evening Robert and Grace joined Jesse on the porch of the Moylan house to gaze at the wonders in the garden. They fell to reminiscing about their dramatic endeavors in their school and college days — particularly Robert as Puck in "A Midsummer Night's Dream," and Grace as Yum-Yum in "The Mikado." Each had learned his lines very quickly, only to forget practically everything a few weeks after the performances.

" 'Ridiculous!' " Jesse snorted. " 'I can remember practically everything I memorized since about the age of ten or twelve.' " Robert and Grace challenged him by dredging up whatever first lines they could remember from Shakespeare, the Psalms, and from Omar's Rubyiat. He responded nobly, usually carrying out the quotation to the last line. Then Grace hunted up an old copy of *101 Best Poems*, thinking to stump him on works less well known than Shakespeare's. But this old philosopher could not be daunted: he completed the quoted first lines with the same unerring swiftness. As Grace reported, "it was incredible." Finally, after several hours of Jesse's feat of memory, she and Robert surrendered.

When inclement weather forced him to remain indoors Jesse would be writing his Philosophy Manuscript, his columns for the Philadelphia *Public Ledger* and *The Liberal Press*, or preparing still more speeches for his many appearances before labor, socialistic, or educational groups within an easy travelling distance of his base in Moylan. But at other times he indulged his hobbies — the creation of oriental rugs and his newly discovered art of wood carving. (These rugs, full of the symbols of various oriental religions, were not among the relics bequeathed to Swarthmore College.) And the wood carving was practiced when he tried to create a more modern set of chessmen from ebony and other hardwoods of appropriate colors. True to his socialist convictions, the pawns were carved as babies, women, old folks, laborers, and a Negro. The medieval knights and bishops were transformed into soldiers and grasping officials; now the rooks were the citadels of modern power — the skyscraper offices of Big Business and the banks. Brand Blanshard remembered him, when he was recovering from a slight stroke, as in a chuckling mood when he displayed his unfinished set of chessmen.   One can see him now, his blue eyes twinkling behind his half-moon rimless glasses as his fingers played with the Phi Beta Kappa key dangling from his watchchain.

The Passing.

Although, as Will Price said, his uncle "never retired from anything up to the day of his death," there were some signs of a slowing down of activities, some glints to show that he knew his sun was slowly setting. After his defeat in the gubernatorial election of 1934, and the generally poor showing of those running for office under the Socialist banner, he suffered a momentary fatigue — and yet one revived by his flashes of conviction that the battle for human uplift must continue. This mood and this conviction were in a lecture he gave to a college audience early in December, 1935. Entitled "The Tired Liberal," the lecture stirred one of his listeners to write "An Open Letter to Professor Jesse Holmes." Published in *The Swarthmorean*, this response showed that at least one of his listeners, while hailing him as a liberal, refused to believe that he was tired — "never, while you seek [the[way of life more blessed."

If this reaction showed that Jesse still had most of the old spirit, there were other signs to show that Jesse felt his advancing age. Three documents in his handwriting, together with the use he gave them, indicate that he was preparing himself, and his relatives and friends, for the certainty of his passing. His lifelong feeling for poetry now led him to compose a poem in his inimitable fashion — a poem undoubtedly read to others in his family circle:

> How vain is life! —
> Love — grave or gay
> Some scraps of strife,
> And then — good day!
>
> How short it seems!
> — Some hopes alight
> Some bits of dreams
> And then — good night!
>
> We give and take,
> We buy and sell,
> We make & break, —
> Hail — & Farewell!

And, while we are not certain that Jesse recited Robert Louis Stevenson's prayer in open meeting, he scribbled it on the back of the Swarthmore Monthly Meeting's *News Letter* of February 10, 1942:

> The day returns, bearing its petty round of irritating concerns and duties. Help us to perform our tasks with laughter and kind faces. Let cheerfulness abound with industry. Give us to go blithely about our business all this day, and bring us at last to our restive beds, weary and content and undishonored, and grant us in the end the gift of sleep. Amen.

The chances are that Jesus did not read the Stevenson prayer in meeting because he had found another prayer in the writings of Louis Untermeyer which expressed more clearly those principles he had taught all his life. Published in the February 20 issue of the *News Letter*, Untermeyer's "Prayer" has a notation scribbled on the Holmes' family copy of it by Robert S. Holmes: "Recited by Dad at meeting on February 15, 1942." One can imagine the scene as the patriarch of the Swarthmorean academic and religious community stood up, adjusted his glasses, and then read Untermeyer's moving poem:

> Lord! [*sic*] tho' [*sic*] our life is but a wraith,
> Altho' [*sic*] we know not how to choose,
> Altho' [*sic*] we grope with little faith,
> Grant me a heart to strive and lose!
>
> Ever insurgent let me be,
> Make me more daring than devout,
> From sleek contentment keep me free,
> And fill me with a buoyant doubt.
>
> Open my eyes to vision, girt
> With beauty, and with wonder lit;
> But always let me see the dirt,
> And all that spawns and dies in it.
>
> Open my heart to music; let
> Me thrill to spring's wild fifes and drums,
> But never let me dare forget
> The bitter ballad of the slums.
>
> From compromise and things half-done,
> Keep me with stern and stubborn pride,
> And if at last a victory's won,
> Lord, keep me still unsatisfied.

And so, having once again inspired his audience to strive for the fulfillment of their best dreams, Jesse Herman Holmes returned to his Moylan home to await his time. "Await" is not quite appropriate here; it was simply not in his nature to sit in a chair and wait for the Call. Instead, in the next three months he did some more carving on his chessmen, wrote more articles to be published in *The Liberal Press,* and tended to his garden and swimming pool.[26]

It was this latter activity which formed the background to his death. He had been painting the inside of his swimming pool in the warm and humid Moylan weather, and came in around supper time feeling uncommonly tired. He said that he thought that he would have his supper in bed from a tray. Rebe served him lamb chops, peas, and potato salad, which he ate while the bedside radio intoned its customary message. After supper, the exact time being undetermined (some sources say about 8 p.m. on May 27, 1942; other sources assert that it was after midnight, i.e., on May 28), Jesse H. Holmes departed this world at age 78 due to a coronary thrombosis. His wife Rebe and daughter-in-law Eloise had heard a noise from his bedroom; they rushed in to find him dead. A doctor was called — Dr. Baker, who had been one of Jesse's students —, but he was only able to confirm the fact of his death.

The Afterglow.

So Jesse almost died with his boots on, a desire he had often expressed to his family. Quite obviously his death had profound effects on Rebe and on Herman and Robert, plus their wives and sons. The rest of his circle of influence searched for ways to express their sorrow, respect, and appreciation for him and his life's work. The Society of Friends, as we have seen in the first chapter of this book, quickly found a pleasant and customary way to celebrate Jesse Holmes' meaning to them. There were, of course, many laudatory obituaries: in *The New York Times,* the Philadelphia newspapers, *The Phoenix, The Swarthmorean* and *The Liberal Press,* plus the *Friends Intelligencer* and the Swarthmore Monthly Meeting's *News Letter.* But some time went by before more formal ways to memorialize him were developed.

The first of these more formal efforts would have pleased Jesse greatly, not only because of its sponsorship by the Philadelphia Federation of Teachers, Local 3, AFT, but by reason of the high

437

caliber of its participants. The Federation organized what they called the "Freedom Forum Lectures in Memoriam — Jesse H. Holmes." Four single lectures and one symposium were to be presented in five Friday night sessions in Philadelphia's New Century Auditorium from November, 1942 through March, 1943. The series was to start with an address by Louis Dolivet, secretary-general to the Free World Association, who would consider "Planning for Freedom." He was followed by Bertrand Russell, world-renowned philosopher, mechematician, and educator, with his thoughts on "Freedom and Organization in Education." Reinbold Niebuhr was to come down from New York's Union Theological Seminary to talk on "Freedom in a Technical Age." And J. Alvare del Vayo, former minister for foreign affairs of the Spanish Republic, would speak on "Political Weapons in the War for Freedom." Perhaps the high spot of this Freedom Forum was the symposium "Freedom for All" — "No issue more grave, no goal more noble. Is not freedom, like peace, indivisible? Can the world exist half slave, half free? . . ." Three men addressed themselves to this universal freedom: Walter White, executive secretary, NAACP, and lobbyist for federal and antilynching bills; Chih Meng, director of the China Institute in America; and Anup Singh, editor of *India Today*. (We may imagine that as these men developed their messages, John Donne was always in the background, peering over their shoulders and whispering, "No man is an Island . . . therefore never send to know for whom the bell tolls; It tolls for thee.")

If the old Longwood Meeting House had ever had a bell it would have rung in joy at the news of the next memorial to Jesse Holmes, even if such news was to be delayed for a while. The road to this memorial started in a time when Jesse was still alive — in July, 1941, when a court decree, it will be remembered, put the proceeds ($5500 after attorneys' fees) from the sale of the Longwood property into a trust fund. But now the road to the memorial entered a detour — an abortive attempt to find an appropriate way to use the income from this trust fund. In November the Longwood Board of Trustees, including Jesse Holmes and W. Waldo Hayes, met at the home of Mabel Foulke in West Chester to try and settle this question. After some discussion it was decided to set up a "Longwood Association Lectureship," which was to plan and finance a series of lectures in the Longwood tradition in one of five communities — either in West Chester, Wilmington, Kennett

Square, Lincoln University, or the State Teachers College at Cheyney. Well-known speakers were to be chosen by a committee including Mrs. Foulke, W. Waldo Hayes, and Jesse Holmes. But the national excitement following Pearl Harbor prevented anything so sane and reasonable as the beginning of this lectureship program in the Quaker manner at this time; the author can find no evidence program was ever actually launched. The trust fund, ironically enough, was probably invested in war-industry stocks or bonds by the West Chester bank; war profits most likely swelled the trust-fund income.

At about the same time, however, a movement was begun in Washington, D.C. which was to have more tangible results in the direction of a memorial to Jesse. Mordecai W. Johnson, president of federally sponsored Howard University, met with William Stuart Nelson, dean of the School of Religion; they agreed upon the desirability of inviting a Quaker to join the theological faculty. Trying to get private funds for such a teacher, they approached Clarence Pickett, of the Friends' Service Committee, and Mrs. Alberta Morris, then secretary of the Committee of Race Relations of the Society of Friends. Quakers in Washington were also informed of the project. The immediate goal was to raise $6000; enough, it was thought, to hire an excellent teacher for two years. And the search for this money was especially acute since the federal government would not support a religious function.

In the fall of 1942, after Jesse had died, the campaign to raise money for this purpose developed more impetus and a fresh focus. Many of his friends wanted to honor his memory and his long years of service. Brand Blanshard was one of these, and he recalled that Jesse had four interests that stood out above all others:

> ... First, he was a devoted Quaker, and for fifty years was a leader in the Society of Friends. Secondly, he loved philosophy with an enthusiasm that proved infectious to numberless Swarthmore students. Thirdly, he was a religious liberal. When religious people were troubled by what was going on in the world of science, and the scientifically minded wanted to make contact with the religiously minded, both groups had a way of turning to Jesse Holmes as their ambassador. And finally, he was a liberal likewise in his social and political views. He was a sort of attorney-at-large for the un-privileged and inarticulate, and was always fighting unpopular up-hill fights on behalf of immigrants, Negroes, and sharecroppers.

Reflecting on this record, and aware of Howard University's need,

Jesse's friends were now inspired to see the obvious. Would they not honor him best by insuring that his work went on? They decided "that if a chair could be founded in *philosophy* and *religion,* held by a *Quaker,* in a *Negro* institution, all four of his great interests would be represented at once."

The idea prospered. Alberta Morris engineered the formation of the National Committee for the Jesse Holmes Memorial Chair, with Brand Blanshard as its chairman, and with herself as secretary. Allen J. White, of the Washington Meeting of Friends, served as leader of the Washington Committee; Clarence Pickett backed up the idea from his AFSC office; and J. Barnard Walton sang the same song for the Friends' General Conference. The Socialist Party, from its national headquarters in New York City, joined in the chorus through its chairman, David H. H. Felix.

Appeals for financial support went out in all directions. David Felix urged his fellow Socialists to send their contributions to Brand Blanshard at Swarthmore since "trade unionists, Quakers ... liberals, teachers and others ..." were all "joining together" to honor Jesse. Blanshard asked the Marshall Field Foundation of New York for $1000, while Allen J. White urged his Washington colleagues to contribute according to their means. And back home in Swarthmore, with college students doing much of the work, 75 donations of an average of $20 had been collected by April 21, 1943.

While the memorial-fund campaign went on a search was being made for a person worthy of being the first to sit in the Memorial Chair. By a "very rare piece of good luck," an admirably equipped young Quaker was found to fill it. He was Dr. Calvin Keene, who, after taking his doctorate at the Yale Divinity School, had gone on to teach philosophy and religion for six years at Colgate University. During his stay there he wrote an article published in the *Friends Intelligencer* entitled "The Negro and Democracy." By the fall of 1943, after careful consideration of the risks and the opportunities at Howard, he had taken up his duties in this Negro community.

On December 17, 1943, a service of dedication for the Jesse Holmes Memorial Chair was held in the Arthur Rankin Memorial Chapel of Howard University. Thirty-seven colleges, universities and theological seminaries from the eastern third of the nation had sent representatives, along with those from thirty-two churches and religious institutions of Washington, D.C. (Jesse would have been

440

amused to note that the thirty-seven schools of religion included a very wide spectrum of religious attitudes, all the way from such sober and prestigious places as Princeton Theological Seminary down to those best described as fundamentalist "colleges of the Bible.") Howard's William S. Nelson presided. After an organ prelude and the singing of a hymn, the Reverend Robert M. Williams, D.D., Asbury Methodist Church, and president of the Interdenominational Ministers' Alliance, Washington, gave the invocation. This was followed by two numbers by the University Choir, rendered with that resonant quality distinguishing Negro voices. And then Dean Nelson introduced Everett Lee Hunt, D. Litt., as an old friend and neighbor of Jesse's and one eminently qualified to tell the assembly of "The Life and Philosophy of Dr. Jesse H. Holmes." We may be sure that, in Everett Hunt's words, Jesse was all there — his wit and humor, his courage, and his unending struggle to elevate mankind.

The second half of the program, interspersed with vocal music, was opened by the Reverend Mordecai W. Johnson, D.D., LL.D., president of Howard University, with an address on "Theology Among University Studies." His place at the lectern was then taken by J. Calvin Keene, Ph.D., who, as assistant professor of the history and philosophy of religion, was already occupying the Memorial Chair. Quite properly, he gave his audience his conception of "The Nature of Religion," something to which Jesse himself had devoted a lot of thought. After a prayer of dedication by the Reverend Howard Thurman, D.D., dean of the Chapel, the ceremonies were brought to a close. If the ceremonies had generated any undue solemnity it was relieved at the informal reception held in the Fellowship Room of the School of Religion.

Although Calvin Keene and his wife had been "strongly drawn" to accept this position at Howard, a university which was "the chief reliance of the colored people for supplying leadership to the forty thousand Negro churches . . . ." in the United States, the financial future of the chair he held was still somewhat in doubt in July, 1944. Only a little more than $4500 of the $6000 needed for the first two years had been raised; and, while Howard University had agreed to meet half the cost of Keene's $3000 salary in the future, Blanshard's Memorial Fund Committee was also obligated to raise $1500 each year. Appeals for money continued to go out; by January 1, 1945 the amount contributed by Jesse's friends, and including $1000 from

441

the Marshall Field Foundation, totalled $5,516.12.

The Longwood Trustees received Blanshard's appeal as a matter of course; and, at a meeting on August 3, 1944, they decided to do something about it. The terms of the trust fund they had set up earlier, however, prevented any direct help to the Memorial Chair: they could give only tangential assistance by maintaining a lectureship "in connection with" it, the "lecture subjects to be confined to religious, moral, scientific and literary purposes, with the design of accommodating, fostering and sustaining the progressive spirit of the age; . . ." The National Bank of Chester County and Trust Company was directed to pay over to Howard University the net income, as it accrued, from the $5500 trust fund set aside for such a purpose. On January 2, 1945, this bank mailed $775 to Mordecai W. Johnson, indicating at the same time that in the future Howard University could expect to receive $261.25 yearly from the fund. By 1970 this had risen to $267.40.

With such slender help one wonders how these two projects — the Memorial Chair and the associated Memorial Lectureship — were able to prosper as well as they did. J. Calvin Keene received fulsome praise for his first year's work, a public-relations release from Howard stating that he had "rendered service of the highest excellence . . . ." As time went on other people filled the Chair; and by the early 1970s Dean William S. Nelson, professor emeritus, occupied it intermittently, teaching such courses as "Non-Violence and Social Change." The memorial lectures continued too, presumably only one a year due to the monetary problem. In 1973, as part of Howard's Thirtieth Annual Institute of Religion, J. Calvin Keene came down from St. Lawrence University, Canton, New York, to speak on "the Hebrew Roots of Christianity and Modern Religion." A year later Nathan A. Scott, Jr., Shailer Matthews Professor of Theology in the Divinity School of the University of Chicago, and the author of twenty-six books, spoke on "Albert Camus and the Christian Faith." (The facts that Dr. Scott was a Negro, a priest of the Episcopal church, and a canon of the Cathedral of St. James in Chicago, would have given Jesse Holmes mixed emotions: joy in seeing how high a Negro could rise if given the opportunity; sadness in that such an intellect should desert the simplicity of the early Christians for the ritualism and ceremony of high-church Episcopalianism.)

If Howard University celebrated Jesse's memory in philosophy

442

and religion, another school got started at the close of World War II to carry on his ideas in the adult-education field. Primarily a socialist-labor venture, the Jesse H. Holmes School opened its evening classes to workers in the Philadelphia area in September, 1945. Six months later it advertised its spring program of studies, with classes to meet in the Friends' Select School, Parkway and Seventeenth Street.

Jesse would have rejoiced at the courses offered in this new school, as well as at the quality of the instructional staff, many of them old friends. David H.H. Felix, who had sent out his appeal for help for the Memorial Chair at Howard on Socialist Party stationery, was to be the instructor for "The World In Which We Live." This was a basic economics course — the "dismal science," which Felix believed was not so dismal, and possibly not a science. Ben Segal, Marjorie Penney, G. James Fleming, and Irving Salert were to combine their talents in a course on "Racial, Religious, and National Minority Problems," a project co-sponsored by the CIO Anti-Discrimination Committee of Delaware and the Philadelphia Industrial Union Council. (Of the four instructors, two were Quakers and the other two Jews.) This course was a prerequisite for the "Institute of Human Relations," sponsored by the Jewish Labor Committee, and would meet every Tuesday for eight weeks. "The Cooperative Movement" would be taught by Robert Z. Willson of the Eastern Cooperative League. A course recalling one of Jesse's major concerns — the "Aims of Our Society" — was to be conducted by Leon Shull, formerly an instructor in workers' education for the ILGWU and the Textile Workers' Union. An "Institute of Labor Relations" was to consist primarily of three interlocking courses: "Parliamentary Law and Public Speaking," conducted by Bernard Backer, executive secretary, Philadelphia Socialist Party, and Burton A. Beck, executive secretary for the Jesse H. Holmes School; "Organizational Techniques" was to be taught by David Schick, educational director for the Upholsterers' International Union, AFL; and the "History of the Labor Movement" would be conducted by Charles Paddock, editor of the *New Party News.*

Nor did the process of memorialization cease with these efforts. Twenty-nine years later (in 1974), Eleanor Stabler Clarke, Swarthmore '18, established the Jesse H. Holmes Prize in Religion, offering $100 annually to that student who submitted the best

443

essay in a competition judged by the Swarthmore department of religion. And so, year after year, his spirit would still go marching on as youth interpreted religion's place and meaning in the modern world.

The Man and His Meaning.

Indeed, these five memorials — the Quaker memorial service on Swarthmore's campus, the Freedom Forum lectures, the Memorial Chair at Howard University and its associated Longwood-sponsored lectureship, plus the Jesse H. Holmes School and the Clarke Prize in Religion — assured that his name and meaning would not soon fade away. The first of these memorials had celebrated his general character, recalling that wonderful combination of wit, humor, courage and idealism which made him such a delightful colleague in reform activities. His friends remarked also on his integrity, noting how all his reform projects seemed to form a harmonious whole, all parts enlightened and bound together by the same set of principles. And these principles certainly included those held up as the ideal for Renaissance Man: to so order one's life as to develop a sound mind in a sound body, to balance intellectual and scientific inquiry with games, sports and physical exercises, and to make a broad range of learning the basis for the duties and responsibilities of effective citizenship. If a revolt against old authority was there, good manners, manliness and morals were also part of the picture; the end produce would be a cultivated gentleman. And those who knew Jesse Holmes thought that few men in the America of his time had approached this ideal as well as he did.

The second memorial had stressed his concern that man, through education, should be freed from all those inherited shackles holding man from the attainment of justice in One World of disparate races and nations. The third had emphasized his deeply held philosophical and religious convictions that man was mortal, that there was no heaven except the one he could produce on earth if he correctly used the pragmatic scientific method. The fourth was but an extension of the third — that the common man, given the opportunity, could attain, through Christian principles of democracy, and again through education, those qualities of mind and leadership which would eventually lead the way to the Promised Land. And the fifth memorial reminded students that an essential

444

part of this quest was the Holmesian investigate spirit applied to a living, evolving religion penetrating all aspects of life.

Why these ideals were not realized more fully in Jesse's lifetime, or in the years that followed, is of course a problem in the infinitely complex calculus of human relations. One major factor lay in the split-personality character of Western civilization, which on given occasions paid lip-service to the principles and practices of Christianity while it more generally followed the principles and practices of a rapacious capitalism. Capitalism emphasized a rough and often immoral competition for finite quantities of Earth's goods; Christianity called for a cooperative spirit in the moderate enjoyment of what was gained by one's own labor. Christian Socialism, with its uncomfortable code of morality, was an ideal too often howled down by the beneficiaries of the other camp — those who applied an infinitely flexible standard of morality to the various situations in which they found themselves.

Jesse Holmes was an advocate of Christian Socialism — better named "Christian Scientific Pragmatic Socialism." And this was a title his friend Norman Thomas could live with: it recalled the principles of Jesus and the inquirying spirit of science; it emphasized the testing of ideas and suggested courses of action to see what practical results would flow therefrom; and it suggested a social justice without which nothing in human society could really succeed. It is a worthy commentary on the lives of Norman Thomas and Jesse Holmes, plus many other progressives, that their ideas have entered the stream of American life, even if only in intermittent and piecemeal fashion — a rivulet here, a brook there. (The young activists of the 'sixties and 'seventies, had they known their history better, might have acknowledged that they were running down some of the lanes of reform marked by older and better-mannered giants before them.) The record from "Teddy" Roosevelt to "Jimmy" Carter is sufficient evidence to show that, despite all odds, and some glaring failures, the people in their democratic might can, if they will, govern themselves to their own advantage. Due to the work of such people as Jesse, the twentieth century may well be called The Century of the Common Man by future historians.

He had his warts and blind spots, of course. It is difficult to reconcile his individualism and opposition to antique social conventions with socialism's restrictions on individual freedom —

with its tendency to make faceless robots out of people. While he liked the principles and theories of socialism, particularly the idea of social planning, he apparently did not foresee how such a program would hamper initiative, foster various forms of dictatorship, and create the bureaucratic tangle and waste seen in modern Russia, England, and in the social-welfare aspects of American life. His tendency to reduce complex social, economic, and political problems to moral issues was a familiar reformers' error; his pragmatic mind should have seen more clearly that, while morality is indispensable among public servants and the people they serve, other ideological and practical factors are also involved — principles which must at times be compromised if anything is to be accomplished in that potpourri of cultures which is America. Indeed, Jesse compromised one of his own principles — that every person should courageously broadcast his basic conclusions and beliefs — when he delayed writing his extremely critical "Our 'Christianity'?" until his life had almost run its course. And even then he didn't publish it. Also, if he had made fewer speeches, devoting more time and energy to the writing of books and articles, his influence would have been more widespread and more lasting. And, if he had concentrated his talents on only two or three closely related reform projects (as was true of Norman Thomas), instead of spreading himself across so many of them, his name might have become known in every household.

Still, as he rested in his sylvan retreat behind his Moylan house, Jesse could look back across his years to a lifetime of achievements. He had always been a humanist, always making his thoughts and actions affirmations for man. He had inspired several generations of Swarthmore students to think for themselves in the light of a larger social commitment. He had helped to redefine the meaning of religion, and had helped to unify the Quakers. He had fought the mindless bigotry of "Back-to-Jesus" movements in his day. He and his more thoughtful Quaker colleagues anticipated the post-Hiroshima effort by philosophical scientists and thinking theologians to find how the rational and the intuitive forces in man, the scientific and the spiritual, could be made to cooperate more effectively to show the way to values and the nature of reality. He had probed the meaning of "free enterprise" in America, asking those who opposed socialism's general welfare just whose welfare they had in mind. And finally he had helped to show that no system

446

can claim to be a working democracy if it denies equality of opportunity in educational, religious, economic or political endeavors. Delighting his friends, paining his enemies, his idealism left no one in his orbit of action unaffected. Robert Browning must have had a man like Jesse Holmes in mind when he wrote:

> One who never turned his back, but marched
>   breast forward,
> Never doubted clouds would break,
> Never dreamed, though right were worsted,
>   wrong would triumph,
> Held, [he fell] to rise, [was] baffled to
>   fight better,
> Sleep to wake.